JUN 10 '94	DATE DUE		

12492

941.084
MAR   Marching to war

MARCHING TO WAR
1933-1939

THE MEETING OF *IL DUCE* AND *DER FÜHRER*: HERR HITLER (LEFT) WELCOMED BY SIGNOR
MUSSOLINI ON HIS ARRIVAL AT VENICE IN 1934 FOR THEIR DISCUSSION OF THE EUROPEAN SITUATION.

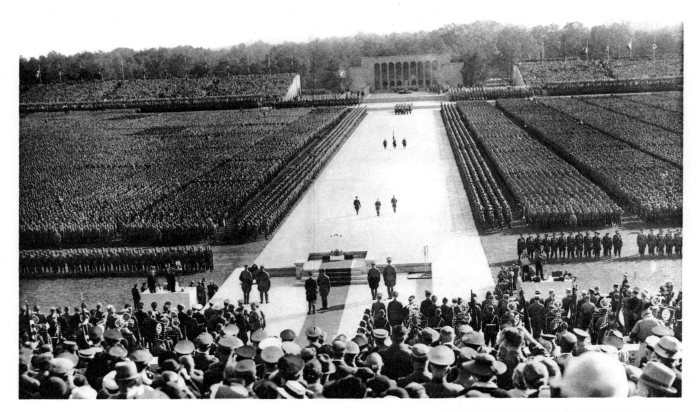

ONE OF THE HUGE MASS DEMONSTRATIONS WHICH CHARACTERISED THE NAZI PARTY RALLY AT NUREMBERG: NAZI SEMI-MILITARY FORMATIONS, SUCH AS THE STORM TROOPERS, PROTECTIVE GUARDS, AND NATIONAL-SOCIALIST MOTOR CORPS, REVIEWED IN THE LUITPOLD ARENA IN 1936 BY HERR HITLER, WHO IS SEEN WITH HERR LUTZE, CHIEF OF STAFF OF THE STORM TROOPERS, AND HERR HIMMLER, LEADER-IN-CHIEF OF THE PROTECTIVE GUARDS.

THE ILLUSTRATED LONDON NEWS

MARCHING TO WAR 1933-1939

INTRODUCTION BY

M A R T I N G I L B E R T

Foreword by James Bishop
Editor-in-Chief, The Illustrated London News

DOUBLEDAY CANADA LIMITED

TORONTO

PUBLISHER'S NOTE

Marching to War is a distillation of 364 issues of *The Illustrated London News* published between the years 1933–1939. It provides a balanced view of this momentous period of history, concentrating essentially on the events, places and people of consequence but also including insights into the social history of the period.

We would like to acknowledge the contribution of two people in this work: Ben Mackworth-Praed who has selected the material to go in and singlehandedly knitted the many strands together into a coherent whole, so that it represents the story in the exact style of *The Illustrated London News* of the time; and of John Watts who undertook the preliminary searches.

We would finally like to thank James Bishop, Editor-in-Chief, *The Illustrated London News* for his encouragement and to Elaine Hart Librarian of *The Illustrated London News* Picture Archive for her co-operation.

This edition published in Canada by
Doubleday Canada Limited
105 Bond Street
Ontario
M5B 1Y3

By arrangement with Bestseller Publications Limited, London

Published by Bestseller Publications Limited
with the permission of *The Illustrated London News*

Copyright © Bestseller Publications Limited 1989

**Printed and bound in Italy
by Milanostampa S.p.A. - Farigliano (CN)**

Canadian Cataloguing in Publication Data

Main entry under title:

Marching to war

Facsimiles from the London illustrated news,
1933–1939.
ISBN 0-385-25217-X

1. Great Britain – History – George V, 1910–1936 –
Sources. 2. Great Britain – History – Edward VIII,
1936 – Sources. 3. Great Britain – History –
George VI, 1936–1952 – Sources.

DA578.M37 1989   941.084   C89-093207-7

CONTENTS

FOREWORD

AN IMPOSING DISPLAY OF GERMAN MILITARY EFFICIENCY: THE GREAT PARADE OF 120,000 STORM TROOPERS BEFORE HERR HITLER IN THE LUITPOLD ARENA AT NUREMBERG IN 1938.

FOREWORD

Until Herbert Ingram came to London in 1842 to produce the world's first illustrated weekly paper the British Press had not known what to do with pictures. Newspapers of the time used occasional woodcut engravings but not one of some 400 newspapers publishing in the early 19th century regularly carried illustrations, nor did they seem to appreciate their significance. As a newsagent in Nottingham Ingram learnt what his customers wanted: they bought the newspapers carrying illustrations, and invariably asked which newspaper contained the news from London. His creation of *The Illustrated London News*, which in its first issue had 30 engravings and thereafter never less and often many more, was thus regarded as a publishing revolution, described by one of its contemporaries, the *Morning Post*, as one of the marvels of the day.

The introduction of halftone photographic reproduction, with the capacity to reproduce photographs within hours, was another revolution, inspiring the rise of the popular and heavily illustrated daily newspapers and ending the pictorial dominance of the ILN, but not its unique qualities as a journal of record, which survive to the present day. The bound volumes provide unrivalled documentary and pictorial evidence of an epoch of social change that has no parallel in British history.

Marching to War recalls seven of these momentous years, from 1933 to 1939, as they were portrayed in the ILN. The title of the book would no doubt have seemed inappropriate to the men who were reporting at that time, when there was so much political emphasis on trying to prevent war, but in the light of history we can see how the march of events was indeed leading inexorably to war, just as we can now recognise how much better it would have been had the politicians in power shared Churchill's percipience. Herbert Ingram did not foresee, when he launched the paper during the long peace that followed Waterloo, that so much of its contents would be reporting wars and the critical events leading up to them. But when the Crimean War broke out in 1853 he showed how it should be done by dispatching six war artists to the front. Eighty years and some 30 wars later his grandson, Bruce Ingram, who was then editing the paper, was equally alert to the requirements of pictorial news-gathering and responsible reporting, as the pages of this graphic book so clearly show.

JAMES BISHOP
Editor-in-Chief
The Illustrated London News
February 1989

THE EIGHT-GUN, SINGLE SEATER VICKERS-SUBMARINE "SPITFIRE" – PROBABLY THE WORLD'S FASTEST STANDARD FIGHTER: A TYPE OF MACHINE WHICH WAS MASS-PRODUCED FOR THE
R.A.F. IN 1939, SEEN ON A TEST FLIGHT.

INTRODUCTION

Hitler's coming to power in Europe on the last day of January 1933 dominated the news in Britain. The picture of him at the window of the Chancellery on the evening of his triumph, greeted by an ecstatic crowd, was clearly the event of the hour, even if the soon to be notorious, but at that moment the unknown cry of 'Heil Hitler' was translated as 'Hail Hitler!'.

Yet there were other dramas in the news that month, particularly the slow but steady Japanese conquest of Manchuria. As Japanese soldiers reached the Great Wall of China, it was clear that in the Far East, as well as in Europe, momentous events, equally full of foreboding, were taking place.

How far the two new powers were bent on conquest was clear enough in the case of Japan. But Germany had been disarmed by the Versailles Treaty, and had neither an army nor an air force with which to wage war. Nevertheless, a new German film portraying a future Anglo-Russian combination against Germany, the hero of which was a German U-boat

THE MUNICH CELEBRATIONS ON THE TENTH ANNIVERSARY OF THE HITLER *PUTSCH* IN NOVEMBER 1923: HERR HITLER AS CHANCELLOR (SEEN FROM BEHIND IN THE SPEAKER'S TRIBUNE), ADDRESSING A VAST GATHERING IN THE SQUARE OUTSIDE FELDHERRENHALLE.

commander, showed that there was a keen new war spirit in Hitler's Germany; one which he, by his speeches, and his call for revenge on Versailles, seemed determined to rouse, and to call to action once Germany was strong enough to seek that revenge.

In Britain, it was not any new army, but the mass of unemployed, many of them former soldiers of the First World War, which gave cause for comment. As Hitler's enthusiastic followers demonstrated their zeal, Britain's unemployed gathered in Hyde Park to demand work, and to protest against recent wage cuts for those in work.

The vulnerability of democracy seemed nowhere more apparent than in the United States, where an assassination attempt was made on the President-elect, Franklin D. Roosevelt, by an Italian-American, Giuseppe Zangara, who fired five shots before being overpowered. But this was no conspiracy against the United States, either internal or external, but a lone assassin. American democracy, though determined to keep clear of all European involvements, was safe.

In Germany, democracy took its greatest blow in March, scarcely a month after Hitler had come to power, when the burning down of the Reichstag by a deranged young man led Hitler to declare that the whole State was in danger of a Communist seizure of power, and to use this fabricated danger to outlaw the vast German Communist party – the second largest Party in Germany – and to arrest and imprison tens of thousands of political opponents – not only Communists, but Socialists, Trade Unionists, liberals, and public opponents of Nazism. That same week, the *Illustrated London News* gave a full page to what it called 'the Human Side of German's Nazi Chancellor', showing him feeding young deer from a bottle, reading a newspaper, patting a small child and – most British of all perhaps – at the sea-side.

The spread of Nazi terror was not hidden, however. Photographs a week later showed the closing down of the Social-Democratic printing works in Munich, and the searching at gun point of Communists in Berlin, 'a typical instance', the caption read, 'of the drastic control exercised in Germany under the Hitler régime'.

No week now passed without some further evidence of Nazi extremism. A boycott of all Jewish shops caused considerable comment, and alarm, in Britain. A week later, the events in distant China were given equal prominents, as the Japanese war machine continued to drive forward. Japan was on the march, her advance marked by a growing number of both Japanese and Chinese dead.

Would Germany also seek to march, that was the question on everybody's lips as Hitler asserted Germany's right to an army and an air force, and an end to the restrictions imposed on her at Versailles by Britain, France and the United States. There were also reports, and photographs, of the growing Nazi movement in Austria, and of its demand for a union with Hitler's Germany.

Not only politics, but natural disasters, made the news in those early months of 1933. First, the most destructive of all volcanoes, Krakatoa, erupted again, its early rumblings giving a fortunate warning. Not so fortunate were the citizens of Long Beach, California, and the adjacent Pacific coast towns, where more than a hundred people were killed, in an earthquake on the San Andreas fault.

The all-present danger seemed, however, as 1933 progressed, to be the Hitler régime in Germany; by the end of May there were detailed reports of how military training – forbidden under the Versailles Treaty, was being carried out in the guise of sport. At the same time, having been forbidden an air force, German anti-aircraft gunners practised their shooting against cardboard models, while, at Nuremberg, a Rally was held in which tens of thousands of Nazis demonstrated by their cheers and salutes the extent of their enthusiasm for the new régime, and, dominating all, the Swastika flag became the most latest symbol of a totalitarian power, as Hitler, contemptuous of democratic value, withdrew Germany from the League of Nations.

As Hitler began to rearm, secretly building up the air force which had been forbidden to Germany under the Versailles Treaty, he also extended the range and severity of his dictatorial rule. Concentration camps were

THE ANTI-JEWISH MOVEMENT IN HITLERIZED GERMANY: POLICE QUESTIONING AN OLD JEW IN THE FOREIGN JEWS' QUARTER IN BERLIN IN 1933.

built to which opponents of the new régime were sent, and where sadistic brutality led to many deaths, and to the cowing of dissent. On 10 February 1934 the *Illustrated London News* showed camp guards on parade at Dachau concentration camp, just outside Munich, noting that a 'force of four hundred men were in control of two thousand five hundred political prisoners'. The caption to this and several other pictures of Dachau, read 'The first authorized Press photographs taken in the great camp at Dachau'.

Hitler's was now 'The Face of the Dictator', set side by side with that of Stalin in a two-page spread of the *Illustrated London News* on 3 March 1934. By contrast, the democratic Government of France, torn by factions and lacking any clear majority party, was a source almost of derision, and of pity too, when riots in Paris followed repeated failures to form a Government, newspaper kiosks and buses being set on fire by the mob during what was described as 'a night of terror'.

There was also terror at night in Vienna, as right-wing Government forces attacked the socialists and turned their artillery fire on workers' houses; these scenes were also captured by the camera and reported, a sign of the spreading political turmoil in Europe as, in Germany, Nazism went from strength to strength. Only in Italy did a German-style discipline prevail, as Mussolini, since 1922 the head of Italy's Fascist régime, opened the twenty-ninth Parliament – 'probably the last Italian Parliament' was the comment in the *Illustrated London News*. This report was on the same page as yet another report of unrest in Paris, as troops were rushed to the French capital in order to prevent Communist violence on May Day.

There were yet more pictures of social unrest in June 1934, when strikers in several American cities were dispersed by the National Guard, which opened fire on them; in Minneapolis a well-known businessman was killed while serving as a special policeman. In Britain, the police were called in that June to prevent violence when 15,000 fascist Blackshirts, led

TYPICAL OF THE MOB-VIOLENCE THAT MARKED THE POLITICAL CRISIS IN PARIS IN JANUARY 1934: A NEWSPAPER KIOSK BEING PUSHED OVER, AS IT WAS SET ALIGHT.

by Sir Oswald Mosley, met in London, amid protests from anti-fascists, many of whom were ejected from the meeting with considerable violence. Scenes of similar disorder, the British Government declared, 'could not be tolerated'.

Britain, France and the United States preserved their democracies. Italy and Germany had lost theirs, and were headed on a course of remilitarization and territorial expansion. The meeting of Hitler and Mussolini at Venice in June 1934 was the first step in the creation of a German-Italian Axis which was in due course to widen its alliance to include Hungary, Rumania, Finland, Slovakia, Bulgaria and Japan.

To tighten his grip on Germany, Hitler moved in July 1934 to purge his rivals and enemies even inside his own Nazi Party. Captain Röhm, hitherto Hitler's Chief of Staff, was shot, as were dozens of other Nazis who, like Röhm, had helped bring Hitler to power. In its report of the 'Night of the Long Knives', as the purge was known, the *Illustrated London News* published its first photograph of Heinrich Himmler, head of the S.S., describing him as 'a bodyguard devoted to Hitler'. Also gaining greater power as a result of the Night of the Long Knives were General

Goering, whom Hitler had chosen to build up Germany's air force, and Dr Goebbels, for several years the head of the propaganda section of the Nazi Party, and now in charge of the German press and radio, the propaganda arm of the Nazi dictatorship.

Death had become a hallmark of the onward march of Nazi power. In August 1934 the Chancellor of Austria, Dr Dollfuss, was shot dead by an Austrian Nazi in the Chancellery in Vienna. But the Nazis failed in their attempt to seize power in the Austrian capital, and four more years were to pass before Austria finally succumbed to the spread of the Swastika.

In September 1934, following the death of the German President, Field Marshal von Hindenburg, it was announced in Berlin that Hitler wished to combine the offices of Chancellor and President. In what the *Illustrated London News* described as 'probably the most vigorous and widespread propaganda effort ever made', the Nazis used mass meetings, film, and the radio, as well as intimidation and threats, to achieve this extension of Hitler's dictatorial power.

There were others, elsewhere, who voted to be a part of Hitler's Germany, first among them the inhabitants of the small Saar region, which had been detached from Germany by the Treaty of Versailles, and which, in a freely held plebiscite in January 1935, turned its back on France, and voted to return to Germany. The lure of Nazism for those who had earlier been detached from Germany was seen in the vote; 90.86 of Saarlanders voted to become a part of Hitler's Reich.

Yet there was also an evil side to the coin. In its issue of 26 January 1935, the *Illustrated London News* had a photograph of 'the exodus of the anti-Nazi element from the Saar since the plebiscite'. Refugees were on the move. A new era had opened, which was to be the curse of the next five years. Already, from within Germany itself, anti-Nazis had sought sanctuary abroad, including hundreds of liberals and democrats, and thousands of Jews. Among those who fled, and were to continue to flee, were many of the leading scientists, doctors and humanitarians of the twentieth century, including Albert Einstein, who found refuge in America, and Sigmund Freud, who, after Hitler's annexation of Austria, was given a safe haven in Britain. But not everyone could get away; two of Freud's sisters were to be among the six million Jews murdered by the Nazis after the outbreak of war.

Other conflicts burst upon the European scene. In Spain, socialist miners and the activist government had, late the previous year, clashed violently in Oriedo, with the Socialists forced to surrender. From Italy, Mussolini's troops now crossed the Mediterranean and sailed through the Red Sea, to attack Abyssinia. But still it was Germany which dominated the headlines of 1935. In March, Hitler announced that there would be military conscription, and the increase of Germany's small army to one which would be among the largest, and certainly the most modern, in Europe. At the first military parade in Berlin following the announcement of conscription, a massive Iron Cross was flanked by two swastikas, the symbol of Nazi power which was becoming increasingly familiar, and – by outside observers – feared. The German air force was also expanding. In England, Winston Churchill, then a member of Parliament but not a member of the Government, warned that German air strength was growing at such a fast rate that it would overtake Britain's within three or four years. The Government dismissed Churchill's warnings as alarmist,

AFTER THE INTENSIVE "YES" CAMPAIGN OF 1934 HAD COME TO ITS CONCLUSION, WITH AN 89.9 PER CENT VOTE IN FAVOUR OF THE LEADER-CHANCELLOR: A TORCHLIGHT PROCESSION OF STORM TROOPERS ON THE MARCH IN BERLIN.

THE GREAT MILITARY PARADE IN BERLIN ON "HEROES DAY" (1935), FOLLOWING THE PROCLAMATION OF GENERAL CONSCRIPTION AND AN INCREASE OF THE ARMY TO 36 DIVISIONS GROUPED IN 12 ARMY CORPS: INFANTRY AND ARTILLARY DRAWN UP IN REVIEW ORDER IN THE LUSTGARTEN, FACING A HUGE IRON CROSS FLANKED BY NAZI SWASTIKAS.

although they were based on facts brought to him secretly by members of the Government's own secret service. The *Illustrated London News* reflected Churchill's concern when, on 12 October 1935, it published a photograph of German bombers over Nuremberg, with the heading: 'The Swastika in the Sky'. The caption to this same picture reflected the British public's concern: 'The German Air Force', it read, 'which still provides considerable field for conjecture'.

Just over a month later, the first of the new German army recruits was sworn in. A photograph of the swearing-in ceremony noted that the soldier's oath of loyalty was taken to Hitler as well as to the nation. Thus the dictatorship gained its military arm.

There was to be no halt in Hitler's triumphs in 1936, a year which was to prove a turning point in his drive for the mastery of Europe. In March, he sent German troops into the Rhineland – the one part of Germany which the Versailles Treaty had declared to be a demilitarized area. Although remaining German after 1918, no troops had been allowed in it. Now Hitler's men rode in on horseback, to be met with flowers. Air force units and artillery followed. In Munich, in a dramatic torchlight procession, 200,000 Nazis gathered to salute Hitler in the city in which, thirteen years earlier, he had founded the Nazi movement, then a small band of scoffed-at cranks, quickly suppressed when they had tried to seize power – and now the rulers of the largest state in Europe.

For the British, there were domestic triumphs to celebrate. That March, 'the stateliest ship in being', the *Queen Mary*, began her first journey from the dockyard to the sea. 'Never in the history of transatlantic travel', declared Winston Churchill, 'has so much been done for those who travel tourist'. That same month, Churchill was warning that any failure to match Hitler's growing military strength could end in disaster for Britain, as the totalitarian régimes of Europe went from strength to strength; in May 1936, Italy conquered Abyssinia, and Mussolini was declared 'founder of the Empire'.

Another exile thus appeared on the pages of the world's press, the former Emperor of Abyssinia, Haile Selassie, who, together with his Empress, was seen arriving by train in Jerusalem, to be the guest of the British Mandate authorities in Palestine, while photographs from his former capital, Addis Ababa, showed corpses in the street.

In Palestine too, where Haile Selassie had found refuge, riots in the streets led during the summer of 1936 to more than twenty Jewish deaths, as Arabs, roused by their leaders to fury against the growing number of Jewish immigrants – including Jewish refugees from Germany – attacked Jewish suburbs in Jerusalem and elsewhere. The British were quick to turn against the rioters, killing six Arabs. This was only the beginning of a spiral of violent incidents. By October 1936, eighty Jews and thirty British soldiers had been killed by Arabs, and more than a hundred Arabs killed by the British.

In a world of violence, sanity as well as safety was still the watchword of the democracies. In June 1936 a Popular Front Government in France, headed by Leon Blum, seemed to hold out a promise both of social justice and resistance to tyranny. But it was quickly put to the test when, in Spain, the recently created republican government, on which similar

democratic hopes had been pinned, was attacked by Nationalist Forces, and the Spanish Civil War began. France, which might have hurried to the aid of the legitimate republican Government of Spain, hesitated to act. The British Government, like the French, decided to stand aside. The word of the hour was 'Non-intervention'. But Hitler and Mussolini knew no such restraints. Italian troops hurried to support the Spanish insurrectionists under General Franco. German pilots were later to bomb cities held by the Spanish Republicans. 'Non-intervention' did not save the republican régime in Spain. But it did reveal the weaknesses of the democracies. Hitler gained confidence from this knowledge of Britain and France's reluctance to act.

On Britain's own border with Spain, at Gibraltar, extra soldiers were called in to ensure that Spanish refugees were kept out, while those refugees who had managed to cross into Gibraltar were sent back to Spain. 'The order was made on the advice of the medical authorities', explained the *Illustrated London News*, 'as the fortress and the town were so overcrowded that there was a risk of epidemic'. As the forces of General Franco slowly gained the ascendence throughout Spain, thousands of Spanish republicans fled across the Pyrenees into France, yet more refugees in a Europe which, with each advance of dictatorial rule, saw the hardships created for those who, leaving in search of safety, often found hostility and uncertainty, as well as a haven.

In dramatic scenes, Hitler now sought to put a peaceful spotlight on Germany, as Berlin played host in August 1936 to the Olympic Games. Those who already had cause to fear the swastika shuddered as they saw the photographs of the Olympic flame being brought into the stadium against a background of swastika banners.

Not Germany, however, but Spain, was the focus of British attention throughout the autumn of 1936, as dramatic pictures showed the battles, the killings, and the destruction of war. As Italians and Germans hurried to support the insurgents – or rebels as they were known – Russian volunteers fought on the Government – the Republican – side. British volunteers were found on both sides of the war, most on the Republican, but a few with Franco. Death came in great numbers to both sides, graphically shown week after week by The *Illustrated London News*, and described in one caption as 'The wastage of young Spanish manhood'.

That October, General Franco was declared 'Chief of the Spanish State', joining Hitler and Mussolini as one of Europe's dictatorial leaders. In Germany, Hitler staged yet another Nazi rally in Nuremberg, the largest yet held, and a potent visual reminder of the formidable drilled ranks of dictatorial power.

There were further visual reminders of the dangers of fascism when, in October 1936, the East End of London saw the clashes between Mosley's gangs and those who were opposed to them. 'Bar the roads to Fascism' was one of the slogans of those who set up barricades in a London street to stop Mosley's men from entering the predominantly Jewish Cable Street.

There was another march in London that winter, when hundreds of unemployed workers marched south from the town of Jarrow to protest in the capital against the lack of jobs. 'Everywhere they were met with friendly feeling', the *Illustrated London News* reported of the arrival of the marchers in London.

The plight of the 'Jarrow Crusaders' was quickly eclipsed, however, by the plight of the citizens of Madrid, as the Republican capital was bombed by General Franco's air force. Each day, news photographs, taken by enterprising – and indeed courageous – photographers, showed bursting bombs and wrecked buildings. For the first time since the end of the Great War eighteen years earlier, terror from the air had fallen on a European capital, but on a far more intensive scale than the German bombing of London and Paris in 1918. Now the forecast of the British poet Siegfried Sassoon was coming true, that 'Fear will be synonymous with Flight'.

In Britain, the end of 1936 saw the first abdication of a British monarch in modern times, when King Edward VIII gave up the throne, rather than give up the woman he loved – Mrs Simpson, an American divorcee. She married Edward, and became Duchess of Windsor; but the throne went to Edward's brother, the Duke of York, who became King George VI. His coronation the following May was a scene of great splendour; at the centre of the official photograph of the Royal Family in their coronation dress were the King's two daughters, Princess Elizabeth and Princess Margaret, the cynosure of all eyes.

One of the first public appearances of the outgoing King was to visit

AT AN ANTI-FASCIST BARRIVADE IN CABLE STREET, E.1., WHERE THE I.L.P. AND THE COMMUNISTS HAD PLANNED A MEETING IN OCTOBER 1936: THE CROWD, WITH STONE-THROWERS AMONG THEM, SCATTERED BY THE POLICE.

Hitler at his Bavarian mountain home, the Bergdorf. But in Britain, opinion was divided as to whether Germany would become a moderate, peace-loving State, or would seek to use its ever-growing military strength to extend its frontiers. That April, the first German stamps with Hitler's head on were issued; underneath them was painted a phrase of Hitler: 'He who wishes to rescue a nation must think heroically'. Not heroism however, in the eyes of most British onlookers, but barbarism, was the act of German aircraft in May 1937, in bombing the Basque town of Guernica, in Northern Spain. At sea, Republican forces bombed the German pocket-battleship *Deutschland*, and in retaliation her sister ship the *Admiral Scheer* shelled the Republican-held coastal town of Almeria.

Momentarily in the autumn of 1937, world attention returned to China, where Japanese warplanes bombed and war ships shelled, the city of Shanghai with an intensity which far surpassed that of Guernica. One photograph showed from the city some of the bodies of more than one thousand Chinese killed at the World Amusement Park in the International Concession to which they had fled to escape the bombardment, only to be hit by stray bombs from one of the few Chinese aircraft that had attempted to counter-attack the Japanese ships; in the photograph can be seen not only the dead, but another of the photographers of the scene. The 'horror of war', as the *Illustrated London News* caption described it, had once more become an object of the cameramen's lenses.

Japan, already the conqueror of the Chinese provinces of Manchuria and Jehol outside the Great Wall, now invaded China itself, capturing many coastal towns amid savage fighting which left hundreds of thousands of Chinese dead.

In Germany, Hitler welcomed Mussolini to a meeting of the two dictators. As they met in Munich, German bombers, piloted by Franco's airmen, bombed the northern Spanish port of Gijon. In Germany itself, opponents of the Nazi régime continued to be seized and sent to concentration camp; British newspapers frequently gave details of the death of a prisoner, or of the severe punishments being meted out in the camps. But not every newspaper took a critical view of Hitler and Nazism. During 1937 the editor of *The Times*, Geoffrey Dawson, wrote to a friend: 'I should like to get going with the Germans. I simply cannot understand why they should apparently be so much annoyed with *The Times* at this moment. I spend my nights in taking out anything which I think will hurt their susceptibilities and in dropping in little things which are intended to soothe them'.

The year 1938 showed that Hitler could not be soothed; that he intended to assert German supremacy in Europe and was not to be deterred from his path either by democratic pleading, or by disapproval and protest. The year began with demonstrations by Austrian Nazis, carrying swastika emblems. The Austrian Government at once banned such demonstrations, but in vain.

When the Austrian Chancellor, Kurt von Schuschnigg, declared in a radio broadcast that 'Austria will remain Free', Hitler determined to march. German troops at once crossed the Austrian border, and on 19 March 1938 the swastika flew over the Chancellery in Vienna. Europe's

first independent State to fall under Nazi rule was now in the grip of a bizarre combination of hysterical jubilation on the part of those Austrians who supported union with Germany, and deep depression on the part of those who, within hours, were to become the victims of all Nazism's anti-democratic and anti-Jewish legislation.

The Austrian army now became an integral part of the Germany army. Austrian refugees joined German refugees in their search for safe havens elsewhere. Austrian Nazis joined German Nazis in imposing discipline and terror. In the *Illustrated London News*, the first photograph of Hitler entering Austria showed, at his side, the head of the S.S., Heinrich Himmler.

Hitler had been born in Austria; in proclaiming the union of Austria and Germany, he told a vast, exhuberant crowd in the centre of Vienna; 'In this hour I can make before the German people the greatest report of my life, of a task carried out. As Leader and Chancellor of the German Reich, I report before German history that my homeland has now entered the German Reich'.

In distant Spain, General Franco's aircraft were bombing Barcelona – the last large city still held by the Republicans who, less than three years earlier, had been the legitimate Government of Spain. Photographs of the bombing still shocked the world; on March 26, the *Illustrated London News* printed one of a tram 'in which all the passengers were killed'.

All Europe now began to look to its air defences; in May, a balloon barrage was organized for London, against which enemy bombers would fly at their peril.

But Hitler had no plans to send his air force over Britain. Instead, he now stirred up fierce pro-Nazi feeling among the German-speaking peoples of the Sudetenland border regions of Czechoslovakia. Marches, flags, the Nazi salute, were each a forwarning of political threats to come. The *Illustrated London News* sent a special artist to Czechoslovakia; at the end of July he drew, and reported on, a 'mysterious gilt symbol' used by the Sudeten Germans 'which', he noted, 'from its semi-swastika design, could obviously be adapted to its more usual form should occasion arise'.

The world did not have long to wait for Hitler's next move. In September 1938, at the annual Nuremberg rally, he told 120,000 soldiers paraded before him: 'Negotiations or conferences did not give us our natural right to the union of us Germans. He had to take it ourselves, and we could do so only thanks to the existence of our army'. Now a new figure appeared in the European headlines and newspaper photographs: Eduard Beneš, the President of Czechoslovakia, who, as Hitler demanded the secession of the Sudetenland province to Germany, appealed to the Czech for calm. But Hitler urged the Sudeten Nazi leader, Conrad Henlein, to demonstrate with mounting fervour, and the two western democracies, Britain and France, pressed the Czechoslovak Government to make the territorial concessions which Hitler demanded in order to avoid war.

In London, trenches were dug in Hyde Park and Kensington Gardens, for those who might be 'caught out of doors' without shelter in the event of war. Gas masks were issued in case of gas bombs being used against

OPERATIONS IN THE SUMMER OF 1937 NEAR LIANSIANG, ON THE RAILWAY, ABOUT 20 MILES SOUTH OF PEKING, WHERE THE JAPANESE DROVE THE CHINESE STEADILY SOUTHWARDS: A COLUMN OF JAPANESE INFANTRY WADING ACROSS A RIVER, THEIR CLOSE FORMATION INDICATING THE ABSENCE OF ANY RESISTANCE.

civilians; a gas proof shelter was even devised for cats and dogs. Half a million schoolchildren were evacuated from London, lest it should suffer the fate of Shanghai, Guernica or Barcelona.

To try to avert a German invasion of Czechoslovakia, the British Prime Minister, Neville Chamberlain, flew twice to Germany to see Hitler. Then after his third flight, at a conference in Munich on the last day of September, he and the French Prime Minister, Edouard Daladier, accepted Hitler's demands for the annexation of the Sudetenland to Germany. The Czechoslovak delegates, who had been kept in a separate room during the final Munich negotiations, were then told of their country's fate. She was to lose her borderlands, with their industry, and their strategic defences, to Germany.

Returning to Britain, Neville Chamberlain declared that he had brought back 'peace in our time'. In the House of Commons, Winston Churchill denounced the Munich agreement as a servile act of appeasement which would only encourage Hitler to make even greater demands. Even as Churchill spoke, tens of thousands of Czechs, and of Czech Jews, fled from the areas about to be annexed. Yet more refugees were on the road. Yet one more region of Europe was about to experience all the rigours of Nazi rule and terror. Yet still, as with the German annexation of Austria, not a shot was fired. The German soldiers entered, not to hostile, but to welcoming crowds. Three years later, the German General who entered the Sudetenland in triumph, General Ritter von Leeb, was to command German Army Group North in Russia to the very outskirts of Leningrad, but was to fight every inch of the way amid terrible slaughter, nor was he to reach his goal.

Hitler, too, entered the Sudetenland in an open car, amid the salutes and plaudits of the onlookers. But henceforth his onward march to European conquest was to be much harder, and, in due course, resisted. Resistance was impossible, however, inside Germany, for the quarter

HERR HITLER WELCOMED IN SUDETENLAND AT WILDENAU IN OCTOBER 1938; WHILE HERR HEINLEIN, NOW COMMISSIONER FOR THE SUDETEN AREAS, WALKS BESIDE HIS CAR (LEFT).

million Jews who had been unable to leave. In November 1938 the Nazi mob turned on them with a hitherto unprecedented savagery. More than ninety Jews were killed. Hundreds of synagogues were burned down. Thousands of Jewish shops were looted. 'The savagery of the mob, it appears', reported the *Illustrated London News* 'was not restrained by the police'.

Europe now awaited with sickening anticipation the next moves of the dictator powers. Even in the United States, President Roosevelt was forced to warn Congress, in January 1939, that the possibility of America remaining isolated from the troubles of the rest of the world had become much reduced. Within a month, General Franco's forces had all but destroyed the Republican forces in Catalonia, and a stream of defeated fighters, Spaniards, democratic Germans and Czechs among them, fled northward across the border into France. Elsewhere along the border, streams of Spanish Catalans, refugees, mostly women and children, sought refuge in France.

In Britain, Royal Air Force Spitfires were under construction, using new techniques of mass-production. In Germany, mass-produced U-boats were photographed on naval exercises, their flotilla named after the U-boat commander who had sunk three British warships at the outbreak

of the First World War. In Belgium, frontier fortifications were manned and gun-emplacements guarded. But it was once more Hitler who took the initiative, invading Czechoslovakia in March 1939 and occupying Prague. The Czechoslovak Government had been unable to resist; half of the country, Slovakia, had broken away to form its own fascist and pro-German Government. Hitler travelled to Prague in a special train, to look down from the Hradschin Castle on his second conquered European capital. Yet not a single German soldier had yet been killed in action.

A new country was now in existence: Greater Germany. Its armies, untested as yet in battle, were masters of two former independent States, Austria and Czechoslovakia. Hitler now turned his anger and his demands on Poland, insisting that the predominantly German-speaking regions which had been given to Poland at the end of the First World War be returned to Germany. The Polish Foreign Minister, Colonel Beck, rejected Hitler's demands.

Coming to London, Beck was given a guarantee by Neville Chamberlain that Britain would not allow Poland to be overrun. In March 1939, Hitler annexed the independent province of Memel, on the Baltic; going by sea to view his conquest. That same month, General Franco entered Madrid, the inhabitants hanging out white sheets as flags of surrender.

Totalitarianism was triumphant, but it had not yet ended its conquests. From Rome, Mussolini now ordered his troops to occupy Albania, on the Adriatic Sea. From Berlin, Hitler called for the annexation of another Baltic port, the Free City of Danzig. In Britain, the Government introduced military conscription, a final, and for some a belated recognition, that war with Germany could not long be avoided.

In Poland preparations were made to resist any German attack. Poland's cavalry, pictured in the *Illustrated London News* on 26 August 1939, was described as 'probably the best in Europe and equipped with sword, lance and machine guns'. That same issue reported that Poland had 3,000,000 trained military reserves, and 3,950,000 horses 'classed as fit for military service'.

In Moscow, the Russians and Germans now signed a non-aggression pact. Henceforth if Hitler were to invade Poland, he need have no fear of a Soviet intervention on Poland's behalf. Unknown to the world, which saw Stalin's smiling face at the signing ceremony, Russia and Germany had agreed to divide Poland between them, once Hitler's armies had done their work of conquest.

On 1 September 1939, less than a week after the Nazi-Soviet Pact, Hitler's troops invaded Poland. That same day, German bombs struck at Warsaw, killing thousands of the city's inhabitants. The Polish forces resisted with tenacity, refusing to yield until driven back by overwhelming German military force and air power. On September 3 both Britain and France, after trying in vain to persuade Hitler to halt his forces, declared war on Germany. For the second time in less than a year 400,000 British children were evacuated from London, together with their gas masks. In Danzig, the citizens welcomed German warships to their port. Trenches were dug on the outskirts of Warsaw as by mid September, German troops reached one of the tram stations on the outskirts of the city. The Second World War had begun.

THE MECHANISED FORCES OF THE GERMAN ARMY ARRIVE AS IF ON PARADE: LIGHT TANKS PASSING THROUGH THE STREETS OF PRAGUE IN MARCH 1939.

THE ILLUSTRATED LONDON NEWS

THE GERMAN LEADER WHOSE WORDS THE WORLD AWAITED: HERR ADOLF HITLER.

It is no exaggeration to say that, in view of the general state of tension in Europe, the world awaited Herr Hitler's speech in the Reichstag on Wednesday, May 17, with a keen interest that was not unmixed with anxiety. It was arranged that the German Chancellor should make this declaration of his country's policy towards disarmament and German rearmament after the crisis in connection with the Disarmament Conference at Geneva had been discussed by the German Cabinet on May 12; and on the evening of that day it was announced that the Reichstag had been summoned to meet on the Wednesday for the particular purpose. Meantime, that meeting of the General Committee of the Disarmament Conference at Geneva which was fixed for the Monday was postponed until the Thursday.

1933

Adolf Hitler appointed Chancellor of Germany — Japanese invasion of China renewed — Japan leaves League of Nations — capture of Jehol province brings Japan to the Great Wall — the Reichstag burned in Germany — the Communists blamed — Nazis triumph in subsequent elections — Nazis order boycott of Jewish traders and professionals — Franklin Delano Roosevelt elected President of the United States — his attempted assassination — British team flies over Everest — Krakatoa erupts — earthquake in California — Germany launches two "pocket battle-ships" — and introduces military training disguised as sport — Nazis suppress Labour unions and all political parties but their own — elections in Irish Free State — Dr Frank, the Nazi Bavarian Minister of Justice expelled from Austria by Chancellor Dollfuss — Nazi party in Austria dissolved — construction of autobahns in Germany to relieve unemployment — the Nazis' first Nuremberg Rally — construction of Maginot Line nears completion — Palestine Arabs protest against Jewish immigration — attempted anarchist rebellion in Spain — Prohibition repealed in United States — Germany withdraws from League of Nations — elections in Spain — Britain's air and naval strengths reviewed.

HITLER, THE NAZI CHIEF,
MADE GERMAN CHANCELLOR:
HIS FERVID ORATORY THROUGH THE MICROPHONE.

Herr Adolf Hitler, appointed Chancellor of Germany on January 30, first became prominent in 1923, through his leadership, along with General Ludendorff, of the Munich rising, after which Hitler was sentenced to five years' imprisonment in a fortress, though released after a few months. He is now only forty-three. By birth he is an Austrian, but his birth place, Branau, is close to the frontier of Bavaria, his father was of Bavarian stock and he has always considered himself a German. In youth he was poor, and worked by turns as builder's painter, labourer, and draughtsman. In August 1914 he joined a Bavarian regiment, and served through the war, winning the Iron Cross, but only reached the rank of corporal. He was seriously wounded and gassed. In 1920, happening to attend a small meeting of the new National Socialist Workers' Party, he decided to join, and next year became its president and leader of the growing Fascist movement. Since 1923, his Nazis have moved from strength to strength until they became the most powerful party, mainly through this forceful leadership and violent, fervid oratory. His Brown Army appealed strongly to German youth and Monarchists look to him to found a new Hohenzollern régime. It is, perhaps, significant that his first Ministry contains a Monarchist element.

THE NEW CHANCELLOR OF THE GERMAN REPUBLIC: HERR ADOLF HITLER, LEADER OF THE NAZIS (NATIONAL SOCIALIST WORKERS' PARTY), WHOSE MINISTRY INCLUDES SEVERAL MONARCHISTS.

MATTERS POLITICAL: OCCASIONS IN BERLIN AND IN LONDON.

THE NEW GERMAN CHANCELLOR ATTENDING THE STATE FUNERAL OF MAKOWSKI AND ZAURITZ IN HIS CAPACITY AS NAZI LEADER: HERR HITLER (R.) RECEIVED BY COUNT HELLDORFF AT THE PROTESTANT CATHEDRAL, BERLIN.

THE FORMER GERMAN CROWN PRINCE CARRYING A WREATH INTO THE CATHEDRAL, WHERE HE ATTENDED THE MAKOWSKI AND ZAURITZ SERVICE.

HONOURING THEIR DEAD COMRADE: NAZIS IN THE GREAT SQUARE BETWEEN THE CASTLE AND THE CATHEDRAL RAISING THEIR HANDS IN A LAST SALUTE TO EBERHARD MAKOWSKI, OF THE NATIONAL SOCIALIST ARMY.

After Herr Adolf Hitler had been heralded as Germany's new Chancellor, there was a great demonstration in his honour in Berlin. At the same time, there was a certain amount of active opposition. On January 30, the night of the announcement, Eberhard Makowski, leader of the 33rd Storm Troop of the National Socialist Army, was shot while he was marching at the head of his men after a parade before the Nazi leader; and Joseph Zauritz, a policeman, was also killed. On Sunday, February 5, a State funeral was accorded to the two men. Herr Hitler attended the service in the Protestant Cathedral, Berlin, but only in his capacity as leader of the Nazis. Much comment was caused by the fact that the former German Crown Prince was also present and stood near the Chancellor during the service.

THE FILM "MORGENROT", WHICH DREW COMMENTS FROM HERR HITLER.

A GERMAN U-BOAT, AFTER HAVING TORPEDOED A BRITISH CRUISER CONVEYING TO RUSSIA BRITAIN'S "BEST-KNOWN ORGANISER AND ARMY LEADER", IS READY TO INTERCEPT AN APPARENTLY HARMLESS SAILING-SHIP: A SCENE FROM THE NEW GERMAN WAR FILM, "MORGENROT".

THE PRODUCTION OF "MORGENROT", THE GERMAN U-BOAT AND "Q"-SHIP FILM, IN BERLIN: HERREN HUGENBERG, HITLER AND VON PAPEN ON THE FIRST NIGHT (LEFT TO RIGHT).

The first night of the German naval war film "Morgenrot" was attended by Herr Hitler, Herr von Papen, the Vice-Chancellor and Herr Hugenberg, Minister for Trade and Food and Chairman of the National Peoples' Party. Later, the "Times" was authorised to say that Herr Hitler by no means approved of the political tinge given to the film.

THE LABOUR DEMONSTRATION OF UNEMPLOYMENT, WHICH WAS WITHOUT SUGGESTION OF DISORDER, ALTHOUGH RIOTING HAD BEEN PREDICTED AND A GREAT FORCE OF POLICE HAD BEEN MOBILISED: MR. GEORGE LANSBURY, LEADER OF THE OPPOSITION, ADDRESSING THE CROWD IN HYDE PARK ON SUNDAY, FEBRUARY 5.

The demonstration was organised by the Trades Union Congress, the Labour Party, and the Co-operative Union. There were those who feared that rioting would occur, owing to the Labour decision to exclude Communist organisations and banners from the procession but, although Communists contrived to slip into the ranks of the marchers, there was no trouble. As a precaution, an unusually large body of Metropolitan Police had been mustered, and in certain districts Special Constables did the work of the regular constables, thus relieving them for duty in the neighbourhood of the Park. The resolution carried demanded a reversal of the "Economy" policy, called for the abolition of the means test and protested against wage-cutting.

LIFE IN JEHOL: THE PICTURESQUE SIDE OF A DISPUTED PROVINCE.

THE MAIN COURTYARD OF THE "TEMPLE OF THE GREAT BUDDHA" IN JEHOL, THE CAPITAL OF THE PROVINCE: A VIEW SHOWING MARBLE STEPS.

THE SONG OF THE LUANG-HO BOATMEN: CHINESE WATERMEN CALLING "HI" AND "HO" AS THEY PROPEL A JUNK FROM JEHOL TO PEKING.

THE JAPANESE IN JEHOL: A SUCCESSFUL CAMPAIGN IN "ARCTIC" CONDITIONS.

A VITAL FACTOR IN THE RAPID CONQUEST OF JEHOL BY THE JAPANESE – LARGELY THE RESULT OF THE MOBILITY AND SUPERIOR EQUIPMENT OF THEIR FORCES: A DETACHMENT OF TANKS WAITING ADVANCE.

RIGHT: AFTER A BIG "BOUND" FORWARD: JAPANESE INFANTRY "DEBUSSING" FROM THEIR MOTOR-TRUCKS AND MOTOR-CARS – MANY OF THEM OF AMERICAN MAKE.

A JAPANESE OFFICER LEADING HIS MEN IN SHOUTS OF "BANZAI!" IN THE CAP-TURED CITY OF SHANHAIKWAN: AN INCIDENT OF THE FIGHTING THAT LED UP TO THE JEHOL SITUATION.

The tense situation that arose recently between the Chinese and the Japanese over the "buffer" province of Jehol, a territory lying between China proper and Manchuria, developed out of the events at the beginning of this year, when the Japanese, on January 3, captured Shanhaikwan. The above photograph, which has just reached us, was taken just after the Japanese had entered the city. It shows a Japanese officer, Major Ochiai, leading his men in their national shout of triumph – "Banzai!" – in front of the ruined tower over the South Gate at Shanhaikwan.

Before the vote on the Committee of Nineteen's Report on Manchuria was taken at the Special Assembly of the League of Nations at Geneva on February 24, Dr. Yen, the Chinese delegate, spoke, stating that his country's delegation would vote for the Report. Mr. Matsuoka made a dramatic speech for Japan, and, having announced that his Government could not accept the Report, urged that the Committee of Nineteen had failed to realise the actual situation in the Far East. He declared, further, his belief that the Powers had long been dealing in fictions regarding China, within which, he argued, there was no constituted Gov-ernment supreme and able to govern. In concluding he asked the delegates, for the sake of peace in the Far East and of peace throughout the world, not to adopt the Report. The vote was then taken: forty-two for the Report; one (Japan) against. After the voting, Mr. Matsuoka said that Japan would make the utmost efforts for peace in the Far East, and for the mainte-nance and strengthening of cordial rela-tions with other Powers. Mr. Matsuoka and his colleagues then walked out.

JAPAN WITHDRAWS FROM THE SPECIAL ASSEMBLY OF THE LEAGUE OF NATIONS AT GENEVA: MR. MATSUOKA (RIGHT) AND COLLEAGUES WALKING OUT AFTER THE VOTE ON THE SINO-JAPANESE DISPUTE OVER MANCHURIA.

THE CHINESE SIDE OF THE CAMPAIGN IN THE LOST PROVINCE

THE CHINESE GOVERNOR OF JEHOL, FOR WHOSE ARREST A WARRANT WAS ISSUED WHEN HE FLED AFTER HAVING ABANDONED THE CAPITAL: GENERAL TANG YU-LIN, RUMOURED LATER TO HAVE BEEN ASSASSINATED.

CAMEL TRANSPORT AS USED BY THE CHINESE FORCES, WHOSE EQUIPMENT WAS SAID TO BE MUCH LESS UP TO DATE AND EFFICIENT THAN THAT OF THE JAPANESE: A SOMEWHAT HEAVILY-LADEN ANIMAL.

SHANSI CARTS HAULING SUPPLIES OVER ROCKY MOUNTAIN PASSES FOR THE CHINESE TROOPS DURING THE OPERATIONS IN JEHOL: VEHICLES WITH SMALL SOLID WHEELS OF A CURIOUSLY PRIMITIVE TYPE.

CHINESE MACHINE-GUNNERS, WITH INFANTRY BEYOND, DURING THE OPERATIONS AGAINST THE JAPANESE IN THE PROVINCE OF JEHOL: TYPES OF A FORCE FITTED AGAINST SUPERIOR MECHANICAL EQUIPMENT.

THE LEG-THEORY CONTROVERSY: LARWOOD AND THE LEG-TRAP IN ACTION.

Throughout the present M.C.C. tour in Australia, there has been evident a certain ill-feeling against the English cricketers' methods, manifested mainly by intense barracking by the crowds, particularly of the captain, D.R. Jardine, and of the fast bowler, Larwood. The methods to which exception has been taken are the use of leg-theory bowling (re-named body-line bowling by the Australians), combined with the setting of a leg-trap – methods which Larwood and Voce have frequently used on the present tour, and with which they have had considerable success. This feeling culminated on January 18, when the third Test Match was in progress, with a telegram from the Australian Cricket Board of Control to the M.C.C. protesting against body-line bowling as unsportsmanlike and as likely to upset the friendly relations existing between Australia and England. The Committee of the M.C.C. met to consider the matter on January 23, and then sent to Australia a strongly worded reply expressing full support of the M.C.C. team, its captain, and its managers. It may be of interest to quote the definition of leg-theory bowling given recently in the "Daily Mail" by Mr. A.P.F. Chapman, formerly the England captain: "It means that the bowler pitches on or a little outside the leg stump, with several fieldsmen placed in a crescent near the wicket on the leg side. His object is not to hit the batsman or to intimidate him. He hopes to cramp the batsman's strokes to such an extent that any attempt to make runs,

LARWOOD IN ACTION: THE ENGLAND FAST BOWLER WHOSE METHODS HAVE CAUSED A STORM OF CRITICISM IN AUSTRALIA, CULMINATING IN AN OFFICIAL PROTEST.

WOODFULL, THE AUSTRALIAN CAPTAIN, STRUCK OVER THE HEART BY A BALL FROM LARWOOD IN THE MATCH AT MELBOURNE BETWEEN THE M.C.C. AND AN AUSTRALIAN XI.

whether by a definite hit or an effort to turn the ball to leg, will lead to a catch by one of the fieldsmen who are clustered so near to him." Such tactics, it is emphasised, are not new, but have been used before by both English and Australian bowlers. Mr. R.H. Lyttelton, in a letter to the "Times", attributed the vulnerability of modern batsmen to the general adoption of the two-eyed stance.

THE REICHSTAG DESTROYED – "A SIGNAL FOR SERIOUS DISORDERS": A FIRE OFFICIALLY DECLARED TO BE DUE TO INCENDIARISM.

The Reichstag fire affected the Parliament Chamber in particular, although much of the building was ruined. Vigorous action followed, and an official proclamation issued on February 28 and signed by Captain Göring, the Nazi Commissioner for the Prussian Ministry of the Interior will rank as one of the most remarkable documents of recent years; a statement whose challenging allegations will long be remembered. Denials and protests followed the publication of this, as might well have been anticipated, more especially as the elections to the Reichstag and the Prussian Diet are due to be held on Sunday next, March 5. It contained the following: "The police found in the Communist headquarters at Liebknecht House, Berlin, during the raid on Friday, instructions according to which Communist acts of terror should start on Tuesday throughout Germany, and general civil war should be let loose. . . . Soon after Captain Göring arrived at the scene of the Reichstag fire, he decided upon drastic measures, since an investigation proved beyond doubt that incendiarism was responsible. Tar products and torches were found in leather bags hidden in the Reichstag, while literature was distributed from the cellar to the top floor. . . . Through discoveries at Liebknecht House, a Bolshevist uprising has been frustrated. Nevertheless the blaze at the Reichstag was intended as a signal for the beginning of serious disorders timed for 4 a.m. to-day (February 28), including wholesale looting in Berlin. . . . It is further established that to-day was the date for the beginning of terrorism against hte life and property of citizens." Other passages read: "Captain Göring orders the detention of deputies and functionaries of the Communist Party. The entire Communist Presss is prohibited for four weeks, and the entire Social-Democratic Press is prohibited for a fortnight." One arrest was made in the building.

SMOKE PORURING FROM THE FAMOUS DOME AND THE WINDOWS LIT UP BY THE FLAMES.

THE FLAMES GLOWING THROUGH THE GILDED-COPPER AND GLASS DOME: A BERLIN LANDMARK.

THE GERMAN ELECTIONS THAT RESULTED IN A NAZI TRIUMPH.

A GREAT PARADE OF NAZIS (NATIONAL SOCIALISTS) IN BERLIN ON THE ELECTION DAY: STORM DETACHMENTS MARCHING THROUGH THE BRANDENBURG GATE.

COUNT HELLDORF, A NAZI LEADER, SWEARING-IN NAZIS AS AUXILLIARY POLICE, ADDITIONS TO A FORCE TO BE INCREASED TO 3000 MEN (INCLUDING ALSO STAHLHELMERS) IN BERLIN.

On Sunday, March 5, elections were held throughout Germany for the Reichstag, and in Prussia for the State Diet as well. In Berlin the polling day passed off with unexpected tranquillity. The result of the elections was a complete triumph for Herr Hitler, the Chancellor, and his Nazi followers. They won 288 seats in the Reichstag (out of a total of 647), as compared with their 195 on the last occasion, and polled a third of all the votes – over 17,000,000 out of 39,162,419. The next largest number of seats (118) was gained by the Socialists, while the Communists obtained 81, the Centre Party 70, the Nationalists 52, and the Bavarian People's Party 21. Six other parties gained a few seats each, totalling among them only 17. Owing to the recent destruction of the Parliament Chamber in the Reichstag building by a fire, officially attributed to incendiarism, it was arranged that the new Reichstag should meet in the historic Garrison Church at Potsdam, within view of the coffin of Frederick the Great. The building is too small to hold all the elected members, but Socialist and Communist Deputies, apparently, were not expected. It was considered probable that, after one meeting, the Reichstag would be adjourned indefinitely and Herr Hitler would proceed to carry out his Four-Year Plan for the regeneration of Germany. In his broadcast speech a few days before the election, he concluded by saying: "Nothing could more fittingly symbolize the beginning of a new Germany than the fact that the Chamber of the old Reichstag lies in ashes, and that the new Reichstag will meet in the Garrison Church." Before the election he made some propaganda flights by aeroplane, and indignation was aroused in Poland by the plan of broadcasting an appeal: "Germans, awake!", while in the air over the Polish Corridor. Before the elections, many Socialists and Communists were arrested for "political offences," and it was stated that the number of arrests throughout Germany must run into several thousands. Large numbers of Nazis and Stahlhelmers were sworn-in as "auxiliary police", of whom there were to be as many as three thousand in Berlin alone, 80 per cent of them being Nazis.

SEARCHING BERLIN PEDESTRIANS ON THE DAY BEFORE THE RECENT ELECTIONS: AN INCIDENT OF A POLICE RAID IN KÖSLINER STRASSE, WHERE MANY HOUSES ARE OCCUPIED BY SOCIAL DEMOCRATS AND COMMUNISTS.

NAZI ACTION – IMPERIAL COLOURS AND THE SWASTIKA FLAG.

A VIGOROUS GOVERNMENT BLOW AT THE WEIMAR CONSTITUTION: THE HOISTING OF THE OLD IMPERIAL FLAG AND THE NAZI SWASTIKA FLAG ON THE LANDTAGS BUILDING, WEIMAR.

With regard to certain of our photographs, we give the following notes:– In a proclamation broadcast by Herr Hitler on the afternoon of March 12, President Hindenburg decreed that, until the flag question was regulated once and for all, the old Imperial colours and the Nazi Swastika flag should be flown side by side. He said: "These flags unite the glorious past of the German Reich with the vigorous re-birth of the German nation."

THE EMBLEM OF THE ALL-CONQUERING NAZIS: THE SWASTIKA FLAG DISPLAYED AT BERLIN'S TOWN HALL.

MUNICH UNDER THE NAZIS: S.A. GUARDS AT THE PRINTING WORKS OF THE SOCIAL-DEMOCRATIC PRESS – ON THE RIGHT, SCATTERED PRINTED MATTER.

ARRESTED COMMUNISTS IN BERLIN LINED UP TO BE SEARCHED FOR WEAPONS UNDER THE SUPERVISION OF NAZI SPECIAL POLICE: A TYPICAL INSTANCE OF THE DRASTIC CONTROL EXERCISED IN GERMANY UNDER THE HITLER REGIME.

THE HUMAN SIDE OF GERMANY'S NAZI CHANCELLOR: HITLER THE MAN.

ADOLF HITLER IN PRIVATE LIFE: INTIMATE ASPECTS OF THE "SPELL-BINDER" WHO IS NOW DOMINANT IN GERMANY.

Herr Adolf Hitler, who has risen from humble origins to be the most powerful man in Germany, and by his appointment as Chancellor and his triumph in the recent elections has now realised his ambition to wield official authority, has hitherto been mainly known to readers in this country as a vigorous party chief and a fiery orator of the "spell-binder" type. His abilities as a constructive administrator have yet to be proved. Meanwhile these interesting photographs reveal another side of his personality – an intimate and human side of which hitherto little has been heard. The photographs were taken by Heinrich Hoffmann, who has been with him since the beginning of the Nazi movement. They show Hitler as a man, in private life, on familiar terms with friends and neighbours, with children, and with animals. His face has shed its public mask of severity, and it is seen that he can laugh and enjoy a joke. In company, it is said, he is charming; while his habits are simple and frugal. According to information supplied, he is a vegetarian, and does not drink or smoke.

THE NAZI BOYCOTT OF THE JEWS: SHOPS AND OFFICES PUT UNDER TABOO.

TYPICAL OF THE WAY IN WHICH NAZIS PREVENTED JEWS DOING BUSINESS ON APRIL 1, WHEN THERE WAS A BOYCOTT FROM 10 A.M. UNTIL MIDNIGHT: A "BUY ONLY AT GERMAN SHOPS" POSTER ON THE WINDOW OF A BERLIN ESTABLISHMENT.

AT A GREAT DEMONSTRATION HELD BY THE BOYCOTTERS OF JEWS IN THE LUSTGARTEN, BERLIN: DR. GOEBBELS, THE MINISTER OF PROPAGANDA, ADDRESSING A BIG MEETING ON "THE FIGHT FOR GERMAN NATIONALISM AND GERMAN TRADE".

The persecution of Jews in Germany entered upon a new phase on March 28, when Nazi Headquarters issued an order for the whole of the machinery of their organisation to be set in motion against the Jews. Personal violence was forbidden; but it was decreed that a national boycott of Jewish goods and of Jews in professions should begin on the following Saturday, April 1. This order, which was represented as a counter-action to anti-German agitation abroad, which, it was alleged, had been inspired by Jewish interests, was duly enforced; save that it would appear that the instructions against personal violence were not obeyed in their entirety. The boycott went on from 10 a.m. until midnight. During that period uniformed Nazis were stationed outside the Jewish shops and other undertakings, and every effort was made – with success – to hold up the work of Jewish traders and professional men. Nazis also posted placards on Jewish shops, telling Germans not to buy from Jews; and kindred notices were pasted over the name-plates of Jewish professional men. By April 3, Berlin, for example, had regained its normal appearance; but, despite expressed opinions that no further move would be made, there was still much fear that the boycott might be resumed on the Wednesday, as threatened. At the same time, it was reported that the German anti-Jewish movement as a whole was continuing.

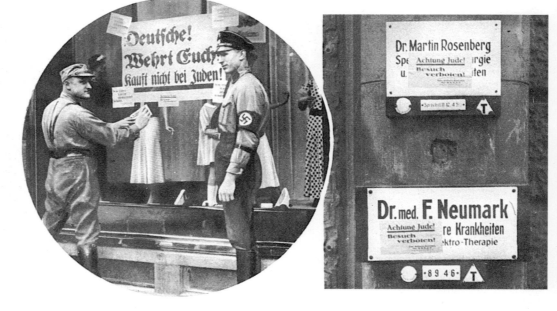

NAZIS AT A JEWISH SHOP: FIXING SUCH NOTICES AS "IT IS FORBIDDEN TO BUY ANYTHING IN THIS JEWISH SHOP" AND "WARNING: JEW! VISITING FORBID-DEN".

THE PRACTICE OF JEWISH PROFESSIONAL MEN HELD UP: "WARNING; JEW! VISITING FORBIDDEN" NOTICES PASTED ON PHYSICIANS' NAME-PLATES.

CARDBOARD AEROPLANES AS TARGETS FOR GERMANS:

Germany, forbidden an air force or anti-aircraft batteries, resorts to substitutes. Just as exercises are carried out with cardboard tanks, so anti-aircraft machine-gunners practise against small cardboard model aeroplanes. To get the "aeroplane" to the desired height, a tower, or pylon, is erected, near which it runs along a wire cable. About midway on the tower, on a platform, is a device by which a soldier moves backwards and forwards the miniature aeroplane slung from the cable. The machine-gunners on the ground try to shoot it down. This cardboard aeroplane, of course, cannot fully replace a real one, which can move from right to left, and up and down, whereas the model, owing to its cable, can only go to and fro. A second apparatus employed by the German anti-aircraft force is even simpler, for the dummy aeroplane turns in the air on a wooden spar. At the same time it is harder to hit because much smaller. The big shield is a bullet-proof protection for the man working it.

A CARDBOARD MODEL AEROPLANE IN THE AIR MOVING ALONG A CABLE. GERMANY, FORBIDDEN AN AIR FORCE OR ANTI-AIRCRAFT BATTERIES, RESORTS TO SUBSTITUTES.

ANTI-AIRCRAFT PRACTICE WITH A CARDBOARD MODEL AEROPLANE IN GERMANY: A MACHINE-GUNNER AIMING AT THE "TARGET".

THE STRONG MAN OF THE UNITED STATES – READY FOR "WAR" POWERS.

MR. FRANKLIN DELANO ROOSEVELT:

THE THIRTY-SECOND PRESIDENT OF THE UNITED STATES, WHO HAS DECLARED FOR ACTION AND ACTION NOW.

It would seem that President Franklin D. Roosevelt is to be the strong man of the United States. When he took the oath of office on March 4, he said: "I am prepared to recommend measures that a stricken nation may require . . . In the event of a critical national emergency, I shall not evade the clear course of duty. I shall ask Congress for the one remaining instrument to meet such a crisis – namely, a broad executive power to wage war against the emergency as great as the power that would be given to me if we were, in fact, invaded by a foreign foe." Within thirty-six hours, acknowledging a national emergency, he had prolonged the United States "bank holiday" until Thursday, March 9, when the new Congress was due to meet in special session, and had made it applicable throughout the country, its territories and insular possessions. Mr. Roosevelt, it may be added, began his career as a lawyer. During the Great War he was Assistant Secretary of the Navy. In 1920 he was Democratic candidate for the Vice-Presidency, but was defeated. He became Governor of New York State in 1928 and was re-elected in 1930. He is fifty-two.

A dastardly attempt was made on the life of Mr. Franklin Roosevelt, President-elect of the United States, who succeeds Mr. Hoover in office today (March 4), when he landed at Miami, Florida on February 15, at the conclusion of a fishing trip on board Mr. Vincent Astor's yacht, "Nourmahal". Mr. Roosevelt was addressing a large crowd at Bay Front Park, and had just ended a brief speech of thanks for his reception. As he sat down in his car, his assistant, an Italian-American named Giuseppe Zangara, opened fire from a few yards away. Five shots, wildly aimed, were fired: at the fifth shot Mrs. Cross, standing near Zangara, managed to knock up his arm, and he was then overpowered. Mr. Roosevelt was unhurt, but five persons near him were injured by bullets, two of them, Mr. Cermak and Mrs. Gill, very seriously. At the time of going to press Mr. Cermak was still very seriously ill. On February 20, Zangara was sentenced to eighty years' imprisonment on four charges of attempted murder, to which he pleaded guilty.

PRESIDENT-ELECT ROOSEVELT, WHO TAKES OFFICE TODAY (MARCH 4), SPEAKING INTO THE MICROPHONE TO THE THRONG THAT GREETED HIM AT MIAMI.

WAVING TO THE CROWD TO SHOW THAT HE WAS UNHARMED AFTER THE ATTEMPT ON HIS LIFE: MR. FRANKLIN ROOSEVELT IN THE CAR WHERE HE WAS SITTING AT THE TIME OF THE OUTRAGE.

THE AIR CONQUEST OF EVEREST: THE CROWNING TRIUMPH OF BRITISH AVIATION ABOVE THE WORLD'S HIGHEST PEAK.

THE MONARCH OF MOUNTAINS CRESTED WITH A SNOWY PLUME: THE GREAT PEAK OF EVEREST (IN THE CENTRE), WITH MAKALU, OF "ARMCHAIR" SHAPE (ON THE RIGHT) – A SOUTH VIEW OF THE MASSIF PHOTOGRAPHED FROM AN APPROACHING AEROPLANE.

In this magnificent air panorama of the Everest range, taken from one of the Houston Flight machines that flew over the summit, we see the tremendous bastions, inaccessible to climbers, that guard the southern approaches to the mighty massif whereon the king of mountains is enthroned. His crest rises to a height of over 29,000 ft. (more than five miles above sea-level). On the right is his imposing neighbour, Makalu (27,790 ft.), whose form has been likened to an armchair, and nearer the foreground are the huge ridges of Chamiang (24,012 ft.) and Lhotse. In Colonel Blacker's first account of the flight (in "The Times"), describing the outward journey, when the aeroplane had attained about 19,000 ft. after clearing the dust-haze, we read: "I soon opened the cockpit roof, put my head out into the slip-stream, and there, over the pulsating rocker arms of the Pegasus (engine), showing level with us was the naked majesty of Everest. I was not able to remain long watching the wonderful sights, as the machine, roaring upwards, unfolded countless peaks to right and left and in front, all in their amazing white mantles, scored and seared with black precipes. Somewhat to my dismay Everest bore that immense snow-plume which means a mighty wind tearing across the summit, lifting clouds of powdered snow and driving it with blizzard force eastward." A little later, as he records in his second account (also in "The Times"), Colonel Blacker opened the floor hatch again and looked down many sheer thousands of feet straight on to a great snow peak which must have been Chamiang. "To my left," he writes, "showed vast and curving glaciers, grimed with ancient deposits and seamed with moraines. All was now bare; the last trees were far below and far behind."

NATURE'S DEPTH-CHARGE: KRAKATOA IN ERUPTION – AND SUGGESTING SUBMARINE WARFARE!

THE BEGINNING OF KRAKATOA'S TERRIFYING DISPLAY: MASSES OF MOLTEN LAVA SHOWING BLACK IN THE PHOTOGRAPH, AND CLOUDS OF STEAM SHOWING WHITE: ONE OF THE EXPLOSIONS FROM A SUBMARINE CRATER WHICH BROKE OUT IN JANUARY OF THIS YEAR.

It was reported on May 4 that Krakatoa, one of the most famous and destructive of volcanoes, situated in the Sunda Strait between Sumatra and Java, had been in eruption again during the early days of the month. This activity followed a severe outbreak that occurred last January – here illustrated by truly astonishing photographs taken at comparatively close quarters – when lava was thrown out, from submerged craters to a height of over 4,000 feet above the sea. For some years there has been an observation station on Lang Island, one of the islands of the Krakatoa group, set up by the Dutch Government to investigate the volcanic activity of Krakatoa, and warn the inhabitants of the neighbouring coasts and islands when an eruption is impending. So the rumbling of the sleeping giant gave warning of the January outbreak; it was possible to predict its approximate date; and an enterprising photographer sought and received permission from the Dutch Government to take photographs of the eruption. A boat and aeroplane were lent by the Government; and the photographer, flying to within about fifty yards of the crater's actual mouth, barely escaped with his life, and lava settled on the wing of the machine.

THE EARTHQUAKE IN CALIFORNIA:
PLEASURE CITIES DEVASTATED.

The earthquake in Southern California began, with a terrific shock, at 5.54 p.m. on March 10, and continued, with more than 20 other tremors, until the following afternoon. An area over 200 miles long and 30 miles wide was affected. The number of dead was put at 119 at the moment of going to press: and the damage to property was estimated at some £15,000,000 (at par). This compares with the thousand fatalities in the great San Francisco earthquake of 1906, when the whole of that great city was wrecked. The greatest losses of life and property were at Long Beach, where over seventy persons were killed, and at Compton, between Long Beach and Los Angeles, where over twenty people were killed.

(LEFT), AFTER THE EARTHQUAKE IN CALIFORNIA: A LEANING SPIRE, ON ST. ANTHONY'S CHURCH, LONG BEACH, WHICH WAS AFTERWARDS RAZED BY FIREMEN – BY WAY OF PRECAUTION.

(RIGHT), A SCHOOL BADLY DAMAGED BY THE SHOCKS: TALL PILLARS (AT THE ENTRANCE OF THE LONG BEACH POLYTECHNICAL HIGH SCHOOL) WHICH REMAINED STANDING, THOUGH THE INTERIOR COLLAPSED.

FUTURIST ARCHITECTURE OF CHICAGO'S "STAR-HITCHED" WORLD'S FAIR.

It was stated recently that the "Century of Progress" Exhibition at Chicago, known as the World's Fair, would be opened officially by President Roosevelt on May 27. According to previous reports, another opening ceremony, of a more unusual character, had been planned for June 1 – nothing less than the switching on of the exhibition lights, the starting of the machinery, and the opening of the science exhibition by means of light from the star Arcturus, 240,000,000,000,000 miles away. The light left the star in 1893, and, after having travelled for forty years at a speed of 186,000 miles a second, is to be focussed on a photo-electric cell by means of the great 40-inch telescope at the Yerkes Observatory at William's Bay, Wisconsin, 100 miles from Chicago. This telescope was illustrated in our issue of May 13. The impact of the light will have an effect on the cell which, when amplified, will convey an impulse to Chicago over wires. It is the first time that an exhibition has been, so to speak, "hitched to a star". The primary purpose of the World's Fair is to demonstrate the great achievements of science during the past century.

THE FIRST LARGE-SCALE APPLICATION TO ARCHITECTURE OF THE SUSPENSION BRIDGE PRINCE PRINCIPLE: THE STRANGELY DESIGNED TRAVEL AND TRANSPORT BUILDING, WITH A ROOF OF METAL PLATES SUSPENDED BY STEEL CABLES HUNG FROM STEEL TOWERS AND ANCHORED BY CONCRETE SLABS.

SYMBOLIC SCULPTURE AT THE EXHIBITION TO BE "OPENED" AGAIN ON JUNE 1 BY MEANS OF LIGHT FROM THE STAR ARCTURUS: TWIN PYLONS GUARDING THE WATER GATE TO THE ELECTRICAL BUILDING.

THE KENTUCKY DERBY INCIDENT: FILM PICTURES ADVANCED AS EVIDENCE.

The Great Race during which Meade, the winning jockey, is alleged to have hindered Fisher, rider of the second, by pulling at his horse's saddle-cloth, and Fisher is alleged to have retaliated by whipping Meade: Head Play (nearer camera) and Broker's Tip, the winner of the Kentucky Derby, racing neck to neck.

A STRICTLY GERMAN POINT OF VIEW AS PICTURED IN ONE OF GERMANY'S LEADING ILLUSTRATED PAPERS: "HOW CAN WORK PROSPER IN SUCH CIRCUMSTANCES? – SINISTER CLOUDS HANG OVER THE WORLD: THE GERMAN AGRICULTURALIST SEES THE FRONTIERS OF HIS NATIVE LAND THREATENED ON EVERY SIDE."

GERMANY AND DISARMAMENT: HERR HITLER SPEAKS; GENEVA RENEWS ACTIVITY: A GERMAN PAPER IS ALARMIST.

In the course of his speech at the meeting of the Reichstag in the Kroll Opera House on May 17, Herr Hitler proved that he can be statesman as well as party leader and popular orator. His tone was most moderate: his statement, reasoned. Naturally, chief interest centred in his policy with regard to disarmament. Among other things, he said: "Germany demands the disarmament of others because her claim is moral, legal and sensible. The advantages of the moment are as nothing when compared with the development of centuries. Germany, France, and Poland will continue to exist. Germany wants nothing that she is not ready to give to others . . . No fresh European War is capable of putting something better in the place of the unsatisfactory conditions which exist today . . . Even by the decisive success of a new European settlement by force, the final result could only be an increase in the destruction of the European balance of power, and thus would contain the seeds for later differences and fresh complications . . . The outbreak of such a madness without end would lead to the collapse of the existing social order in Europe. A Europe sinking into Communistic chaos would bring about a crisis in the development of the world of unimaginable extent and duration." As a sequel to this, Herr Nadolny, Germany's chief representative at the renewed meeting of the General Committee of the Disarmament Conference at Geneva on the 19th, said that the German Government accepted the British Draft "not only hitherto as a basis of discussion, but as a basis for the future Convention itself".

GERMAN BATTLESHIPS LAUNCHED COMMISSIONED.

THE LAUNCH OF GERMANY'S SECOND POCKET BATTLE-SHIP: THE "ADMIRAL SCHEER" TAKING THE WATER AT WILHELMSHAVEN.

On April 1, Germany's second 10,000-ton "pocket battle-ship" was launched. A guard of honour and groups of the nationalist associations were drawn up to meet General von Blomberg, Minister of Defence, and Admiral Raeder, at Wilhelmshaven. Admiral Raeder, in his speech, said that the spirit of Jutland had become a symbol of the nation's future. It was this spirit, he added, which had inspired Admiral Scheer and his crew and enabled them to carry off the laurels of victory from the biggest fleet in the world! The new battle-ship was named after the "Victor of Jutland", Admiral Scheer, by Frau Bessor, Admiral Scheer's daughter. At the same time as the "Admiral Scheer" was christened, Germany's other "pocket battle-ship", the "Deutschland", was commissioned.

GERMANY'S FIRST "POCKET BATTLE-SHIP": THE MUCH DISCUSSED "DEUTSCHLAND" ON HER TRIALS.

The "Deutschland", Germany's first "pocket battle-ship", and the most discussed of the world's war-ships, began her trials in Kiel Bay on January 19. It may be recalled that she was launched by President von Hindenburg in May 1931. She combines the gun-power of a small battle-ship with the speed of a cruiser, and has been constructed in accordance with the terms of the Treaty of Versailles, by which it was agreed that Germany should not build battle-ships of over 10,000 tons. She is the first of four vessels of her class. According to the latest "Jane's Fighting Ships", she is the first ship of her size to have an electrically welded hull.

MILITARY TRAINING AS A "SPORT" IN GERMANY: A STEP TOWARDS A REVIVAL OF CONSCRIPTION? A NATIONAL SYSTEM DECREED BY HINDENBURG: THE "DEFENCE-SPORT" COURSE FOR GERMANS.

VISUAL TRAINING: YOUNG GERMANS BEING TAUGHT TO IDENTIFY POINTS IN A LANDSCAPE, USING FINGERS OR THUMBS TO JUDGE DISTANCES BY A FAMILIAR MILITARY METHOD.

PRACTISING THE ART OF TAKING ANY AVAILABLE COVER ON THE BATTLEFIELD: A YOUNG GERMAN UNDER MILITARY INSTRUCTION WHO HAS CAMOUFLAGED HIS HEAD WITH A BASIN.

THE TRAINER AT THE ORTELSBURG AVIATION SCHOOL, WITH EAGLE ON WRIST, INSTRUCTING A YOUNG ENTHUSIAST BEFORE SHE GOES UP.

These photographs indicate how Germany is preparing for the day when, as she hopes, it may again be possible to develop her military forces without the restrictions at present imposed by the Versailles Treaty. Under the heading "New Germany: German Youth and 'Defence Sport'" (Wehrsport), an explanatory note supplied with the photographs here given states: "President Hindenburg created by special decree the Defence-Sport system which gives young men from sixteen to twenty-one, during a course of three weeks, the elements of military training after the manner of sport. They are provided with free lodging and uniform, and receive instruction in the study of landscape, judging distances, map-reading, finding their way by compass and similar matters. This systematic training course for German youth, on military lines, is an important symptom of Germany's national aspirations. The courses are now held in all the German States." The recruits, it will be noted, are uniformed but unarmed.

THE SHAPE, HEIGHT, AND WIDTH OF THE EAGLE'S SPREAD WINGS TAKEN AS THE TEXT FOR GLIDING LESSONS: STUDENTS OF AN ART WHICH IS FOUNDED ON THE NATURAL MOVEMENTS OF SOARING BIRDS.

CLASSED WITH FIRE-BRIGADES – BY HERR HITLER: GERMAN "WEHRSPORT".

THE WEHRSPORT MOVEMENT IN GERMANY, WHICH IS REGARDED BY THE CHANCELLOR AS NO MORE MILITARY THAN A FIRE-BRIGADE OR A ROWING CLUB: YOUTHS, IN THEIR FULL EQUIPMENT, AT "CROSS-COUNTRY" EXERCISES.

"ALL'S WELL IN THE RANKS. WE SING OUR MARCHING SONG": WEHRSPORT VOLUNTEERS, HEADED BY AN INSTRUCTOR, ON A ROUTE-MARCH.

In his famous declaration of policy in the Reichstag the other day, Herr Adolf Hitler, the Chancellor and Nazi leader, claiming that his country had disarmed and arguing that German disarmament should be the signal for general disarmament, went on to say that the Nazi Storm Troops were without military training, were equipped solely for party needs, had as their purpose only the removal of Communist danger, and were organised only for reasons of propaganda. Likewise, he argued, the Steel Helmets were in being only to foster the tradition of comradeship among those who had been in the trenches, and to protect Germany against Communism, "a danger which other nations cannot estimate". He continued: "If the statesmen at Geneva claim that these are military units, they might just as well include fire-brigades, gymastic clubs, rowing clubs, and other sport organisations." Among "other sport organisations" must, we presume, be reckoned the Wehrsport movement here illustrated, in which connection it may be recalled that German sport as a whole shows every sign of being "militarised": it has been asserted authoritatively that, so long as compulsory service is lacking, "military sports must be the common property of the entire youth of Germany".

MOSCOW – WHERE BRITISH SUBJECTS WERE ARRESTED.

In view of the arrest of British subjects in Moscow, on a charge of sabotage, and the consequent protests by this country, general conditions in the Russian capital are of exceptional interest at the moment. "A city unique among the cities of the world, the cultural, social, and political centre of a country occupying one sixth of the entire surface of the earth, the capital of the first Socialist State – the U.S.S.R. – which has preserved many interesting relics of all stages of its growth through eight long centuries although continually changing its aspect – such is Moscow." So says the official guide-book. Let us now see what a matter-of-fact American observer – and one with a confessed affection for the Russian people – found in Moscow. Mr. Will Durant gave his impressions of Russia in a series of exceedingly lucid and well-informed articles in the "Saturday Evening Post". "Some of the avenues were smoothly paved," he writes: "in 1912 they were content with cobblestones. Private automobiles were few, but buses were many, and the trams were frequent and full. Shacks and palaces passed by us in chaotic alternation: the bizarre grandeur of old churches mingled with the crude boxes and parallel lines of modernistic monstrosities; the great stores that had given colour to this thoroughfare twenty years before were closed, and white sheets draped their vast windows dismally. Dingy tenements opened their sleepy portals and sent forth streams of workers to shops and factories, majestic, spacious, clean; already at nine in the morning, a line of pilgrims was waiting to enter the tomb of Lenin." As to the first hotel

PROPAGANDA IN MOSCOW, WHERE THE MOTIVES OF INDIVIDUAL ENTER-PRISE ARE REPLACED BY PRAISE AND COLLECTIVE ENTHUSIASM: A BOARD ON WHICH THE CHARACTERISTICS OF VARIOUS FACTORIES ARE PUBLICLY DISPLAYED – A SNAIL SYMBOLISES SLOW WORKERS; AND SO FORTH.

he tried, an American business man assured him that every room was taken, and congratulated him, because the food was terrible, the water was undrinkable, there was no beer to be had, there was no water in the shower-baths, and there were too many cockroaches on the floor. "But in the end," continues Mr. Durant, "we are fortunate. At noon, eight hours after our arrival at the Mecca of our dreams, room is found for us at the Savoy Hotel. It is a relic of the old regime, well managed and maintained under the new. At last order and quiet, cleanliness and a bath! White sheets, hot water, and vast bourgeois towels."

(RIGHT), WHERE A CERTAIN MODICUM OF FOOD IS A WORKER'S RATION – SO LONG AS HE DESERVES WELL OF THE SOCIALIST STATE: A PATIENT FOOD-QUEUE WAITING TO PRESENT THEIR FOOD "COUPONS".

RUSSIAN BALLET – HAMMER AND SICKLE VERSION.

Russian Ballet has attracted enormous interest in Western Europe ever since that memorable day in 1907 on which Diaghilev, Bakst, and Fokin opened their season at the Chatelet Theatre, in Paris, with a Russian company. Far from declining, Russian Ballet has enjoyed a revival of popularity this year. The "Ballets Russes de Monte Carlo", which began at the Alhambra on July 4, recently reached the hundredth performance. Meanwhile, ballets are still being performed in the Grand Theatre at Moscow, a city whose Russian Ballet flourished as a branch of that in St. Petersburg and, later, gained recognition on its own account; and it is of great interest to see how the ballet has developed under the Soviet régime. This art form – probably the most "artificial" of all (with the possible exception of the cinema) – with its traditions going back to the eighteenth century, is a curious anomaly in the land of the Five-Year Plan. Yet its popularity there seems unquestionable.

THE DEVELOPMENT OF THE MOSCOW BALLET – ONE OF THE MOST BRIL-LIANT ORNAMENTS OF THE IMPERIAL REGIME – UNDER THE SOVIETS: AN EFFECT OF "MASS-PURPOSE" IN A BAL-LET WITH THE FRENCH REVOLUTION AS ITS BACKGROUND – "THE FLAME OF PARIS".

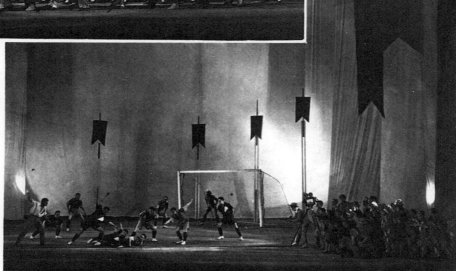

(RIGHT), DOUBTLESS OF GREAT TOPIC-AL INTEREST IN RUSSIA, WHERE "FUT-BOL", FORMERLY ANATHEMATISED AS CALCULATED TO FOSTER A SPIRIT OF ANTAGONISM AMONG PROLETARIANS, WAS RECENTLY SANCTIONED BY THE SOVIET AUTHORITIES AS A VALUABLE GYMNASTIC EXERCISE: A FOOTBALL-LERS' BALLET: WITH THE ACTIONS OF PLAYERS AND SPECTATORS STYLISED IN AN ODD MANNER.

THE ARREST OF BRITISH SUBJECTS BY THE OGPU IN MOSCOW.

INCIDENTS AND PERSONALITIES; AND A "FANTASTIC" CHARGE.

THE BRITISH AMBASSADOR, SIR ESMOND OVEY (LEFT), AND M. LITVINOFF, SOVIET FOREIGN COMMISSAR (RIGHT), TO WHOM HE PROTESTED AGAINST THE ARRESTS: A PHOTOGRAPH TAKEN WHEN SIR ESMOND PRESENTED HIS CREDENTIALS IN 1929.

MR. ALLAN MONKHOUSE IN THE ROOM IN WHICH HE WAS ARRESTED; WITH A UNION JACK BEHIND HIM.

BRITISH AND RUSSIAN ACCUSED LISTENING TO THEIR SENTENCES IN THE MOSCOW COURT: (CENTRE FOREGROUND – LEFT TO RIGHT) MR. WILLIAM MACDONALD (TWO YEARS' IMPRISONMENT); M. ZORIN (EIGHT YEARS); AND MME. KUTUSOVA (EIGHTEEN MONTHS) – (BACKGROUND) MR. CHARLES NORDWALL (EXPULSION).

The six British subjects who were recently arrested by the Ogpu in Moscow are all members of the Metropolitan-Vickers organisation, a well-known electrical engineering company. The first four arrested were Mr. Allan Monkhouse, the manager in Russia; Mr. W.H. Thornton; Mr. John Cushny; and Mr. W.H. Macdonald. Mr. Charles Nordwall and Mr. Gregory were arrested later. Mr. Monkhouse and Mr. Nordwall were subsequently released, but were required to remain in Russia. Strong protests were made by the British Ambassador, Sir Esmond Ovey, on the instructions of the British Government. On March 19 the Metropolitan-Vickers Electrical Co. Ltd. issued an official statement concerning a report that the charges against the company's engineers were connected with the building of the Dnieprostroy Dam, declaring that there was no truth in it. The statement continued: "The idea of damaging these huge turbines by pouring in sand or acid is manifestly absurd. Each blade used in these machines weighs ab-

THE HUGE TURBINES OF THE DNIEPROSTROY DAM: MACHINERY WHICH, IT WAS REPORTED, THE ARRESTED MEN MIGHT BE ACCUSED OF DAMAGING BY POURING IN SAND – A FANTASTIC CHARGE.

out five tons and millions of gallons of water pass through the turbines daily which would prevent any acid or sand remaining in them. The statement that the charge against the arrested men is of such a nature, therefore, is fantastic . . ." It was announced in Parliament on March 20 that the Government would suspend negotiations with the Soviet Government for a commercial treaty. Full details of the charge against the arrested men had not been received, but it had been described as one of sabotage in the electrical industry.

The trial ended on April 19. The six British engineers and eleven Russians, employees of the Metropolitan-Vickers Company, were accused of counter-revolutionary activities, bribery, espionage, and sabotage. The sentences on the British engineers were as follows: Mr. Leslie C. Thornton, 3 years' imprisonment; Mr. William Macdonald, 2 years; Mr. Allan Monkhouse, Mr. Charles Nordwall and Mr. John Cushny, expulsion. Mr. A.W. Gregory was acquitted.

THE MAY DAY MILITANT IN MOSCOW.

SOME OF THE 350 AEROPLANES THAT TOOK PART IN THE MILITARY AND AIR DISPLAY ON MAY DAY IN MOSCOW: THE MACHINES LEAVING THEIR AERODROME FOR THE RED SQUARE.

NOT CHEERED BY THE SPECTATORS IN THE RED SQUARE, WHO SHOWED LITTLE ENTHUSIASM: M. STALIN, THE RUSSIAN DICTATOR (RIGHT), ON THE WAY TO THE PARADE, WHICH WAS THE MOST ELABORATE IN THE HISTORY OF SOVIET RUSSIA.

May Day in Moscow was chiefly notable for a great military and air display, the most elaborate in Soviet history. Over 350 aeroplanes – fifty per cent of them new bombers – flew over the Red Square in formation; and much was made of a parade of 300 tanks, including heavies, racers, Soviet-constructed Carden-Lloyds, amphibians, and twelve exceptionally large models, some equipped with five guns. According to the "Daily Telegraph's" correspondent, the crowd showed little enthusiasm and did not even cheer Stalin, contenting themselves with mild applause. The same writer noted that the military march past Lenin's tomb seemed less spontaneous than it used to be. This year's conscripts repeated the oath to defend the Soviet Union and the cause of world revolution. Then a salute was fired within the walls of the Kremlin. Voroshiloff's harangue to the Army was of a distinctly cautious nature. Foreign military attachés attended: and all the Diplomatic Corps were present, save Mr. Strang, the British Chargé d'Affaires, and other officials of the Embassy.

FROM THE WORLD'S SCRAP-BOOK:
NEWS ITEMS OF TOPICAL INTEREST.

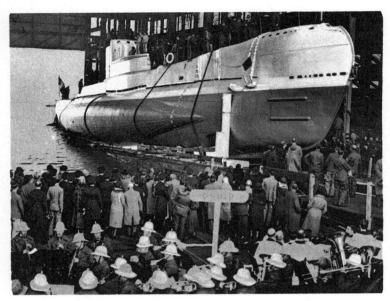

THE LAUNCH OF A NEW BRITISH SUBMARINE: *THE STARFISH*, SISTER VESSEL OF *SEAHORSE*, LEAVING THE STOCK AT CHATHAM DOCKYARD.

H.M. Submarine "Starfish", the last of the three submarines authorised in 1930, was launched at Chatham Dockyard on March 14, the ceremony being performed by Mrs. S.O. Summers, Mayoress of Gillingham. The new submarine cost £250,000, is equipped with anti-aircraft guns, has a standard displacement of 640 tons and is 187 feet long. She was designed by Mr. A.W. Johns, C.B., C.B.E.

ONE OF THE ARMOURED CARS WHICH, AT THE DICTATOR'S ORDERS, PATROLLED THE STREETS OF ATHENS AND FIRED MACHINE-GUNS ON THE CROWDS.

An attempt to set up a military dictatorship in Athens, with scarcely a pretence of popular backing, failed inevitably after a mere fourteen hours. When, on March 6, the general election went against the Republican National Union, of M. Venizelos, General Plastiras, on the pretext that there was no chance of a stable Government, proclaimed a dictatorship and martial law. He arrested M. Tsaldaris, the Opposition leader, whose Popular Party had won the elections and cleared the streets of Athens with armoured cars and machine-guns when the people gathered to protest. His triumph was short-lived. Late on March 6 a provisional military Cabinet, backed by the most influential statesmen of Athens, turned out General Plastiras, deciding to govern until order was restored. By March 8 all was quiet; the military Government, having done its work, resigned: and M. Tsaldaris took up office and formed his Cabinet in a constitutional way. Leaders of the coup d'état were arrested, with the exception of General Plastiras, who had succeeded in escaping.

THE FLYING CORPS OF THE NAZI "BROWN" ARMY: MEN AND MACHINES OF THE BERLIN SECTION ON PARADE AT A GERMAN AERODROME.

"Hitler's army", writes a correspondent, "has its own flying corps; applicants are first required to attend a school where they are taught aeroplane construction and theoretical work. The fact that they are not allowed to have military aeroplanes means that practical work is very limited."

(BELOW). NOT A FILM STUNT OR AN OBSTACLE RACE, BUT LONDON DOCKS POLICEMEN CARRYING OUT THEIR DUTIES! – JUMPING INTO THE WATER IN OVERCOATS TO TEST THE LIFE-JACKETS WHICH THEY WEAR WHEN ON PATROL IN FOGGY WEATHER.

BEFORE MR. J.A. MOLLISON'S START FOR BRAZIL: HIS WIFE (AMY JOHNSON) EXAMINES HIS ENGINE WHILE HE LIFTS THE COWL.

Mr. J.A. Mollison left Lympne on February 6 to fly to Brazil in 3½ days, via West Africa and the South Atlantic, using the Puss Moth "Heart's Content" in which he crossed the North Atlantic last year. His wife (Amy Johnson) escorted him across the Channel in her own machine. By February 7 he had reached Agadir and left for Villa Cisneros, Rio de Oro.

(LEFT), PROFESSOR EINSTEIN AND M. HERRIOT, ON THEIR WAY TO RECEIVE HONORARY DEGREES AT GLASGOW.

(RIGHT), IRISH TROOPS WEARING STEEL HELMETS FASHIONED AFTER THE GERMAN MODEL, DURING THE IRISH FREE STATE GENERAL ELECTION: INFANTRY STANDING BY IN RATHMINES TOWN HALL, DUBLIN.

A number of distinguished persons received honorary degrees from Glasgow University, when Commemoration Day was celebrated on June 21. Among them were two very distinguished foreigners, Professor Albert Einstein and M. Edouard Herriot, ex-Premier of France and Mayor of Lyon, who received Honorary L.L.D.s.

On the whole, the Irish Free State Election passed off without any very serious disturbances. For all that, there were outbreaks of political enmity from time to time, and the authorities had to take certain precautions. The men shown in our photograph were among those who stood by and did not have to use their authority. it should be noted that they wear steel helmets, of the German style and also that they are equipped with gas-masks.

MRS. BEETON, OF THE COOKERY-BOOK: A PORTRAIT AC-
QUIRED BY THE NATIONAL PORTRAIT GALLERY.

A portrait of Mrs. Beeton (1836–1865) has been acquired by the
National Portrait Gallery. The famous author of the cookery-book
was born ninety-seven years ago, and wrote her book seventy-four
years ago. Her portrait is a tinted photograph.

GENERAL SANDINO.

After maintaining, for six years, the revolt
against the Nicaraguan Governments supported
by United States Marines, General Augustino
Sandino has made peace with the newly-
inaugurated Nicaraguan President, Dr. Juan
Bautista Sacasa. The last United States Marines
departed recently from Nicaragua.

THE DEATH OF A FLYING PIONEER: HERR
GUSTAV LILIENTHAL.

Gustav Lilienthal, brother of Otto Lilienthal,
another pioneer of flying, had a life-long ambition to construct a machine that would fly
naturally like a bird, with flapping wings. This
aim was never fulfilled, but many important
discoveries were made as the direct result of his
work. Herr Lilienthal has died, while at work
on his experiments, at the age of eighty-four.

THE U.S.A.'S FIRST WOMAN AMBASSADOR:
MRS. OWEN TAKING THE OATH AT
WASHINGTON.

President Roosevelt, having already appointed
the first woman to hold Cabinet rank in the
U.S.A., subsequently selected Dr. Ruth Bryan
Owen as Ambassador to Denmark. She is the
daughter of the late William Jennings Bryan,
who was three times a candidate for the Presidency. Mrs. Owen is the widow of Major
Reginald Owen, of the Royal Engineers.

MARINUS VAN DER LÜBBE: THE
ALLEGED INCENDIARY OF THE REICH-
STAG.

This Communist, who, according to the
official reports, admitted to having set fire
to the Reichstag, is Dutch. He has studied
in Russia.

SIR HENRY ROYCE.

The great motor and aeroplane engineer died
April 22, aged seventy. Designed engines
which gained for Britain the world speed
record on land, sea, and air; including that
which enabled Flight-Lieutenant Stainforth
to make his air speed record of 407 m.p.h.

TO WORK IN THE NEW MOND LABORATORY: PRO-
FESSOR KAPITZA.

Professor Kapitza will continue his valuable researches
on the properties of matter in the Royal Society Mond
Laboratory, officially opened at Cambridge on February 3 by Mr. Baldwin, Chancellor of the University.

LIEUTENANT-GENERAL NAGAOKA, A PIONEER OF JAPANESE
AVIATION.

The death occurred at Tokyo recently of Lieutenant-General Gaishi
Nagaoka, a pioneer of aviation in Japan, and often called "The
Father of Japanese Aviation", at the age of seventy-five. He claimed
to have the longest moustachios in the world. These, it is said,
measured some twenty inches from tip to tip.

THE 1933 DERBY WON BY THE 17TH EARL OF DERBY, AFTER WHOSE
ANCESTOR, THE 12TH EARL, THE FIRST DERBY WAS NAMED.

THE CAMERA AS RECORDER:
PEOPLE IN THE PUBLIC EYE.

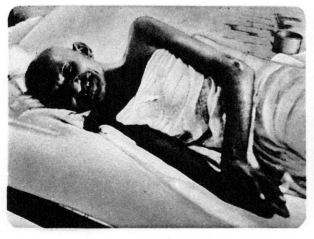

MR. GANDHI AT THE BEGINNING OF HIS THREE WEEKS' FAST, SINCE COM-
PLETED: A SELF-IMPOSED PENANCE IN AID OF THE UNTOUCHABLES.

Mr. Gandhi's fast ended on May 29. Lady Thackersey's house, where he had been
staying, was besieged by people of all classes, and nearly 200 gathered in the hall. At
noon Mr. Gandhi's bed was wheeled in. He was much wasted, but smiled a greeting.
After a devotional ceremony, during which a special poem by Rabindranath Tagore
was recited, Mr. Gandhi drank some orange juice presented by an Untouchable boy.

THE WINNING OWNER: LORD DERBY SHAKING HANDS WITH HIS JOCKEY, T. WESTON, BEFORE LEADING-IN HIS HYPERION.
ON THE RIGHT, S. DONOGHUE, WHO RODE LORD DERBY'S SECOND STRING, THRAPSTON.

The Derby – "the 150th renewal of the Derby Stakes" – was run on Wednesday, May 31. It was won by Lord Derby's Hyperion
(Gainsborough-Selene); trained by Lambton; T. Weston up. Hyperion won by four lengths in 2 min. 34 sec., a record. The first
Derby was run on May 4, 1780, and the "Evening News" has noted that it arose out of wagers at a convivial meeting of sportsmen held
at the house of the twelfth Earl of Derby. "These jovial spirits dined so gloriously under the hospitable roof of their host that they
departed at the dawn pledged to celebrate the occasion by running a race for stakes to be named after Lord Derby."

GERMANY AND AUSTRIA IN THE NEWS: NAZI AND ANTI-NAZI DEMONSTRATIONS.

DR. FRANK IN VIENNA, DESPITE THE AUSTRIAN GOVERNMENT'S INTIMATION THAT HIS VISIT WAS NOT WELCOME: AUSTRIAN NAZIS SALUTING AS THE GERMAN NAZI LEADERS DROVE THROUGH THE CITY.

Despite having been informed that the Austrian Government did not consider his visit very desirable, the Nazi Dr. Frank, the Bavarian Minister of Justice, drove through the city "in state" on May 13; and in the evening addressed Austrian Nazis. Later, at Gratz, he made a speech which caused the Austrian Government to ask him to leave the country.

THE SHORT AUSTRIAN CHANCELLOR AND THE TALL HEIMWEHR COMMANDER-IN-CHIEF: DR. DOLLFUSS (LEFT CENTRE) AND PRINCE RUDIGER VON STARHEMBERG (NEXT TO HIM) AT THE SCHONBRUNN PARK HEIMWEHR PARADE.

For many hours Dr. Dollfuss, Europe's smallest Chancellor, dressed in his war-time uniform, took the salute with, at his side, the tall Prince Rudiger von Starhemberg. In connection with the request that Dr. Frank should leave Austria without delay, Dr. Dollfuss has said that Austria's action was not directed against the German Government, but against Dr. Frank personally.

ANTI-GAS TRAINING IN PARIS: PERSONS ATTENDING THE PUBLIC COURSE AT A LOCAL MAIRIE, WEARING THEIR GAS-MASKS.

Paris is taking its anti-gas training very seriously. The Prefect of Paris recently announced that instruction of the civilian population in defence against gas attack would begin on May 29. Our photographs illustrate the course of anti-gas training organised by a local Parisian section of the "Ligue de Défense Aérienne".

A NAZI TOP-HAT PARADE THROUGH VIENNA: SWASTIKA-ADORNED HEADGEAR WORN BY STUDENTS AS A PROTEST AGAINST THE BANNING OF THE BROWN SHIRT.

Dr. Dollfus, the Austrian Chancellor, in his vigorous campaign against the Nazi Party in Austria, recently banned the wearing of uniforms of political organisations. On May 7 Nazis held a big demonstration in Vienna, with the Swastika sign prominent on their top-hats; but the Government then forbade the wearing of badges as constituting a uniform.

THE ITALIAN ARMADA OF THE AIR: THE ROME–CHICAGO FLIGHT.

ANTI-NAZI-ISM IN ENGLAND: THE MME. TUSSAUD'S WAXWORK FIGURE OF HERR HITLER DAUBED WITH RED PAINT AND PLACARDED.

On May 12, the figure of Herr Hitler at Mme. Tussaud's was disfigured. On the following day it was taken to Marylebone Police Court and three men were charged with damaging the model. They pleaded Not Guilty and were remanded in custody for seven days. This was one of several demonstrations during the visit to England of Dr. Rosenberg, representing Herr Hitler.

THE ITALIAN FLYING-BOAT SQUADRON AT NEW YORK: THE MACHINES MOORED OFF THE FLOYD BENNETT FIELD AFTER THEIR JOURNEY FROM CHICAGO.

The formation flight of twenty-four Italian "Savoia S55X" flying-boats from Rome to Chicago – the most ambitious undertaking of its kind hitherto – began, under the command of General Balbo, on July 1. The arrival at Amsterdam was marred by an accident to one of the machines which, landing at the wrong angle on shallow water, crashed and overturned. One man was killed and three slightly injured. The flight continued by way of Reykjavik and Montreal to Chicago, returning via New York.

POLITICAL FERMENT IN EUROPE: OUTSTANDING PHASES AND PERSONALITIES.

THE INITIATOR OF THE PROPOSAL FOR A FOUR-POWER PACT: SIGNOR MUSSOLINI – HERE SEEN ON A MOTOR-CYCLE, INSPECTING MOTOR-CYCLISTS IN ROME.

A CONTRAST TO THE ADJOINING PHOTOGRAPH: SIGNOR MUSSOLINI ON HORSE-BACK, AT A FASCIST MILITARY CEREMONY BEFORE THE FORUM OF AUGUSTUS.

Signor Mussolini's proposal for a Four-Power Pact between Great Britain, France, Italy and Germany was first announced, it may be recalled, when he was visited by Mr. MacDonald in March. The suggestion caused disquiet among the smaller Powers, especially those of the Little Entente, but latterly the prospect of removing opposition has improved. On May 28 the Paris correspondent of the "Times" reported that, in view of the progress made during the discussions held there, towards smoothing away objections, he understood that a virtual agreement had been reached, and that the Pact in its amended form would shortly be initialled. The misgivings of the Little Entente appeared to have been overcome on the understanding that the Pact did not affect their relations with France, and that the revision of territorial questions, if it arose, would be left to the normal procedure of the League of Nations.

THE DISARMAMENT CONFERENCE AT GENEVA: M. PAUL-BONCOUR RESTATING THE FRENCH CONDITIONS.

MR. NORMAN DAVIS, AMERICAN AMBASSADOR-AT-LARGE, MAKING A MOMENTOUS DECLARATION AT GENEVA.

HERR NADOLNY, THE GERMAN DELEGATE AT GENEVA, WHO WITHDREW A DISRUPTIVE AMENDMENT.

The recent work of the General Committee of the Disarmament Conference was reviewed by Sir John Simon in Parliament on May 26. Referring to the British Draft Convention, he said: "We have now had most gratifying and helpful declarations, first of all, I think, from Italy, subsequently from France and from America, and recently from Germany, recognising that it is along the lines of this draft that progress is most likely." He emphasised the great significance and importance of the fact that, with the full authority of the United States Government, their leading representative, Mr. Norman Davis, had indicated that America was prepared to modify the law of neutrality. Alluding to Herr Hitler's recent pronouncement, Sir John attached equal value to a recent incident at Geneva when "the German representative withdrew an amendment which would have had a shattering effect on the prospects of the Disarmament Conference."

AUSTRIA'S REMARKABLE "LITTLE NAPOLEON" WHO HAS DE-FIED HITLERISM: CHANCELLOR DOLLFUSS.

MR. DOLLFUSS TAKING THE SALUTE ON THE 250TH ANNIVERSARY OF VIENNA'S DELIVERANCE FROM THE TURKS.

"THE MICROSCOPIC MODERN METTERNICH OF EUROPE": CHAN-CELLOR DOLLFUSS MAKING A POLITICAL SPEECH.

Dr. Engelbert Dollfuss, the present Austrian Chancellor, is a remarkable personality. After a recent interview with him, Mr. George Slocombe wrote (in the "Evening Standard"): "Four feet eleven inches is the stature of Chancellor Dollfuss, who has astonished the world by his defiance of Germany and his peremptory expulsion of the Nazi Ministers. The President of the Republic described him to me as 'our little Napoleon' ". Dr. Dollfuss himself said: "I have no fear of Nazis either here or in Germany. I shall protect Austria's independence from attacks within the country or without. You have witnessed a veritable risorgimento in Austria. We desire only to live in peace and friendship with Germany, but we shall not suffer any threats to our independence. I am not a Dictator. I am a democrat. I do not intend to establish a dictatorship in Austria or to restore the monarchy."

ROAD-MAKING FOR UNEMPLOYED; AND OTHER PHASES OF NAZI GERMANY.

At Frankfurt on September 23 Herr Hitler inaugurated the construction of a new system of motor-roads all over Germany. With a spade handed to him by Herr Dorpmuller, President of the Reichbahn, the Chancellor personally cut the first sod for the first section of road to be made from Frankfurt to Mannheim and Heidelberg. The ceremony was attended by most of the prominent Nazi leaders. This road project is one of the large economic schemes devised by the Government to provide employment for several hundred thousand men during the next five to ten years. Herr Hitler said in his speech that the object was to fight the curse of unemployment and alleviate the distress of millions.

CROSS-ROADS, WITH CENTRAL BRIDGE, DESIGNED FOR THE GOVERNMENT'S MOTOR-ROAD CONSTRUCTION SCHEME: AN "ISLAND" ENABLING VEHICLES TO CHANGE DIRECTION WITHOUT INTERRUPTING FAST TRAFFIC.

GERMAN UNEMPLOYED "REGIMENTED" AS SPADE-MEN FOR ROAD-MAKING.

"THE GERMAN WOMAN DOES NOT SMOKE": ONE OF THE NOTICES PLACED IN RESTAURANTS IN ULM, ON THE DANUBE, BY ORDER OF THE CITY COMMISSIONER – A HINT TO THE "RE-BORN".

"WAR AGAINST THE UN-GERMAN SPIRIT": WHITE-SHIRTED NAZIS COLLECTING "UN-GERMAN" BOOKS AND PAMPHLETS THROWN FROM A LIBRARY'S WINDOWS BY THEIR FELLOWS: WITH A BAND IN ATTENDANCE.

HITLER-WORSHIP: THE NAZI LEADER PORTRAYED FOR THE PEOPLE OF GERMANY.

HERR HITLER'S FORTY-FOURTH BIRTHDAY HONOURED BY THE STATE PORCELAIN FACTORY AT MEISSEN: THE PORTRAIT PLAQUE IN CHINA WHICH HAS JUST BEEN ADDED TO THE POPULAR WARES.

METAL HITLER RELIEFS READY FOR DISTRIBUTION THROUGHOUT GERMANY, WHERE THOUSANDS HAVE ALREADY BEEN SOLD TO ARDENT FOLLOWERS OF THE CORPORAL WHO BECAME NAZI LEADER AND GERMAN CHANCELLOR.

THE NAZI RALLY AT NUREMBERG:

THE FIRST SINCE THE NAZI REVOLUTION IN GERMANY – AN IMMENSE DEMONSTRATION OF ORGANISED POWER.

AN ENORMOUS CONCOURSE OF NAZIS ON THE LUITPOLDHAIN AT NUREMBERG: THE STAGE SET ON A VAST SCALE FOR THE DEDICATION OF STANDARDS BY HERR HITLER (THE LEFT-HAND FIGURE OF THE TWO ADVANCING IN THE CENTRE TOWARDS THE WAR MEMORIAL).

THE "GRAF ZEPPELIN" IN FLIGHT OVER NUREMBERG: THE FAMOUS AIRSHIP WHOSE PRESENCE CAUSED GREAT ENTHUSIASM AT A RALLY OF YOUNG NAZIS (HERE SEEN MARCHING TO THE STADIUM).

REFORMED GERMANY AT FEVER HEAT.

THE SPECTACULAR MARCH-PAST OF THE BROWN ARMY, IN ITS FULL STRENGTH, THROUGH THE STREETS OF NUREMBERG ON THE CONCLUDING DAY OF THE GREAT NAZI RALLY: A SOLID PHALANX OF STORM-TROOPERS IN COLUMNS OF TWELVE.

NAZIS SALUTING THEIR LEADER AMID A GREAT DISPLAY OF FLAGS BEARING THE SWASTIKA: HERR HITLER (STANDING AT THE TOP OF A HIGH PLATFORM) ABOUT TO ADDRESS A VAST ASSEMBLANCE.

The fifth national rally of the Nazi Party in Germany was held at Nuremberg from August 30 to September 3. It was the first since the Nazi revolution, and was organised on a vast scale eclipsing any of its predecessors. The total number of Nazis present, from all parts of the Reich, was estimated to be some 500,000 including 150,000 storm troops. On his arrival, Herr Hitler announced that future bi-annual rallies would always be held in "the super-German town of Nuremberg". On September 2 he addressed 160,000 of the party functionaries assembled on the Zeppelinwise, a great meadow on the outskirts, and later he spoke at a gathering of 60,000 young Nazis in the Nuremberg Stadium. Their enthusiasm rose high when the "Graf Zeppelin", just arrived from Friedrichshafen, flew low over the stadium. On the concluding day there was a great march-past of the Brown Army through the streets, lasting five hours. Herr Hitler took the salute in the old market square, now renamed "Adolf Hitler Platz". Near him, in a place of honour, sat Herr Franz Hofer, the Tyrolese Nazi leader who recently made a dramatic escape from prison at Innsbruck.

DEVICES THAT BRING "MICKEY MOUSE" AND THE "SILLY SYMPHONIES" TO LIFE – AND TO SCREEN STARDOM.

MICKEY MOUSE, THE "STAR" COMEDIAN WHO HAS RAISED THE ANIMATED CARTOON FROM THE POSITION OF A "SHORT", TO THAT OF A LEADING FEATURE: THE "WORLD'S MOST FAMOUS RODENT"; WITH HIS CREATOR, MR. WALTER DISNEY.

THE MAN WHO PRODUCES MOST OF THE STRANGE NOISES THAT ARE HEARD IN A "MICKEY MOUSE" FILM: PINTO COLVIG (ONCE A "BARKER" – OR ANNOUNCER – WITH A CIRCUS) EMITTING A HOWL FOR "PLUTO", MICKEY'S CANINE FRIEND.

Mr. Disney's film career commenced in 1920, when he was working in the American Middle-West in a commercial art-studio. For a period he was on a night shift, and towards midnight he often heard scratching against the metal wires of the waste-baskets which held the discarded lunch-boxes of the staff. It was the mice, nibbling their evening meal. From being merely interested in the rodents, Disney became fascinated, tamed a number of them, and soon had a dozen of them living happily in a cage, where he fed them regularly. One became so friendly that the artist allowed it on his desk while he worked. Then, one day, soon after the war, Disney and his brother, Roy, hit on the idea of making moving-picture cartoons in an empty box-room which happened to be handy. Fifteen hundred drawings went to the making of each cartoon, and Walter drew them all. He also wrote the scenarios (which detail every action and change of scene in a story) and built the sets. Soon their work began to attract notice, and, after selling their first film for £300, which meant about a hundred per cent profit, Walter was asked to make a series of the cartoons, with a rabbit as the central character: you may, perhaps, recall 'Oswald the Rabbit'. Disney made twenty-six of them, but his heart was not really in the work. A rabbit is rather a dumb creature and he could not conceive it expressing or conveying joy, or any emotion at all. If only he could use another animal, such as . . . Then inspiration came to him. He thought of the pets he had made in 1920. Why not a mouse? Like Chaplin, Mickey refuses to talk, recognising that by speaking no language he is understood in all languages. That is why the Germans adore their Michal Maus, the French their Michel Souris, the Spaniards the Miguel Ratoncito and Miguel Pericote, the Italians Michele Jopolino, the Greeks (they have a word for it!) Mikel Mus, and the Japanese Miki Kuchi. More, Mickey has now reached the pinnacle of fame – he is 'in' Madame Tussaud's! Mickey has even earned the attention of various censorships. Germany objected that it was offensive to her national dignity for an army of cats wearing German military helmets to chase an army of mice. One American censor 'cut' not Mickey, but his friend Clara the Cow, just because she was reading Elinor Glyn's 'Three Weeks'! Yet another came down heavily because he deemed Mickey to be the victim of mental delusions! But such things do not hinder his triumphal progress. The garage in which the first Mickey saw the light of celluloid has become a £100,000 motion-picture producing plant, and his progenitor, Mr. Disney, has just announced a budget of £160,000 for the making of thirty-one films in the coming year.

A HIGH-POWERED CAMERA WHICH PHOTOGRAPHS EACH SEPARATE MOVEMENT OF THE HAND-DRAWN CARTOON ON A FRESH EXPOSURE: SHOWING, ON THE TABLE, THE FRAME WHICH HOLDS DOWN THE SUPERIMPOSED DRAWINGS ON TRANSPARENT CELLULOID.

THE GERM OF AN ANIMAL DANCE: MR. DISNEY WATCHES HIS ASSISTANTS DO A BOISTEROUS BIT OF REHEARSING.

THE CALIFORNIA LYNCHING: THE MOB IN ACTION; BREAKING INTO SAN JOSE GAOL.

One of the most hideous lynchings in the history of California occurred on the night of November 26. A crowd of about 100 men battered in the doors of the county gaol at San José, beat the sheriff into insensibility, and, in spite of the clubs and tear-gas bombs of policemen and deputy sheriffs, carried off Thomas Thurmond and Jack Holmes, who were alleged to have confessed to the kidnapping and murder of Mr. Brooke Hart, the twenty-two-year-old son of a local merchant. The two men were stripped, beaten, and hanged on a tree in a neighbouring park. Some 6,000 other people looked on, cheering the lynchers. When Mr. James Rolph, Jnr., the Governor of California, heard the news he said: "This is the best lesson California has ever given the country. We show the country that the State is not going to tolerate kidnapping." These expressions of approval were generally condemned. Lynching is rare in California. It is mainly confined to the South, where the victims are usually negroes.

A CALIFORNIAN "INFERNO": THE MOST TRAGIC FOREST FIRE ON RECORD.

AFTER THE FIRE: THE SCENE OF AN APPALLING HOLOCAUST IN GRIFFITH PARK, WHERE 72 MEN WERE REPORTED TO HAVE PERISHED, TRAPPED IN A WOODED CANYON, WHICH BLAZED FIERCELY OWING TO A LONG DROUGHT.

THE BREAKING-IN OF THE GAOL DOOR AT SAN JOSÉ – THE BATTERING-RAM OF IRON PIPING IN ACTION, WIELDED BY A CROWD OF LYNCHERS INCLUDING AT LEAST ONE WOMAN (WEARING A FUR COAT WITH LIGHT COLLAR).

PROOF OF FRANCE'S POLICY – DEFENCE, NOT ATTACK: MAKING HER EASTERN FRONTIER SECURE FOR THE FUTURE.

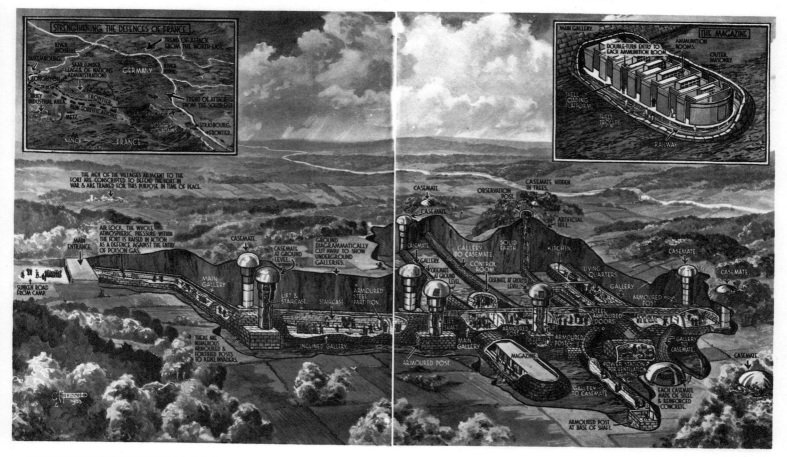

A SUBTERRANEAN FORTIFICATION TYPICAL OF THOSE THE FRENCH ARE COMPLETING BETWEEN LUXEMBOURG AND THE VOSGES: A DIAGRAMMATIC DRAWING TO SHOW THE CONTROL POSTS, LIVING QUARTERS AND OTHER WORKS BURIED DEEP UNDERGROUND: AND DETAIL SHOWING AN UNDERGROUND MUNITIONS MAGAZINE (INSET RIGHT).

This diagram clearly shows the workings of the underground fortification system on the eastern frontier of France. The diagram is based upon all the permissible official information, but is not meant to represent any particular fort: it is to be regarded as typical of those that have been built. The essential points of the French system, which has been conceived and carried out on a gigantic scale and is the strongest ever evolved, are as follows: a line of fortified casemates giving each other mutual protection by cross-fire and inter-connected by underground galleries safe from bombardment. All the key positions, normally vulnerable to aerial and other attack, are, in this case, buried underground, such as living quarters, magazines, stores, power stations and control posts. Measures have been taken to permit of a sudden concentration of troops, and to allow the whole frontier to be completely closed within a few hours of alarm being given; and the position has been chosen with such care and rendered so strong in defence that any known form of attack would undoubtedly have the utmost difficulty in penetrating it. Plans for the "Maginot Line", so called after the late War Minister, M. André

Maginot, who was in charge of the works, were first submitted in 1925, when it was decided to make a stretch of about 200 kilometres – country undefended by natural obstacles – as far as possible impregnable. A commission under the chairmanship of Marshal Joffre and subsequently of General Guillaumat, was appointed to study the question. The Commission considered that the industrial basin of Briey, whose productive work is of extreme importance to national defence, was immediately accessible to an enemy force issuing between Lauterbourg and Longuyon and that two natural roads of invasion, one from the south-east, the other from the north-east, converge at this point. These and similar strategic considerations determined the choice of terrain to be fortified; the lessons of the last war decided the character that the fortifications should take. Modern military technique renders possible the rapid cross-country transport of troops in motor vehicles and includes the possibility of sudden attack by heavy artillery and gas. Against all such weapons the new system should be proof.

A CAMOUFLAGED DOUBLE CASEMATE NESTLING IN A WOOD: ONE OF THE DEFENSIVE WORKS THAT BLEND WITH THE SURROUNDING COUNTRY: THE ESSENTIAL PARTS BEING SAFE AND HIDDEN UNDERGROUND.

A very great deal of interest has been aroused by the fact that France has recently strengthened the military fortifications along her eastern frontier; and there has been considerable speculation as to the nature of these defences. We are able here to publish photographs and a diagram illustrating certain of the typical works constructed, and to show that the fortifications, besides being on a gigantic and, probably, unprecedented scale, are, in many respects, of a completely novel type. It is important to realise that they are wholly defensive in character, and could be put to no other purpose than that of protecting the soil of France. Since it is understood that a sum exceeding £30,000,000 – a considerable portion of France's total military expenditure – has been devoted to these purely defensive works, no better proof could be desired of that country's essentially pacific outlook. In any case, the fortifications should be singularly competent to achieve the object of

FRANCE'S CAMOUFLAGED DEFENCE WORKS ON HER EASTERN FRONTIER: A PEACEFUL-LOOKING COUNTRYSIDE WITH NO SIGN, EXCEPT A LINE OF BARBED WIRE, TO INDICATE THE ELABORATE FORTIFICATIONS AT THE HILLOCK IN THE MIDDLE.

protecting France from invasion along the Saar district; in the face, that is, of any form of ground attack hitherto known. Each defence work is so constructed as to have two main sectors of fire, roughly parallel to the frontier. Thus the whole line is continuously defended by cross fire, and each fortification defends its neighbour's flank. Protection against shell fire is ensured by a great depth of reinforced concrete and by armour-plated turrets.

These interesting photographs give further details of the vast defensive system which, after three-and-a-half years' work, France has now almost completed along her eastern frontier north of the Vosges. In outline, the system consists of a series of strongly protected, camouflaged casemates, armed with the most up-to-date weapons and connected with each other by subterranean galleries. All that is essential is buried deep underground – control posts, living quarters, stores, power stations, and other adjuncts. The underground galleries form a veritable labyrinth so that should a fort be invaded, it could still be defended in sections. Near each fort camps have been constructed for the officers and men of the Regular Army who would occupy it if the alarm were given. Reserve troops consisting of inhabitants of neighbouring villages are trained together with the Regulars to ensure effective co-ordination, and to allow each section of the line to have among its defenders those whose home it is. Thanks to all these measures, a few hours would suffice to close the frontier completely.

IN NAZI GERMANY: THE HAMMER BREAKS; AND THE VOTE ON GERMANY'S WITHDRAWAL FROM THE LEAGUE OF NATIONS.

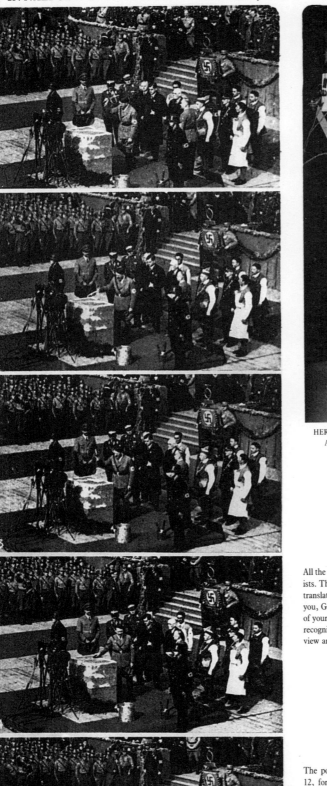

HERR HITLER SPEAKING TO THE GERMAN PEOPLE AFTER GERMANY'S WITHDRAWAL FROM THE LEAGUE OF NATIONS AND THE DISARMAMENT CONFERENCE: THE CHANCELLOR AT THE MICROPHONE ON THE NIGHT OF OCTOBER 14.

Billigst Du, deutscher Mann, und Du, deutsche Frau, die Politik Deiner Reichsregierung, und bist Du bereit, sie als den Ausdruck Deiner eigenen Auffassung und Deines eigenen Willens zu erklären und Dich feierlich zu ihr zu bekennen?

Ja   **Nein**

THE "YES" OR "NO" REFERENDUM PAPER GERMAN VOTERS WILL MARK ON NOVEMBER 12.

All the candidates will be National Socialists. The question to be answered may be translated: "Do you, German man, and you, German woman, approve the policy of your Government and are you ready to recognise it as the expression of your own view and your own will and solemnly to pledge yourself to it?"

The polling in Germany, on November 12, for the Reichstag elections and the Referendum on the foreign situation resulted, as was generally expected from the conditions, in a sweeping victory for Herr Hitler and his policy, described as the most overwhelming triumph ever obtained anywhere in a Parliamentary election. In the plebiscite no less than ninety-two per cent voted for the Nazi candidates. No opposition candidates were allowed to stand.

AN HOUR'S "SILENCE" OBSERVED THROUGHOUT GERMANY TO LISTEN TO HERR HITLER'S FINAL ELECTION BROADCAST APPEAL: A TYPICAL SCENE IN THE POTSDAM PLATZ, BERLIN, WITH ALL TRAFFIC STOPPED AND PASSERS-BY GIVING THE NAZI SALUTE.

THE BREAKING OF THE "SYMBOLIC" HAMMER IN HERR HITLER'S HAND: "CUTS" FROM THE FILM OF THE MUNICH INCIDENT; SHOWING HOW THE HAMMER'S HEAD AND HANDLE CAME APART.

During the laying of the foundation stone of the new Gallery of German Art, in Munich, by Herr Hitler, on Sunday October 15, the day after Germany had announced that she would withdraw from the League of Nations and from the Disarmament Conference, a most dramatic incident occurred: a happening that has given rise to much talk, more especially on the part of those who believe in portents! The "Daily Telegraph's" correspondent reported the incident fully. He stated that on the arrival of Herr Hitler the Bavarian Minister of the Interior handed him a silver hammer, saying: "The Munich Upper Bavarian Nazi Corps, with which the Nazi movement was founded, presents you with this hammer, with the desire that you will use it not only today to lay the foundation-stone of the Gallery of German Art, but also for laying the foundation-stones of all new buildings and that you will regard it as the sign and symbol of the future of the Nazi movement." Thereupon,

Herr Hitler took the hammer. He was to have tapped the stone three times, but at the first blow the hammer broke in two, the handle remaining in his hand, the head resting on the stone. Without a word, the Chancellor turned and resumed his seat. The same correspondent pointed out that the German Press had been forbidden to report the incident, and that orders had been issued that photographs showing it should be destroyed. On the following day, the "Telegraph" repeated that elaborate precautions were being taken in Germany to keep the affair as secret as possible. It also asserted that a Press photographer who had circulated a photograph taken after the breaking of the hammer had been threatened with internment in a concentration camp if he did not prevent publication.

ANTI-BRITISH ARAB RIOTS IN PALESTINE: DRAMATIC SCENES AT JAFFA.

THE ARAB RIOTS AT JAFFA IN WHICH ONE CONSTABLE AND TEN CIVILIANS WERE KILLED, AND OTHERS SERIOUSLY INJURED: A BATON CHARGE AGAINST THE MOB BY THE PALESTINE POLICE. (ABOVE)

(RIGHT), ARAB RIOTERS AT JAFFA HURLING STONES AND IRON BARS AT THE POLICE (DRAWN UP IN THE BACKGROUND), WHO WERE AFTERWARDS FIRED AT AND REPLIED: A DRAMATIC PHOTOGRAPH AT THE HEIGHT OF THE DISTURBANCES.

The Arab disturbances in Jerusalem on October 13 were followed later – there and elsewhere in Palestine – by more serious trouble, arising again from demonstrations of Arabs against increased Jewish immigration. At Jaffa, on October 27, they organised a procession, in defiance of the Government's prohibition. The crowd attacked the police and eventually fired upon them and the police returned the fire. The casualties were officially stated as 1 constable and 10 civilians killed and 2 constables and 10 civilians seriously injured. Order was restored and many arrests were made. Several Arab leaders arrested were taken to prison at Acre. The High Commissioner (Sir Arthur Wauchope) stated that the police force (including Arabs and Jews as well as British members) "throughout acted with the greatest control and forbearance". In Jerusalem on the same day a crowd attacked the police station and when baton charges failed to disperse them the police fired. One demonstrator was killed. Further disorders occurred in Jerusalem on October 29, when 2 people were killed and 17 injured. The Arabs had arranged a general strike. At Haifa on the 28th the police were compelled to fire on a mob which stoned the police barracks and the railway station. One constable and 6 rioters were taken to hospital.

A WINDOW ON THE WORLD:
EVENTS AT HOME AND ABROAD.

GOVERNMENT AID FOR THE NEW GIANT CUNARDER: "NO. 534" LYING, HALF COMPLETED, ON THE STOCKS AT CLYDEBANK.

Great interest was aroused by the announcement made by Mr. Chamberlain in the House of Commons, on December 13, that the Government intended to provide financial facilities for the completion of the new Cunard liner lying on the stocks at Clydebank. The announcement was cheered by M.P.s. Mr. Chamberlain explained that the decision had been made possible by the fact of a forthcoming merger of the North Sea Fleets of the Cunard and the White Star lines.

(RIGHT), THE EXPRESS WRECKED BY ANARCHISTS NEAR VALENCIA: THE SCENE OF THE DISASTER, WHEN FOUR COACHES WERE THROWN DOWN INTO A GULLY.

Attempts at anarcho-syndicalist rebellion were made in many towns and villages in Spain on December 9 and 10. The authorities, who were forewarned, took prompt action and proclaimed "a state of alarm", and the situation was soon well in hand. Perhaps the worst outrage occurred when the daily Barcelona–Seville train was wrecked, some distance from Valencia, by a contact bomb placed on a bridge. The bomb blew the tender of the train to pieces and hurled four coaches into the gully below. Five people were killed and thirty-eight injured – mostly third-class passengers. There were acts of arson and violence in the provinces of Valencia and Granada and a general strike began at Coruñna. A determined attempt was made at Saragossa to assault the police headquarters, but it was repelled. A partly successful attempt was made to set Granada ablaze. Bands of youths fired convents and attempts were made to set the theatre and the Law Courts on fire.

(LEFT), NEW YORK'S DEMAND FOR LIQUOR THE DAY AFTER THE REPEAL OF PROHIBITION: BRISK BUSINESS IN A WINE AND SPIRIT STORE.

The repeal of the Eighteenth Amendment was completed, by the deciding vote of Utah, on December 5 and Prohibition was thus ended in the United States. Its passing was celebrated in New York that night with restraint and decorum. The State Alcoholic Beverage Control Board of New York arranged to grant some 3500 licences, while hotels and restaurants made elaborate preparations for special dinners.

THE AEROPLANE IN WHICH ADMIRAL BYRD INTENDS TO FLY OVER THE SOUTH POLE: A NEW TWIN-ENGINED CURTIS-CONDOR MACHINE.

Rear-Admiral Byrd's new Antarctic expedition is to make a stay of a year or more in Polar regions. The barquentine "Bear of Oakland" left Boston on September 25 for the Antarctic, carrying the scientists of the expedition, their equipment and much of the food supply. The Admiral himself is following in the "Jacob Ruppert", on board of which is the big twin-engined aeroplane shown here, an autogyro and various supplies.

"WE CANNOT ACCEPT THE CONTINUANCE OF OUR INFERIORITY."

SECURITY IN THE AIR: COMPARISONS ILLUSTRATING THE PRESENT WEAKNESS OF GREAT BRITAIN, WHICH HAS DROPPED FROM FIRST TO FIFTH OF THE WORLD'S AIR POWERS.

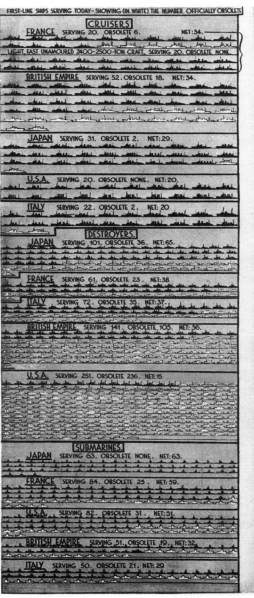

The vital subject of Britain's dwindling air strength in relation to that of other Powers was discussed recently in both Houses of Parliament and an important statement was made by the Air Minister, Lord Londonderry. Having declared that a race between nations in armaments must be avoided at all costs, he continued: "When the war closed, we were the first Air Power in the world. After the Armistice we dispersed the greater part of our vast air fleets, until this country is today fifth only of the world's Air Powers in terms of first-line strength. Our example has, unhappily, elicited no response, and we must abandon the policy of unilateral disarmament. We cannot accept the continuance of our present inferiority and, if parity cannot be secured by reductions elsewhere, then the converse proposition must follow and we shall have no option but to begin to build upwards. The appropriate steps to ensure that the British Empire is at least as strong in the air as any other great nation are at the present moment under examination by his Majesty's Government." The above illustration shows clearly the present comparative position. In home defence we are dangerously weak; and our first-line strength consists of only 488 machines. The conversion of large commercial aircraft into heavy bombers is a comparatively simple matter and the drawing shows the approximate numbers of such aircraft ready for instant conversion. It also shows how the forces of the first five great Air Powers are subdivided and illustrates the most popular types in use. In view of Navy Week and of the First Lord's statement that the British Navy has been cut to the bone, while others have made no step towards "universal brotherhood", it is also of value to re-examine the position of the chief Powers with regard to warships old and new. The life of a cruiser is officially reckoned as sixteen years; that of a destroyer as twelve years; and that of a submarine as thirteen years. We here suggest diagrammatically what would happen if it were decided to scrap all the obsolete vessels. It would be realised, for example, that, although Great Britain has fifty-two cruisers of the first-line in service, eighteen of these are obsolete; and that Japan, the U.S.A. and Italy have now removed practically all their old ships. The detail of the ships now building is from the latest edition of the official Return of Fleets, which shows France with a great battleship, seven cruisers and twelve fast, unarmoured cruisers on the stocks. In addition, France is building no fewer than twenty-five submarines. Italy, it will be observed, also has an ambitious submarine programme. Whereas Great Britain, Japan and Italy are building cruisers of 8000 tons or less, the United States still concentrates on the powerful 10,000-ton ships. There is, of course, another influence at work in naval construction; and that is the building of the German 10,000-ton cruisers, which have now been classed as battleships. Meanwhile, as a result of the one-sided concessions made by our representatives at the London Treaty, the British Navy now finds itself in the extraordinary position of being unable to replace obsolete cruisers and having to be content with ships inferior in gun-power, speed, and protection to those building abroad.

FLEETS OLD AND NEW: SHIPS OF THE GREAT NAVAL POWERS – OBSOLETE, BUT IN SERVICE AND BUILDING.

A 'PLANE THAT CAN LAND IN A TENNIS COURT: SEÑOR DE LA CIERVA'S AUTOGIRO

THE "AUTOGIRO" LANDS ALMOST VERTICALLY AT 13 FEET PER SECOND.

THE WONDERS OF THE "GET OFF" (DRAWN TO SCALE WITH FULLY LOADED & IN AN ABSOLUTELY DEAD CALM THE MACHINE CAN GET OFF IN 25 YARDS.

& LANDING OF THE AUTOGIRO. THE SIZE OF THE AIRCRAFT.)

WITH THE WIND BLOWING AT 5 MILES PER HOUR THE MACHINE CAN GET OFF IN ABOUT 5 YARDS.

PILOT ONLY.

RUN 3 YARDS (OR LESS).

LENGTH IN YARDS.

AN AEROPLANE THAT CAN LAND IN A TENNIS COURT AND CAN TAKE OFF, FULLY LOADED AND IN A DEAD CALM, IN TWENTY-FIVE YARDS: THE AUTOGIRO WHICH IS EXPECTED TO BE AVAILABLE TO THE PUBLIC BY NEXT APRIL AT £1200 OR LESS.

After tests carried out at Hanworth on November 8, it was announced that the Autogiro without fixed wings, elevators or rudder should be available to the public by April next. This type of machine, now equipped with a more powerful engine, has passed definitely out of the experimental stage and is to be put on the market at a price probably not greater than £1200. The new engine is of 140 h.p., and the machine is now capable of a top speed of nearly 120 miles an hour and a lowest speed of fifteen miles an hour. Control is obtained in this model simply by tilting the rotors, the effect of which is to alter the line of lift in relation to the centre of gravity. Of particular interest is its method of landing. The machine is brought in at its normal gliding or sinking speed until about ten feet from the ground: then full engine is put on with the nose set up at a sharp angle. As soon as the tail wheel touches the ground, the engine is shut off, the under-carriage wheels flap down and the machine scarcely moves forward at all. The machine is a two-seater with open cockpit. It is almost automatically stable, and has an advantage in cloud flying because there is only one control level and if that is central the machine must be flying straight. It has a range of three hours.

FROM THE WORLD'S SCRAPBOOK:
NEWS
ITEMS
OF
TOPICAL
INTEREST

LANDING ON THE TAIL FIRST, THE FRONT WHEELS THEN FLOPPING DOWN TO THE GROUND WITH SCARCELY ANY FORWARD MOTION; THE WHOLE MANOEUVRE BEING DONE AT A WALKING-PACE UNDER PERFECT CONTROL.

THE PRINCE ON SOCIAL SERVICE IN YORKSHIRE: HIS ROYAL HIGHNESS AMONG THE UNEMPLOYED.

The Prince of Wales arrived at Hull on December 13 to begin his three-day visit to centres for the unemployed in various parts of Yorkshire. His Royal Highness conducted the tour in his capacity as Patron of the National Council of Social Service. He stayed at Harewood House, as the guest of the Princess Royal and the Earl of Harewood. On the first day of the tour he spent a busy morning in Hull, and later visited Beverley, York, Otley, and Shipley. The second day, December 14, was devoted to the older mining areas of the West Riding – for instance, Pontefract, Hemsworth, Featherstone and Barnsley – and to the towns of Rotherham and Sheffield. On the third day the Prince, accompanied by the Earl of Harewood, visited centres for the unemployed at Penistone, Bradford, Morley, Huddersfield, Wakefield and Leeds. In a speech at Barnsley, his Royal Highness expressed again his interest in the social service work with which he has so prominently identified himself.

453 SEATS; 20 PARTIES; 7000 "CANDIDATES": THE SPANISH ELECTION.

A General Election for the first ordinary Cortes of the second Republic – the first General Election since the abdication of King Alfonso – was held in Spain on Sunday November 19. In Madrid things were quiet, but there were a number of disturbances in the provinces and there was some loss of life. Women voted for the first time and there is no doubt that it was they who caused the swing to the Right, away from the Radicals of the Centre Party and the Socialists, Radical Socialists and Communists of the Left. There are 453 seats to be filled in the new Parliament. For these there were 7000 declared candidates; but only 2000 were actually voted for. The official Parties numbered 20 and there were some 60 or 70 unofficial so-called Parties. A second ballot will be necessary in thirty-five out of the fifty electoral districts; in those districts, that is, in which none of the parties received the necessary forty per cent of the votes cast. This second ballot will be held on December 3. It is of interest to add that General Sanjurjo, Marquis del Riff, who was sentenced to death for leading the Royalist revolt last year, but had his sentence commuted to life imprisonment, and is now in prison, polled many votes at Melilla, Spanish Morocco.

WOOING THE ELECTORS BY PLACARDING THE WALLS OF A SACRED BUILDING: POSTERS ON THE SEVENTEENTH-CENTURY CHURCH OF THE ORDER OF CALATRAVA, IN MADRID.

THE PRINCE OF WALES'S TOUR OF SOCIAL SERVICE: WATCHING UNEMPLOYED AT PHYSICAL TRAINING IN THE LONDESBOROUGH DRILL HALL AT HULL.

THE ILLUSTRATED LONDON NEWS

THE TRAGEDY OF DOLLFUSS: THE AUSTRIAN CHANCELLOR, MURDERED BY AN AUSTRIAN NAZI, LYING DEAD IN HIS STUDY IN THE CHANCELLERY IN VIENNA; WITH SOLDIERS OF THE FEDERAL ARMY ON GUARD.

Dr. Dollfuss, Chancellor of Austria, shot by an Austrian Nazi in the Chancellery in Vienna on July 25, when an armed rebel band of that party entered the Ballhausplatz building disguised in the uniform of the regiment on guard duty there, received two wounds. It was stated in evidence during the trial of Otter Planetta and Franz Holzweber. One shot was fired at a distance of not more than eight inches and passed through the neck: the other injured the spine. Soon after 4.30 in the afternoon Major Fey, one of the members of the Government who had been taken prisoner, speaking from the Chancellery window, informed the commander of the police detachment outside that Dr. Dollfuss had been seriously wounded; but death is said to have occurred at about a quarter to four. The Chancellor's last words, after he had asked that further bloodshed might be avoided, were, said Major Fey at the Planetta-Holzweber trial: "Rintelen will make peace. I resign in his favour." And he asked that greetings might be given to his wife and children. After the Chancellery was once more in Government hands, the body was placed on a table in the Chancellery's own study, and there it lay in an open coffin until the removal to the City Hall for the public lying-in-state before the State funeral. At the Chancellery, on July 26, President Miklas received the widowed Frau Dollfuss on her arrival from Italy by aeroplane and conducted her to the study, where she knelt for a while in prayer.

1934

Fascists and Communists riot in Paris — Government coup against the Socialists in Austria — unemployed march from Glasgow — first photographs of Dachau — Albert I, King of the Belgians, killed while rock-climbing — succeeded by his son Leopold III — Hitler and Mussolini meet for the first time in Venice — Blackshirt meeting at Olympia raises question of excessive violence — Hitler "purges" Nazi Party in Germany with over seventy summary executions — Chancellor Engelbert Dollfuss of Austria assassinated by Austrian Nazis — succeeded by Dr Kurt Schuschnigg — President Hindenburg of Germany dies — Hitler confirmed as Leader and Chancellor — the "Queen Mary" launched — abortive left wing risings in Madrid and Catalonia — assassination in Marseilles of King Alexander of Yugoslavia and M. Barlton, French Foreign Minister — the Gran Chaco War between Bolivia and Paraguay enters its third year.

THE FACE OF THE DICTATOR:

HITLER OF GERMANY

Herr Adolf Hitler, leader of the National Socialist Party. The portraits on this page are given for comparison of facial types among existing Dictators. Herr Hitler, who became German Chancellor in January 1933, after the Nazi electoral triumph, is by birth an Austrian, and is now aged forty-four. At fifteen he was left an orphan and worked for a time as a builder's labourer in Vienna. He served in the war and was wounded. Afterwards he was one of the earliest members of the German Labour Party, which developed into the great Nazi organisation. He is a compelling speaker and a master of propaganda.

STALIN OF SOVIET RUSSIA

Joseph Vissarionovitch Stalin, General Secretary of the Russian Communist Party, is regarded as a virtual Dictator. He was born in 1879, the son of a Georgian cobbler, at Gori in Tiflis. At seventeen, having been expelled from a religious seminary where he was educated he began a career of political agitation. Between 1902 and 1917 he was several times arrested and exiled. At the Revolution he became a Commissar and later fought against Denikin and the Poles. From 1920 to 1923 he was on the Military Council. After Lenin's death he became dominant in Russia and secured the exile of Trotsky and other rivals.

DOLLFUSS OF AUSTRIA

Dr. Engelbert Dollfuss, Chancellor of Austria and champion of her independence against Nazi Germany, comes of an old Catholic peasant family and was born in 1892 at the village of Texing. He served in the war in a Tyrolese regiment. In 1919 he became Secretary of the Lower Austrian Peasant League; in 1931 Minister of Agriculture; and Chancellor after the crisis of 1932. He has governed without a Parliament, though repudiating the term Dictator. He makes up for small stature (he is only 4 ft. 11 in.) by immense energy and has great charm of manner. Last October he narrowly escaped assassination.

MUSSOLINI OF ITALY

Known to his compatriots as "Il Duce", Signor Benito Mussolini, who has ruled Italy (under King Victor Emmanuel) for more than eleven years, was born at Predappio, Forli, the son of a blacksmith, in 1883. Before the war he was engaged in political journalism. He served and was wounded in the war, and subsequently founded the Fascist movement to combat Bolshevism. The famous March on Rome gave him the power of a Dictator, and he first became Premier in 1922. This porphyry bust, the first of its kind to be made in Florence since the seventeenth century, was carved by Professor Amedeo Orlandini from a gesso model by Professor Graziosi.

A CONDITION OF THINGS WELCOMED BY THE WORKLESS: UNEMPLOYED CLEARING SNOW FROM THE STEPS OF THE CITY HALL, NEW YORK; A FRACTION OF THE LABOUR DONE BY THE 21,000 MEN ADDED TO THE 10,000 REGULAR STREET-CLEANERS OF THE CITY.

THE BITTER END OF 1933 IN THE STATES.
CHRISTMAS-TIDE SNOW AND ICE ONLY THE UNEMPLOYED WELCOMED.

A SIXTY-TWO-TON CHAPEL OF ICE BUILT ON THE LAWRENCE COLLEGE CAMPUS AT APPLE-TON, WISCONSIN: A STRUCTURE EIGHTEEN FEET HIGH AND LIT BY COLOURED ELECTRIC LIGHTS.

NEW YORK'S PRISON SCANDAL.

"THE WORLD'S WORST PRISON", WHERE GANGSTERS ARE SAID TO LIVE LIKE RESIDENTS IN A COUNTRY CLUB: THE WELFARE ISLAND GAOL, NEW YORK.

A surprise "raid" on Welfare Island Prison on January 24 by Mr. MacCormick, the new Commissioner of Correction in New York, and other officials is reported to have disclosed an almost unbelievable state of affairs. Gangster chiefs are said to be armed with knives and to enjoy their own wireless, special food, pet

IN THE NEW YORK PENITENTIARY SAID TO BE "RULED BY BIG GANGSTER INMATES": SOME OF THE WEAPONS SEIZED DURING THE POLICE RAID.

dogs, cigarettes and telephones in their cells connected with the outside world. They are never reproved, it is asserted, let alone made to obey prison rules; and it is alleged that they spend at least one night a week in New York, and carry on an extensive traffic in drugs!

THE CALIFORNIAN STORM-FLOODS.

Many lives were lost and enormous damage was done in California by floods following a terrific rainstorm on the night of December 30–31. The number of deaths was given on January 2 as thirty-one, with thirty-five people seriously injured and nineteen still unaccounted for. Some 3500 persons were driven from 1200 homes; houses and streets were half buried in mud, rocks and debris and more than twenty bridges were destroyed.

ONE OF SEVERAL CARS ENGULFED WITH THEIR OCCUPANTS DURING THE FLOODS: THE VEHICLE AFTER PARTIAL EXCAVATION, SHOWING HOW DEEPLY IT WAS SUBMERGED.

THE "NAZI" CRISIS IN AUSTRIA.

On February 2, 120,000 farmers and peasants gathered in Vienna. They had come from 1700 parishes in Lower Austria after they had heard of the difficulties besetting Dr. Dollfuss. Their purpose, in the words of the resolution passed at the meeting which led to the demonstration, was to give the reply of "iron-fisted peasants to the barbarous methods of Nazi agitators", and to show their high regard for Dr. Dollfuss. They marched round the Ringstrasse eight abreast, with bands and banners and passed a stand, in front of the Ministry of Defence, on which the Chancellor and members of the Government had gathered. Later, they were addressed by Dr. Dollfuss, who reviewed the sufferings of Austria since the break-up of the Monarchy; recounted the efforts of the Government to improve the condition of the people, and explained the present emergency. "We are fighting for the honour and freedom of this country", he declared. In the course of the same weekend the Tirolese Heimwehr intervened at the provincial seat of Government with demands for the establishment of semi-military authoritarian rule.

THE GREAT DEMONSTRATION OF LOYALTY TO DR DOLLFUSS BY 120,000 LOWER AUSTRIAN PEASANTS: ENTHUSIASTIC ACCLAMATIONS FOR THE CHANCELLOR DURING THE MARCH ALONG THE RINGSTRASSE IN VIENNA.

FIERCE RIOTING AND FIRING IN THE STREETS OF PARIS.

ELOQUENT TESTIMONY TO THE DESTRUCTIVE ENERGY OF THE RIOTERS IN PARIS: A PILE OF MISCELLANEOUS WRECKAGE COLLECTED AFTERWARDS ON A QUAY-SIDE NEAR THE CHAMBER OF DEPUTIES.

TELEPHOTOGRAPHS OF A NIGHT OF TERROR.

TOP: POLICE ATTEMPTING TO EXTINGUISH A BURNING BUS IN THE PLACE DE LA CONCORDE, BENEATH THE FAMOUS EGYPTIAN OBELISK: THE SCENE OF THE WORST RIOTING IN PARIS SINCE THE DAYS OF THE COMMUNE. BOTTOM: THE MINISTRY OF MARINE, AT THE CORNER OF THE RUE ROYALE AND THE RUE DE RIVOLI, SET ON FIRE: THE PRINCIPAL ITEM IN THE MANY MILLIONS OF FRANCS WORTH OF DAMAGE DONE.

BROKEN HEADS A RESULT OF COMING INTO COLLISION WITH THE POLICE: A WOUNDED DEMONSTRATOR ARRESTED DURING THE COMMUNIST RIOT; AND OTHERS COWERING ON THE GROUND.

AND OF ITS AFTERMATH.

A RIOTER HURLING A MISSILE FROM BEHIND AT MOUNTED POLICE IN THE PLACE DE LA CONCORDE.

THE TRAGIC SIDE OF INSURRECTION: PARIS CROWDS IN REFLECTIVE MOOD AT THE FUNERAL OF ONE OF FIFTEEN CIVILIANS WHO LOST THEIR LIVES IN THE FIRST RIOT.

Political rioting of extraordinary violence took place all over Paris on the evening and night of February 6, and a certain number of troops were brought into action to support the police. The fiercest fighting was centred in the Place de la Concorde and outside the Hotel de Ville, where the rioters were fired on and there were many casualties. The Ministry of Marine was set on fire, and the Chamber of Deputies, where a session was in progress, was in a state of siege. The rioters were drawn from extremists of the Right and of the Left. Royalists on the one hand, including members of the Camelots du Roy and of Jeunesse Patriote and Communists on the other, attacked Police, Gardes Civiles, Gardes Mobiles, and Gardes Republicains, engaging them in an attack, while more fighting took place between rival bands of demonstrators. About ten thousand ex-Servicemen, with war flags flying, marched in convoy down the Champs Elysees, towards the Place de la Concorde, shouting "Mort à Daladier!" and were charged by mounted Gardes Republicains with drawn swords. In all, the rioters were estimated, by the Prefect of Police, as being 50,000 strong. About fifty private motor-cars, ten buses and trams, and forty newspaper kiosks were burned; and the streets, the next morning, remained littered with iron bolts, bricks and lengths of iron piping used as weapons. Meanwhile, M. Daladier, who faced pandemonium in the Chamber of Deputies, obtained three votes of confidence. It was considered very doubtful, however, that his Government would survive long.

THE INTERIOR OF A LIVING-ROOM IN ONE OF THE GREAT BLOCKS OF FLATS FOR WORKMEN WHICH WERE USED AS SOCIALIST STRONGHOLDS DURING THE FOUR DAYS' FIGHTING: TYPICAL EFFECTS OF BOMBARDMENT.

CIVIL WAR IN AUSTRIA:
THE GOVERNMENT "COUP D'ETAT".

A CASUALTY ON THE SOCIALIST SIDE AT LINZ: A DEAD MACHINE-GUNNER IN A ROOM IN THE HOTEL SCHIFF, BESIDE THE GUN WHICH HE HAD FIRED FROM THE WINDOW AT THE TROOPS AND POLICE.

Very serious fighting between Government forces and armed Socialists broke out in Austria on February 12. Even the earliest news made it clear that in Vienna, Linz, Graz, Styr, and other cities, casualties on both sides had been heavy, and that several hundred had been killed. Howitzers, machine-guns, rifles, and revolvers were freely used in the streets, and in Vienna, Karl Marx House, a huge block of industrial flats which was a Socialist stronghold, was shelled into surrender. The conflicts arose through a sort of Government *coup d'etat* which aimed at the complete suppression of the Socialist party – a party which was supreme in Vienna, though not in the rest of Austria. On February 12 the Socialist party was declared illegal: the Rathaus, the centre of the Socialist Government in Vienna, was captured and the Heimwehr (Austrian Fascist) flag was flown from its tower: the Socialist Government was forcibly evicted, and its leaders, except a few who escaped into Czechoslovakia, were arrested; Dr Karl Seitz, the Socialist Burgomaster, was confined in the Rathaus, and martial law was declared in Vienna, Upper and Lower Austria, Styria, Carinthia, and, on February 13, in the Austrian Tirol. The movement was initiated during Dr. Dollfuss's absence the previous week in Hungary, its leaders being Major Fey, Vice-Chancellor, and commander of the Heimwehr in the State of Vienna, and Prince Starhemberg, the head of the Heimwehr. The Heimwehr is a Fascist organisation, looking to Italy for its inspiration. It fully supported Dr. Dollfuss when he assumed dictatorial powers, and is as hostile to the Nazi party which receives support from Germany, as to the Socialists. The Nazis took no part in the *coup*, hoping no doubt that both the Socialists and the Government party would be weakened. It appeared, however, that if order could be restored, Dr. Dollfuss's position would be strengthened. The desperate Socialist resistance was probably made possible by secret organisations replacing their Schutzbund, officially banned last March.

The civil war ended in a triumph of the Government forces and the Heimwehr over the Socialist Schutzbund, and in the complete suppression of the municipal rule of socialism in Vienna. It was stated on February 15 that the Schutzbund fighting squads had abandoned organised resistance, and that order had been restored both in Vienna and in the provinces. Herr Dollfuss, the Chancellor, had broadcast an appeal to those who were still in revolt to make their submission, promising a free pardon to all, except the leaders. This offer met with an immediate response and by the stipulated time there were surrendered 34 machine-guns, over 400 rifles, 40,000 rounds of ammunition, and many hand grenades. The Government troops then returned to barracks,

GOVERNMENT TROOPS ADVANCING AT THE DOUBLE DURING THE FIGHTING AGAINST THE SOCIALIST FORCES IN VIENNA: PART OF A CINEMATOGRAPH FILM OBTAINED BY A LATVIAN OPERATOR WHO WAS REPORTED TO HAVE BEEN ARRESTED, IMPRISONED, AND SENTENCED TO DEATH.

THE USE OF ARTILLERY BY THE GOVERNMENT FORCES, THE DECISIVE FACTOR IN BREAKING DOWN THE SOCIALIST RESISTANCE: GUNS BEING PREPARED FOR ACTION AND TRAINED ON THE KARL MARX HOF, AN IMMENSE BLOCK OF 1400 FLATS AT HEILGENSTADT, A DISTRICT OF VIENNA.

while the cordon round the city of Vienna, and the wire barricades, were withdrawn so that the streets began to resume their normal aspect. The losses on the Government side were estimated at 102 dead and 319 wounded (115 seriously). The breakdown was 29 soldiers, 29 police, 11 gendarmes, and 33 Heimwehr or other soldiers. Out of the total of 102 dead, 42 were killed in Vienna, the rest in the provinces. Civilian losses throughout Austria were put at the surprisingly low figures of 137 dead and 339 wounded. Out of these losses, 315 were said to have occurred in Vienna. The fiercest fighting took place in the Floridsdorf district of Vienna on February 14. Howitzers were pouring shells into Floridsdorf for five hours from four different positions. The Government's prompt use of artillery proved the decisive factor. The centre right-hand photograph is a section of cinema-film taken by John Dored, a Latvian photographer. He was arrested and his camera was smashed, but he had already managed to send away part of the film which was conveyed to London by air. It was reported that he had been condemned to death, and that diplomatic efforts were being made to save him.

CASUALTIES ON THE GOVERNMENT SIDE, WHICH INCLUDED 102 DEAD, 88 BELONGING TO THE HEIMWEHR AND OTHER ANCILLARY FORCES: TWO HEIMWEHR MEN FALLEN IN A DOORWAY IN THE FLORIDSDORF DISTRICT.

"CATHERINE THE GREAT": A SCENE FROM THE FAMOUS BRITISH FILM (ACCLAIMED ALIKE HERE AND IN NEW YORK) – SHOWING FLORA ROBSON (CENTRE) AS THE EMPRESS ELIZABETH.

THE FILM VOGUE FOR ROYAL ROMANCES: BRITISH AND AMERICAN SUCCESSES.

"THE SCARLET EMPRESS": AN AMERICAN FILM ABOUT CATHERINE THE GREAT – A SCENE SHOWING MARLENE DIETRICH (CENTRE) AS CATHERINE, AND GROTESQUE STATUES OF APOSTLES AND SAINTS.

"QUEEN CRISTINA": A SCENE AT THE SWEDISH COURT, SHOWING GRETA GARBO AS THE WHIMSICAL QUEEN, SEATED ON HER THRONE – (INSET ABOVE) A PORTRAIT OF MISS GARBO.

THE HEROINE OF "THE SCARLET EMPRESS": MARLENE DIETRICH AS THE YOUNG GERMAN PRINCESS WHO AFTERWARDS BECAME CATHERINE THE GREAT OF RUSSIA.

"QUEEN CHRISTINA": A FILM VERSION OF AN ECCENTRIC PERSONALITY – GRETA GARBO AS THE QUEEN OF SWEDEN ADDRESSING A CROWD GATHERING IN THE PALACE COURTYARD.

In the screen world of late there has been a remarkable spate of historical films concerning romantic or picturesque images of the past, which have proved immensely popular. Prominent among them is "Catherine the Great", a British drama recently produced at the Leicester Square Theatre, in which Miss Elisabeth Bergner has made such a success in the name part. Later, it was given in New York, and received with great enthusiasm. An American film version of the story originally bearing the same title, but subsequently entitled "The Scarlet Empress", is a Paramount production, in which Miss Marlene Dietrich plays Catherine. "Queen Christina", recently produced at the Empire, is a Metro-Goldwyn-Mayer picture dealing with the eccentric daughter of Gustavus Adolphus, impersonated by Miss Greta Garbo. Other historical films projected include "Nell Gwyn", with Sir Cedric Hardwicke as Charles II; "Marie Antoinette", with Charles Laughton as Louis XVI., and a screen version of Bernard Shaw's "St. Joan".

THE LAST EMPEROR OF CHINA, WHO IS TO BE ENTHRONED AS THE FIRST EMPEROR OF MANCHUKUO.

A NEW EMPIRE IN AN AGE OF REPUBLICS.

The inauguration of a new Empire is remarkable, in a world where the general tendency is rather towards republican forms of rule. The ex-Emperor of China, last of the Ching Dynasty, who abdicated in 1912, is to be enthroned on March 1 as the first Emperor of Manchukuo (formerly Manchuria), established as an independent State on March 1, 1932, with the ex-Emperor as its Chief Executive, or Regent. On abdicating the Chinese throne, he had retained his status as sovereign of the Manchu Bannermen. He was born in 1906. His enthronement will take place at Hsinking (Changchun), Manchukuo's new capital.

THE CONSORT OF THE FUTURE EMPEROR OF MANCHUKUO: THE EX-EMPRESS OF CHINA.

A WINDOW ON THE WORLD: THE NEWS IN PICTURES.

THE CHIEF OF THE CUBAN ARMY AND HEAD OF THE REVOLUTIONARY JUNTA, TO WHOM PRESIDENT HEVIA TENDERED HIS RESIGNATION: COLONEL FULGENCIO BATISTA IN OVERCOAT AND PEAKED CAP, (FOURTH FROM RIGHT), WITH SOME OF HIS STAFF.

Yet another political change in Cuba, this time with hopes of permanent settlement, occurred on January 18, when the Provisional President, Dr Carlos Hevia, after holding office for only two-and-a-half days, presented his resignation to the Revolutionary Junta, headed by Colonel Batista, Chief of the Army. The same day, Colonel Carlos Mendieta, leader of the Nationalist Party, described as the most popular man in Cuban politics, was sworn in as the new Provisional President. He had the full support of all parties, except Labour, and of the Army. The Labour Federation tried to call a general strike, which failed. There were great rejoicings in Havana over his appointment, and the prospect of relief from the strife of the last six months. Further enthusiasm greeted the recognition of the new Government on January 23 by the United States, Great Britain and the Dominions, France, Italy, and other countries.

"I SWEAR TO ADOLF HITLER UNDYING LOYALTY AND STRICT OBEDIENCE."

On the morning of February 25, in the Konigsplatz at Munich, Herr Hitler's deputy, Herr Rudolf Hess, administered to some 30,000 Nazis a remarkable oath of loyalty and obedience to the Nazi leader, and this was broadcast to over a million of the political leaders and officials of the Nazi Party through the agency of all the German wireless stations. The words of the oath were: "I swear to Adolf Hitler undying loyalty and strict obedience to him and his appointed leaders"; and Herr Hess said of it: "You have taken the greatest oath in the history of the German Nation. See that you keep it." In Berlin some 70,000 persons assembled in the Lustgarten – the scene of so many political mass meetings – repeated the oath as it was received by radio, in the presence of President Hindenburg and the Chancellor himself. Kindred procedure was followed at various other centres.

WHEN OVER A MILLION LEADERS AND OFFICIALS OF THE NAZI PARTY SWORE ALLEGIANCE TO HERR HITLER: TAKING THE "GREATEST OATH IN THE HISTORY OF THE GERMAN NATION" IN BERLIN.

THE UNEMPLOYED MARCHERS FROM THE NORTH: THE GLASGOW CONTINGENT (HEADED BY MR McGOVERN M.P.) SETTING OUT FOR LONDON.

Mr John McGovern, M.P., headed a detachment of about 400 unemployed marchers when they set out from Glasgow for London to take part in the mass conference of unemployed there next month. The Glasgow marchers were joined by fully 300 marchers from Aberdeen, Perth, Dundee and other Northern towns. Each contingent carried its distinguishing banner and was headed by a flute band.

THE DEATH OF A FAMOUS NICARA-GUAN REBEL FIGHTER.

General Don Augustino Sandino, who for more than five years opposed the Nicaraguan Governments which were supported by US Marines, was shot dead at Managua on February 21 by Nicaraguan National Guards, who, it was assumed, had exceeded their instructions.

THREE ROYAL "STORM-TROOPERS", THE SONS OF HIGHER RANK THAN THEIR FATHER: (LEFT TO RIGHT) PRINCE HUBERTUS, THE EX-CROWN PRINCE, AND PRINCE FRIEDRICH.

A POLITICAL TURN GIVEN TO THE MUNICH CARNIVAL: A FLOAT SHOWING "HONEST GERMAN MICHAEL" IN A CAGE, ESCORTED BY FRENCH BLACK TROOPS.

HOSTILITY TO THE DISARMAMENT CONFERENCE DEMONSTRATED IN THE MUNICH CARNIVAL: AN IRONICAL TABLEAU REPRESENTING "DEFENCELESS FRANCE".

The first Munich carnival procession under Nazi auspices took place on February 11, and contained several features of a highly political character. One of the chief sections consisted of an elaborate pastiche of the League of Nations and the Disarmament Conference. This was headed by a float representing Peace mounted on an enormous tank, and immediately followed by "defenceless France" and "re-armed Germany". The former group was made up of tanks, heavy guns, and French colonial troops armed to the teeth; while the latter was made up of German youths wearing paper cocked-hats, and armed with sticks and wooden guns. A car escorted by heavily-armed French colonial troops bore an iron cage in which the rustic figure of the German "Michael" was confined. This was accompanied by a long banner inscribed "Michael, are you going back to Geneva?" Among the non-political features was the Loch Ness monster.

LIFE IN A GERMAN CONCENTRATION CAMP FOR POLITICAL OPPONENTS OF THE NAZIS.

THE FIRST AUTHORISED PRESS PHOTOGRAPHS TAKEN IN THE GREAT CAMP AT DACHAU.

CAMP GUARDS ON PARADE AT DACHAU: MEMBERS OF A FORCE OF FOUR HUNDRED MEN IN CONTROL OF TWO THOUSAND FIVE HUNDRED POLITICAL PRISONERS.

RECREATION, *EN DESHABILLE*, FOR POLITICAL PRISONERS IN THE CONCENTRATION CAMP AT DACHAU: A GAME OF CHESS, AND A PIPE, OUTSIDE THE BARRACKS, APPARENTLY DURING THE PREVALENCE OF A HEAT-WAVE.

Hitherto little has been available by way of illustration of the German concentration camps for political prisoners under the Nazi régime, about which there has been so much rumour and discussion. Unique interest consequently belongs to these photographs, lately to hand from a French source, and secured, it is stated, on the first occasion on which a journalist has been authorised to take pictures in the camp at Dachau. Although, as far back as last October, a message from Berlin stated that the camps were to be abolished, and that "most of them had already been closed down", recent news does not fulfil that prophecy. On January 26 Herr Gerhardt Seger, former secretary of the German Peace Society, was reported to have said that there were still sixty concentration camps in Germany, containing 50,000 political prisoners. Meanwhile, however, there seems to be no doubt that large numbers of prisoners have been released from time to time, partly in view of the Nazi electoral triumph, and also as a gesture of goodwill at Christmas, preference being given to prisoners of good behaviour and especially to fathers of large families. Those released were urged to enter the Nazi fold, and at the same time were warned that any relapse on their part into hostility towards the Government would meet with "rigorous, unrelenting, and final measures". A recent sidelight on the question was thrown by the case of three Roman Catholic priests, arrested last November, who were sentenced on January 24, at Munich, to several months' imprisonment. One of the priests was accused of having fabricated stories of atrocities said to have been committed in the camp at Dachau, and the others of having passed on these stories. It may be recalled also that, some few months ago, attention was drawn, by Major-General Sir Neill Malcolm, to alleged ill-treatment of a well-known prisoner, Herr Ebert, son of the first President of the German Republic, "to whom (said General Malcolm) Germans owe far more than many of them are now willing to admit". In a letter to "The Times", all the more impressive from its sympatic tone towards Nazi rule, General Malcolm made the following statements (here somewhat abridged); "I am not one of those who can see no virtue in the Hitler régime. To me it seems that his Government, like most other Governments, has done much that is good. It has certainly restored to a great majority of Germans that feeling of national self-respect which is perhaps the most precious possession of a great people. Nevertheless, in common with other revolutionary movements, the Hitler régime has an unpleasant side, which is doing Germany much harm in the eyes of the outside world. I believe that there are very many right-minded Germans who know little or nothing of the administration of the concentration camps. I believe there are others who do know and heavily disapprove." Some three weeks later General Malcolm made known, "without comment", an account of a visit to Herr Ebert, at the Börgemoor camp, by a member of the Prussian Ministry of the Interior, to whom Ebert said he had experienced no ill-treatment. At the same time it was reported from Berlin that, while no denial of General Malcolm's statements, or reference to them, had apparently been published in Germany, Herr Ebert had suddenly appeared at another camp, at Lichtenburg, where he was seen, looking physically fit and well-fed, by a group of foreign visitors including a British journalist. The correspondent from whom the above photographs came, describing his visit to Dachau, writes: "To this camp the Hitler Government has sent its most formidable opponents. Dachau is a little village on a hill thirty kilometres from Munich. The motor-bus from the station is always full, for the camp commandant allows the prisoners' parents to bring them, from time to time, food, linen, and tobacco. All about the camp were guards in green uniform armed to the teeth, and from a turret in a corner two machine-guns point towards the gate. 'There are here,' said the Commandant, '2500 prisoners and only 400 hundred guards. That is why our men are armed and we have the wire charged with electricity. So far we have set free, provisionally, nearly 600 prisoners, of whom only about 50 have returned. The prisoners were ordered to build a memorial to Horst Wessel, and hang the barrack walls with portraits of Hitler, and the swastika sign, which also appears on workshop walls, work-tables and even tools. The administration of the camp is excellent, and when inspecting the dormitories, the living quarters, the kitchens, and the hospital, one recalls that meticulous preparation is the chief virtue of the Germans. The workshops are provided with modern machinery, and Dachau is, in effect, a highly up-to-date factory.' "

ELABORATE PRECAUTIONS IN ORDER TO PREVENT THE ESCAPE OF PRISONERS: USE OF A FORMIDABLE SYSTEM OF BARBED WIRE, ELECTRICALLY CHARGED, ROUND THE DACHAU CAMP.

A MEMORIAL TO HORST WESSEL, THE NAZI "MARTYR-POET" WHICH THE PRISONERS AT DACHAU WERE ORDERED TO BUILD: AN EFFORT TOWARDS POLITICAL CONVERSION.

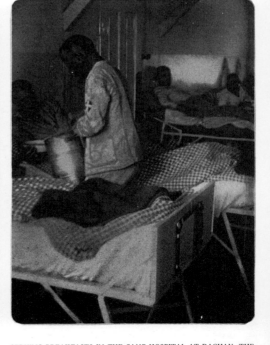

SERVING BREAKFASTS IN THE CAMP HOSPITAL AT DACHAU, THE JOB OF A SOCIALIST DOCTOR, WHO IS ONE OF THE PRISONERS – GOING ROUND THE BEDS WITH FOOD.

THE GREAT INDIAN EARTHQUAKE:
RUIN AT MUZAFFARPUR & JAMALPUR.

MATERIAL DAMAGE IN A DISTRICT IN WHICH NEARLY TWO THOUSAND PEOPLE LOST THEIR LIVES: A TEMPLE AT MUZAFFARPUR.

CRACKS IN THE SURFACE OF THE EARTH LIKE WAVES OF THE SEA: A GENERAL VIEW OF FISSURES IN THE POLO GROUND AT MUZAFFARPUR, IN BIHAR, WHICH PRODUCED A TERRACED EFFECT.

The official return issued as we write gives the number of the killed as follows but it may be taken as certain that still more lives were lost: Patna, 138; Gaya, 34; Shahabad, 16; Samaran, 435; Saran, 170; Darbhanga, 1887; Muzaffarpur, 1929; Bhagalpur, 111; Monghyr, 1318; and Purnea, 2: while 2900 were killed in Nepal. A recent Exchange message stated that for several days scores of lorries were employed in Monghyr removing corpses which were thrown into the Ganges, and that many hundreds of bodies remained to be collected. In the bazaar alone hundreds were killed by buildings collapsing. The hospital was destroyed.

FROM THE WORLD'S SCRAP-BOOK:
NEWS ITEMS OF TOPICAL INTEREST.

THE PACT OF ROME: SIGNOR MUSSOLINI (LEFT) SIGNING THE PROTOCOLS, WITH HERR DOLLFUSS (SECOND FROM RIGHT) AND GENERAL GOMBOS (RIGHT) LOOKING ON.

The new three-Power agreement between Italy, Austria and Hungary, known as the Pact of Rome, was signed there on March 17 by Signor Mussolini, Herr Dollfuss, Chancellor of Austria and General Gombos, Prime Minister of Hungary. It consists of three Protocols. The first is a political agreement by which the three nations undertake to "concert together on all the problems which particularly interest them". The other two are designed to develop economic relations.

THE RETURN OF THE MONSTER? A PHOTOGRAPH OF A STRANGE MOVING OBJECT IN LOCH NESS, TAKEN BY MR. R.K. WILSON AT A RANGE OF UNDER 200 YARDS – A QUARTER-PLATE SNAPSHOT AS TAKEN; NOT RETOUCHED.

A London surgeon, Mr. R.K. Wilson having noticed an object moving in the water, took this photograph on April 19 from the shore of Loch Ness near Invermoriston. Zoologists to whom it was submitted were of the opinion that it did not represent any bird, animal, or fish known to frequent British waters: but a later suggestion was that the apparent head and neck were really the high dorsal fin of a partly submerged killer-whale.

(LEFT), THE TRAGIC DEATH OF KING ALBERT WHILE ROCK-CLIMBING: HIS LATE MAJESTY WITH QUEEN ELISABETH.

Albert I, King of the Belgians, who met his death so tragically on the evening of February 17 by falling while rock-climbing at Marche-les-Dames, near Namur, will be remembered not only as a wise ruler, but, especially, for the determined and heroic part he played at the outbreak of the Great War and during those years of conflict which enabled him successfully to defend the integrity of the national territory; as well as for his devotion and statesmanship during the difficult period of recovery. He was born in Brussels on April 8, 1875, second son of Prince Philip, Count of Flanders, younger son of King Leopold I, and brother of King Leopold II. He became Heir Apparent in 1891, on the death of his brother, Prince Baudouin; and he succeeded to the Throne on the death of King Leopold II, in December 1909. His marriage to the Duchess Elisabeth, daughter of the late Duke Charles Theodore of Bavaria, took place on October 2, 1900. The Queen was ever her husband's truest helpmate in peace and war.

THE FRENCH GOVERNMENT READY FOR ANY MAY DAY DISTURBANCE: A DETACHMENT OF MOBILE MACHINE-GUNS IN PARIS, FOR THE PREVIOUS DAY'S REVIEW.

In view of the appeal to strike and demonstrate on May Day, launched by the trade unions and the Communist paper, "Humanité", the Paris garrison was reinforced by detachments of troops from places as far distant as Brittany. As a demonstration of the forces at their disposal the Government held two reviews on April 30, one at the Esplanade des Invalides, and the other at the Porte Dorée, where the Communists had proclaimed their intention to hold a mass demonstration.

THE RED SEA PORT OF THE YEMEN RECENTLY OCCUPIED BY IBN SA'UD'S FORCES: THE INNER HARBOUR AT HODEIDA.

THE CAMEL CORPS IN THE ARMY OF THE CROWN PRINCE AHMAD, ELDEST SON OF THE IMAM OF THE YEMEN: PART OF THE FORCE ON THE MARCH.

THE ARABIAN WAR:
"AN ARAB FAMILY QUARREL".

THE RULER OF SAUDI ARABIA (NEJD AND THE HEJAZ), WHO IS AT WAR WITH HIS NEIGHBOURS, THE IMAM OF YEMEN: KING IBN SA'UD, THE HEAD OF THE WAHABIS.

SECOND SON OF THE IBN SA'UD, AND LEADER OF THE TROOPS WHO RECENTLY ENTERED HODEIDA: THE EMIR FPISAL, VICEROY OF MECCA.

IBN SA'UDS ELDEST SON AND HEIR TO THE SAUDI ARABIAN THRONE, WHO IS IN CHIEF COMMAND OF THE WAHABI FORCES IN THE FIELD: THE AMIR SA'UD (LEFT), WITH HIS UNCLE.

According to the account given by Mr H. St. John Philby, the explorer and friend of Ibn Sa'ud, printed in the "Daily Telegraph", war broke out in Arabia in the first weeks of April. Following a breakdown of negotiations regarding disputed territory, King Ibn Sa'ud informed the Imam Yahya of the Yemen that the heir to the Sa'udi Arabian throne, the Amir Sa'ud (Viceroy of Nejd), had orders to advance with his troops to the Yemen frontier. After turning the Imam's forces out of the Tihama coastal district, the Sa'udi troops occupied Hodeida on May 5. The Yemeni civil and military authorities had already withdrawn: and the Emir Feisal, commanding on this sector of the front, entered the town on May 6, and assumed responsibility there. He is Viceroy of Mecca, and heads the Ministry of Foreign Affairs.

THE PRINCE OF WALES IN NORTH WALES:
A THREE-DAYS' TOUR AMONGST UNEMPLOYED.

H.R.H. VISITING THE SITE OF THE NEW OCCUPATIONAL CENTRE IN BANGOR: A PHOTOGRAPH SHOWING THE PARTLY ERECTED BUILDING, WHICH IS BEING CONSTRUCTED BY UNEMPLOYED FROM MATERIAL FROM AN OLD CINEMA GIVEN TO THEM.

The Prince of Wales arrived in north Wales on May 16, to begin a three-days' tour, with the object of visiting certain occupational and other centres for the unemployed and seeing what is being done in connection with their social needs: this in his capacity as Patron of the National Council of Social Service. The following notes concern our photographs: – In Bangor unemployed are on voluntary work in which the Prince was much interested. They are building a new occupational centre, using material from an old cinema that was given to them by its owner on condition that they removed it from its site to the scene of their own labours. H.R.H. signed the plans and also the Visitors' Book. – The Carnarvon Castle function was arranged chiefly that the Prince might be greeted by the Welsh League of Youth, a national, but not nationalist body.

WHERE HE WAS INVESTED AS PRINCE OF WALES TWENTY-THREE YEARS AGO: THE PRINCE AT CARNARVON CASTLE, WITH MR LLOYD GEORGE, CONSTABLE OF CARNARVON CASTLE, AND MEMBERS OF THE WELSH LEAGUE OF YOUTH.

"INTENSITY OF WAR-MINDEDNESS" IN SOVIET RUSSIA: MILITARY AND NAVAL STRENGTH AND MAN-POWER – A COMPOSITE PHOTOGRAPHIC IMPRESSION OF A PARADE IN RED SQUARE, MOSCOW.

This impressive display of the Red Army's strength is significant in view of recent developments in Russian foreign policy. It was rumoured lately that the Soviet might apply for admission to the League of Nations, with a view to a mutual assistance pact with France, extending the present pact of non-aggression concluded in 1932. There have also been exchanges of views between the Soviet and the Little Entente, tending towards resumption of regular relations. Last February an Anglo-Soviet temporary commercial Agreement was signed at the Foreign Office. It has been suggested that Russia is seeking security in Europe in view of possible, though not necessarily imminent, trouble in the Far East. The above photographs were sent to us by Major Ralph Rayner, prospective National Conservative candidate for Totnes, who writes, "The great parade I saw in the Red Square, Moscow, stupendous as a mass demonstration, was equally impressive as a military spectacle. The drill and technical efficiency of the Red forces on parade filled us with admiration of the staff work, which

secured that more than a million people passed the saluting base without any perceptible hitch. It is the ordinary everyday life of Soviet Russia, however, which gives away the intensity of her war-mindedness. One cannot move far without meeting bodies of regular troops, of khaki-clad young Communists or of armed workers marching under slogans of 'War to the Death'. One cannot linger at a bookstall without observing war literature of every kind. On flaming posters in the streets, workshops, and the Law Courts, workers and soldiers are represented fighting shoulder to shoulder amid gas, tanks, and aircraft. Every factory and village seems to have its rifle-club. In gliding, the U.S.S.R. is now, perhaps, leading the world – one wonders whither! At any rate, two humble observers, totalling forty years Army and Navy service between them, are convinced that Russia is more openly and more intensely preparing for future war than any other country in Europe."

EUROPE'S LEADING DICTATORS MEET:
HITLER–MUSSOLINI SCENES IN VENICE.

A GROUP ON THE BALCONY OF THE DOGE'S PALACE: DURING THE ASSEMBLAGE IN ST. MARK'S SQUARE: (LEFT TO RIGHT, IN FRONT) HERR HITLER, BARON VON NEURATH (GERMAN FOREIGN MINISTER), AND SIGNOR MUSSOLINI.

After meeting at the Venice aerodrome Herr Hitler and Signor Mussolini went by motor-launch to the Grand Hotel. Subsequently they had many conversations on political affairs, both in the Doge's Palace and in the Villa Pisani at Stra, formerly owned by Napoleon. Signor Mussolini's sudden decision not to sleep there on the night

THE GERMAN CHANCELLOR'S ARRIVAL AT THE GRAND HOTEL, VENICE: HERR HITLER (CENTRE) STEPPING ON THE GANGWAY FROM THE LANDING STAGE, AND SIGNOR MUSSOLINI (EXTREME RIGHT) LEAVING THE MOTOR-LAUNCH.

of June 14, it was reported, caused rumours that the building was haunted, and it was recalled that Napoleon only slept one night there. A more prosaic explanation was that the villa consists of large untenanted rooms and has the depressing air of an empty hotel. At the great assemblage in St. Mark's Square on the 16th, Herr Hitler and Signor Mussolini took their stand on a special stage erected near the Campanile, and watched a march-past of troops. The Dictators were on excellent terms with each other. Later they ascended to the balcony of the Doge's Palace, where Signor Mussolini addressed the vast crowd, his speech being amplified by loud-speakers. "Herr Hitler and I have met," he said, "not to re-make the political map, nor add new reasons of unrest, but to attempt to dispel the clouds which obscure the European horizon . . . In these days that we have spent together our spirits have been in intimate communion." An official communiqué issued later said, "The personal relations thus initiated between the two heads of Governments will be continued in the future."

KIDNAPPING – THE WORST "RACKET" IN THE USA: NOTORIOUS CASES.

(LEFT), THE CORRUGATED-IRON "BOX" WHICH WAS SUNK IN THE ARIZONA DESERT, IN WHICH KIDNAPPERS KEPT LITTLE JUNE ROBLES FOR NINETEEN DAYS; AND MR HOUSTON, WHO FOUND HER, HOLDING UP THE CHAINS BY WHICH SHE WAS SECURED.

(BELOW), WHERE MR WILLIAM GETTLE, THE WEALTHY OIL-MAGNATE, WAS KEPT FOR SIX DAYS BY KIDNAPPERS: THE HOUSE IN LA CRESCENTA, NEAR LOS ANGELES, FROM WHICH HE WAS RESCUED BY THE POLICE.

One of the most shocking of all the kidnapping outrages from which the United States have been suffering during recent years was perpetrated when June Robles, the six-year-old daughter of Mr Fernando Robles, a wealthy cattle-rancher of Arizona, was kidnapped and kept in a pit in the desert for nineteen days. At the end of this time a mysterious letter from Chicago to the local County Attorney gave a hint of the child's whereabouts. The hole in which she was found was hidden under a spiked bush of cactus. An attempt had been made to construct inside the pit a cage of corrugated iron sections. Motor-chains and dog-chains were fastened to the victim's ankles and to an iron pipe rammed in the earth. The sacks on which she slept were infested with vermin. The desert country of Arizona is, of course, subject to violent alterations of temperature, the cold at night being piercing, while the temperature on the day on which June Robles was found reached 110 degrees, the inside of the pit being even hotter. At the time that little June Robles was restored to her family in Tucson, Mr William F. Gettle, the wealth oil magnate, was rescued by the police, who found him confined in a little house in La Crescenta, a town a few miles from Los Angeles. He was bound hand and foot to a rough bed, and his face was encased in a mask of court-plaster. A singular coincidence had enabled the police to get on the trail of Mr Gettle's kidnappers. The police had installed a secret voice-recording apparatus in the walls of a house in Los Angeles, suspecting the occupants of having taken part in a bank robbery. They heard nothing about the bank robbery, but got a clue which led to Mr Gettle's rescue. Subsequently, four men were arrested in connection with the crime.

AN IMPRESSION OF AMERICA'S MIGHT AT SEA: THE GREAT NAVAL REVIEW.

One of the biggest displays ever staged in the New World took place on May 31 off the Ambrose Lightship, at the entrance to New York Harbour. President Roosevelt, on board the heavy cruiser "Indianapolis", held a review of the United States Fleet – the first in New York waters since 1918 – at which eighty-six vessels, ranging from battle-ships to a submarine tender, took part, the ships forming a column twelve miles long and taking over an hour to pass the reviewing base. It was a most majestic spectacle. Our photographs show: (Fig. 1) naval aeroplanes, nearly 200 of which gave an aerial display, flying over the heavy cruiser "Indianapolis", from which the President took the salute; (Fig. 2) the heavy cruiser "Louisville" (left) and the battle-ship "Pennsylvania" in the Hudson River, beneath the skyscrapers of Manhattan.

RUSSIA'S MIGHT ON LAND: SOVIET TANKS NEAR MOSCOW

A PARADE OF RUSSIA'S MILITARY MIGHT; A GREAT CONCOURSE OF TANKS NEAR MOSCOW WITH MECHANICS MAKING THEIR LAST PREPARATIONS FOR AN ADVANCE IN FORMATION.

This remarkable photograph just arrived from Russia makes a worthy addition to the composite photographic impression of Soviet Russia's "intensity of war-mindedness" which aroused great interest in our last issue. It shows a tremendous array of tanks gathered in preparation for a recent military review. In connection with these giant military displays, it is interesting to recall the words of M. Litvinoff on May 29th, when as mentioned on another page, the Soviet Foreign Commissar proposed that the Disarmament Conference should be transformed into a permanent and regularly assembling Conference of Peace. M. Litvinoff said that the Conference he had in mind "should work out, extend and perfect the measures of strengthening security. It should give a timely response to warnings of impending dangers of war and to appeals for aid; to S.O.S. from threatened States; and it should afford the latter timely aid within its power, whether such should be moral, economic, financial, or other kind". It should not, of course, be assumed that in Russia military displays are inconsistent with a pacific outlook, anymore than they are elsewhere.

"CIVIL WAR" SCENES IN THE USA: STRIKERS DEFY OFFICIAL FORCES.

(LEFT), THE TROUBLE IN TOLEDO, OHIO, WHERE STRIKERS BESIEGED LOYAL WORKERS IN A FACTORY, AND WERE DISPERSED BY THE NATIONAL GUARD, THREE BEING SHOT: MEN OF THE NATIONAL GUARD CHARGING THROUGH A HAIL OF STONES.

(RIGHT), MINNEAPOLIS TRUCK STRIKERS, WHO ATTEMPTED TO PREVENT THE MOVEMENT OF TRUCKS IN THE MARKET AREA, FIGHTING WITH THE POLICE: TRADE UNION MEMBERSS ARMED WITH CLUBS, METAL BARS, AND LENGTHS OF GAS-PIPING.

A serious clash occurred in Minneapolis on May 21 between the police and trade union truckmen who were on strike. There were many casualties on both sides, and it was not until the strikers were threatened with short-barralled shot-guns that the police succeeded in getting the upper hand. The affray was the result of some 300 strikers trying to prevent city produce firms from using motor trucks to distribute their goods. In the course of the fighting, Mr Francis H. Shoemaker, a Farmer-Labour Member of the House of Representatives, was taken into custody. Fighting between the strikers and police continued for some days, while the Regional Advisory Manager of the American Ball Company, was so badly injured while acting as special policeman that he died. A truce was at last proclaimed. The Concessions demanded by the strikers included a forty-hour week and a 30 dollar a week wage. The Labour Board's terms were approved by the employers, but rejected by the drivers. While the Minneapolis strike remained still unsettled, serious rioting, which ended with National Guards firing on a mob of strikers, broke out at Toledo, Ohio. Three people were killed. Workers who had been on strike for some days at the plant of the Electric Autolite Company besieged 1800 loyal employees, who were in danger of being overwhelmed. National Guardsmen arrived in Toledo and succeeded in dispersing the strikers and liberating the loyal workers after a night of terror in the wrecked factory, besieged by the mob. Serious rioting went on for several days. Mr Charles P. Taft was carrying on negotiations, but progress towards an agreement was hindered by the strikers' insistence that the militia be withdrawn before a settlement be made. It was announced on June 3 that the strike had been settled, the employers agreeing to a 5 per cent wage increase and virtual recognition of the men's union for purposes of bargaining in future disputes.

UNREST IN THE UNITED STATES: LABOUR TROUBLES; AND THE END OF PUBLIC ENEMY JOHN DILLINGER.

The general strike which had been imminent in San Francisco for many days began on the morning of July 16. It was called in sympathy with the strike of longshoremen and other maritime workers, which had been going on since early May. It is the object of the longshoremen to wrest from the steamship companies control of the employment of labour; and an obstinate attitude by both employers and employed brought about the general strike. Until July 19 and 20, when the sympathy strikes were called off and most of the transport workers returned, San Francisco, which has a population of 1,300,000, was paralysed, transport was at a standstill, and the food shortage became acute.

THE SHOOTING OF JOHN DILLINGER, AMERICA'S FOREMOST MURDERER AND ROBBER: "PUBLIC ENEMY NO. 1" (IN SHIRT-SLEEVES), WHEN IN PRISON.

The sordid career of John Dillinger, who is known to have been concerned in at least fourteen murders and numberless robberies, came to an end on July 22, when he was ambushed and shot dead by Federal detectives as he came out of a cinema in Chicago. A woman associate of the outlaw is said to have betrayed him to Mr Melvin Purvis, chief of the Chicago detectives of the Department of Justice, and sixteen men were stationed outside the cinema. It was hoped that he would be taken alive, but he sought to "draw" and was shot dead.

THE SAN FRANCISCO GENERAL STRIKE: A MOUNTED POLICE OFFICER IN THE "ARMOUR" OF HIS COUNTRY'S CIVIL DISPUTES – HELMET AND GAS MASK; AND A MASK FOR THE HORSE'S EYES.

THE BLACKSHIRT MEETING: A QUESTION OF EXCESSIVE VIOLENCE.

An audience of 15,000 people was present at a meeting of the British Union of Fascists held in the main hall at Olympia on the evening of June 7. Sir Oswald Mosley was the only speaker. His speech, which lasted for two and a quarter hours, was continually interrupted by those hostile to the Blackshirt movement, and by strife between them and Blackshirt stewards, male and female. Every few minutes throughout the meeting there was a clash, since a campaign of interruption had clearly been planned in advance; and numbers of interrupters were violently ejected. Demonstrations also took place outside the hall, and led to such obstruction of those entering that the meeting started forty minutes late. Police were in force outside Olympia. They had a difficult task in keeping the peace between groups of Blackshirts and anti-Fascists, and during the evening made twenty-three arrests. The question whether excessive violence was used by the Blackshirt stewards at the meeting has aroused much controversy, and has even been taken up in Parliament. In a statement in the House of Commons on June 11, the Home Secretary said that scenes of disorder such as those witnessed on this occasion could not be tolerated.

THE SCENE INSIDE OLYMPIA DURING SIR OSWALD MOSLEY'S SPEECH: A MEETING CONSTANTLY INTERRUPTED BY SHOUTS, FREE FIGHTS, AND THE EJECTION OF INTERRUPTERS WITH A VIOLENCE THAT SOME THOUGHT JUSTIFIED AND SOME THOUGHT EXCESSIVE.

HITLER'S "PURGE":
SOME OF THE MOST PROMINENT VICTIMS;

PROTAGONISTS IN THE GERMAN POLITICAL TRAGEDY: HERR HITLER (RIGHT), WITH CAPTAIN ROHM (CENTRE), LATE CHIEF OF STAFF, SAID TO HAVE BEEN PERSONALLY ARRESTED BY HIM AND AFTERWARDS SHOT; AND GENERAL GORING (LEFT), WHO CONDUCTED THE COUP IN BERLIN – A GROUP TAKEN IN DAYS WHEN ALL THREE WERE CLOSE COLLEAGUES AND BEFORE HERR HITLER BECAME CHANCELLOR.

CHIEF GROUP-LEADER HEINES, FOUND BY HERR HITLER IN CAPTAIN ROHM'S COUNTRY HOUSE, AND AFTERWARDS EXECUTED.

LIEUT.-GENERAL VON FRITSCH, COMMANDER-IN-CHIEF OF THE ARMY – REPORTED ARRESTED AND CONDEMNED TO DEATH.

GROUP-LEADER KARL ERNST, COMMANDANT OF THE BERLIN-BRANDENBURG STORM TROOPERS. ONE OF THE S.A. LEADERS EXECUTED.

The schism among the Nazi leaders came to a dramatic head on June 30, when Herr Hitler and his chief lieutenant, General Goring, struck suddenly at those suspected of preparing a "second revolution". The Chancellor himself flew by night to Munich and drove thence to the country house of Captain Rohm (Chief of Staff, formerly commander of the Brown Army, and Minister without Portfolio) at Bad Wiessee. There it was reported that Fuhrer personally arrested Captain Rohm, who was given the chance of committing suicide, and, having refused, was afterwards shot. In the same house Herr Hitler also found Chief Group-Leader Heines, in shameful circumstances, and he also was later executed. Meanwhile, in Berlin General Göring had been taking similar measures against those believed to be involved in a conspiracy against the Hitler régime. Captain Rohm,

who was severely wounded in the war, was at Hitler's side in the Munich *Putsch* of 1923. Later, he served with the Bolivian Army, but was recalled by Hitler in 1930 and appointed Chief of Staff. He organised the Brown Army. Edmund Heines, who was Chief Group-Leader for Silesia, had also taken part in the Hitler *Putsch* at Munich. He was one of the first to receive the Nazi "dirk of honour". Group-Leader Ernst, Commander of the Berlin-Brandenburg S.A. (Storm Detachments), was arrested at Bremen as he was about to leave for a holiday in Madeira, and was subsequently shot. Several of the Nazi leaders had attended his marriage recently. He is said to have been formerly a junior employee in a Berlin hotel.

ON THE EVE OF THE CRISIS IN GERMANY:

HERR HITLER'S UNSUSPICIOUS ACTIVITIES WHILE PLANNING THE "PURGE"; AND OTHER PERSONALITIES.

LEADING PERSONALITIES INVOLVED IN THE NAZI CRISIS IN GERMANY: (FROM LEFT TO RIGHT) HERR VON PAPEN, GENERAL VON BLOMBERG, HERR HITLER, GENERAL GÖRING, AND DR. GOEBBELS.

WHEN IT WAS DOUBTFUL WHETHER THEIR THOUGHTS WERE ON THE CEREMONY: A WEDDING ATTENDED BY HERR HITLER (BEHIND THE BRIDE) AND GENERAL GÖRING (RIGHT, AS BEST MAN), AT ESSEN, JUST BEFORE THE COUP.

PRESIDENT OF THE SUMMARY COURT-MARTIAL IN BERLIN: HERR HIMMLER, HEAD OF THE S.S. (*SCHUTZSTAFFEL*), A BODYGUARD DEVOTED TO HITLER.

THE NEW NAZI CHIEF-OF-STAFF: HERR VICTOR LUTZE, APPOINTED TO SUCCEED CAPTAIN ROHM, WHO WAS EXECUTED.

Some of the above illustrations throw an interesting light on Herr Hitler's cautious proceedings during the few days immediately before his sudden descent on Munich, where he is said to have arrested Captain Rohm and Herr Heines. In a report of the dramatic events of June 30 in Germany, the "Times" stated, citing an official, but anonymous, eye-witness; "The latest tidings about the plot against him made Herr Hitler resolve to take drastic action. While the 'purification' was being prepared, a visit to Western German labour camps was arranged in order to lull the plotters into a sense of security. At 2 am on Saturday (June 30), the Führer,

though he had hardly slept for some days, ordered the journey to Munich; with Dr Goebbels, Herr Lutze, and others unnamed, he took an aeroplane from the Hangelar aerodrome, near Bonn. His attitude during this nocturnal flight into the unknown was one of tremendous resolution." Another incident calculated to allay suspicion was his attendance at the wedding of Councillor Terboven and Fraulein Ilse Stahl, at Essen. General Göring acted as the bridegroom's "best man". After the ceremony, the Chancellor continued his tour of labour camps.

GERMANY "CARRIES ON AS USUAL" AMID AN ORGY OF EXECUTIONS.

PUBLIC CURIOSITY IN BERLIN ON JULY 1; CROWDS OUTSIDE THE CHANCELLERY IN THE SILHELM-STRASSE, WAITING TO CATCH A GLIMPSE OF HITLER.

HERR HITLER (IN THE CAR, SALUTING) ON HIS WAY TO THE REICHSTAG MEETING: DRIVING THROUGH STREETS WITH SIGNIFICANTLY FEW ONLOOKERS BEHIND THE S.S. NAZI GUARDS.

HITLER'S "APOLOGIA":

THE FUHRER DEFENDS HIS ACTS AS GERMANY'S "SUPREME COURT".

Hitler's "purge" of the Nazi party, by eliminating alleged conspirators against him, was not completed by the dramatic events of June 30. It was reported later that at least sixty persons were shot in Berlin on Sunday, July 1, and that further executions took place the next day. Among the killed, it was stated, was Herr von Müldener, a member of the ex-Crown Prince's *entourage*. Another report stated that Prince August Wilhelm of Prussia, the ex-Kaiser's third son, had been expelled from the Storm Troops. The most poignant tragedy was the death of Frau Elizabeth von Schleicher, ex-Chancellor General von Schieicher's wife, who was shot in an endeavour to shield him. One version of the story is that, after the order for his arrest had been signed by General Göring, four truckloads of Nazi police suddenly arrived at his villa near Potsdam as the family were sitting down to lunch. On being informed that he was under arrest, the General made to reach his revolver, and the police replied with a volley. Frau Schleicher sprang towards their Commander, beseeching him to cease firing, and fell mortally wounded.

All Germany listened, through the radio, to Herr Hitler's momentous speech on July 13 (at the Reichstag meeting in the Kroll Opera House, Berlin) when he told the story of the "plot" suppressed on June 30 and July 1, and gave a list of seventy-seven summary executions. As he drove to the meeting, with a heavily armed bodyguard, there were unusually meagre crowds behind the S.S. Nazi guards lining the streets. General Göring, the Speaker's chair, appeared for the first time not in Nazi uniform but in that of the Air Sport Federation, or future German Air Force. The climax of the Führer's speech came when he declared: "There was only one course open – lightning action. Only ruthless and bloody intervention could perhaps crush the revolt . . . If I am reproached with not leaving condemnation to the legal courts, I would answer; 'In this hour I was responsible for the fate of the German nation, and in these twenty-four hours I was therefore the supreme court of the nation in my own person' . . . I gave the order to shoot the main culprits . . . and I further gave the order to shoot down the mutineers at the least sign of resistance to arrest . . . Everyone must know for the future that certain death will be his lot if he raise his hand against the State."

THE TERRIBLE SNOWSCAPES OF NANGA PARBAT, REPUTED THE MOST DIFFICULT PEAK IN THE WORLD TO CLIMB: MEMBERS OF THE ILL-FATED GERMAN EXPEDITION, ROPED TOGETHER, CROSSING A CREVASSE, 18,000 FEET UP.

The German Himalayan Expedition which ended in tragedy on the upper slopes of Nanga Parbat was led by Herr Willi Merkl, a Munich railway official. The Expedition was organised by the German railways and paid for by subscriptions from railwaymen. Herr Merkl had been the leader of the German attempt on Nanga Parbat in 1932, when storms forced the climbers to abandon the assault at a height only slightly less than that reached on the last occasion. Only once before had an attempt to climb the peak been made in 1895, when the famous mountaineer Mr A.F. Mummery led an expedition and lost his life. Herr Merkl, with Dr. Wieland, Dr. Welzenbach, and several porters, was overtaken by a terrific snow-storm when at Camp 8, on July 8, and was forced to turn back. Dr Wieland died before reaching Camp 71; but Herr Merkl struggled on to Camp 6, and there, according to a porter who accomplished the descent, sheltered in an ice-hole for some days, huddled up against another porter for warmth. Although without food and very weak, Herr Merkl was still alive on July 14; but soon all hope of saving him had to be abandoned, since the atrocious weather made rescue impossible.

"IN THESE 24 HOURS I WAS THE SUPREME COURT OF THE NATION. . . . I GAVE THE ORDER TO SHOOT THE MAIN CULPRITS": HERR HITLER AT THE REICHSTAG MEETING DELIVERING HIS MOMENTOUS "APOLOGIA" ON THE RECENT NAZI "PURGE", FROM THE CENTRAL TRIBUNE IN FRONT OF GENERAL GÖRING (SEATED IN THE SPEAKER'S CHAIR).

A WINDOW ON THE WORLD
EVENTS AT HOME AND ABROAD

THE KING OPENS THE LARGEST UNDER-WATER TUNNEL IN THE WORLD.

An historic occasion took place at Liverpool on July 18 when the £8,000,000 Mersey Tunnel was opened by the King and named "Queensway". The Lord Mayor offered the city's welcome, and an address was read by the chairman of the Mersey Tunnel Joint Committee, Sir Thomas White.

WORK RESTARTS ON THE GIANT CUNARDER: "NO. 534" ON THE STOCKS AT JOHN BROWN AND CO.'S SHIPBUILDING YARD AT CLYDEBANK.

There was rejoicing on the Clyde on April 3, when work, suspended owing to the slump since December 12, 1931, was restarted on the hull of the 73,000-ton liner, "No. 534". Six hundred men who, with few exceptions, had done no work in their own trades for more than two years, were piped to work and cheered by a laughing crowd. Two hundred more men were engaged the following day. The liner will probably be launched in the autumn.

A SCENE IN THE JORDAAN DISTRICT – THE "EAST END" OF AMSTERDAM – AFTER THE RIOTS ENGINEERED BY COMMUNISTS: A STREET LITTERED WITH PAVING-BLOCKS AND BRICKS; AND A DAMAGED TREE.

On July 5, desperate fighting occurred in Amsterdam between large bodies of Communists and police in the district of Jordaan, Amsterdam's "East End". When barricades were set up by the rioters the police opened fire. The trouble continued on July 6. A desperate attempt was made to set a bridge on fire, but was frustrated by the fire brigade. The rioters also opened a number of bridges to hinder the police. By this time armoured cars were patrolling the streets; marines were guarding the docks; and the city police had been reinforced by national and military police. The riots were engineered by Communist agitators, and the most serious fighting took place in the Jewish and poorer quarters. The occasion of the trouble was the reduction in the "dole" given to the unemployed. When rioting was renewed during the week-end, Dr. Colijn, the Premier, arrived in Amsterdam to take charge of the situation. It was stated in some quarters that the police had shown want of vigour in suppressing the disorders.

THE GERMAN CRUISERS "KONIGSBERG" (LEFT) AND "LEIPZIG" AT PORTSMOUTH: THE FIRST VISIT OF GERMAN ARMED VESSELS TO AN ENGLISH NAVAL PORT SINCE 1914.

The German cruisers "Konigsberg" and "Leipzig" arrived in Portsmouth Harbour on the morning of July 11 for a four days' visit; and there was an exchange of salutes between them and the naval and military shore batteries, the German Rear-Admiral's flag-ship firing twenty-one guns in honour of the country and seventeen in honour of the commander-in-Chief of the port. The occasion was remarkable from the fact that German armed vessels were visiting an English naval port for the first time since 1914.

A FRENCH RIVAL TO "NO. 534": THE "NORMANDIE", WHOSE GROSS REGISTERED TONNAGE WILL BE ABOUT 79,000, BEING COMPLETED AT ST. NAZAIRE.

On the left we give a picture of the British liner, "No. 534", which unless the "Normandie" eclipses her, will be the largest in the world. Here is a general view of the French ship, with two funnels already in position, and work on the third proceeding. Her estimated gross tonnage will be 79,280 – 6000 greater than that of "No. 534", which, however, may be re-estimated at a much higher figure before the vessel is completed.

TRAGEDY OF DOLLFUSS: AT THE CHANCELLERY AND THE RADIO STATION.

THE SCENE OF DR DOLLFUSS'S DEATH: IN THE MURDERED CHANCELLOR'S STUDY IN THE CHANCEL-LERY; WITH THE DIVAN ON WHICH HE DIED IN THE BACKGROUND.

THE WIRELESS STATION FROM WHICH AN ANNOUNCER WAS FORCED TO BROADCAST "THE GOVERN-MENT WAS RESIGNED": HEIMWEHR AND POLICE ATTACKING THE BUILDING OF THE RAVAG (THE AUSTRIAN BROADCASTING CO.) IN VIENNA.

In his broadcast account of the *putsch* of July 25 in Vienna, Major Fey said: "Terrible events have happened in Austria. At 11 a.m., a Cabinet Council was held, and at 11.30 it was informed that supposed Heimwehr men and 150 Nazis, disguised as members of the police, were assembling in an athletic club in the 7th Vienna district and were planning some action against the Government. I at once informed the Chancellor, and the Cabinet meeting broke up, leaving the Secretary of Security and National Defence to take over in their place. Suddenly a detachment of what were thought to be police and army troops entered the Chancellery, where we were sitting. They had rifles in their hands, and forced their way into the main room. Karwinsky and I were arrested, as was Dollfuss in another room. At 2.30 I was escorted into another room, where I found Dollfuss lying wounded on a sofa . . . We were escorted to a room where we were kept for several agonising hours, during which the Nazis, armed with rifles, threatened several times to kill us. Later in the day Herr Neustaedter-Stuermer was taken to the Chancellery to commence negotiations with the rebels."

We quote the "Daily Telegraph": When Herr Schuschnigg, now the Chancellor, broadcast on the night of July 25, he said "This terrible day was started by a lie. The announcer of the broadcasting station, with a revolver placed at his head, was forced to say: 'The Government has resigned. Dr. Rintelen has taken over power.' " This was at about the time the rebel Nazis were entering the Chancellery. The Heimwehr and police were in action immediately, and there was brisk fighting with machine-guns, rifles, pistols, and hand-grenades, while the Ravag (the building of the Austrian Broadcasting Company) was being cleared. Meantime, a director had been shot dead. Three police and two Nazis were killed. The wounded were numerous. A number of arrests were made. On July 26 the "Times" correspondent in Graz stated: "The false announcement of the Government's resignation broadcast from Vienna was the signal for a Nazi revolt throughout Styria . . . The Nazis, where they felt themselves strong enough, set out to storm police stations and Government buildings. They have been encouraged in their resistance by reports that their fellows are still fighting in Vienna and that the revolt will soon spread over Austria." In other words, they believed the false announcement, and not the official broadcast accounts.

By the end of July the Austrian Government had succeeded in getting the Nazi rising in the provinces thoroughly under control. The worst disturbances took place in Styria and Carinthia, where the insurgents were well supplied with machine-guns and casualties were heavy on both sides. A large number of Nazi prisoners was taken and numbers of fugitives took refuge across the Yugoslav border, where most of them were taken to concentration camps. The hardest fighting in Carinthia took place round Klagenfurt and Villach, the two chief towns of the Province, and there was also much guerilla warfare in country districts. In some small towns the Nazis only continued their resistance through ignorance of the failure of a general insurrection.

On July 28 the body of Herr Dollfuss was buried, in accordance with his wish, in the cemetery at Heizing, Vienna.

OTTO PLANETTA   FRANZ HOLZWEBBER

The trial of two Austrian Nazis on charges in connection with the entry into the chancellery on the occasion on which the chancellor, Dr. Dollfuss, was killed, ended in Vienna on July 31. The prisoners were Otto Planetta, 35, charged with high treason and with the Murder of Dr. Dollfuss, and Franz Holzwebber, 30, charged with high treason on the ground that he was the leader of the rebels in the chancellery. Both were ex-soldiers. Both were sentenced to death by hanging and the sentence was carried out within three hours.

THE STATE FUNERAL IN VIENNA.

PRINCE STARHEMBERG MAKING HIS FUNERAL ORATION AT THE CITY HALL: THE VICE-CHANCELLOR IN THE NEW SCHUSCHIGG CABINET SPEAKING OF THE MURDERED CHANCELLOR, DECLARING THAT HIS POLICY WOULD BE CARRIED ON, AND SAYING: "YOU WILL ENTER INTO AUSTRIAN HISTORY BECAUSE OF THE SUCCESS OF YOUR WORK."

THE LYING-IN-STATE: GREAT CROWDS LINED UP IN VIENNA TO PASS BEFORE THE COFFINED BODY OF THE CHANCELLOR IN THE CITY HALL.

THE DEATH OF FIELD-MARSHAL VON HINDENBURG SECOND PRESIDENT OF THE GERMAN REPUBLIC.

THE VICTOR OF TANNENBERG, MOST FAMOUS OF THE GERMAN WAR LEADERS, HONOURED IN DEATH AS IN LIFE: IN BERLIN, AT NEUDECK, AND AT TANNENBERG.

THE FUNERAL OF PRESIDENT VON HINDENBURG: THE COFFIN – COVERED WITH A WAR FLAG AND BEARING THE FIELD-MARSHAL'S HELMET – BEING DRAWN FROM NEUDECK, THE SCENE OF DEATH, TO THE TANNENBERG MEMORIAL, THE PLACE OF BURIAL.

THE DEAD PRESIDENT LYING IN STATE AT NEUDECK: FIELD-MARSHAL VON HINDENBERG WEARING THE MANTLE OF THE ORDER OF ST. JOHN ON THE RIGHT, THE EX-KAISER'S WREATH.

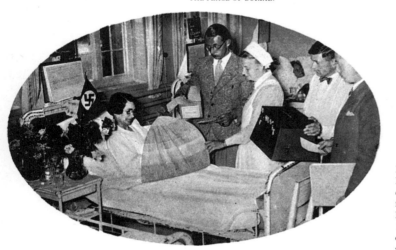

A PATIENT RECORDING HER VOTE IN A BERLIN HOSPITAL: A PHOTOGRAPH SHOWING THE PORTABLE SCREEN USED TO ENSURE SECRECY AND THE SEALED BOX FOR THE RECEIPT OF THE FILLED-IN VOTING PAPER.

HERR HITLER CONFIRMED AS LEADER-CHANCELLOR. THE VITAL "YES" OR "NO" PLEBISCITE IN GERMANY

Immediately after the death of President von Hindenburg, when it became known that the office of the Reich President had been united with that of the Reich Chancellor, it was announced that the Leader and Chancellor desired that the post combining the offices of President and Chancellor in his person should be submitted forthwith to a national plebiscite. A most intensive campaign began almost at once to reach its height at Hamburg on the 17th, when Herr Hitler broadcast an appeal to the people to support him. Then, on August 19, as arranged, the polling took place. The vote was secret – much has been made of that – and there was but one question to answer: the voter was required to put a cross against "Yes" or "No", according to whether he or she was or was not in agreement with Herr Hitler's new position and powers. The result was overwhelmingly in favour of the Leader-Chancellor. The provisional figures (as issued on the Monday) were: votes for Hitler, 38,362,760; votes against Hitler, 4,294,654; spoiled papers, 872,296. Every effort was made to persuade all to poll, and 95 per cent of the electorate voted; 2,034,846 did not vote.

DURING THE PLEBISCITE CAMPAIGN – PROBABLY THE MOST VIGOROUS AND WIDESPREAD PROPAGANDA EFFORT EVER MADE: A RAILWAY ENGINE INSCRIBED: "EIN VOLK, EIN FÜHRER, EIN 'JA' " (ONE PEOPLE, ONE LEADER, ONE "YES".)

HERR HITLER'S FIRST ACT AS GERMAN LEADER AND CHANCELLOR: THE FUHRER PAYING TRIBUTE TO THE MEMORY OF PRESIDENT VON HINDENBURG, THE FORMER HEAD OF THE STATE, IN THE FLOWER-LINED REICHSTAG.

GIANT "534" LAUNCHED – AS THE "QUEEN MARY".

"THE STATELIEST SHIP NOW IN BEING": AT THE END OF THE VITAL 54 SECONDS OF THE LAUNCH BY THE QUEEN.

The great thrill of the day at the launch of the Cunarder "Queen Mary", was, of course, the spectacle of her vast bulk gliding down the slipways immediately after the Queen had named her and actuated the launching mechanism. This, the first voyage of the giant liner, occupied just 54 seconds. Just afterwards, the above photograph was taken from the air. The bad weather conditions, it need hardly be said, made photography very difficult. When the six triggers holding the ship fast were released, and the six hydraulic rams gave her an initial thrust, she started forward with a grinding noise and moved, slowly at first but smoothly and gathering speed, towards the Clyde. As her stern entered the water a white-capped wave arose and for a moment flooded a little of the shore, but soon dispersed. When the bow took the water, the vessel gave one violent lunge, and lay afloat on an even keel, to be taken in charge by tugs.

FROM THE WORLD'S SCRAP-BOOK:
NEWS ITEMS OF TOPICAL INTEREST.

THE TEXTILE STRIKE IN THE UNITED STATES: NATIONAL GUARD SENTRIES BEHIND A SHIELD AT THE MILLS AT KANNAPOLIS, NORTH CAROLINA.

The United States textile strike, which began on September 1, when over 600,000 workers were called out, was still continuing nearly three weeks later. The dispute concerned wages and hours of work. On September 5, Mr. Roosevelt intervened by appointing a board of three members to mediate on the strike. There were serious riots in North and South Carolina, Georgia, and Rhode Island, troops were called out, and numbers of people were injured and killed. On September 17 Mr. Francis Gorman, leader of the strikers, issued a public warning that unless the dispute was settled that week, all divisions of the industry, involving a further 100,000 workers, would be ordered out. It was thought that 13,000 troops were then on duty trying to maintain order.

The Fascist demonstration and the anti-Fascist counter-demonstration in Hyde Park on Sunday, September 9, yielded one more proof of the fact that the British people retain their sense of proportion; for, taking it as a whole, the event passed off without any incident that could be regarded as in the least serious. The crowd was essentially orderly and good-humoured; and the official organisation was such that the two Parties concerned were divided from one another by a "No-Man's Land" kept by mounted and foot police. Mr. Will Rogers, the shrewd American humorist, observer, and journalist, whose comments are printed in six hundred of his country's papers cabled from London: "The English are the smartest white people there is; they'll never have Communism, Fascism, Hitlerism or nudism in this country. They have a park here – Hyde Park – which was built for people that are 'agin' something. Yesterday I was there when it had the biggest crowd that has ever been there. The Blackshirts were holding their meeting. Two hundred yards away the Communists were holding theirs. And in between was all of London laughing at both of them."

THE FASCIST DEMONSTRATION AND THE ANTI-FASCIST COUNTER-DEMONSTRATION: THE "NO-MAN'S LAND" IN HYDE PARK DIVIDING THE TWO PARTIES FROM ONE ANOTHER AND KEPT BY THE POLICE.

THE GRAVE DISORDERS IN SPAIN:
STRIKES AND FIGHTING IN MADRID.

CAPTURED REVOLUTIONARIES, WITH RAISED HANDS, BEING SEARCHED BY CIVIL GUARDS ARMED WITH RIFLES: A SCENE AFTER A FIGHT IN THE CENTRAL DISTRICT OF MADRID DURING THE RECENT DISTURBANCES.

The outbreak of the grave disorders in Spain is said to have been due to the fact that the Prime Minister, Señor Lerroux, in forming his coalition Cabinet, included three members of the semi-Fascist Catholic Party. The Socialists saw in this the first step towards crushing the Labour movement, and promptly called a general strike throughout Spain, with a view to upsetting the Government and turning out the Fascist element. The strike began on the night of Friday, October 5, and on the following day the trouble developed into a revolutionary movement and firing began in Madrid. The Government offices and Civil Guard barracks were attacked, shots were fired at the Chamber of Deputies, and attempts were made to seize the telephone building. These attacks were repulsed, but sniping at the police from side streets and the roofs of houses continued for several hours. At 10.00 pm Señor Lerroux delivered a broadcast address, proclaiming a state of war throughout Spain, and the presence of troops in the streets had a reassuring effect. The casualties in Madrid were estimated at 12 dead and 50 wounded. Several hundred arrests were made. On the 9th it was reported that there had been further fighting, and that there was no sign as yet of the collapse of the revolt in the capital. The revolutionaries had adopted guerrilla tactics, which the Government forces found very difficult to deal with.

ARTILLERY BOMBARDMENTS IN BARCELONA:

A NIGHT OF BATTLE THAT ENDED THE TWELVE-HOUR CATALAN REPUBLIC.

THE CAPTURE OF THE CITY HALL, IN WHICH SEÑOR COMPANYS AND MEMBERS OF THE MUNICIPAL ADMINISTRATION, SUPPORTERS OF THE SEPARATIST MOVEMENT, AHD FORTIFIED THEMSELVES: INFANTRY OF GENERAL BATET'S FORCES ENTERING THE BUILDING, WHICH WAS MUCH DAMAGED BY BOMBARDMENT AND WAS FLYING THE WHITE FLAG. (TOP LEFT.)

On the 6th, the Regional Government in Barcelona endeavoured to establish a Provisional Spanish Republic, in opposition to the powers in Madrid. At 8.15 on the night of October 6, the Catalan President, Don Luis Companys, proclaimed the Catalan State of the Spanish Federal Republic, in which the Catalan Government and leaders had fortified themselves, just as the Mayor and Members of the Municipal Government had in the City Hall across the square. While the Catalans were rejoicing, two hours after the Proclamation, General Batet's troops appeared on the scene. Thereupon, reported "The Times," soldiers of the Separatist Party, the Estat Catala, in citizens' clothing but wearing the Separatist Insignia on their sleeves, attempted to oppose their passage, and firing began. The troops advanced on the Generalitat Palace, driving back the Catalan police. They reached the Square and were met by firing, which began a battle lasting through the night until 6 a.m. The troops trained trench-mortars on the palace, and also on the City Hall. The facades of both were much damaged. About 8 a.m. a heavy bombardment of the City Hall began, and those in the Generalitat, knowing that the City Hall would soon be taken and fire directed from it against themselves, decided to surrender and sent out a uniformed guard with a white flag. The attacking troops then entered the building, and the leading Separatists within were detained. Among those taken prisoner was Señor Companys. He and others were placed on board a ship in the harbour.

THE ENGLAND–AUSTRALIA AIR RACE:
OVER ELEVEN THOUSAND MILES IN UNDER THREE DAYS.

The most remarkable air race that has ever been held – that from Mildenhall Aerodrome, Suffolk, to Melbourne, in connection with the Victorian centenary celebrations started on the morning of Saturday, October 20. The first machine off was the D.H. Comet (Gipsy VI.) flown by Mr. and Mrs. J.A. Mollison, which was started at 6.30 a.m., and the last machine took off at 6.43 a.m. The speed race was won by C.W.A. Scott and T. Campbell Black, who made the flight of 11,300 miles in a little under three days. Their aeroplane was a de Havilland Comet – a twin-engine (Gipsy VI.) two-seater, low-wing cantilever monoplane with a fully retracting undercarriage – specially made to meet the conditions and regulations governing the particular event, and, of course, the conditions likely to be encountered between England and Australia. So new in design is it that there was no time for it to be thoroughly tested before it started on the great enterprise. Mr. and Mrs. Mollison flew a similar machine. They made a record non-stop flight to Baghdad, covering 2530 miles in 12 hours and 40 minutes, and then a flight to Karachi which lowered the England–India record to 22 hours, 13 minutes, but they had to give in at Allahabad, owing to cracked pistons. A most impressive performance was put up by the Douglas DC2 "air hotel" entered by the Dutch airline K.L.M. which arrived second at Melbourne, having carried seven passengers as far as Albury, one hundred and sixty miles short of the finish.

A BEAM WIRELESS PHOTOGRAPH OF THE WINNING COMET ON ITS ARRIVAL AT MELBOURNE: THE MONOPLANE PILOTED BY SCOTT AND CAMPBELL BLACK IMMEDIATELY AFTER THE LANDING.

THE ROUTE FLOWN BY THE COMPETITORS IN BOTH SPEED RACE AND HANDICAP: A MAP SHOWING THE CONTROLS AT WHICH ALL HAD TO LAND, AND THE CHECKING POINTS, WHERE LANDING WAS NOT NECESSARY.

THE DUTCH "AIR HOTEL" WHICH ARRIVED SECOND IN THE RACE: THE DOUGLAS D.C.2 (WRIGHT CYCLONE), PILOTED BY MESSRS. K.D. PARMENTIER AND J.J. MOLL AND CARRYING SEVEN PASSENGERS AS FAR AS ALBURY, BEING FLAGGED OFF FROM MILDENHALL AT THE START.

ASSASSINATION

THE SCENE OF THE ASSASSINATION OF KING ALEXANDER OF YUGOSLAVIA AND M. BARTHOU IS VIVIDLY SHOWN IN THIS WONDERFUL PHOTOGRAPH. THE ASSASSIN IS BESIDE THE CAR, JUST AFTER HE HAD FIRED THE FATAL SHOTS, BEING CUT DOWN BY LIEUT. COL. PIOLLET (ON HORSEBACK) OF THE 141ST INFANTRY REGIMENT, WHO HAD BEEN RIDING AT THE SIDE OF THE CAR. THE BLADE OF THE COLONEL'S SWORD IS FAINTLY VISIBLE, AND THE ASSASSIN HAS HIS HAND TO HIS HEAD, WHILE THE CHAUFFEUR HAS SEIZED HIS COAT TO PREVENT HIM GOING. THIS PHOTOGRAPH FORMS A UNIQUE RECORD OF THE TRAGEDY, AND IS A REMARKABLE ADDITION TO THE MANY HISTORIC PHOTOGRAPHS PUBLISHED IN OUR PAGES.

THE UNCLIMBED AND "UNCLIMBABLE" MOUNT MYSTERY:
OUTWORKS AND "SENTINELS" THAT GUARD THE HIGHEST PEAK IN CANADA.

ON THE WAY TO MOUNT MYSTERY: THE HEAD OF DAIS GLACIER, WHERE THERE IS A "GREAT GLEAMING BASIN, THREE MILES ROUND THE RIM"; AND A CAMPING SITE USED IN THE RECENT ATTACK ON MOUNT WADDINGTON (INDICATED BY AN ARROW).

THE PROFILE OF MOUNT MYSTERY: THE PEAKS OF MOUNT WADDINGTON – THE SECOND HIGHEST OF WHICH THE MUNDAY-HALL PARTY CLIMBED, THOUGH ITS HIGHEST DEFEATED THEM – SEEN FROM AGUR GLACIER.

MOUNT MYSTERY – UNCLIMBED AND "UNCLIMBABLE": THE HIGHEST PEAK OF MOUNT WADDINGTON (13,260 FT.), CONSIDERED VIRTUALLY UNCLIMBABLE BY THE MUNDAY-HALL EXPEDITION, WHICH RECENTLY ATTEMPTED IT – A ROCKY FLAG OF PECULIAR FORMATION, COVERED WITH ICE-SCALES, "ALMOST A NIGHTMARE IN ITS GRIM INACCESSIBILITY."

ARMISTICE DAY STILL DRAWS ITS UNFORGETTING MYRIADS.

ARMISTICE DAY MAINTAINS ITS HOLD ON THE HEART OF THE EMPIRE, AND LONDONERS STILL GATHER IN THEIR THOUSANDS ROUND THE NATIONAL MEMORIAL: A GENERAL VIEW OF THE SCENE AT THE CENOTAPH, LOOKING NORTH UP WHITEHALL TOWARDS THE WAR OFFICE (RIGHT, BACKGROUND) AND SHOWING THE WHOLE ROADWAY BEYOND THE MONUMENT PACKED WITH PEOPLE.

THE ROYAL WEDDING: THE BRIDAL COUPLE ON THE PALACE BALCONY.

Acknowledging the cheers from those gathered outside the Palace, the Duke and Duchess of Kent came out on to the balcony and waved their thanks. From left to right are Princess Elizabeth of York; the bride and bridegroom, with Princess Margaret Rose of York behind them; Prince Nicholas of Greece, father of the bride: and the Queen. In the small photograph, the King is holding up Princess Margaret Rose, who hides him from the camera, and the Queen is lending a hand to steady her.

AFTER THE MARRIAGE IN WESTMINSTER ABBEY: THE DUKE AND DUCHESS OF KENT WAVING THEIR THANKS TO THE CROWD FROM BUCKINGHAM PALACE.

FROM THE WORLD'S SCRAP-BOOK:
NEWS ITEMS OF TOPICAL INTEREST.

AN ANTI-AIRCRAFT UNIT, HEAVILY CONCEALED WITH FOLIAGE, AWAITING AN "ENEMY" AEROPLANE IN JAPANESE ARMY MANOEUVRES: AN ANCIENT DEVICE IN MODERN WAR.

"BIRNAM WOOD COMES TO DUNSINANE" IN MODERN WARFARE: CAMOUFLAGED MEN AND A CAR CAREFULLY HIDDEN WITH NETS AND FOLIAGE IN JAPANESE MANOEUVRES.

The necessity of concealment is, of course, as great in the warfare of today (both mock and serious) as it ever was; but it is interesting to find much the same device in use now as that immortalised in "Macbeth", where Malcolm ordered his troops hew down and carry boughs so as to "shadow the numbers of our host and make discovery err in report of us." These photographs were taken last month in Japan, where, from November 11 to 14, the annual Army manoeuvres were held in the plains north of Tokyo. More than fifty thousand troops took part, under the personal direction of his Imperial majesty the Emperor Hirohito. Soon after these manoeuvres, on November 22, the Japanese Cabinet accepted a majority of the Army's and Navy's demands for new expenditure. The Army's appropriations from the 1934–35 Budget were fixed at £28,583,000 and the Navy's at over thirty millions. It is Japan's largest Budget.

(LEFT), THE DEEPEST DESCENT INTO THE OCEAN EVER MADE: DR. WILLIAM BEEBE'S TWO TON STEEL BATHY SPHERE BEING UNLOADED AT BERMUDA.

(RIGHT), THE "BIRD'S EYE" THAT WILL VIEW LONDON'S TRAFFIC PROBLEMS FROM ALOFT: SCOTLAND YARD'S NEW AUTOGIRO FOR OBSERVING TRAFFIC.

Dr. William Beebe, the American scientist, with Mr. Otis Barton, his assistant and film photographer, descended in their bathysphere 3028 feet into the ocean depths off Bermuda on August 15, beating their own record of a few days before by 518 feet. The deeper they went the larger seemed the fish. Dr. Beebe reported one monster 20 ft. long and "glittering with lights like a skyscraper at night." The presssure on the sphere at the lowest depth was about half a ton to the square inch.

An expedient that was originally, we believe, adopted as a means of controlling traffic on Derby Day, has now been tried in the metropolis. Scotland Yard's new autogiro will be used for carrying out observations over traffic-congested areas. The observers will be in wireless touch with the Yard's traffic department. The machine will be permitted to hover low over London. It is also suggested that it might be used for tracking car-bandits.

THE PLIGHT OF HUNGARIAN REFUGEES
EXPELLED FROM YUGOSLAVIA.

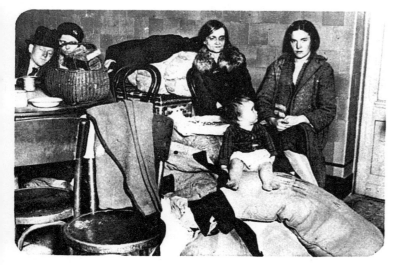

It was reported from Budapest, on December 7, that the number of Hungarian refugees expelled from Yugoslavia was about 2500; but the exodus ceased a few days later, following an order issued by Prince Paul, First Regent of Yugoslavia, immediately on his return to Belgrade from the Royal Wedding ceremonies in London. It was understood that he expressed himself most strongly concerning the deportations, pointing out the bad effect they had on public opinion in London and Paris. At the same time, at Geneva, the Yugoslav-Hungarian dispute was allayed, after anxious negotiation in which Mr. Anthony Eden played a conciliatory part, by a resolution accepted by both parties, and passed by the League Council. Mr. Eden was nominated as *rapporteur* to conduct investigations.

ONE OF THE HUNGARIAN FAMILIES DEPORTED FROM YUGOSLAVIA INTO HUNGARY: A TYPICAL GROUP AFTER THEIR ARRIVAL IN BUDAPEST.

POLITICALLY DANGEROUS? YUCIKA VAROSSY, AGED FOUR, EXPELLED FROM YUGOSLAVIA; A LITTLE GIRL WITH HER MOTHER'S ADDRESS IN BUDAPEST ATTACHED TO HER COAT.

A COAL-MINING REGION THAT MUST CHOOSE BETWEEN UNION WITH FRANCE OR GERMANY, OR ELECT TO REMAIN UNDER THE CONTROL OF THE LEAGUE OF NATIONS.

IN READINESS FOR THE SAAR PLEBISCITE:
THE INTERNATIONAL FORCE.

THE NETHERLANDS CONTINGENT OF THE INTERNATIONAL FORCE TO BE QUARTERED IN SAARBRÜCK-EN TO KEEP ORDER DURING THE PLEBISCITE: A BODY OF DUTCH MARINES DRILLING AT ROTTERDAM IN PREPARATION FOR DUTY IN THE SAAR.

SOME OF THE BATTALION OF CARABINIERI DETAILED FOR SERVICE IN THE SAAR AS MEMBERS OF THE SAAR INTERNATIONAL FORCE: A FAMOUS BODY OF ITALIAN TROOPS.

THE ADVANCE PARTY OF THE BRITISH CONTINGENT OF THE SAAR INTERNATIONAL FORCE IN SAARBRÜCKEN: SOME OF THE EIGHTY MEN OF THE EAST LANCASHIRE AND ESSEX REGIMENTS AND 120 R.A.S.C., R.A.M.C., AND "ODD DETAILS" MARCHING THROUGH THE TOWN TO THEIR QUARTERS.

GERMAN PROPAGANDA FOR THE PLEBISCITE: "THINK OF THE WELFARE OF YOUR CHILDREN; SAY 'YES' FOR GERMANY!" PLACARDED ON THE WALLS.

Although the Saar plebiscite is not due till early next year, the question of procedure is already being anxiously discussed and the various parties interested, especially the Nazis, are pursuing active propaganda. The position in the Saar is thus explained in "The Stateman's Year Book": "According to the Treaty of Versailles, France obtained from Germany, as a compensation for the destruction of the coal mines in the North of France, the exclusive rights of exploitation of the coal mines in the Saar Basin. The area of this district is about 751 square miles and the population 657,870. For fifteen years the Saar Basin is to be governed by a Commission of Five, chosen by the league of Nations. At the end of these years the population will decide by vote one of three alternatives – maintenance of the rule set up by the Treaty, union with France, or union with Germany." The Committee of Three appointed by the League to investigate the plebiscite position – Baron Aloisi (Italy), Señor Cantilo (Argentina) and Señor de Madariaga, Spanish Ambassador in Paris – recently arranged to have a scheme of Saar government framed by a committee of jurists, in case the electorate decide to remain under the League. The International Governing Commission at present consists of a British President (Mr. G.G. Knox) and a French, a Saar German, a Yugoslav and a Finnish member, with a Saar German bureaucracy. Their administration has been described as "an astonishingly successful experiment". Order has been maintained with only 1000 gendarmes and a small police force and finance has been well managed. Up to a year ago, it was regarded as a foregone conclusion that the Saar people would vote for return to Germany but the Nazi revolution raised new problems. There is unrest among Catholics and all depends, it is said, on the issue between the Nazis and the Catholic Church in Germany. The International Force, approved by the League of Nations, for preserving order in the Saar before, during, and after the Plebiscite of January 13, is composed of 1500 British, 1300 Italians, 260 Swedish, and 250 Dutch troops. The British contingent will consist of the 13th Infantry Brigade, 1st Battalion East Lancashire Regiment, and 1st Battalion Essex Regiment. The Italian contingent will comprise two battalions of Grenadiers and one of Carabinieri. Holland is sending a body of Marines. The Swedish contingent is being recruited from volunteers, as the constitution forbids sending conscripts abroad without the sanction of the Riksdag, which is not now sitting.

EVIDENCE OF THE FUTILITY OF WAR:
A MORTALITY OF ONE IN FIVE IN FIGHTING FOR A "GREEN HELL".

TWO AND A HALF YEARS' WAR FOR A SEMI-SWAMP:
WITH THE PARAGUAYANS IN THE GRAN CHACO.

A PARAGUAYAN PATROL IN THE "GREEN HELL" THAT FORMS THE FIGHTING ZONE IN THE GRAN CHACO WAR: AN ALARM IN THE SEMI-SWAMP, WHERE ADVANCE IS ONLY POSSIBLE AT TIMES BY CUTTING A WAY THROUGH THE JUNGLE GROWTH WITH MACHETES.

EVIDENCE OF THE FUTILITY OF WAR: TWO AND A HALF YEARS' FIGHTING FOR A SEMI-SWAMP: A PARAGUAYAN SOLDIER IN THE GRAN CHCO, ARMED WITH RIFLE AND MACHETE.

Dr. J.W. Lindsay, who has been working from the beginning of hostilities as a doctor of the Paraguayan Red Cross and Director of one of the military hospitals of the Paraguayan Army, said of the fighting he had witnessed: "The war in its history and strategy has been a replica in miniature of the Great European War, but the slaughter has been more frightful than in any modern war. The South African War had a mortality of one in twenty; fourteen years' improvement in armaments gave the European War a mortality of one in ten; and exactly fourteen more years of scientific improvement in the machinery of war has in the Chaco War given a mortality of one in five." When the strife started between Bolivia and Paraguay – both members of the League of Nations – there were no roads in the war zone. Now there are roads; there are motor-lorries instead of bullock-waggons for the transport of troops, food supplies, and war material; and ambulance aeroplanes carry the wounded to properly equipped hospitals. Further, said Dr. Lindsay, "both armies have imported all the most modern weapons of war: tanks, light artillery, light and heavy machine-guns, rifles and bayonets, and aeroplanes of every kind." The tanks were tried, but the terrain defeated them. Gas has not been used because the terrible heat prevents the wearing of gas-masks. For the same reason, there are no steel helmets. Otherwise, civilisation has done its best! And what is the war for, this war in a "Green Hell" of swamp and jungle? Writing

to "The Times" Lord Luke gave the answer: "A country like Bolivia, with 594,000 square miles would not trouble about a semi-swamp like the Gran Chaco (the precise area in dispute is known as the Chaco Boreal and covers about a hundred thousand square miles of "No Man's Land") but for the fact that she wants a port on the Paraguay River, the great waterway that leads down to the River Plate. Even if she were successful in obtaining a strip of land through the Gran Chaco, down to a point opposite Asuncion, the building of a railway, without which transport would be impossible, would entail years of construction and probably present serious financial difficulties." Yet, as we write, a "Times" cable from New York says: "The Paraguayans and Bolivians are both reported to be determined to fight out the war in Gran Chaco to a finish. Neither side, it is said, is really expecting peace to be brought about by the latest formula of the League of Nations. Bolivia has ordered the mobilisation of the nation's entire man-power for service in the field and behind the lines." At the same time, the "Daily Telegraph" correspondent in Geneva reported that heavy reverses had induced Bolivia to accept the League of Nations' recommendations as a basis for establishing peace. Paraguay had not then replied. Possibly – just possibly – something will have been settled before these pictures are published.

WOUNDED AND SICK WAITING TO BE REMOVED TO HOSPITAL: CASUALTIES TYPICAL OF THE MANY WHO HAD TO TRAVEL BETWEEN 250 AND 300 MILES IN BULLOCK-WAGGONS BEFORE AMBULANCE AEROPLANES WERE IMPORTED INTO THE TERRIBLE GRAN CHACO FIGHTING ZONE.

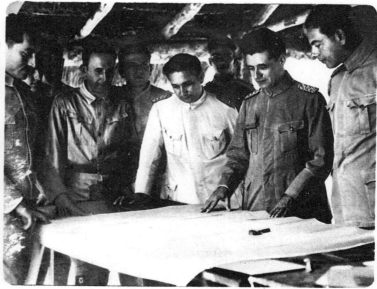

A COMMANDER-IN-CHIEF IN THE WAR THAT IS THE LATEST EVIDENCE OF THE FUTILITY OF WAR: GENERAL DON JOSE ESTIGARRIBIA, OF PARAGUAY; WITH HIS STAFF.

General Don José Estigarribia saw service during the Great War, which was to end war! He was associated with Marshal Foon, whose tactics he employed during the fighting against the Bolivians in the Gran Chaco. Indeed, as Dr. J.W. Lindsay has pointed out, "The war in its history and strategy has been a replica in miniature of the Great European War."

THE ILLUSTRATED LONDON NEWS

RULER OF A LAND, NEVER YET SUBJUGATED, MENACED BY WAR THAT MIGHT HAVE FAR-REACHING EFFECTS: THE EMPEROR HAILE SILASSIE I. OF ABYSSINIA WATCHING A MARCH-PAST OF HIS TROOPS.

Abyssinia, it has been pointed out, has been independent of foreign control for 5000 years, never having been conquered by Ancient Egypt, Rome or Islam, and any attack on its independence by Italy would mean a war with far-reaching effects on international affairs. Hence the great efforts being made to keep the peace between the two countries. Not long ago the Emperor Haile Silassie was reported to have said: "In the event of further frontier incidents, and in view of the Italian mobilisation and arming, while we have steadfastly avoided taking any defensive steps that might be misinterpreted, we shall feel compelled in the last measure to defend our frontiers." The Emperor, formerly known as Ras Taffari, was born in 1891 and became King (Negus) in 1928. In 1930 he was crowned Emperor of Ethiopia (Abyssinia). He is progressive in his ideas and has striven to modernise his country and abolish slavery.

1935

The Saarland votes over-whelmingly to return to Germany after 15 years under League of Nations mandate — fervent welcome to Hitler — the Lindbergh murder trial begins in the U.S.A. — tension mounts between Italy and Abyssinia over Italian Somaliland — Germany introduces conscription — the Stresa Conference (Italy, France, Great Britain) and the League of Nations condemn the action — Silver Jubilee of King George V and Queen Mary — Italy invades Abyssinia — the League of Nations imposes sanctions — Italy walks out — the battle of Adowa refought and Makale captured.

THE DECISIVE SAAR PLEBISCITE: 90.36 PER CENT VOTE FOR THE RETURN OF THE TERRITORY TO GERMANY.

SAAR PLEBISCITE ENTHUSIASTS DEFY RAIN AND SNOW: A VAST PHALANX OF UMBRELLAS AT AN OPEN-AIR MEETING OF THE NAZI DEUTSCHE FRONT, NEAR SAARBRÜCKEN – SHOWING A SPEAKER'S TRIBUNE (ON THE RIGHT).

THE ANTI-NAZI "CLENCHED-FIST" SALUTE: DEMONSTRATORS AT AN OPEN-AIR RALLY, IN SAAR-BRÜCKEN, OF THE EINHEITSFRONT, WHO STAND FOR THE *STATUS QUO* AND THE MOTTO "DOWN WITH HITLER!"

PRO-HITLER SAARLANDERS GIVE THE NAZI SALUTE TO PROSPECTIVE SUPPORTERS: A TUMULTUOUS WELCOME FOR 300 COMPATRIOTS FROM AMERICA, ENTITLED TO VOTE IN THE PLEBISCITE, ON THEIR ARRIVAL IN SAARBRÜCKEN.

Rival factions in the Saar, the Nazi Deutsche Front and the anti-Nazi Einheitsfront, each held a great open-air meeting at Saarbrücken on Sunday, January 6, just a week before the date of the Plebiscite. Their ardour was not damped by the rain, which turned to sleet and snow. The Deutsche Front met in the morning, at the suburb of St. Arnual, where about 150,000 people stood beneath a vast phalanx of umbrellas, greeting the arrival of flags and leaders with shouts of "Heil!" It was a middle-class crowd, mostly men, in contrast to the artisan and feminine element among the anti-Nazis. The Einheitsfront meeting was held at 3 p.m. at a sports ground, and a company of the East Lancashires was stationed near to deal with any attempt at molestation, but none occurred. The rival crowds were in close juxtaposition at Saarbrücken station, as the Nazis were leaving and their opponents arriving, but skilful police arrangements and a show of force – Italian army lorries with a machine-gun – prevented a clash. As they passed each other, the Nazis sang the Horst Wessel Song and their rivals replied with the Internationale.

The first stage of the Plebiscite took place at Saarbrücken on January 7, when certain classes of voters unable to attend on polling day (January 13) – officials, members of essential public services, patients in hospital, and convicts in prison – were given special facilities to vote. The voting cards set out the three choices – (1) *Status quo*; (2) Union with France; (3) Union with Germany – with a blank circle opposite each for the voter's cross. There was no disorder, but several voters were disqualified for announting their intentions.

The result of the plebiscite was announced officially on January 15. Of the 539,541 persons entitled to vote, 97.9% went to the poll. The voting was as follows: For union with Germany, 477,119 (90.36 per cent); for the *status quo*, otherwise the maintenance of the rule set up by the Treaty of Versailles, 46,513 (8.81 per cent); for union with France, 2,124 (0.4 per cent). There were 2249 invalid papers, and 1256 blank papers. In connection with these figures, it is well to recall that the Saar, which is rich in coal and iron, was German until the end of the Great War. By the Treaty of Versailles France obtained (as compensation for the destruction of the coal mines in the North of France) the exclusive rights of exploitation of the coal mines in the Saar Basin, which it was arranged should be governed for fifteen years by a Commission of Five chosen by the League of Nations; with a plebiscite to follow. After the result of Sunday's voting had been announced, Herr Hitler broadcast an appeal to Saarlanders to maintain discipline and said: "With the return of the Saar, there are no more territorial claims by Germany against France, and I declare that no more such claims will be raised by us. We are now certain that the time has come for appeasement and reconciliation." With regard to certain of the pictures here given, some additional notes may be useful. The Deutsche Front – that is, the Nazi Party – were always certain of victory and did not disguise the fact. "The Times" made an interesting point when describing the voting: "The voters everywhere showed remarkable care to avoid infringing the rules against party cries and gestures within the polling stations, but the Deutsche Front officials outside them ostentatiously greeted each other and their friends among the voters with the Nazi salute and the words 'Heil Hitler!' " Incidentally, as one of our photographs shows, there was much anticipatory rejoicing in the Saar Territory and in Germany. As to the voting and the counting, everything was carried out in the most thorough and disciplined fashion. British troops of the International Force played their part in the general arrangements securing order, notably at Saarbrücken goods station when ballot-boxes were being unloaded, in the removal of the boxes to the Wartburg, and outside the Wartburg, where they were on duty outside the counting.

(RIGHT), ANTICIPATORY REJOICING: MEMBERS OF THE DEUTSCHE FRONT, CERTAIN OF AN OVER-WHELMING VOTE IN FAVOUR OF THE RETURN OF THE SAAR TERRITORY TO GERMANY, DEMONSTRAT-ING IN SAARBRÜCKEN ON MONDAY, JANUARY 14.

FROM THE WORLD'S SCRAP-BOOK:
NEWS ITEM OF TOPICAL INTEREST.

TELEVISION ARRIVES: PLANS FOR A LONDON SERVICE – A HOME RECEIVING SET.

We illustrate here the latest type of home receiver for vision and sound, with a fluorescent screen 9 by 6 in., costing about £50 (another, with 12 by 9 in. screen, costs about £80) – here showing a "Mickey Mouse" picture – for which the Postmaster General (Sir Kingsley Wood) recently announced the Government plans for a television service, expected to begin in the latter part of this year.

AN EXTRAORDINARY PHOTOGRAPH OF A MOTOR-RACING MISHAP IN CALIFORNIA: A CAR UPSIDE DOWN IN THE AIR AFTER A SKID.

The correspondent who sends us this extraordinary photograph notes: "Pierre Bertrand skidded into the mushy ground during the main event at the Los Angeles Legion Ascot Speedway. His car turned completely over, coming to a stop with Bertrand still nonchalantly perched in the cockpit! He was found to be suffering only from minor bruises!"

TRAINING IN HAND-TO-HAND FIGHTING: JAPANESE SOLDIERS IN THEIR HEAVILY PADDED "FENCING-SUITS", REMINISCENT OF THE TRADITIONAL JAPANESE BODY ARMOUR.

THE GREAT UNITED STATES NAVY DIRIGIBLE WHICH HAD TO COME DOWN AT SEA OFF POINT SUR, WITH STERN CRUMBLED AND TWO GAS CELLS GONE: THE 785-FT. "MACON" IN FLIGHT OVER THE 600-FT. BATTLE-SHIP "NEW MEXICO".

On February 13, a report was received that the U.S. Navy's Airship "Macon", the world's largest dirigible, had crashed in the Pacific off the California coast during a strong gale. This was confirmed later by a report from Commander H.T. Wiley, of the "Macon", quoted by British United Press. Commander Wiley has now survived three airship disasters, having been in the wreck of the "Shenandoah", as well as in those of the "Akron" and the "Macon".

THE IRAQ PIPE-LINE INAUGURATED: BRINGING OIL ACROSS THE DESERT.

Our photograph shows the treeless desert country through which the pipe-line passes on most of the 600-odd miles from Kirkuk to the Mediterranean. Also to be noted are the telegraph poles which accompany it throughout to ensure good communications.

The news that fighting had again broken out between Chinese and Japanese forces on the boundaries of Jehol once more focussed world-attention on the Japanese army. The training of this force differs in many respects from that of the armies of other Powers, though it owes something to German ideas. The outstanding points in the making of a Japanese soldier are the importance attached to moral and to tactical training. The former is thought to necessitate his instruction in the "seven duties of the soldier" – loyalty, valour, patriotism, obedience, humility, morality and honour – and insistence on frugality, simplicity, and spartan existence generally.

THE LINDBERGH CASE: A TRIAL WITH AMAZING PRESS AND RADIO PUBLICITY.

(ABOVE), THE SCENE OF THE TRIAL OF BRUNO HAUPTMANN FOR THE ALLEGED MURDER OF COLONEL LINDBERGH'S SON IN MARCH 1932: THE COURTHOUSE AT FLEMINGTON.

(LEFT), ACCUSED OF MURDERING COLONEL LINDBERGH'S BABY SON "WHILE ATTEMPTING A BURGLARIOUS ENTRY": BRUNO RICHARD HAUPTMANN, A GERMAN CARPENTER.

(RIGHT), MISS BETTY GOW, WHO RETURNED FROM SCOTLAND TO GIVE EVIDENCE: LEAVING THE "AQUITANIA" WITH A SHIP'S OFFICER.

It is probably safe to say that no murder case has ever obtained such amazing Press and radio publicity, even in the United States, as the trial of Bruno Richard Hauptmann, a German carpenter, aged thirty-four, on a charge of murdering the infant son of Colonel and Mrs. Lindbergh, "while attempting a burglarious entry into the Lindbergh home on March 1, 1932." The trial opened on January 2, before Mr. Justice Trenchard, at Flemington, a country town in New Jersey, a few miles from Colonel Lindbergh's estate from which the baby was kidnapped. The old-fashioned Courthouse, built 100 years ago and only accommodating some 300 to 400 people, was packed, and there were over 800 applications for 135 newspaper seats. Part of the American Press, it may be noted, has shown signs of dissatisfaction with the excessive publicity aroused by the trial and with the methods of procedure in general. It was reported that counsel, both for the defence and the prosecution, gave long interviews to the Press, every day, announcing their plans for the next day's hearing; and, further, that on January 3 Mr. Reilly delivered a broadcast talk in which he said the defence would attempt to show that the kidnapping was planned in the Lindbergh home, though no member of the family was implicated. The witnesses for the prosecution included Colonel and Mrs. Lindbergh and Miss Betty Gow, the child's Scottish nurse. In the course of the trial, Amandus Hochmuth testified that he had seen Hauptmann near the Lindbergh estate on the day of the kidnapping and Mr. A. Osborn, a handwriting expert, alleged that "the ransom notes were all written by the writer of various papers signed 'Richard Hauptmann' ".

THE SAAR'S FERVENT WELCOME TO HITLER IN ITS "FIRST HOUR OF LIBERTY": A DAY OF REJOICING IN GERMANY.

Since the result of the Saar plebiscite was declared, in favour of Germany, there has been a large exodus of refugees from the anti-Nazi element in the population. It was reported on January 22 that, with a view to limiting this movement, the management of the Saar mines had placarded Baron von Neurath's declaration of December 3, that the German Reich would guarantee the life and property of all persons in the Saar territory. At the same time, it was estimated that, up to January 21, the French Consulate at Saarbrücken had issued about 8000 visas for refugees, and that nearly 1000 more people had made their way to the French frontier without visas. Many of them had been granted the necessary passports at Forbach. According to a report, however, the refugee movement had begun to slow down. The German Front in the Saar, it was said, were doing everything possible to prevent intimidation.

THE EXODUS OF THE ANTI-NAZI ELEMENT FROM THE SAAR SINCE THE PLEBISCITE: REFUGEES ARRIVING AT FORBACH, NEAR THE FRENCH FRONTIER.

HERR HITLER (STANDING IN HIS CAR, BAREHEADED AND WITHOUT HIS WATERPROOF IN PELTING RAIN), TAKING THE SALUTE AT A MARCH-PAST THAT LASTED OVER AN HOUR: A GENERAL VIEW OF THE PROCESSION THROUGH SAARBRÜCKEN OF TROOPS AND VARIOUS UNIFORMED ORGANISATIONS FROM GERMANY.

Friday, March 1, the day on which the Saar was formally handed back to Germany, was an occasion of fervent rejoicing not only in that district but throughout Germany and in Saarbrücken, the capital of the territory, the climax of enthusiasm was reached when Herr Hitler himself unexpectedly arrived in the town. As his car moved slowly through the streets, the crowd broke into wild cheers; as one eyewitness puts it, "the succession of Heils shouted in unison by thousands of voices sounded like gun-fire". Noticing that everyone was soaked with rain, Herr Hitler removed his hat and waterproof, a dramatic gesture to which was attributed the cold that caused him to postpone Sir John Simon's visit to Berlin. Then the Chancellor stood for over an hour in heavy rain taking the salute at a march-past. In the evening Herr Hitler addressed the crowd from the Town Hall. "I am happy to be with you", he said, "in the first hour of your liberty. It is a day of happiness for all Germany. I believe that it is also a happy day for all Europe, for it has removed the crisis under which two great nations have suffered most. Let us hope that our great neighbour is also ready, together with us, to seek peace. It must be possible for two nations to grasp hands and to remove all the obstacles in the way of peace."

ITALIAN TROOPS LEAVE FOR E. AFRICA: ITALY'S "ULTIMATUM" TO ABYSSINIA.

THE TENSION BETWEEN ITALY AND ABYSSINIA: FASCIST MILITIA (BLACKSHIRTS) IN SERVICE KIT LEAVING ROME FOR EAST AFRICA, AND A CHEERING GROUP AT THE STATION AS THEY ENTRAINED FOR NAPLES.

At the moment of writing, the situation between Italy and Abyssinia is reported to be somewhat easier, the Abyssinian Government being inclined to accept the proposal of a neutral zone on the border of Italian Somaliland. Meanwhile, however, Italy's military precautions have gone a step further. On February 16 two battalions Blackshirts (Fascist Militia), in full service kit with khaki Colonial helmets, marched through Rome and entrained for Naples, whence they sailed for East Africa. Before leaving Rome they were reviewed by Signor Mussolini, who told them that they were going to the defence of their fatherland, and commended their soldierly appearance. Another battalion had previously left for East Africa, after inspection by the Prince of Piedmont.

Tension between Italy and Abyssinia, due to clashes on the border of Italian Somaliland, recently reached an acute stage. On February 12 it was reported that Signor Mussolini had sent an "ultimatum" to Abyssinia demanding a bare-headed salute to the Italian flag, an indemnity, and a formal apology for the frontier "incidents" in which Italian soldiers had been killed, also the appointment of a mixed commission to fix the frontier, and an undertaking from the Abyssinian Government to guarantee and respect it. On February 11, we may recall, it was officially announced in Rome that, "as a precautionary measure", two divisions had been mobilised, numbering in all about 25,000 men. To counteract alarmist rumours however an informal declaration was made to the foreign Press, emphasising the fact that this mobilisation was purely precaution-

ary, not one soldier had sailed from Italy and it was hoped there would be no need to send any troops to Abyssinia. The Abyssinian Chargé d'Affaires in Rome, M. Jesus Afework, was reported to have said in an interview: "If Italy really intends to make war on Abyssinia the Abyssinians will defend their country to the last. We have 500,000 men under arms and we can raise one million. Abyssinia does not want war, but if we are attacked we shall fight. Meanwhile negotiations for a settlement were proceeding at Addis Ababa, between the Emperor and the Italian Minister, Count Vinci. Regarding the military position of Abyssinia the latest edition of "The Statesman's Year-Book" says: "The standing army comprises the nucleus, and the remainder of the forces are formed from the chiefs and their retainers summoned in time of war, a sort of feudal levy, every man except the priests, being an actual or potential soldier.

The regular army amounts to something under 100,000 men. Both they and the militia, amounting to perhaps 300,000–400,000 men, are very loosely organised and have nothing in the shape of transport and little modern equipment. A Belgian military mission was engaged in 1929 and is now at work training some 2500 men of the Royal Bodyguard. The latter is armed with a certain amount of modern armament, including a 5-ton tank given to the King by the Duke of the Abruzzi during his visit to Abyssinia in May 1927. A beginning has been made with the formation of an Air Force, started under French auspices."

RUSSIA'S ARMY: A FORCE WITH A 940,000 PEACE STRENGTH.

THE SOVIET AIR FORCE INCREASED 330 PER CENT DURING RECENT YEARS, ACCORDING TO M. TUKHACHEVSKY'S SPEECH IN THE SOVIET CONGRESS: A PARADE OF BIG MACHINES.

FURTHER EVIDENCE OF THE EFFICIENT INDUSTRIAL ORGANISATION WHICH NOW EQUIPS THE RED ARMY: A PARADE OF MOTOR MACHINE-GUNS IN THE RED SQUARE, MOSCOW.

AEROPLANES OF A FORCE WHICH HAS NOT ONLY BEEN ENORMOUSLY ENLARGED IN THE COURSE OF RECENT YEARS, BUT HAS HAD THE FLYING SPEED AND RANGE OF ITS BOMBERS AND PURSUIT 'PLANES MUCH INCREASED: AN IMPOSING ARRAY OF SOVIET FIGHTERS – FITTED WITH SKIS FOR WINTER FLYING.

M. Tukhachevsky, Soviet Deputy Commissar for Defence, recently informed the Congress of Soviets that the Red Army's real peace strength was 940,000 not 562,000. The announcement was received with enthusiasm. The new total does not include the frontier guards, the territorials on short-term training, the military preparation battalions, or the semi-military "Osoviakhim" organisation. M. Tukhachevsky said that in the last four years the Air Force had been increased by 330 per cent; and that the flying speed of pursuit 'planes and bombers had been nearly doubled, while their fighting range had been increased three to four fold. The number of light tanks had increased in the same period by 760 per cent, and medium tanks by 792 per cent, with a three to six fold increase in speed. Air machine-guns showed an increase of 800 per cent and heavy artillery one of 210 per cent. The quality of the latter arm, he said, was now extremely high, both in guns and ammunition. Last year an enormous system of permanent concrete frontier fortifications was completed; both on the East and the West. The great distances from the western to the eastern frontiers of Russia made the efficient transfer of divisions from one front to another impracticable in peace time and this explained the increase in the peace strength of the army and the heavy sacrifices made for the full garrisoning of frontier fortifications. Another point touched on by M. Tukhachevsky was that the object was now to produce the maximum of mobility in the Red Army. He claimed that he had already achieved "lightning marching speed" compared with a few years ago. He also spoke of the Red Army as "a force for peace". Another fact divulged by M. Tukhachevsky was that since 1931 the number of submarines had increased 435 per cent; and that of light torpedo craft 370 per cent.

MECHANISED ANTI-AIRCRAFT DEFENCE IN RUSSIA: A WINTER MANOEUVRES STUDY OF AN OFFICER AND MACHINE-GUNNERS; WITH A WEAPON MOUNTED ON A LORRY.

SOLDIERS OF RUSSIA, WHOSE PEACE STRENGTH IS ACKNOWLEDGED TO BE 940,000, NOT 562,000, AS OFFICIALLY REGISTERED IN GENEVA: INFANTRY MARCHING IN MASSED FORMATION DURING A CEREMONIAL PARADE IN MOSCOW.

CONSCRIPTION PROCLAIMED IN GERMANY:

HERR HITLER SEEN LEAVING A GREAT CELEBRATION IN THE BERLIN OPERA HOUSE ON THE WAR HEROES COMMEMORATION DAY, FOLLOWING THAT OF THE PROCLAMATION.

On March 16, Herr Hitler announced the institution of compulsory military service in Germany and an increase in the Army involving repudiation of the military clauses in the Versailles Treaty. In the evening of that day a crowd collected outside the Chancellory in the Wilhelmplatz, Berlin, and acclaimed Herr Hitler when he appeared at a window. The proclamation itself was read by Dr. Goebbels, Minister of Propaganda, at a gathering of some 15,000 people in the Sport Palast, Berlin's largest public hall. The reading caused unbounded enthusiasm, and was followed by continuous applause. In explaining the reasons for the Government's action, the proclamation referred, among much else, to the menace of Russia's army of 101 divisions (960,000 men), and to the recent increase in the period of French military service. There were also allusions to the fact that, while Germany had disarmed in accordance with the Versailles Treaty, other nations had failed to do so. The proclamation ended, however, on a conciliatory note. "The German Government" (it concluded) "expresses the confident hope that it may be granted to the German people, now recovering its honour, in independent equality of rights, to make its contribution to the pacification of the world in a free and open co-operation with the other nations and their Governments." Herr Hitler and some of his principal supporters are here seen leaving after the memorial ceremony in honour of Germany's two million war dead, on the day for the Commemoration of Heroes (March 17), which followed that on which the dramatic proclamation was issued. In the above photograph Herr Hitler is seen walking between Field-Marshal von Mackensen, a famous veteran of Germany's war leaders (wearing the Death's Head Hussar uniform), as the representative of the old Imperial Army, and General von Blomberg, the Minister of Defence, representing the present armed forces of Germany. Behind them are the heads of the three fighting services – (from left to right) General von Fritsch, Commander-in-Chief of the Army; General Göring, Air Minister; and Admiral Raeder, Commander-in-Chief of the German Navy.

THE GERMAN ARMY: TO BE RAISED TO 36 DIVISIONS

THE COLOURS OF THE OLD GERMAN ARMY, WHICH FOUGHT IN THE GREAT WAR, BORNE, IN THE MARCH THROUGH BERLIN, BY SOLDIERS OF THE PRESENT FORCES, ON THE DAY OF COMMEMORATION OF WAR HEROES, AFTER THE PROCLAMATION OF CONSCRIPTION OF THE PREVIOUS DAY: A GENERAL VIEW, SHOWING FLAGS ON PUBLIC BUILDINGS AT HALF-MAST IN HONOUR OF GERMANY'S TWO MILLION DEAD.

On March 15 – the day before the German declaration of conscription and a largely increased Army strength – a vote in the French Chamber authorised an extension of the period of military service, in view of German re-armament. Addressing the Chamber, M. Flandin said: "As the result of plans known to all, Germany will have available at the beginning of 1936 at least 600,000 men. . . . We should have 208,000 men. Such a difference cannot be tolerated." After the German declaration of March 16, Marshal Pétain commented: "Approximately this news is what we knew long ago. It makes official a state of affairs which already existed." A Paris report on other French views stated: "Germany's military strength will exceed 600,000 men, with an air force far stronger than that of France, but a much less formidable Navy." The question of air forces will, of course, be one of the principal matters for discussion during Sir John Simon's coming visit to Berlin.

Commenting on the effect of the new German conscription scheme, "The Times" military correspondent stated recently: "Before Germany left the League her proposal was for an expansion of the Versailles Treaty army of 100,000 long service troops to 300,000 short-service troops. It has been generally assumed that she has since carried out this expansion. The declaration that her peace-time Army will now consist of 12 Army corps headquarters and 36 divisions will naturally suggest that the total strength is considerably larger. In automatic weapons the new army is certainly well equipped, having nearly 400 machine-guns. These assure the divisions a high defensive value. But it is hardly to be expected that an army . . . long restricted in developing heavy artillery and tanks, should have anything like an equivalent power of taking the offensive."

THE ANGLO-GERMAN CONVERSATIONS IN BERLIN: THE BRITISH FOREIGN SECRETARY AND THE GERMAN CHANCELLOR FACE TO FACE IN "EXPLORATORY" DISCUSSION OF EUROPEAN PROBLEMS. (FROM LEFT TO RIGHT): MR. ANTHONY EDEN (THIRD FROM LEFT), SIR JOHN SIMON, HERR HITLER, HERR SCHMIDT, BARON VON NEURATH (GERMAN FOREIGN MINISTER), SIR ERIC PHIPPS (BRITISH AMBASSADOR), AND HERR VON RIBBENTROP (THE CHANCELLOR'S DISARMAMENT AFFAIRS).

The visit of the British Foreign Secretary (Sir John Simon) and the Lord Privy Seal (Mr. Anthony Eden) to Berlin duly took place, notwithstanding momentary doubts aroused by the recent German proclamation of conscription. As Sir John Simon pointed out in Parliament a few days previously, this visit, like those arranged to other European capitals, was "purely exploratory in character". The Anglo-German conversations opened in the Chancellery at Berlin at 10.30 a.m. on March 25, and continued until 7.30 p.m., with a break of about two hours, during which the British delegates, with Sir Eric and Lady Phipps, were entertained to lunch by Baron von Neurath. During his recent statement in the House of Commons describing his conversation with Herr Hitler in Berlin, Sir John Simon mentioned that in regard to naval armaments Germany claimed, with certain reserves, 35 per cent of British tonnage.

THE GERMAN NAVY: A FORCE WHICH GERMANY CLAIMS SHOULD EQUAL 35 PER CENT OF BRITISH TONNAGE.

ONE OF FIVE PRE-DREADNOUGHTS ALLOWED TO GERMANY UNDER THE VERSAILLES TREATY: THE OLD BATTLESHIP "SCHLESWIGHOLSTEIN", FLYING A VICE-ADMIRAL'S FLAG AT GUNNERY PRACTICE DURING NAVAL MANOEUVRES.

ONE OF FIVE POST-WAR 6000-TON CRUISERS, WHICH CARRY NINE 6-INCH GUNS, BUILT ACCORDING TO TREATY LIMITATIONS: THE "LEIPZIG" – A STARBOARD SIDE VIEW, SHOWING THE STERN ON THE LEFT.

STRESA: THE CONFERENCE BETWEEN GREAT BRITAIN, ITALY AND FRANCE.

ISOLA BELLA, THE BEAUTIFUL LITTLE ISLAND IN LAKE MAGGIORE, SEEN FROM STRESA: THE SITE OF THE FAMOUS VILLA BORROMEO, WHERE THE THREE-POWER STRESA CONFERENCE BEGAN ON APRIL 11.

THE BRITISH PREMIER AND THE ITALIAN "DICTATOR": MR. MACDONALD WITH SIGNOR MUSSOLINI, WHO HAD JUST WELCOMED HIM ON HIS ARRIVAL AT STRESA STATION, LEAVING FOR ISOLA BELLA.

THE SCENE OF THE CONFERENCE: THE MUSIC SALOON (NOW RENAMED THE CONFERENCE HALL) IN THE BORROMEO CASTLE, ADORNED WITH PAINTINGS BY TEMPESTA, TO WHICH OTHER WORKS OF ART WERE ADDED FOR THE OCCASION.

DELEGATES AT PALLANZA TO VISIT FIELD-MARSHAL CADORNA'S MONUMENT: MR. MACDONALD (SECOND FROM LEFT) WITH M. FLANDIN (FRENCH PREMIER; SECOND FROM RIGHT) AND M. LAVAL (FRENCH FOREIGN MINISTER; EXTREME RIGHT).

The Stresa Conference on the European situation, which brought together for the first time the Premiers and Foreign Secretaries of Great Britain, Italy and France, began on April 11 and ended on the 14th, when a joint *communiqué* was issued giving details of the discussions and stating that the delegates "found themselves in complete agreement". The Conference took place in the Borromeo Castle on Isola Bella, one of the Borromean islands in Lake Maggiore, and the meetings were held in the Music Saloon, henceforth to be called the Conference Hall. This fine chamber contains fifty paintings by Pieter Molyn the Younger (1632–1701), known from his storm pictures as Tempesta, who was sheltered by Count Vitaliano Borromeo when he had fled from Genoa, falsely accused of murdering his wife. In honour of the Conference the Borromeo family brought to the

Castle for the occasion many art treasures from their palace in Milan, including works by Titian and Leonardo. Signor Mussolini, who presided at the Conference, reached Stresa by seaplane. After the first session the British and French delegates visited Pallanza, on the opposite side of the lake, and laid wreaths at the monument of Field-Marshal Cadorns.

HERR HITLER'S BIRTHDAY GIFT OF 41 AEROPLANES: BERLIN CELEBRATIONS.

April 20 was Herr Hitler's forty-sixth birthday – the first since he succeeded the late President von Hindenburg as Head of the State – and in that capacity he was accorded due military honours. The Colour Company of the Berlin Guard Regiment, carrying the Colours of Herr Hitler's old regiment (the 16th Royal Bavarian Infantry), paraded before him in the Wilhelmstrasse. On the aerodrome at Staaken he accepted as a gift from the S.A. (Nazi Storm Troops) a squadron of 27 fighter aeroplanes, and 14 others from the Kyffhauserbund (Veterans' League). Among the congratulatory messages received by Herr Hitler was one from King George.

A SQUADRON OF 27 AEROPLANES, AND 14 OTHER MACHINES, GIVEN TO THE FÜHRER ON HIS BIRTHDAY: HERR HITLER, WITH GENERAL GÖRING (RIGHT) SHAKING HANDS WITH OFFICERS OF THE NEW GERMAN AIR FORCE ON THE OCCASION OF THE PRESENTATION.

THE LEAGUE OF NATIONS COUNCIL DISCUSSING THE RESOLUTION THAT CONDEMNED GERMANY'S UNILATERAL ACTION IN RETURNING TO CONSCRIPTION: A MOMENTOUS SESSION AT GENEVA. (FROM LEFT TO RIGHT, AT FAR SIDE OF TABLE) BARON ALOISI (ITALY), M. LAVAL (FRANCE), M. TEWFIK RUSHDI ARAS (TURKEY, PRESIDING), M. AVENOL (SECRETARY-GENERAL), SIR JOHN SIMON (GREAT BRITAIN), M. LITVINOFF (SOVIET RUSSIA), AND M. BENES (CZECHOSLOVAKIA).

Our photograph illustrates the League of Nations Council Meeting at Geneva, on April 16, held to discuss the French appeal against the German conscription decree of March 16. A resolution was submitted by Sir John Simon, M. Laval and Baron Aloisi, representing respectively Great Britain, France and Italy (the three Powers which had met at Stresa), in the course of which it was stated: "The Council . . . declares that Germany has failed in the obligation which lies upon all the members of the international community to respect the undertakings which they have contracted, and admits no unilateral repudation of international obligations." The resolution further stated that the Council requested a committee to propose measures which might be applied if, in the future, any State should endanger peace by such action. The resolution was read by M. Laval, and supported by Sir John Simon and Baron Aloisi. Next day (April 17) it was passed unanimously. Of the fifteen States represented on the Council, thirteen voted for the resolution, Denmark abstained, and Germany was absent. During the debate before the voting, M. Litvinoff (Soviet Russia) made a forceful speech, as a reply to Herr Hitler's statement to Sir John Simon in Berlin about the Russian menace. On April 20, the British Government received a Note from the German Government contesting the League Council's right to judge Germany, rejecting the resolution and reserving the right shortly to make known its own attitude regarding the various questions touched on. In the above photograph, Germany's empty chair is seen to the left of Baron Aloisi.

A WINDOW ON THE WORLD: EVENTS AT HOME AND ABROAD.

AFTER DROUGHT, DUST: A KANSAS FARMER LOOKING AT HIS TRACTOR, HALF-BURIED IN DUST BROUGHT BY STORMS THAT HAVE SWEPT THE MIDDLE WEST.

The drought which caused millions of dollars' worth of damage in the mid-western States of the U.S.A. last year has been followed by dust storms. In the week ending March 27, storms in Kansas, Colorado, and Wyoming have killed nineteen people, hundreds of head of livestock have perished and immense damage has been done to farming country. Railway and air traffic was, in places, almost unable to proceed. At Dighton, Kansas, on March 26, a goods train collided with a passenger train in a fog of dust and thirty-two people were injured. Numerous cases of "dust pneumonia" are reported. A message from Springfield, Colorado, said that humans and beasts could not survive if the storms continued. The herds will not eat the dust-laden pasture.

THE TITHE WAR IN KENT: EFFIGIES OF THE ARCHBISHOP OF CANTERBURY AND QUEEN ANNE ABOUT TO BE BURNED ON A BONFIRE NEAR ASHFORD.

Effigies of the Archbishop of Canterbury and Queen Anne were burnt on April 5, amid the cheers of some 200 tithe-payers, after a fruitless sale of siezed goods at Beechbrook Farm, Westwell, near Ashford. The sale followed the fourth distraint on the same farm. A procession marched to the spot with donkeys bearing placards ridiculing the tithe system, and other signs were fixed to the effigies, such as "Tithe did for us; now we've done with tithe". The tenant of the farm set fire to the pile, while the crowd pelted the effigies with mud.

THE FIRST VISIT OF A BRITISH MINISTER TO SOVIET RUSSIA: MR. EDEN'S INTERVIEW WITH M. STALIN. (FROM LEFT TO RIGHT) MR. ANTHONY EDEN (LORD PRIVY SEAL), M. STALIN (THE SOVIET "DICTA-TOR"), M. MOLOTOFF (PRESIDENT OF THE COUNCIL OF PEOPLE'S COMMISSARS), AND M. MAISKY (SOVIET AMBASSADOR IN LONDON).

Mr. Anthony Eden, the first British statesman to visit Russia since the Revolution, arrived in Moscow on March 28, and the same afternoon discussed the European situation with M. Litvinoff, Soviet Commisar for Foreign Affairs, on the basis of the Anglo-French *communiqué* of February 3 and its four points – Security, Armaments, the Air Pact, and the League of Nations. On the following day, Mr. Eden, with the British Ambassador for Russia, Lord Chilston, was received by M. Stalin, General Secretary of the Communist Party and popularly known as the Soviet "Dictator". Their conversation (interpreted by M. Litvinoff) lasted for about an hour. M. Stalin wore his habitual dress, consisting of a grey blouse, blue trousers and black top-boots. The British visitors, it was reported, were impressed by "the weight and tranquility of their host's manner, and by his wide knowledge and deep insight into international affairs". A joint Anglo-Soviet *communiqué* issued afterwards stated that "the conversations were conducted throughout in an atmosphere of complete friendliness and frankness" and that "there is at present no conflict of interest between the two Governments on any of the main issues of international policy."

The Nazis failed to obtain complete political control of the Free City of Danzig in the elections for the Assembly on April 7. They secured 44 seats, with 139,043 votes; increasing their percentage by eight only. They did not gain the two-thirds majority which would have enabled them to amend the constitution. The Nazi election propaganda was of the most intense order. Herr Hess, Herr Hitler's deputy, arrived by aeroplane on April 5 and addressed a meeting at Zoppot in the evening. General Goring had delivered an address on the previous day. The height of the Nazi "campaign" was reached on April 8, when Dr. Gobbels, Reich Propaganda Minister, addressed a meeting in the Heumarkt, amid regimented Nazis, and flags and banners waving in the glare of searchlights. The result of the Danzig election may be considered as one of the biggest disappointments the National Socialist movement has experienced since it came into power.

HERR HITLER'S DEPUTY IN DANZIG FOR THE ELECTION CAMPAIGN: HERR RUDDOLPH HESS (CENTRE) WITH HERR FÖRSTER, LEADER OF THE DANZIG NAZIS (LEFT), AND DR. GREISER, PRESIDENT OF THE SENATE (RIGHT).

THE SILVER JUBILEE PROCESSION AND THANKSGIVING SERVICE.

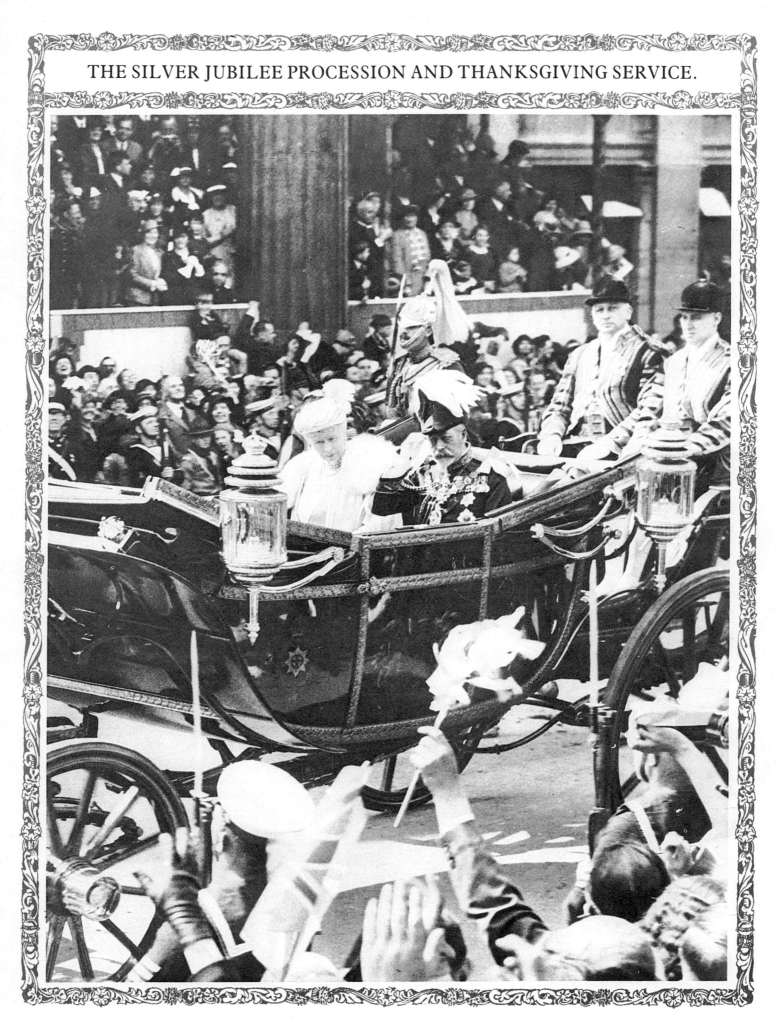

ACCLAIMED BY THE REALM AND THE EMPIRE: THEIR MAJESTIES THE KING AND QUEEN ON THEIR WAY TO ST. PAUL'S CATHEDRAL.

Their Majesties are seen as they drove to St. Paul's Cathedral on May 6, for the Thanksgiving Service to commemorate the twenty-fifth anniversary of the King's accession to the Throne. All along the route they were cheered and cheered again, with that real personal emotion which, in the words of the Archbishop of Canterbury, today fills the heart of the Realm and Empire.

SUNLIT ST. PAUL'S: IN THE CATHEDRAL DURING THE JUBILEE SERVICE – THEIR MAJESTIES UNDER THE DOME.

The Silver Jubilee Service of Prayer and Thanksgiving in St. Paul's was not only a solemn occasion, but a spectacle of great beauty and magnificence. The sunlight gleaming down from the clerestory windows, through the tranquil spaces of the great Cathedral, touched the splendid uniforms of the assembled congregation and evoked patches of brilliant colour. Against the majestic background of Wren's architecture was displayed the vivid splendour of gold and scarlet and blue; while the elegance of the ladies' gowns mingled with garbs from far distant lands, many coloured turbans and bright saris, plumed helmets and jewelled headdresses.

THE KING AND QUEEN DRIVING THROUGH LONDON: ROYAL PROGRESSES – FORMAL AND INFORMAL.

THEIR MAJESTIES' SURPRISE VISIT TO THE EAST END: THE ROYAL CAR CONTAINING THE KING AND QUEEN, AND ALSO THE PRINCESS ROYAL AND PRINCESS ELIZABETH, WITH AN IMPROMPTU LOCAL ESCORT IN PENNYFIELDS, POPLAR.

OUTSIDE THE GATES OF BUCKINGHAM PALACE DURING THE ASSEMBLAGE OF 70,000 SCHOOL CHILDREN TO SEE THEIR MAJESTIES START FOR THEIR DRIVE IN NORTH LONDON: PAVEMENT POSITIONS KEPT BY PILES OF CLOTHES, SATCHELS AND OTHER BELONGINGS.

THEIR MAJESTIES' SURPRISE VISIT TO SOUTH-WEST LONDON: AN INFORMAL DRIVE THROUGH BATTERSEA, LAMBETH, WANDSWORTH, AND KENNINGTON TO SEE THE LOCAL DECORATIONS – THE ROYAL CAR CREATES EXCITEMENT IN A BATTERSEA STREET.

The King and Queen have given London wonderful opportunities of greeting them, apart from ceremonial occasions. On May 10 they took an informal drive in the royal car through Battersea, Lambeth, Wandsworth and Kennington. On Saturday, May 11, their Majesties made the first of the four Processional Drives on their official programme (to North, South, East and West London respectively) taking a circular route and halting at St. Marylebone Town hall where eight North London Mayors were presented. This was the children's day of the Jubilee celebrations, for in the Mall, Constitution Hill, the Green Park and St. James's Park, accommodation had been provided, at their Majesties' own desire for some 70,000 boys and girls drawn from London schools. On Sunday, May 12 their Majesties made another informal tour, this time paying a surprise visit to East London, accompanied by the Princess Royal and Princess Elizabeth.

THE SECOND ROYAL JUBILEE DRIVE THROUGH LONDON SUBURBS: THEIR MAJESTIES PASSING THE HEADQUARTERS OF A SOCIETY OF WHICH THEY ARE PATRONS.

On May 18 the King and Queen, accompanied by a Captain's escort of the Life Guards, drove through several miles of streets in South-east London and were most enthusiastically greeted by thousands of cheering spectators. At Camberwell Green the Mayors and Mayoresses of seven South London boroughs were presented to their Majesties. Our photograph shows them passing the Kennington Road building of the Waifs and Strays Society, of which their Majesties are patrons.

THE KING AND QUEEN AMONG THE FLOWERS OF SILVER JUBILEE YEAR AT CHELSEA: THEIR MAJESTIES AT THE ROYAL HORTICULTURAL SOCIETY'S GREAT SPRING SHOW.

The King and Queen paid their customary visit to the Chelsea Flower Show, in the grounds of the Royal Hospital, at a special view on May 21. The Show was open to the public from the 22nd to the 24th. Every effort had been made to ensure a worthy display for Jubilee year, despite difficulties caused by recent cold weather. Behind the Queen in our photograph is Lady Aberconway, wife of Lord Aberconway, President of the Royal Horticultural Society.

THE EMPIRE CELEBRATES THE ROYAL JUBILEE: FLOODLIGHTING AND PAGEANTRY IN FOUR CONTINENTS.

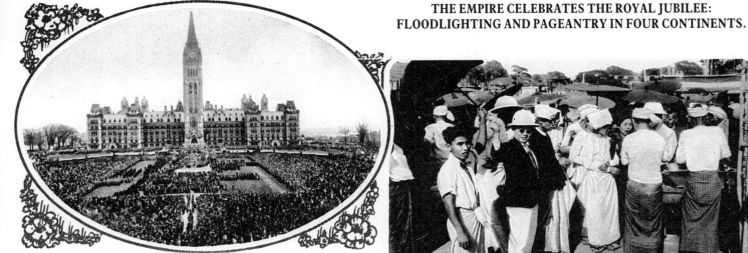

OTTAWA: THE GREAT CROWD THAT GATHERED ON PARLIAMENT HILL IN ORDER TO PARTICI-PATE IN THE ROYAL SILVER JUBILEE CELEBRATIONS LED BY THE GOVERNOR-GENERAL.

On this page we illustrate certain of the Empire's celebrations of the King's Silver Jubilee. In Canada the Ottawa ceremony was the focal point. In addition to this, the Canadian radio commission had mapped out a special broadcasting programme, which began with the Ottawa ceremony; while, in the afternoon, the King's broadcast to the whole British Commonwealth was heard distinctly throughout Canada by millions of his subjects. At five o'clock there was a B.B.C. re-broadcast of the Thanksgiving Service at St. Paul's. At Malta the celebrations included the floodlighting of numerous important buildings, particularly the Auberge de

BURMA: A SILVER JUBILEE DAY DISTRIBU-TION OF RICE TO BUDDHIST NUNS AT PROME, WHO OFFERED PRAYERS FOR THEIR MAJESTIES THE KIND AND QUEEN.

MALTA: THE BRILLIANT FIREWORK DISPLAY OVER THE ST. ANGELO FORTRESS: WITH H.M.S. "QUEEN ELIZABETH" SEEN IN THE FOREGROUND.

CALCUTTA: BOYS DANCING THE BATRACHARI – A RECENTLY REVIVED BENGALI FOLK DANCE.

SOUTH AFRICA: A ZULU WAR DANCE IN HONOUR OF THE ROYAL JUBILEE, WITH CHANTING AND STAMPING AND THE BRANDISHING OF STICKS AND SPEARS: TWO TRIBES IN A COMBINED DANCE; THE CHIEF ON THE RIGHT WAVING A UNION JACK.

Castille (the Army G.H.Q. in Malta), St. John's Cathedral, Medina Cathedral, and the Opera House. The enthusiasm throughout the Indian Empire was remarkable. Newspapers invariably hostile to the Administration, though indicating their dissatisfaction with British political leaders for failing to implement royal promises, all spoke in the highest terms of the King-Emperor and his House. The illuminations in Bombay were on the most ambitious scale. For about a mile along the Island the principal public and private buildings, including the Rajabai clock tower, were brilliantly outlined by electric light. In South Africa a chain of bonfires along the hills was one of the displays arranged by the capital of the Union; while other arrangements included the floodlighting of all Government buildings.

BOMBAY: A LORRY DISGUISED AS A CAPARISONED ELEPHANT, COMPLETE WITH MAHOUT AND HOWDAH, IN THE MOTOR PARADE.

STRENGTH OF THE HOME DEFENCE AIR FORCE TO BE TREBLED.

HAWKER "DEMONS" OF NO. 41 SQUADRON DIVING THROUGH THE CLOUDS AT A SPEED OF OVER 200 MILES AN HOUR: REHEARSING AN INCIDENT FOR THE R.A.F. DISPLAY AT A HEIGHT OF 9000 FT. OVER NORTHOLT.

In his recent speech explaining the Government's air policy, Lord Londonderry, Secretary of State for Air, said: "By March 31, 1937, the strength of the Royal Air Force based at home, irrespective of the Fleet Air arm, will be 1500 first-line machines. . . . In short, we are nearly trebling the present strength of the Royal Air Force at home today. There follows from this a tremendous expansion of our activities over the whole field". In consequence of the Government's decision, the Royal Air Force is to be rapidly increased, and vigorous efforts are being made to provide the large body of skilled pilots and tradesmen required. The total number of entries needed in the present and succeeding years is approximately 2500 pilots and 20,000 tradesmen and unskilled men. A large proportion of the pilots will be entered as officers on short service commissions. Increased numbers of airmen pilots will also be wanted. An entry of 1300 men a quater will be necessary for duties in connection with the maintenance of aircraft. Men who are skilled fitters in civil life and men of superior intelligence will be accepted for training as mates, flight mechanics, or flight riggers. Then 400 men a quarter are required for training as armourers, wireless operators, and photographers. In addition to the above classes, a large number of unskilled men over eighteen and under twenty-six years of age will be accepted for entry as aircraft hands. The air defence of Great Britain has its headquarters at Uxbridge, and from that centre are administered at present thirty-four stations. Under the new scheme, provision has been made for thirty-one new stations, and this fact means the selection and preparation of the necessary new aerodromes, with the erection of the requisite buildings and hangars. Generally, a station consists of two squadrons of aircraft, with approximately twenty-four officers and 450 men. Large additions to the existing number of home defence aircraft will be required. No fewer than seventy-one new squadrons are to be formed, and new aircraft will also have to be provided for the numerous additional flying schools, in addition to the re-equipment of existing units.

"NORMANDIE" WINS THE "BLUE RIBAND".

THE STATUE OF LIBERTY (WHICH WAS A GIFT FROM FRANCE TO THE UNITED STATES) SEEMS TO WAVE GREETINGS TO THE "NORMANDIE".

The "Normandie" arrived at New York on the afternoon of June 3 on the completion of her maiden voyage across the Atlantic. Her time between Southampton and the Ambrose Light set up a new record of 4 days 11 hours 33 minutes, her average speed being 29.68 knots. The best previous average had been made by the Italian "Rex", with 29.64 knots. On her return voyage the "Normandie" had the average speed, when she reached Plymouth on June 12, of 30.31 knots. Her best day's run averaged 30.91 knots. The "Queen Mary" is expected to do even better!

THE GREAT QUETTA EARTHQUAKE.

THE WHOLE OF QUETTA CITY HAS BEEN DESTROYED: IN DEVASTATED BRUCE ROAD, MAIN STREET OF QUETTA, WHERE THOUSANDS OF DEAD ARE STILL BENEATH THE RUINS.

The great earthquake that devastated Quetta, in Baluchistan, and the district about it, occurred at 3 hours 3 minutes 2 seconds on the morning of May 31. Quetta, it will be realised, was the headquarters of the Western Command. On June 2 a statement by the Government of India said: "The whole of Quetta City has been destroyed and is being sealed under military guard from today on medical advice. It is estimated that 20,000 corpses remain buried under the debris. There is no hope of rescuing any more living." An India Office statement issued later estimated that the total death toll, including that of Quetta, is probably in excess of 40,000.

THE KING'S JUBILEE REVIEW OF THE R.A.F.

THE INSPECTION AT MILDENHALL: HIS MAJESTY THE KING MOTORING THROUGH THE LINES OF THE THIRTY-EIGHT SQUADRONS DRAWN UP ON THE AERODROME IN A GREAT ARC, WITH A FRONTAGE OF FOUR SQUADRONS.

THE KING'S SILVER JUBILEE REVIEW OF THE TROOPS OF THE ALDERSHOT COMMAND.

THE INFANTRY MARCH PAST: RUSHMOOR ARENA, DURING THE REVIEW OF JULY 13.

THE KING'S SILVER JUBILEE REVIEW OF THE FLEET: AT SPITHEAD

THE ROYAL YACHT "VICTORIA AND ALBERT", WITH HIS MAJESTY AND HIS SONS ON BOARD, SEEN FROM THE "HOOD" AS SHE ENTERED THE LINES – FROM LEFT TO RIGHT: "IRON DUKE", "RESOLUTION", "REVENGE", "RAMILLIES", "ROYAL SOVEREIGN", "QUEEN ELIZABETH", AND THE ROYAL YACHT.

ITALY'S GREAT MILITARY DISPLAY

"WE WILL BRING TO THE HIGHEST POSSIBLE LEVEL THE POWER OF THE NATION'S ARMED FORCES": SIGNOR MUSSOLINI MAKES A STIRRING SPEECH TO THE ITALIAN TROOPS, AT THE CONCLUSION OF THE MANOEUVRES, FROM AN OBSERVATION POST OVERLOOKING THE ADIGE VALLEY.

ITALY'S STRENGTH IN LIGHT TANKS: AN IMPOSING PARADE, WITH THEIR CREWS BESIDE THEM, AT THE REVIEW HELD AFTER THE MANOEUVRES.

HEAVY ARTILLERY OF THE ITALIAN ARMY USED DURING THE RECENT MANOEUVRES HELD ON A GREAT SCALE IN THE MOUNTAIN REGION NEAR BOLZANO: STRENUOUS WORK IN MAN-HAULING A BIG GUN INTO "ACTION".

PROOF OF EXTENSIVE MECHANISATION IN THE MODERN ITALIAN ARMY: A TRACTOR-DRAWN BATTERY OF ARTILLERY ON A WINDING ROAD DURING THE MANOEUVRES.

THE DUCE AND HIS SOVEREIGN: AN INTERESTING GLIMPSE OF KING VICTOR AND SIGNOR MUSSOLINI AT THE MANOEUVRES.

The great Italian manoeuvres, with Signor Mussolini in supreme command, which began at midnight on Saturday, August 24, and are to end today, the 31st. Their function was not only for the italian forces to receive their customary training, but to show the world that Italy is a power very much to be reckoned with in Europe. In this connection, Il Duce, interviewed for the "Daily Mail", said at the end of last week: "In addition to the army which we have concentrated on the Red Sea and the Indian Ocean, we have at the present moment almost another army of 500,000 men, which is mobilised around Bolzano for manoeuvres, and which will remain ready to confront any eventuality." In the same spirit General Balstrocchi, speaking to foreign journalists at Bolzano, was emphatic that, in spite of her commitments in Africa, Italy was as strong as ever; and he added that Signor Mussolini was determined that his country should be second to none of the Great Powers.

WARRIORS IN ADDIS ABABA:
THE ABYSSINIAN EMPEROR REVIEWS HIS TROOPS.

THE EMPEROR OF ABYSSINIA, SILENT, IMPASSIVE, AND DIGNIFIED AS EVER, WATCHING A MARCH-PAST OF SOME 80,000 WARRIORS FIERCELY PROTESTING THEIR LOYALTY BEFORE LEAVING FOR THE FRONT.

HAILÉ SILASSIE'S RIGHT-HAND MAN: THE ABYSSINIAN WAR MINISTER, RAS MULUGBTA (SEATED) – A TOWERING, GRIZZLED FIGURE WHO EXPRESSED HIS FEALTY TO HIS EMPEROR AS HE PASSED BEFORE HIM AT THE END OF HIS TROOPS.

ABYSSINIA'S ARMY:
WEAPONS AND EQUIPMENT IMPORTED FOR DEFENCE.

ABYSSINIAN FIELD ARTILLERY.

SAVAGE WARRIOTS IN UNCONTROLLED FRENZY RUSHING TOWARDS THE EMPEROR TO HURL THEIR WEAPONS AT HIS FEET, BEG FOR AMMUNITION, AND PROTEST THEIR LOYALTY; WHILE GUARDS PROTECT THE EMPEROR FROM THEIR FERVOUR.

MEN OF RAS NASIBU'S CAMEL CORPS ON THE SOUTHERN FRONT.

AN ANTI-AIRCRAFT GUN IN A PIT OUTSIDE ADDIS ABABA.

On October 17 the Emperor of Abyssinia held a gigantic review in the military field beside the palace at Addis Ababa. the Emperor, dressed in field uniform, sat enthroned in a great tent. Around him was his staff, including the impressive figure of Ras Mulugeta, the War Minister, who also led his men past the Emperor. In all, some 80,000 men marched past, and the review lasted four hours. The troops taking part ranged from the Imperial Guard, armed with modern rifles and bayonets and followed by machine-guns of the Vickers pattern carried on mules, to fierce fighting men from the provinces, armed with nothing better than sticks and rifle belts. At times it was difficult to keep in bounds the tribesmen's demonstrations of patriotic fervour. Some rushed shouting and gesticulating before the Emperor, brandishing their weapons, pleading for ammunition, and loudly swearing allegiance. After the parade most of the troops marched out on the Dessie road to a camping place, before leaving in batches for the northern front. Ras Mulugeta's men were said to be bound for Makale.

ALL ROME ANSWERS THE CALL FOR NATIONAL "MOBILISATION" IN ITALY: CROWDS AT THE VICTOR EMMANUEL MONUMENT LISTENING TO SIGNOR MUSSOLINI'S SPEECH RELAYED BY LOUD-SPEAKERSS FROM THE PALAZZO VENEZIA.

ITALY'S EMPTY CHAIR AT THE LEGUE OF NATIONS COUNCIL AFTER HER REPRESENTATIVES HAD WALKED OUT RATHER THAN LISTEN TO THE ABYSSINIAN DELEGATE: A GENERAL VIEW, SHOWING MR. EDEN AND M. LAVAL.

Excitement rose to fever pitch when Signor Mussolini appeared on the balcony of the Palazzo Venezia. He was greeted with a roar of cheering. Then there was a blast of trumpets and, amid a tense hush, he began to speak. "Twenty million Italians", he said "are at this moment gathered in the squares throughout Italy. It is the most gigantic demonstration which the history of mankind records". Referring to events in East Africa, he declared: "With Ethiopia we have been patient for years. Now, enough! At the League of Nations, instead of recognising the rights of Italy, they dared to speak of sanctions . . . But let it be said once more, in the most categorical manner, as a sacred pledge . . . that we will do everything possible to avoid a colonial conflict assuming the character and bearing of a European conflict."

On the second day (September 5) of the momentous session of the League Council at Geneva, held to seek a settlement of the Italo-Abyssinian crisis, the Italian delegation caused an atmosphere of acute tension by walking out of the Council Chamber. As Professor Jeze was about to begin his reply, for Abyssinia, to the Italian accusations presented on the previous day by Baron Aloisi, the Baron rose and left his place. It was then occupied for a time by the second Italian delegate, Signor Rocco, but presently, after listening to Professor Jeze in great embarrassment for about ten minutes, Signor Rocco also got up and left the hall, leaving Italy's seat vacant. In our photograph it is next to M. Laval (seen in the centre, with hand to head). The other empty chair, to the left, is that formerly used by Germany. To the right of M. Laval (from left to right) are Señor Rulz-Guinazu (Argentina, presiding), M. Avenol (Secretary-General of the League), Mr. Eden, M. Litvinoff (Russia), and Colonel Beck (Poland), who is on the Committee of Five. On the extreme left in the same row is Mr. S.M. Bruce (Australia).

A COLOSSAL PORTRAIT OF SIGNOR MUSSOLINI, AN INSPIRATION FOR "ETHIOPIAN FORCES" ORDERED TO EAST AFRICA: AN EMBARKATION SCENE AT NAPLES.

Headed by the Duce, as Minister of the Armed Forces, Italy is devoting herself whole-heartedly to what is called "the intense military preparations of the nation". Apart from mobilisation, there is much stir among the air forces in Eritrea; Signor Mussolini has witnessed "naval exercises of a new type", flying to Spezia for the purpose, embarking in the "Zara", and seeing bombing exercises by seaplanes and land 'planes; and there have been special air exercises in the Veneto-Tridentina-Padana zone.

OBEYING THE WORDS OF MUSSOLINI: "THE BRAVE YOUTH OF ITALY WILL PROVE EQUAL TO EVERY BATTLE AND WILL AFFIRM TO THE WORLD THE GREATNESS AND POWER OF THE EMPIRE OF ANCIENT ROME"; TROOPS LEAVING NAPLES FOR EAST AFRICA.

THE ENORMOUS INFLUENCE OF ONE MAN OVER A PEOPLE: SIGNOR MUSSOLINI'S MAGNETIC POWER IN SWAYING THE ITALIAN POPULACE.

A scene such as that here illustrated makes it easier to understand how Signor Mussolini has succeeded in imposing his will on a whole nation. The photograph proves his immense popularity, and his extraordinary power of compelling the devotion of vast crowds by the magnetism of his personality and the inspiring force of his oratory. This particular speech, which is typical of many another, was delivered in the town square at Trento, where some 70,000 people had assembled to hear him, shortly after the great manoeuvres of the Italian Army in the north, near Bolzano. On this occasion he was reported to have said, in addressing the citizens of Trento and Blackshirt militiamen: "The time is approaching for effort and sacrifice. The nation will face them wholeheartedly, because he who fails to arrest fortune's wheel at the historic moment will never perhaps be able to touch it again. . . . Any man who imagines that he can stop or slacken the gallant march of this young Fascist Italy with some miserable policy is under a delusion." He had recently announced that, in the near future, "a general assembly of the forces of the regime shall take place in the provines and the colonies." Details of the plan indicated that it would amount to a kind of levie *en masse*, and that on the chosen day some 10,000,000 Italians would take part in a vast national demonstration.

"ANY MAN WHO IMAGINES HE CAN STOP THE GALLANT MARCH OF YOUNG FASCIST ITALY WITH SOME MISERABLE POLICY WILL BE DISAPPOINTED": SIGNOR MUSSOLINI (THE FRONT FIGURE ON THE TRIBUNE) ADDRESSING A VAST CROWD AT TRENTO.

THE DICTATOR OF GERMANY AND HIS MASSED FORCES: THE GREAT NAZI RALLY HELD AT NUREMBERG – HERR HITLER ADDRESSING A VAST ASSEMBLAGE.

Herr Hitler arrived at the Nazis' third Nuremburg rally by air from Munich. The rally was formally opened on the 11th with a proclamation of Nazi policy, at the Luitpoldhalle, and a procession of about 100,000 storm troops, special guards, and other Nazi organisations through the streets. On the 12th, Herr Hitler took the salute at a grand parade of 50,000 members of the Labour Corps, who all shouldered their spades and stood at attention while he addressed them. Next day he drove several times through the city, which was crowded with visitors brought by special trains and estimated to number nearly 600,000. The rally reached its height on Sunday, September 15. The proceedings began with a vast assembly in the Luitpoldhain, a park converted into a great stadium. The enclosure was filled with 75,000 storm troops (S.A.), 16,000 special guards (S.S.), and 10,000 members of the Nazi motor-corps. There were present also nearly 100,000 spectators. Herr Hitler paid a tribute to Germans who fell in the Great War. A special session of the Reichstag was held in the Chamber of Culture at Nuremberg, where Herr Hitler made a short speech, and, at his suggestion, three new laws were passed, including a declaration that the Swastika flag, the emblem of the National-Socialist (Nazi) movement, will be the sole official flag of the German Reich.

(LEFT) HERR HITLER (SPEAKING BEFORE MICROPHONES) ADDRESSING A VAST MULTITUDE OF HIS ADHERENTS AT AN OPEN-AIR STADIUM IN NUREMBERG DURING THE THIRD NAZI RALLY HELD SINCE THE PARTY CAME INTO POWER: AN INTERESTING PARALLEL TO OUR ILLUSTRATION OF SIGNOR MUSSOLINI SPEAKING TO A GREAT CROWD AT TRENTO.

THE NEW BATTLE OF ADOWA: ACTION PHOTOGRAPHS OF THE ITALIAN ATTACK ON NORTHERN ABYSSINIA.

MOUNTED ITALIAN TROOPS ADVANCING ON ADOWA: THE ATTACK WHICH WON FOR ITALY HER "SENTIMENTAL VICTORY", AVENGING THE DISASTER OF 1896; THOUGH LATER REPORTS DENIED THE EARLIER STORIES OF FIERCE FIGHTING AND SUGGESTED THAT THE ABYSSINIANS MADE NO ATTEMPT TO HOLD THE TOWN IN FORCE.

ITALIAN TANKS PROCEEDING OVER ROUGH COUNTRY DURING THE ATTACK ON ADOWA – TWO OF THE NINETY-TWO WITH WHICH THE FORCES ADVANCING FROM ERITREA ARE SAID TO BE SUPPLIED: A PHOTOGRAPH VIVIDLY SUGGESTING THE NATURAL OBSTACLES IN THEIR PATH.

The lull in the Italians' advance in northern Abyssinia, after their establishment on the line Aksum-Adowa-Adigrat, lasted longer than had been generally expected. Few people had realised what extraordinary difficulties the country of Tigré province puts in the way of a modern army, or had foreseen that the determination of the Italian command to risk no unsupported advance would make necessary a most arduous work of consolidation before the attack could be safely resumed. Apart from the obviously limited capacity of aircraft for transporting supplies, General de Bono's army depends for all its needs on the roads from Asmara.

They are described as tortuous, narrow, congested, and dangerous, and the casualties to vehicles and personnel incurred in traversing them are said to be considerable. Major General Fuller, writing in the "Daily Mail", said that in 31 miles out of the 80 on which he travelled a few days ago between Asmara and Adi Kaie, there have been counted no less than 1700 hairpin bends. For mile after mile there is a sharp turn every fifty to seventy yards, and in places the road is nothing but a track of loose boulders resembling the dry bed of a zigzagging torrent. It is not surprising that General de Bono hesitated before lengthening a line of communications such as

THE ITALIANS ADVANCE TOWARDS MAKALE.

A LONG COLUMN OF ITALIAN INFANTRY, WITH MACHINE-GUN COMPANIES, MOVING SOUTH ACROSS THE PLAIN FROM ADIGRAT: A STRETCH OF EASY COUNTRY, WHICH GRADUALLY GIVES PLACE TO HIGH MOUNTAINS AND DEEP GORGES.

THE FALL OF MAKALE:
RAS GUGSA, THE DESERTER, HOISTS ITALY'S FLAG.

Makale was occupied by Italian forces on November 8, and the tri-colour flew once more over the fort of Enda Jesus, where it had been pulled down in the war of 1896. No resistance was offered, but it was found that Ras Gugsa's residence had been ransacked by the retreating Abyssinians, in revenge for his desertion, and many houses had been set on fire. Ras Gugsa took part in the entry into Makale, and hoisted the flag over the citadel. It was on October 9 that Gugsa, then Governor of Makale, went over to the Italians and surrendered to General Santini near Adigrat. At a review in Adigrat on October 17, General de Bono appointed him, as a reward, Governor of the Tigré Province in the name of King Victor Emmanuel. Gugsa is a nephew of Ras Seyyum and great-grandson of the Emperor John. His defection caused great perturbation at Addis Ababa, where at first no one could believe that this young chief of a famous line could have turned traitor.

RAS GUGSA, THE ABYSSINIAN CHIEF WHO WENT OVER TO THE ITALIANS AND WAS APPOINTED GOVERNOR OF THE TIGRÉ PROVINCE. HOISTING THE ITALIAN FLAG AT THE CITADEL AT MAKALE, WHICH HE FORMERLY GOVERNED IN THE NAME OF THE EMPEROR HAILE SILASSIE.

this. Water shortage in the Tigré is another enemy which the Italians have to face. Although they can to some extent make use of native wells in the occupied districts of Abyssinia, they are said to be carrying with them portable well-boring apparatus on lorries accompanying their advance. Fresh wells can be sunk a few yards away from sources that are polluted, for pollution apparently affects only the upward gush of the waters. However, in spite of all natural obstacles, preparations for a further advance, with Makale as the main objective, were pushed forward, and there was a general impression, premature as it turned out, that October 28, the anniversary of the Fascist march on Rome, would be the day of its launching. Already the Italians had made considerable headway on their left flank, where General Santini commands the first National Army Corps, and had penetrated some distance beyond Adigrat. The photograph at the top of this page shows vividly the manner of their advance in this sector. The plain which the Italian troops are seen crossing with such ease is not typical of the country south of Adigrat, which is mostly mountainous.

THE ILLUSTRATED LONDON NEWS

"CHIEF OF THE SPANISH STATE" AND COMMANDER-IN-CHIEF: GENERAL FRANCO, LEADER OF THE ATTACK ON MADRID.

General Franco, who was Governor of the Canaries when the war broke out, was generally regarded as the leader of the rising. He gained control of the troops in Morocco, calling himself "Chief of Forces in Africa". With Morocco as a base, he began shipping from the Straits to Spain, and put himself at the head of an offensive.

His pre-eminence was acknowledged when he was proclaimed Chief of the Insurgent Forces and "Chief of the Spanish State" at Burgos on October 1. General Franco, it is thought, did not actually organise the revolt. This is supposed to have been done by the "Military Brotherhood", who, when their plans were ready, offered him the leadership. General Franco made his career in Morocco, and at the time of his promotion was stated to be the youngest Spanish general. Later, he was appointed Governor of the Canary Islands by the Republican Government, which had reason to fear his ambition and ever-growing popularity. He is forty-five.

1936

Funeral of King George V — Prince of Wales becomes Edward VIII — left-wing successes in French and Spanish elections followed by strikes in France and extreme-left riots throughout Spain — Germany reoccupies the demilitarized Rhineland — France mans the Maginot Line — Haile Silassie, the Emperor of Abyssinia, flees to British protection in Jerusalem after his armies collapse in the North — King Victor Emmanuel proclaimed Emperor of Abyssinia by Mussolini — Haile Silassie in person warns League of Nations that the fate of Abyssinia could be repeated in Europe — drought in the U.S.A. — military uprising breaks out in Spanish Morocco and Spain — suppressed in Madrid and Barcelona but successful in Morocco, Seville and Burgos — grave unrest in Palestine — the Berlin Olympic Games — Italian aircraft ferry Moroccan troops to Spain — General Franco assumes charge of the Spanish rebellion — Toledo, Iran and San Sebastian fall to the insurgents — the capture of Badajoz links Seville and Burgos — King Edward VIII abdicates and is succeeded by his brother George VI — Zinovieff and other leaders of the Russian revolution executed in Moscow — President Roosevelt re-elected in the U.S.A.

"THE KING IS DEAD.
GOD SAVE THE KING."

HIS LATE MAJESTY KING GEORGE V.

THE HIGH AND MIGHTY PRINCE EDWARD – OUR ONLY LAWFUL AND RIGHTFUL LIEGE LORD EDWARD
VIII: HIS MAJESTY IN NAVAL UNIFORM, FOR THE FUNERAL OF KING GEORGE V.

To the profound regret of his people here and beyond the seas, his Majesty King George V., who had been lying ill since January 17, died at Sandringham House, his Norfolk home, at five minutes to midnight on Monday, January 20. His late Majesty was born on June 3, 1865, at Marlborough House.

In the Accession Proclamation it was written: "The High and Mighty Prince Edward Albert Christian George Andrew Patrick David is now, by the death of our late Sovereign of happy Memory, become our only lawful and rightful Liege Lord Edward the Eighth, by the Grace of God, of Great Britain, Ireland and the British Dominions beyond the Seas. King, Defender of the Faith, Emperor of India." Addressing the Privy Council at the Court of St. James on January 21, the new King said: "When my father stood here twenty-six years ago he declared that one of the objects of his life would be to uphold constitutional Government. In this I am determined to follow in my father's footsteps . . . I place my reliance upon the loyalty and affection of my peoples throughout the Empire, and upon the wisdom of their Parliaments, to support me in this heavy task, and I pray that God will guide me to perform it."

KING GEORGE'S LAST JOURNEY FROM HIS NORFOLK HOME TO LONDON: THE FUNERAL PROCESSION
LEAVING THE CHURCH OF ST. MARY MAGDALENE AT SANDRINGHAM.

This photograph shows the coffin of his late Majesty leaving Sandringham Church on its journey of two and a half miles to Wolferton Station. Along the road stood dense silent crowds in the winter sunshine. The coffin, borne on a gun-carriage which six bay horses drew, was covered with the Royal Standard of England. On it rested two wreaths – a white cross of flowers from Queen Mary and a wreath of white and red carnations from King Edward and his brothers and sister. A short service had previously been held in the church, conducted by the Bishop of Norwich and the Rector of Sandringham, who was a domestic chaplain to King George.

THE EMPTY SADDLE: KING GEORGE'S WHITE PONY, JOCK, WHICH HE RODE ONLY A FEW DAYS BEFORE
HIS DEATH, BEING LED IN THE PROCESSION CONVEYING THE COFFIN.

In the procession conveying the body of King George from Sandringham Church to Wolferton Station, on January 23, the first stage of the journey to London, a pathetic sight was his Majesty's favourite shooting pony, Jock, saddled but without the familiar figure of his royal master. Only a few days before his death, the King had been riding Jock through the woodlands, and to the people of the neighbourhood watching the cortege the empty saddle was a poignant reminder of their well-beloved "Squire". The pony, beautifully groomed, his milk-white coat a dazzling contrast to the prevailing black, was led by a groom from the Sandringham stables immediately behind the carriages containing the royal ladies. Officially Jock belongs to Windsor, where all the greys are kept, but always accompanied King George to Sandringham or Balmoral, and had carried him at every shoot on those estates during the past twelve myears. At Windsor, he was much in demand, for the King liked to walk in the park and ride home after a rest. He resumed his habit of taking rides on Jock after his recovery from his serious illness in 1928, and he is said to have spoken about the pony while he was lying on his death-bed.

THE LEFT CELEBRATES SPANISH ELECTION RESULTS

A TRAIL OF ARSON IN SPAIN: THE BURNING OF CHURCHES.

A BRUSH WITH MOUNTED POLICE, SOME OF WHOM FRATERNISED WITH THE CROWD: IN MADRID, WHERE A "STATE OF ALARM" WAS PROCLAIMED; ONE PERSON HAVING BEEN KILLED AND A NUMBER INJURED – A MARCH TO THE GAOL TO DEMAND THE RELEASE OF POLITICAL PRISONERS.

EXCITED CROWDS IN THE PUERTA DEL SOL, MADRID, CELEBRATING THE VICTORY OF THE LEFT IN THE ELECTIONS: DEMONSTRATORS DEMANDING AN IMMEDIATE AMNESTY FOR POLITICAL PRISONERS.

LEFT-WING EXTREMISTS NEAR MADRID GIVING THEIR CLENCHED FIST SALUTE AFTER BURNING OF CONVENT PROPERTY: AN EXAMPLE OF THE ANTI-CATHOLIC FEELING WHICH HAS INSPIRED THE BURNING OF MANY CHURCHES AND CONVENTS THROUGHOUT THE COUNTRY.

ONE OF SEVERAL RIGHT-WING SPANISH NEWSPAPERS THAT HAVE SUFFERED DURING THE RECENT DISORDERS: THE WRECKED OFFICES OF "LA NACION" AFTER AN ATTACK BY RED EXTREMISTS.

THE SPIRES OF THE CHURCH OF SAN LUIS BLAZING FIERCELY IN THE NIGHT: A BUILDING SITUATED IN THE CENTRE OF MADRID, CLOSE TO THE PUERTA DEL SOL AND THE MINISTRY OF THE INTERIOR.

RIOTERS SETTING FIRE TO THE PRIVATE MOTOR-CAR OF SEÑOR JUAN CAYON, A MEMBER OF THE RIGHT PARTY: A PHASE OF THE DISORDERS AT PUENTE VALLECAS, ON THE OUTSKIRTS OF MADRID, WHERE SHOPS WERE LOOTED AND BURNT.

Serious disturbances throughout almost the whole of Spain followed the victory of the Left in the recent elections. At first the riots were mainly caused by left-wing supporters excitedly celebrating their victory; but later the extremists turned against the new Prime Minister, Señor Azaña, and indulged in an orgy of anti-Catholic and anti-Fascist outrages. At a Cabinet Council on March 16 it was decided to adopt a firm attitude towards the disturbers of law and order, who were stated not to belong to the proletarian parties forming the Left Coalition, but to less responsible and more extreme groups. The Government was authorised to prolong the "state of alarm" in Spain for a further period of thirty days from March 16. As these photographs show, the typical form of outrage has been incendiarism. More than twenty churches were damaged or destroyed by fire, and convents, schools, and newspaper buildings have also suffered. A number of people were killed. It was difficult to obtain accurate news from various parts of the country, for a rigorous censorship was imposed on the Spanish Press, especially on the organs of Conservative opinion.

GERMANY REOCCUPIES RHINELAND:
ACTION DESCRIBED BY THE GERMAN FOREIGN MINISTER AS MERELY SYMBOLIC.

AFTER HERR HITLER HAD REPUDIATED THE LOCARNO TREATY: FLOWERS FOR GERMAN TROOPS ENTERING DÜSSELDORF, IN THE DEMILITARIZED RHINELAND ZONE, AS "SYMBOLS" OF EQUALITY OF RIGHT.

GERMAN ARTILLERY BY THE RHINE IN THE REOCCUPIED RHINELAND ZONE: ARTILLERY ON THE MARCH IN DÜSSELDORF DURING THE "HISTORIC HOUR" IN WHICH GERMAN TROOPS TOOK POSSESSION OF THEIR "FUTURE PEACE-TIME GARRISONS IN GERMANY'S WESTERN PROVINCES".

The troops began to move during the early hours of March 7 and some of them crossed the Rhine bridges as the Leader was addressing his followers but the march of reoccupation did not end then. By the Sunday, however, Cologne, Coblenz, Mainz, Bonn, Mannheim, Düsseldorf, and Saarbrücken had been garrisoned. In Cologne the inhabitants were taken by surprise but they soon had their flags flying and were extending an enthusiastic welcome. The German Air Force marched into Düsseldorf on Sunday, followed by field artillery and other units. There, as elsewhere, the troops were decorated with flowers. It was there, also, that General Kuhne addressing the airmen, said: "The Rhine is Germany's river and shall never be a German boundary" – a sentiment common to all parts of the Reich.

As Herr Hitler, speaking in the Reichstag on March 7, was announcing that Germany was no longer bound by the Locarno Treaty, which must be regarded as having practically ceased to be in view of the signature of the Pact between France and the Soviet Union, German troops were entering the demilitarized Rhineland Zone and garrisoning it. The Leader's reference to this *fait accompli* was: "In this historic hour, when German troops are taking possession of their future peace-time garrisons in Germany's western provinces, we unite to testify to two holy, innermost articles of faith: First, to the oath to yield to no Power or force in the re-establishment of the honour of our nation and sooner honourably to succumb to direct distress than to capitulate: and, secondly, to the affirmation that we shall now all the more work for European understanding and particularly for an understnding with the Western nations and our Western neighbours."

THE AGREEMENT WHICH FORMED GERMANY'S PRETEXT FOR THE RHINELAND OCCUPATION: THE FRANCO-SOVIET PACT RATIFIED BY A LARGE MAJORITY IN THE FRENCH SENATE.

MR. EDEN MAKING HIS STATEMENT IN THE HOUSE OF COMMONS ON MONDAY, MARCH 9: THE GOVERNMENT'S DECLARATION AS TO THIS COUNTRY'S ATTITUDE TOWARDS THE SITUATION CREATED BY THE GERMAN GOVERNMENT.

The Franco-Soviet Pact was presented to the French Senate for ratification on March 12. As Herr Hitler had already ordered the reoccupation of the Rhineland, basing his move on the pretext that the pact was contrary to the letter and spirit of the Locarno Treaty, all doubt was removed as to the Senate's decision, most of the Senators feeling that a reply was needed to an attempt at intimidation. Ratification was in fact carried by 231 votes to 52. Here M. Paul-Boncour (left) is seen speaking.

Defining British policy with regard to the situation arising out of Herr Hitler's speech and the action of the German Government in sending troops into the demilitarized Rhineland zone, Mr. Anthony Eden, the Secretary of State for Foreign Affairs, made a statement in the House of Commons on March 9. In the course of it he said: "There is, I am thankful to say, no reason to suppose that the present German action implies a threat of hostilities . . . But in case there should be any misunderstanding about our position as a signatory of the

Locarno Treaty, his Majesty's Government think it necessary to say that, should there take place, during the period which will be necessary for the consideration of the new situation which has arisen, any actual attack upon France or Belgium, which would constitute a violation of Article 2 of Locarno, his Majesty's Government in the United Kingdom, notwithstanding the German repudiation of the Treaty, would regard themselves as in honour bound to come, in the manner provided in the Treaty, to the assistance of the country attacked". Later, he said: "If peace is to be secured there is a manifest duty to rebuild. It is in that spirit that we must approach the new proposals of the German Chancellor. His Majesty's Government will examine them clear-sightedly and objectively with a view to finding out to what extent they represent the means by which the shaken structure of peace can again be strengthened."

FRANCE'S MAGINOT LINE MANNED

AS A SEQUEL TO GERMANY'S MARCH INTO THE DEMILITARIZED RHINELAND ZONE.

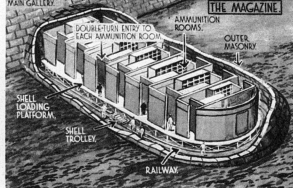

CASEMATES IN THE MAGINOT DEFENSIVE LINE OF FRANCE'S EASTERN FRONTIER; OFFICIALLY REPORTED TO HAVE BEEN MANNED AS A SEQUEL TO GERMANY'S MARCH INTO THE DEMILITARIZED ZONE.

\ FEATURE OF THE VAST UNDERGROUND WORKS OF THE MAGINOT LINE, BY WHICH FRANCE'S EASTERN FRONTIER CAN BE CLOSED IN A FEW HOURS: AN UNDERGROUND MAGAZINE.

THE ENTRANCE TO ONE OF THE NUMEROUS SHELTERS FOR PERSONNEL AND MUNITIONS IN THE MAGINOT LINE; GIVING PROTECTION FROM BOMBARDMENT AND SITUATED SOME WAY BACK FROM THE FRONTIER.

Opposite we illustrate events which accompanied Germany's reoccupation of the demilitarized Rhineland zone. Though much anger was aroused in France by this step, no sweeping military measures were taken. The chief precaution adopted was stated to be the return to the French fortifications of the frontier defence groups, which, for purposes of convenience, had been training a few miles further from the frontier. Troop movements on the French eastern frontier continued throughout March 9; and that night the French military authorities announced that the strategic Maginot Line had been manned with "speed and efficiency". This line of strong points, stretching from Belfort to Montmedy and connecting with the Belgian frontier, would be, it was stated, as difficult to cross by air as by land. The essential points of the French system, which has been conceived and carried out on a gigantic scale and is the strongest ever evolved, are as follows: a line of fortified casemates giving each other mutual support by cross-fire, and interconnected by underground galleries safe from bombardment. All the key positions, normally vulnerable to attack from the air or a break-through by mechanized forces, are in this case buried underground.

A 99 PER CENT VOTE FOR HERR HITLER: THE GREAT ELECTION CAMPAIGN FOR GERMANY.

EXPOUNDING THE PROPOSALS OF THE LOCARNO POWERS IN PARIS: M. FLANDIN SPEAKING IN THE CHAMBER OF DEPUTIES.

M. Flandin, the French Foreign Minister, read a full statement on the attitude of his Government towards the proposals drawn up by the Locarno Powers in London, in the French Chamber of Deputies, on March 20. He gave reasons why these proposals, although admittedly a compromise between the English and French points of view, were regarded as satisfactory.

The great Reichstag election campaign culminated in the official announcement after the polling on Sunday, March 29, that 45,431,102 persons were eligible to vote and that 44,954,937 votes had been cast. The votes for the Party List, which means for Herr Hitler and a "Sovereign State" Germany, were 44,411,911; and there were 543,026 votes against and invalid. The "contest" was conducted with intensity and ingenuity, for the present state of European affairs made it particularly necessary for Nazi Germany to demonstrate not only unity and agreement with the reoccupation of the Rhineland zone, but complete confidence in the Leader and his policy of "freedom, honour and peace". A note or two may be given in amplification of the captions under our pictures. The photograph of decorated Ludwigshafen emphasises the obedience paid to such orders as that given by the Minister for Propaganda in connection with March 27. Referring to this, "The Times" Berlin correspondent wrote: "The beflagging of houses, one minute's silence, and the hearing of a speech by the Führer were the national duties for the afternoon. At a quarter to four a rash of red Swastikas broke out in every city, town, and village in response to the order by wireless, 'Hoist flags'. No public building, no mansion or cottage was to be without one, Dr. Goebbels had ordered." That was for the occasion of Herr Hitler's speech at the Krupp Works in Essen, during which shops remained closed and work indoors and outdoors was suspended while the nation listened; and when the Leader declared: "We must be masters in our own house". Previously, at Ludwigshafen, in the Rhine zone, he had said, on March 25, that he regarded the Locarno Powers' proposals as an insult to German honour and dignity.

A SYMBOL OF THE OBEDIENCE DR. GOEBBELS ANTICIPATED WHEN HE ORDERED THAT, AT A SIGNAL BY WIRELESS, EVERY CITY, TOWN AND VILLAGE SHOULD HOIST FLAGS WHILE THE LEADER SPOKE AT ESSEN: LUDWIGSHAFEN ARRAYED IN HERR HITLER'S HONOUR.

WITH MALLET, HAMMER, SWORD AND SWASTIKAS BEHIND HIM – NOT THE HAMMER AND THE SICKLE!: HERR HITLER SPEAKING AT THE KRUPP WORKS IN ESSEN, STANDING ON A PLATFORM PLACED ON THE UNDERCARRIAGE OF A LOCOMOTIVE AND WITH A CYLINDER AS READING-DESK; DECLARING, FOR ALL THE WORLD TO HEAR, "WE MUST BE MASTERS IN OUR OWN HOUSE".

THE WAR IN ABYSSINIA: THE SCENE OF THE NEW ITALIAN

THE BATTLE OF ENDERTA, WHICH ENDED IN THE CAPTURE OF AMBA ARADAM.

ITALIAN ARTILLERY IN ACTION IN THE BATTLE OF ENDERTA, WHICH ENDED IN THE CAPTURE OF AMBA ARADAM ON FEBRUARY 15.

THE ITALIAN BOMBARDMENT OF AMBA ARADAM, THE MOUNTAIN STRONGHOLD SOUTH OF MAKALE WHICH FELL ON FEBRUARY 15: A PHOTOGRAPH FROM A GAUMONT-BRITISH NEWS FILM OF THE ATTACK; SHOWING A SHELL BURSTING.

THE CAPTURE OF AMBA ALAJI –
THE LIMIT OF THE 1895 ADVANCE.

ABYSSINIAN DEAD IN THE CAVERNOUS FASTNESSES OF AMBA ARADAM: THE NATURAL FORTRESS DESCRIBED AS AN "INTRICATE MASS OF CAVERNS, VALLEYS, PEAKS, CRAGS AND RUGGED GROUND, WHICH OFFER DEFENSIVE POSITIONS AT EVERY TURN."

AMBA ALAJI, WHICH HAS FALLEN TO MARSHAL BADOGLIO'S FORCES: THE MOUNTAIN WHERE THE ITALIANS SUSTAINED A REVERSE IN 1895, WHEN 2000 OUT OF 2400 MEN UNDER MAJOR TOSELLI FELL FIGHTING AGAINST THE ONSLAUGHT OF 50,000 SHOANS.

The battle of Enderta was the prelude to an Italian victory on the northern front. The advance was southward again from Amba Aradam, which fell in the battle of Enderta. It ended in the occupation, apparently without resistance from Ras Mulugeta, of Amba

Alaji, the last of the great natural obstacles which bar the road leading to Dessie and the South. Amba Alaji marked the limit of the Italian advance in 1895, when, a few months before the Adow disaster, 2000 out of a force of 2400 men under Major Toselli fell fighting against 50,000 Abyssinians. The battle began at dawn on February 28, the III Corps attacking northwards from Gaela and the Taraghe Pass (West of Amba Aradam), and the Eritrean Army Corps, aided by Italian troops, attacking from the North and East near Abbi Addi. The Italian reports claimed that the Abyssinians were entrapped and that artillery fire and aircraft attacks rendered their only path of escape, westwards towards the Takkare River, almost impossible. Both Abyssinian armies were said to have been heavily defeated.

THE OBJECT OF ITALIAN BOMBING RAIDS: DR. MELLY'S RED CROSS UNIT IN ABYSSINIA.

On the morning of March 4 the British Ambulance Service Unit of the British Red Cross in Abyssinia was bombed at Alamata, near Kworam, by an Italian Caproni aeroplane, No. 62. Serious damage was done; four patients were killed and three were wounded. Dr. Melly, the medical officer in charge, stated in his preliminary report that the ambulance was encamped two miles from the nearest troops on open ground. The Italian aeroplane repeatedly flew over the camp at a low altitude, dropping in all forty bombs. Three tents used as hospital wards, operation and sterilisation tents, and one lorry was destroyed. There were no casualties among the personnel. Dr. Melly added that, besides the red crosses on tents and on the flagstaff, a ground flag 40 ft. square, bearing a large red cross, lay in the centre of the camp. The bombing was repeated on March 5 and on March 6, although little by then remained of the camp. The staff and patients had moved overnight by lorry to a place of relative safety unmarked by the Red Cross. The doctors continued their work as best they could after the loss of much of their equipment. The Italian allegations were that in the centre of the camp a large sheet was spread bearing a Red Cross, but that otherwise the encampment was not provided with any Red Cross sign; and that reconnoitring Italian aeroplanes were met with anti-aircraft fire from the neighbourhood of the camp on March 3, 4 and 5. The British reply stated that the identity of the ambulance camp was plain, and emphatically denied the allegation that fire was opened from it on aircraft or that it was used as cover for troops. It ended by saying that the Government reserved the right to claim compensation for the losses suffered.

DISPLAYING ITS GROUND FLAG, FORTY FEET SQUARE – AS IT WAS WHEN BOMBED BY AN ITALIAN AEROPLANE ON MARCH 4: AN ENCAMPMENT OF THE BRITISH RED CROSS UNIT UNDER DR. MELLY.

VICTORIES IN THE NORTH; AND BOMBING FROM THE AIR

THE VICTOR OF ASHANGI: MARSHAL BADOGLIO, COMMANDER-IN-CHIEF OF THE ITALIAN FORCES IN ABYSSINIA.

THE BATTLE OF LAKE ASHANGI: THE EMPEROR OF ABYSSINIA, WHO LED HIS TROOPS, AT FIELD HEADQUARTERS.

Marshal Badoglio, whose victory at Ashangi followed many other successes, succeeded General de Bono, last November, as Italian High Commissioner in East Africa and Commander of the Abyssinian Expedition. He claims that the recent advance on the northern front added another 23,000 square miles of territory to the 15,000 square miles previously occupied. He has been officially thanked for each of his victories, but as he already holds all the highest orders and decorations, including the Order of the Annunciation (the Italian equivalent of the Garter and Order of Merit combined), he is a difficult man to reward. It was thought probable that the King of Italy, advised by the Duce, might confer on him the one high distinction he lacks – the Grand Cross of the Colonial Order of the Star of Italy. Marshal Badoglio fought in the Adowa campaign of 1896, the Tripoli war of 1911, and the Great War, for his services in which he was made Marchese di Sabotino. In 1919 he became a Senator, and he has also been Governor of Libya, Colonial Minister, Ambassador to Brazil, and Chief of the General Staff.

On March 31 a battle began in the neighbourhood of Lake Ashangi, on the Italians' left flank in the North. The Emperor of Abyssinia, at the head of the Imperial Guard, himself took part in the fighting. In two *communiqués* of April 4 Marshal Badoglio reported that the battle reached its final stage that morning, with the troops commanded by the Emperor in flight towards the South. "All our aeroplanes", he added, "are engaged in bombing and machine-gunning this disorderly mass." The Abyssinian losses were described as very heavy and the Italian casualties were given at about forty dead and wounded. By April 5 the I Army Corps was said to be in full occupation of the entire district surrounding Kworam, South of Lake Ashangi. From Addis Ababa the Emperor was reported on April 4 to be still holding his own in the fighting. The message added that for five days there had been desperate onslaughts on the Italian positions south of Amba Alaji, against superior numbers, superior equipment and superior organisation. The Italians were said to be trying to place a belt of gas round the Emperor, and to be subjecting him and his men to continual bombardment by hundreds of aeroplanes.

THE AIR RAID ON UNFORTIFIED HARRAR:

NATIVE HOUSES IN RUINS AFTER THE RAID: THE DESTRUCTION OF THE SECOND CITY OF ABYSSINIA, THE CENTRE OF THE EMPEROR'S PROVINCE, BY THREE HUNDRED ITALIAN BOMBS.

THE ABYSSINIAN COLLAPSE IN THE NORTH: ITALY'S RAPID ADVANCE.

WHAT THE MECHANIZED COLUMN SHOWN FROM THE AIR ON THE OPPOSITE PAGE LOOKS LIKE FROM THE GROUND: LORRIES UNDER GENERAL STARACE IN THE SWIFT ADVANCE ON GONDAR AND LAKE TANA.

Harrar, the second largest town in Abyssinia, was heavily bombed from the air on March 29. The Italians appeared to direct their attacks particularly on hospitals and missions in the town. There were few casualties, since the alarm had been given in time, and most of the population were able to take refuge outside the town. The sudden and unexpected collapse of Abyssinian resistance in the north enabled the invaders to sweep Southward along the whole of their front. On the right the Italian mechanised flying column under General Starace occupied Gondar on April 1, and, joining with other

detachments, advanced to the northern shores of Lake Tana on April 12. Meanwhile an Italian detachment moving southward from Noggan along the Sudanese border entered Metemma, which is the local name for the Abyssinian half of the frontier post of Gallabat. On the left flank the Italian successes were still more spectacular. The battle of Lake Ashangi, fought in the first few days of April, ended all Abyssinian resistance in that sector. Kworam was occupied; then Kobbo; then Waldia; and on April 15 the Italians entered Dessie without opposition. This town was the Emperor's headquarters during the early part of the war.

ADDIS ABABA – NOW IN ITALIAN HANDS: THE CITY LEFT LEADERLESS BY THE BEATEN EMPEROR'S FLIGHT.

By May 4 the Italian advance guard had reached the outskirts of Addis Ababa, and their occupation of the city occurred on the following day. With the flight of the Emperor, all organised resistance ceased. General Graziani had not won his decisive victory in the Ogaden, and on May 4 unbroken armies still blocked his way to Jijiga and Harrar: but their continued resistance depended on the local chiefs and not on any centralised command. In these circumstances it was thought that serious fighting was at an end. On the main line of attack in the North the advance Southward from Dessie was made at considerable speed, for the town fell as lately as April 15. The French Government on May 4 requested the Italians to hasten their entry, so that the inhabitants might be protected from the dangerous riots that broke out there after the Emperor's departure. Bands of desperate Galla warriots were roaming the city. Before leaving late on the night of May 1, the Emperor gave orders that the Gibbi (Imperial Palace) should be thrown open, and the people were allowed to help themselves. The uncontrolled mob ran riot, pillaging, burning, and shooting, and many lives were lost. One message said that half the town was in flames on May 3.

THE RULER OF ABYSSINIA, WHO FLED FROM ADDIS ABABA, HIS CAPITAL, TO JIBUTI, IN FRENCH SOMALILAND, AND LEFT FOR HAIFA IN H.M.S. "ENTERPRISE": H.M. HAILE SILASSIE I., EMPEROR OF ETHIOPIA.

PROCLAIMED EMPEROR OF ABYSSINIA: KING VICTOR EMMANUEL OF ITALY, WITH SIGNOR MUSSOLINI, WHO WAS HAILED BY THE FASCIST GRAND COUNCIL AS FOUNDER OF A RE-BORN ROMAN EMPIRE.

Mr. Eden announced in Parliament on May 4 that the Emperor of Ethiopia had left Addis Ababa on May 2, accompanied by other members of his family, and arrived at Jibuti, the port of French Somaliland, on May 3. "The Emperor made it clear", continued Mr. Eden, "that his wish was to proceed with his family to Palestine. His Majesty's Government felt it incumbent on them to grant this request and facilitate their passage to Jerusalem". Mr. Eden added that the British cruiser "Enterprise" had been ordered to Jibuti to convey the Emperor's party to Haifa.

In an announcement made in Rome on May 9, and greeted with wild enthusiasm, Signor Mussolini said: "Italy has finally her empire . . . Here is the law, O Italians, which closes one period of our history and opens up another. (1) The territories and the peoples that belonged to the Empire of Abyssinia are placed under the full and entire sovereignty of the Kingdom of Italy. (2) The title of Emperor has been assumed for himself and for his successors by the King of Italy . . . Blackshirts, legionaries, the salute to the Re-Imperatore!" The Fascist Council officially expressed "the gratitude of the fatherland to the Duce, founder of the Empire".

THE DIGNITY AND CHARACTER OF THE EMPEROR HAILE SELASSIE I.: A NOTABLE PORTRAIT BRONZE IN EPSTEIN'S BEST MANNER.

"I AM HERE TODAY TO CLAIM THAT JUSTICE WHICH IS DUE TO MY PEOPLE": THE EMPEROR HAILE SILASSIE OF ABYSSINIA MAKING HIS PROTEST AGAINST ITALY BEFORE THE LEAGUE OF NATIONS AT GENEVA – (SEATED TOGETHER AT THE BACK, LEFT TO RIGHT) M. VAN ZEELAND (PRESIDING) AND M. AVENOL, SECRETARY-GENERAL OF THE LEAGUE.

The Emperor Haile Silassie addressed the League Assembly at Geneva on June 30 in a speech of impressive dignity. After recalling the decision of fifty nations that an aggression had been committed, he described, as a warning to Europe, the deadly effects of Italian poison-gas sprayed from aircraft over densely populated area. He then traced the successive stages of the conflict. "I refused", he said, "all proposals to my personal advantage made to me by the Italian Government if only I would betray my people and the Covenant. I was defending the cause of all small peoples threatened with aggression . . . The problem today is a much wider one than the removal of sanctions. It is the very existence of the League of Nations. It is the confidence that each State is to place in international treaties. It is the value of promises made to small States . . . God and history will remember your judgement . . . Placed by the aggressor face to face with the accomplished fact are States going to set up a terrible precedent of bowing before force? Representatives of the world, I have come to Geneva to discharge in your midst the most painful of the duties of a Head of a State. What reply shall I have to take back to my people?"

DISASTROUS
U.S.A. FLOODS

(LEFT), THE OPENED "SLUICE-GATES" OF THE PITTS-
BURGH PRESS! WHERE THE WATER LAY 15 FT. DEEP

(ABOVE), A SECTION OF STEEL BRIDGE CARRIED AWAY
BY FLOOD-WATERS AND ICE, IN MAINE.

(RIGHT), THE POPULATION OF WILKESBARRE, PENN-
SYLVANIA, FORCED TO TAKE TO BOAT TRANSPORT.

Disastrous floods which, in the middle of March, caused the death of some two hundred people in the eastern United States, rendered several hundred thousand homeless, and inflicted damage estimated at £20,000,000 at least. The great steel centre of Pittsburgh, Pennsylvania, which has some 700,000 inhabitants, was the city hardest hit. The waters of the Alleghany and Monongahela rivers, which converge there, reached a height of 17½ feet on the night of March 18, ten feet higher than in Pittsburgh's worst previous flood, that of 1913. For several days the city was without gas or electricity, and with little more than one day's supply of drinking-water. Transport, except in boats or canoes, was almost non-existent, and there were several serious fires, which the brigades were helpless to stem, in and about the city. In "The Golden Triangle", the main shopping and business centre, water lay from ten to fifteen feet deep. Of the immense damage done there, amounting to several million pounds, it was said that only a small part was covered by insurance. In the Pittsburgh area, including Johnstown, where a dam burst, the toll of deaths reached about a hundred. In order to avert epidemics, the public health service sent thousands of units of typhoid vaccine by air to Pittsburgh, and the crisis passed without any outbreak occurring.

THE THIRD WORST TORNADO DISASTER ON RECORD IN THE UNITED STATES:
MANY TOWNS AND VILLAGES WRECKED WITH A LOSS OF SOME 500 LIVES.

EVIDENCE OF THE TORNADO'S TERRIFIC FORCE: A PARTLY DEMOLISHED GEORGIA HIGH SCHOOL.

A series of tornadoes, described as the third worst in the history of the United States, swept across the South-eastern States on the night of April 5 and during the next day, causing great loss of life and enormous material damage. The first tornado struck Mississippi and Alabama without warning and reduced towns and villages to ruins. Further storms followed, moving eastward across Georgia and North and South Carolina towards the Atlantic. In Mississippi alone the number of dead was officially estimated at 250. The town that suffered most was Tupelo, where 184 bodies were counted. Another town severely stricken was Gainesville, in Georgia, where the number killed was given as 183. Here also scores of buildings were blown down and outbreaks of fire increased the peril. By April 7, the bodies of 408 persons had been recovered in the region affected, but it was feared that the total death-toll would be at least 500. Some 2000 other people were injured. At Gainesville the damage to property was about £3,000,000 and at Tupelo £1,600,000. To prevent looting, 2000 National Guardsmen were on duty. At Gainesville convicts worked with members of this force and firemen in clearing wreckage.

CONVICTS (IN STRIPED CLOTHES) AT WORK WITH FIREMEN AND NATIONAL GUARDSMEN: SEARCHING THE DEBRIS OF A HARDWARE COMPANY'S WRECKED BUILDING IN THE TOWN SQUARE AT GAINESVILLE.

GREAT DROUGHT IN THE UNITED STATES: £100,000,000 DAMAGE TO CROPS.

AN OAT-FIELD RUINED BY THE DROUGHT IN BISMARK, NORTH DAKOTA.

A SALE-ROOM IN NEBRASKA: FARMERS HAVE HAD TO SELL THEIR BELONGINGS.

REFUGEES FROM OKLAHOMA CAMPING BY THE ROAD AT BAKERS-FIELD, CALIFORNIA.

THE FRENCH STAY-IN STRIKES

HERR HITLER'S 47TH BIRTHDAY:

THE GALLERIES LAFAYETTE PARALYSED BY A STAY-IN STRIKE: THE EXTRAORDINARY SCENES WHEN EMPLOYEES CAMPED IN THEIR DEPARTMENTS AND SHOP-GIRLS TURNED IN TO SLEEP ON THEIR COUNTERS.

BERLIN BECOMES AN ARMED CAMP FOR HERR HITLER'S FORTY-SEVENTH BIRTHDAY: THE NEW MECHANIZED ARMY ASSEMBLING FOR THE GREAT PARADE – INFANTRY IN LORRIES TOWING QUICK-FIRING ANTI-TANK GUNS AND OTHER UNITS.

HOW THE FRENCH STAY-IN STRIKERS WERE MAINTAINED IN THEIR FACTORIES: FAMILIES AND SYMPATHISERS ARRIVING WITH PROVISIONS AT THE ENTRANCE OF A BIG CHOCOLATE WORKS.

A remarkable "epidemic" of stay-in strikes began in France after the victory of the Front Populaire in the elections. By June 4, over 500,000 workers were "occupying" 350 factories. The prospects for M. Blum's Socialist Government, still only in the process of formation, looked grave; much anxiety began to be felt in French financial circles, and a flight from the franc set in. M. Blum took office on June 4 and on June 5 the new Government announced the introduction of immediate legislation to meet the situation. The measures promised included an amnesty, a 40-hour week, holidays with pay and a programme of public works to relieve unemployment.

A MYSTERY STREAM OF ILL OMEN REAPPEARS: "WOE WATERS" HELD TO PRESAGE DISASTER!

THE SWIFTEST UNITS OF THE MECHANIZED ARMY: MOTOR-CYCLISTS WHO TOOK PART IN THE GREAT BIRTHDAY PARADE, WHICH INCLUDED MOTOR-CYCLE BATTALIONS EQUIPPED WITH BOTH LIGHT AND HEAVY MACHINE-GUNS.

THE SOURCE OF THE WOE WATERS OF THE WOLDS THAT FORM THE GYPSEY RACE, A MYSTERIOUS STREAM NOW FLOWING AGAIN AFTER HAVING BEEN DRY FOR SEVERAL YEARS: A SPRING RISING AT WHARRAM-LE-STREET, YORKSHIRE.

The forty-seventh birthday of Herr Hitler, the German Leader, Chancellor, and Supreme Commander-in-Chief, on April 20, was marked in Berlin by a parade of armed forces of a kind Germany had not seen since the days of the Kaiser. As "The Times" had it, "fifteen thousand officers and men of the Army, Navy, and the Air Force, with 1000 horses and 1500 armoured cars, tanks, and other mechanical vehicles, turned Berlin into an armed camp from early morning. For an hour and three quarters they marched, rode, and drove past the Führer in the Tiergarten". Included in the parade were infantry, machine-guns and mortars, horse artillery, infantry in lorries, anti-aircraft detachments, pioneers, a thousand seaman, detachments of the Air Force, light tanks, armoured cars (the largest types equipped with both pom-poms and machine-guns) and motor-cycle battalions. Before the parade, Herr Hitler announced certain promotions – General von Blomberg to Field-Marshal; Generals Göring and Baron von Fritsch to Colonel-General and Admiral Raeder to General-Admiral. Colonel-General von Fritsch and General-Admiral Raeder were also given the rank of Reich Minister. King Edward sent a congratulatory telegram to Herr Hitler.

A MILITARY REVOLT IN SPAIN: PEOPLE AND PLACES
THE SUPPRESSION OF THE REBEL RISING IN MADRID

DEAD HORSES, KILLED IN THE STREET FIGHTING, USED AS BARRICADES IN MADRID: REBEL TROOPS FIRING FROM BEHIND THEIR BODIES AT GOVERNMENT SUPPORTERS – A LAST STAND BEFORE THEY WERE OVERCOME BY THE LOYALISTS.

THE CAPTURE OF THE CHIEF REBEL STRONGHOLD IN MADRID: THE SURROUNDING DEBRIS BEARING WITNESS TO THE INTENSITY OF THE FIRING: LOYALISTS BEATING DOWN THE DOOR OF LA MONTANA BARRACKS, WHICH, IN THE REBELS' PLANS, WAS TO HAVE FURNISHED THE SPEARHEAD FOR A FINAL THRUST AGAINST THE GOVERNMENT.

FIGHTING IN THE STREETS OF BARCELONA.

YOUNG COMMUNISTS CROUCHING BEHIND A BARRICADE OF STONES IN BARCELONA: A PHASE OF PROLONGED STRUGGLE WHICH ENDED IN THE LOYALISTS' VICTORY.

A GIRL, ARMED WITH A RIFLE, PATROLLING A STREET IN BARCELONA.

"THE WOMEN KEPT CALLING ON THEIR MEN TO TAKE NO PRISONERS BUT TO SLAUGHTER ALL": A GIRL WITH THE LOYAL FORCES IN BARCELONA.

THE FLEET IN ACTION AGAINST THE REBELS.

THE SPANISH BATTLE-SHIP "JAIME I": REPORTED TO HAVE BEEN DAMAGED BY GUNFIRE FROM THE SHORE BATTERIES WHEN BOMBARDING REBELS. THE SHIP IN THE HANDS OF HER CREW WHO KILLED THE OFFICERS.

FIELD ARTILLERY IN ACTION AGAINST REBEL FORCES NEAR TOLEDO: AN ENGAGEMENT WHICH HELPED TO TIGHTEN THE GOVERNMENT'S CONTROL OVER CENTRAL SPAIN: THE INSURGENTS, MAINLY MILITARY CADETS, BEING DEFEATED AND FORCED TO RETREAT.

A Right Wing revolt, described as openly Monarchist in its aims, broke out in Spain and Spanish Morocco early in the morning of July 18. It seems to have been almost completely military in origin. The rebellion had evidently been planned with extreme care. First came the revolt in Morocco, where the insurgents succeeded in occupying the principal towns of the Protectorate. Contingents were smuggled across the Straits to Spain itself by sea and air. Simultaneous insurrections throughout the country were calculated to draw a circle of violence round Madrid and intimidate the Republican Government. Then there was to be a rising in Madrid, the rebels hoping to seize power and, presumably, to set up a military dictatorship which would stamp out Socialism in Spain. Of the provincial insurrections not all were successful, that in Barcelona in particular being suppressed after two days of bitter fighting. In Madrid the rebels also failed. The civilian population hastily armed by the Government, came to the support of the troops that remained loyal; and on July 20 La Montana barracks, a large building on the edge of the hillside above the River Manzanares which was to have been the rallying point

for the rising, was shelled into submission. A number estimated at a thousand were killed or wounded before the fighting ceased in Madrid. The rebel officers were deserted by many of the rank and file, which at heart remained loyal to the Republic. After their success the Government had immediately to organise the defence of the capital against a rebel army advancing south from Burgos under General Mola. A battle was fought on July 24 in the pass at Somo-sierra (about fifty miles north of Madrid), and, though both sides claimed the victory, it seemed that the threat to the capital was thereby diminished. Later the Government captured Albacete from the rebels – an important success which ensured that Madrid would not be starved into surrender since Albacete commands the communications with the towns of the Mediterranean littoral, Murcia, Alicante, Cartagena and Valencia. At the time of writing much of the South of Spain, as well as Spanish Morocco, remained in rebel hands, and General Mola's forces were still in strength at Burgos and Pamplona in the North.

CIVIL WAR IN SPAIN: A REIGN OF TERROR AT MALAGA.

ARMED PEASANTS ON PATROL IN MALAGA: MEN OF THE KIND THAT FORMED SMALL BANDS AND MARCHED OUT TO MEET THE ADVANCE OF WELL-TRAINED AND WELL-EQUIPPED MOROCCAN TROOPS, OPPOSING THEM WITH WHATEVER WEAPONS THEY COULD FIND.

RUINS OF A BUILDING IN MALAGA: THE INTERIOR OF A WRECKED DEPARTMENT STORE AFTER AN ARSON ATTACK.

A BURNED THEATRE IN MALAGA, DESTROYED BECAUSE IT REPRE-SENTED TO THE COMMUNISTS A PHASE OF BOURGEOIS ART, NOW DEFUNCT.

The suppression of the rebellion in Malaga, accomplished after severe fighting in the early days of the civil war, gave power to the extremists of the Left wing – as in Barcelona and other Spanish cities. Malaga then underwent a reign of terror. A Soviet was established and incendiarism and destruction of property became rife. Many people took refuge in the surrounding mountains and hundreds of refugees sailed to find scantu-ary in Gibraltar. Foreigners were taken off by H.M.S. "Brazen" and other British warships. British residents of Ronda who escaped via Malaga told of atrocities committed by Reds. Suspects were taken to a cemetery, ordered to walk towards a hole and shot in the back. Everyone in the city was made to have a permit. Malaga was vital to the rebels because it was almost the only harbour in the Straits available to the loyal Spanish fleet. Warships attempted to shell the only road from Algeciras to Malaga, met by bands of ill-armed citizens.

CIVIL WAR IN SPAIN: SEVILLE IN REBEL HANDS.

STUBBORN FIGHTING NORTH OF MADRID.

WOMEN PLEADING WITH REBEL TROOPS FOR THE LIVES OF THEIR MENFOLK, AS THE REBELS ENTER THE TOWN OF CONSTANTINA, BETWEEN SEVILLE AND CORDOBA; WITH WHITE FLAGS OF SURRENDER HANGING FROM THE WINDOWS.

VOLUNTEERS ARMED BY THE GOVERNMENT LEAVING MADRID IN MOTOR-COACHES TO FIGHT AGAINST THE REBELS IN THE MOUNTAINS NORTH OF THE CITY: CITIZENS OF THE CAPITAL GIVEN AN ENTHUSIASTIC SEND-OFF BY CHEERING CROWDS.

Rebel successes during the week ending August 15 enabled the Northern forces under General Mola to join up with the Southern forces under General Franco and General Quelpo de Llano. General Mola flew to Seville to meet General Franco. Their plan was said to be a joint attack by the Northern and Southern armies on Madrid and an attempt to starve the capital into surrender. The capture of Badajoz by the rebels on August 14 gave them control of almost the whole Portuguese frontier and of the Western approaches to Madrid. Their Southern army was continually reinforced by Moroccan troops. The position at the end of the fourth week of civil war had taken a distinct turn in favour of the rebels. The Badajoz fighting in particular had shown the advantage of possessing the majority of trained and equipped troops, for the Govern-ment's militia-men were more than once worsted by a weaker force of Moroccans.

(LEFT), THE REBEL COMMANDER IN THE NORTH AT AN INSPEC-TION IN BURGOS: GENERAL MOLA, WHO SECURED HIS COMMUNICA-TIONS WITH GENERAL FRANCO BY ADVANCING TO THE WEST OF MADRID AND JOINING WITH HIM AT MERIDA.

(RIGHT), GENERAL FRANCO IN SEVILLE: THE LEADER OF THE REBELLION WITH HIS PILOT AFTER FLYING FROM MOROCCO TO TAKE CHARGE IN SOUTHERN SPAIN AND ORGANISE THE ATTACK ON MADRID.

CIVIL WAR IN SPAIN: "TERRIFYING RESPONSIBILITY"
MOROCCAN TROOPS WITH THE REBELS: WAR MATERIALS FROM ITALY

ONE OF THE THREE ITALIAN AEROPLANES WHICH CRASHED ON THE WAY FROM SARDINIA TO MOROCCO: IT APPARENTLY RAN OUT OF PETROL, THREE OF THE FOUR OCCUPANTS BEING KILLED.

MOORISH REGULARS HELPING THE SPANISH REBELS LANDING AT AN AERODROME IN SPAIN: ADDITIONS TO A FORCE REPORTED TO HAVE FALLEN OFF THROUGH DISSATISFACTION IN MOROCCO, STIMULATED BY SPANISH GOVERNMENT PROPAGANDA.

From the beginning of the war General Franco brought over Moroccan troops to help his cause. The superior training and equipment of the Moroccans gave them a great advantage over the Government militia. They were of special value in the attack on Badajoz, and they took part in the advance on Malaga. A battalion of them reached Burgos on August 22, and after a parade through the town went up to the Guadarrama front, North of Madrid. Dreadful atrocities were reported and in case they escaped the rebels' action in using Moroccans to fight against the Spaniards has been described as a "terrifying responsibility", alleviating foreign sympathy. An incident which created much interest was the flight of five Italian machines from Sardinia on July 30. They

were laden with war material and were bound for Spanish Morocco, where the rebels were supreme. Three of the machines made forced landings, apparently from lack of petrol. The incident rendered much more difficult the negotiations in Europe for universal neutrality in the Spanish war. In the Balearic Islands, Majorca fell to the rebels, Minorca to the Government. Aeroplanes from Mahon daily raided the bigger island, and most of the foreigners in Palma were taken to Marseilles in H.M.S. "Repulse".

SOVIET RUSSIA'S SYMPATHY FOR SPAIN:
A MOSCOW DEMONSTRATION IN FAVOUR OF THE FRENTE POPULAR

REBELS COURT-MARTIALLED:
GENERALS GODED AND BURRIEL CONDEMNED.

GENERAL GODED (LEFT) AND GENERAL BURRIEL SITTING BETWEEN CIVIL GUARDS AT THEIR TRIAL: REBELS WHO LED THE REVOLT IN BARCELONA AND FELL INTO THE HANDS OF THEIR ENEMIES WHEN THE LEFT WAS VICTORIOUS.

"GREETINGS TO THE SPANISH PROLETARIAT, HEROICALLY FIGHTING AGAINST FASCISM": BANNERS ABOVE THE CROWD AS THEY LISTEN TO ONE OF THE SPEECHES AT THE MASS MEETING IN MOSCOW.

A military court composed of colonels, lieutenant-colonels and majors sat in the prison ship "Uruguay" as she lay in Barcelona harbour on August 11 and condemned to death General Manuel Goded and General Alvaro Fernandez Burriel, who were accused of military rebellion. The officers were executed in public by a firing squad in the fortress of Montjuich early the following morning. It was possible to dispense with some of the ordinary formalities of a court-martial because Barcelona and other Catalan cities have been declared in a state of siege for the purpose of administering military justice. This fact permitted the accused to be tried by persons of lower rank than themselves. Otherwise no legal requirements were omitted. The sentence was approved by the local military judge-advocate, and the warrant was sent by air to Madrid for confirmation by the Cabinet, who also signified their approval. General Goded was accused of organising rebellion in both Majorca and Barcelona. He had flown to Barcelona to take charge of the rebel forces there when war began. General Burriel commanded the Barcelona cavalry garrison.

The sympathies of Soviet Russia are naturally with the Government and the workers of Spain in their war against the Fascist uprising. These sympathies were shown in a most practical way when, after a great meeting in the Red Square, Moscow, on August 3, a fund for the "Defence of the Spanish People" was instituted. About 120,000 people had gathered in the Red Square to listen to speeches on the Spanish crises and to demonstrate their solidarity. The text of a telegram to Madrid, "hoping for the victory of the people's front which is certain if unity is preserved", was unanimously approved. The undisguised sympathies of the Russian people, however, did not prevent the Government of the U.S.S.R. from supporting the French proposals for non-intervention in Spain – proposals which have also the strong support of the British Government. On August 10, the French Chargé d'Affaires in Moscow was informed of the official Russian adhesion to the French text.

THE BERLIN OLYMPIC GAMES

THE OPENING OF THE OLYMPIC GAMES AT BERLIN: THE HUGE STADIUM CROWDED WITH SPECTATORS FOR THE INAUGURAL CEREMONIES – SEEN FROM THE AIRSHIP "HINDENBURG".

JESSE OWENS, THE WONDERFUL AMERICAN NEGRO ATHLETE, WITH HIS OAK TREES AND OTHER OLYMPIC TROPHIES: THE WINNER OF THREE CHAMPIONSHIPS – THE 100 METRES (10.2 SEC), THE 200 METRES, AND THE LONG JUMP.

The eleventh Olympiad was opened in the Reichsportsfeld, Berlin, on August 1. The great stadium was packed with 100,000 people. At nearly four o'clock, bugles sounded and Herr Hitler appeared and was enthusiastically greeted. "Deutschland Uber Alles" and the "Horst Wessel" song were sung; the flags of the nations were hoisted round the stadium; and the Olympic bell was rung. This was the signal for the athletes to enter. They marched in alphabetical order of their countries' names, except for the Greek team, which came first, and the German team, which, as representing the hosts, brought up the rear. A number of ceremonies followed, in the course of which Herr Hitler declared the Olympic Games open. The last of the torch-bearers from Greece ran in with the burning torch and ignited the Olympic fires. The great airship "Hindenburg" flew over the arena during the inaugural ceremonies, and came down so low that the faces of those looking out of the gondolas could be plainly seen from the ground.

The athletic events of the Olympic Games at Berlin ended on August 9. By then most of the Olympic records had been beaten and a number of new world records had been set up. There was no doubt that Jesse Owens, the American negro, had put up the most wonderful of many performances. He won three championships – the 100 metres (in 10.2 seconds), the 200 metres (in 20.7 seconds), and the long jump (with 8.06 metres, or 26 ft. 6½ in.). Others of America's negro team, notably Metcalfe and Woodruff, also covered themselves with glory. Great Britain's first championship was won by H.H. Whitlock in the 50-kilometre walk; and on the last day of the athletics, this country won a track event, the 1600 metres relay. The team was F.F. Wolff, G.L. Rampling, W. Roberts, and A.G.K. Brown. They won by 2 seconds from the USA. J.E. Lovelock, the great New Zealand miler, had already achieved a magnificent victory in the 1500 metres, setting a new world record of 3 min. 47.8 seconds. He finished five yards ahead of the American, G. Cunningham, who also broke the previous world's record. The USA and Germany were the most successful nations in the athletics. The Olympic Games end to-morrow, August 16.

THE OLYMPIC WINTER GAMES

CANADIAN COMPETITORS GIVING THE NAZI SALUTE AS THEY MARCHED PAST HERR HITLER AT THE OPENING OF THE FOURTH WINTER OLYMPIC GAMES AT GARMISCH-PARTENKIRCHEN, BAVARIA.

The fourth winter Olympic Games had been opened by Herr Hitler at the Ski Stadium in Garmisch-Partenkirchen, Bavaria, on February 6. The total number of spectators was estimated close on fifty thousand. The heavy snow which fell throughout the ceremony, came just in time to fulfil the hopes of all those concerned in the Games, for before that, lack of snow had threatened to spoil several of the events. The ceremony began with a march into the enclosure by the twenty-eight national teams competing.

THE "QUEEN MARY" WINS THE BLUE RIBAND: A RECORD ATLANTIC PASSAGE.

The "Queen Mary" regained for Britain the Blue Riband of the atlantic when, at 8.12 pm on August 30, she passed the Bishop Rock in the Scilly Isles as here homeward voyage after having covered the 2939 miles from the Ambrose Light, New York, in 3 days 7 hours 57 minutes, thus beating the previous record for the eastward passage, made by the French liner "Normandie", by 3 hours 31 minutes. The "Queen Mary's" average speed for the voyage was 30.63 knots, compared with the "Normandie's" 30.31. Only a week ago, it will be recalled, the "Queen Mary" had broken the record for the westward crossing with a time of 4 days 49 minutes (from the Bishop Rock to the Ambrose Lightship) at an average speed of 30.14 knots. The "Normandie" on her maiden voyage last year, made the westward passage at an average speed of 29.94 knots. When noting the "Queen Mary's" westward record in our last issue, with illustrations

of earlier Atlantic crossings and their times, we pointed out that, in order to capture the Blue Riband, she would have to perform the homeward run at an average speed exceeding 30.31 knots. This feat, as mentioned above, she triumphantly accomplished, in spite of fog on her last lap. There was great excitement among the passengers as the ship neared the Bishop Rock lighthouse, marking the eastern end of the officially recognised "record course". She left Southampton for New York on August 19, and thus she completed the double journey in 11 days. On her arrival back at Southampton she received a welcome such as that port had never before seen. The shores were thronged with cheering crowds, sirens sounded, and aircraft roared overhead, while scores of pleasure-boats and steamers packed with holiday-makers escorted the "Queen Mary" to her berth in the Ocean Dock.

RACIAL BITTERNESS IN PALESTINE WHERE THE OUTLOOK IS STILL GRAVE: BRITISH ATTEMPTS TO CURB THE OUTBREAK OF LAWLESSNESS.

THE PALESTINE DISTURBANCES: THE SMALL POLICE FORCE, ARMED ONLY WITH BATON AND SHIELD, FACING A DENSE ARAB MOB.

Racial disturbances broke out recently in Palestine, when, April 15, a Jew was killed at Nablus. Subsequently, two Arabs were killed there, and it was assumed that Jews were responsible for the death. On April 19 there were clashes between Jews and Arabs which involved police intervention. Since the outbreak at Jaffa the racial bitterness between Arabs and Jews in Palestine has increased. The Arab demand for a reduction in the number of Jewish immigrants led first to an Arab strike and then to rioting, shooting, and the firing of property both in the towns and in the country districts. On May 18 the High commissioner, Sir Arthur Wauchope, approved the Labour Schedule of 4,500 Jewish immigrants for the half-year ending September 30, thereby showing the official intention not to yield to the Arab demands. On the same day the Colonial Secretary announced in the House of Commons that the King would be advised to appoint a Royal Commission which, after order had been restored, would visit Palestine and, without bringing into question the terms of the mandate, would inquire into the causes of unrest and the alleged grievances of the Arabs and the Jews. Meanwhile, at the High Commissioner's request, reinforcements were sent from Egypt to supplement the Palestine garrison. Police and supporting British troops were forced to fire on demonstrators at Nablus, Acre, and elsewhere. A curfew was imposed and the police were empowered to control all motor traffic on the roads south of Haifa and Tiberias, so as to prevent the movement of agitators. The first death among British police and troops since the beginning of the trouble occurred in Jerusalem on May 28, when a constable was shot dead while walking back from duty along through the Old city. On the same day a party of Seaforth Highlanders was fired on near Jemin and returned the fire, killing two Arabs and wounding four.

A serious outrage occurred on the Jerusalem-Jaffa line during the night of June 18–19, when unknown Arabs unscrewed and removed one of the rails. A train running from Jaffa was derailed; the engine, followed by eight waggons, crashing on its side. On June 22 a British detachment was engaged when a train which it was escorting was stopped by boulders on the line between Deir esh Sheikh and Artuf and was attacked by Arabs with rifles, shot-gun fire and bombs. On the previous day a fight lasting several hours was fought near Tulkarm between armed Arabs and men of the Seaforth Highlanders and Royal Scots Fusiliers. A British Sergeant and Private and ten Arabs were killed. Four aeroplanes co-operated with the troops.

On July 27 elaborate police and military precautions were taken throughout Palestine, in case the Arabs might celebrate the hundredth day of their strike by a special display of lawlessness. The continued need for precautions had been demonstrated on the previous day by an Arab attack on a convoy from Tel Aviv to Jerusalem. The escort, however, signalled for assistance by wireless. In response came aeroplanes and a detachment of the Dorsets. Most of the assailants were killed.

The danger that Arab extremist would get out of hand and continue their campaign of violence even though the Arab leaders were ready to parley became a reality during the week ending August 15. Armed bands infesting the hills were with great difficulty followed and suppressed; and there were a number of engagements with British troops.

Following the announcement that a whole division of British troops was being sent to Palestine, the Colonial Office, on September 7, issued a "statement of policy" concerning that country. After describing the development of the situation from a political strike, through murder and outrage to guerilla warfare, the report stated that neither the forbearance of the authorities nor the appointment of the Royal Commission to enquire into the situation as soon as the disorders ceased had produced any amelioration. The Arab leaders had refused to call off the strike unless the British Government changed its policy entirely; and the efforts of the King of Saudi Arabia, of the Amir of Transjordan, and of General Nuri Pasha, Foreign Minister of Iraq, to persuade them to take a more reasonable attitude had all failed.

The Palestine strike was called off on October 12, after having lasted for six months. The decision was reached after the Arab Higher Committee had consulted with local committees; and followed an appeal issued by the Kings of Iraq and Saudi Arabia and the Emirs of Transjordan and the Yemen. A manifesto published in the Arab Newspapers stated that the perseverance of the strike had proved in a way which had astonished the world its conviction that British policy in Palestine must be changed. On October 12 shops opened again in Palestine, markets were thronged, and the roads were filled with vehicles. A new military policy was announced by the British General Staff, involving the provisional adoption of defensive tactics, with a view to reducing precautionary measures if the situation improved. The casualties in Palestine between April 19 and October 9 were, approximately, 29 British killed and 142 wounded; 80 Jews killed and 200 wounded; and at least 200 Arabs killed and over 800 wounded.

THE IMMIGRATION OF JEWS INTO PALESTINE – AGAINST THE ARAB'S COMPLAINT, CAUSING PRESENT TROUBLES: A MAP SHOWING THE POSITION OF JEWISH AGRI-CULTURAL SETTLEMENTS (DARK SHADING).

A TRAIN DERAILED BY ARABS ON THE JERUSALEM-JAFFA LINE: THE ENGINE AND TRUCKS LYING IN WRECKAGE.

(ABOVE) IN TURBULENT PALESTINE: A BRITISH POLICE PATROL, SEARCHING ARABS FOR FIRE-ARMS ON ONE OF THE WAR-TIME TURKISH ROADS.

(RIGHT) THE PRESIDENT OF THE HIGHER ARAB COMMITTEE HAJ AMIN EL HUSSEIN . . .

A RAILWAY LINE NEAR LYDDA RENDERED IMPASSABLE BY ARABS, WHO TORE UP THE TRACK: BRITISH TROOPS CHANGING FROM ONE TRAIN TO ANOTHER TO CIRCUMVENT THE OBSTRUCTIONS.

CIVIL WAR IN SPAIN: IRUN CAPTURED BY REBEL FORCES.

THE FALL OF IRUN: A BODY OF REBEL TROOPS ENTERING THE TOWN AMID THE BURNT AND BATTERED RUINS IF ITS BUILDINGS, WHICH HAD BEEN SET ON FIRE BY THE GOVERNMENT FORCES DEFENDING IT BEFORE THEY LEFT.

A TYPICAL INSTANCE OF "MOPPING-UP" OPERATIONS BY THE REBELS IN IRUN AFTER THEY HAD CAPTURED THE TOWN: REBEL RIFLEMENT ATTACKING A FARM-HOUSE WHICH WAS BELIEVED STILL TO BE OCCUPIED BY GOVERNMENT SNIPERS.

The town of Irun, in Northern Spain, between San Sebastian and the French frontier, was captured and occupied on September 5 by rebel troops under Colonel Beorlegui. He entered the town with a regiment of mixed infantry, two companies of the Spanish Legion, and four armoured cars. The rest of the attacking force remained outside, and some of them were engaged in "mopping-up" operations, including attacks on outlying farms believed still to harbour snipers. In a report of the same date, from Hendaye, just across the frontier in France, it was stated that Irun, which twenty-four hours before had been a town of 12,000 inhabitants, had that

morning become a heap of blazing ruins. It had been destroyed by the Government troops defending it, when they realised that they could no longer hold out. "The defenders," wrote Mr. Christopher Martin (in "The Daily Telegraph"), "contested every house and doorway, but they were forced back remorselessly. Refusing to surrender, they destroyed every building as they abandoned it. Some premises were blown up with dynamite. Others were soaked with petrol and set on fire. Within two hours practically every building in the town was ablaze."

THE CIVIL WAR IN SPAIN:

THE CAPTURE OF SAN SEBASTIAN – SAVED FROM THE FATE OF IRUN BY THE BASQUES AMONG THE DEFENDING FORCE.

A GOVERNMENT SUPPORTER BEING TAKEN TO THE REBEL HEADQUARTERS BY A FASCIST MILITIA MAN AND A REGULAR SOLDIER: AN INCIDENT IN SAN SEBASTIAN AFTER ITS OCCUPATION BY THE INSURGENTS.

FEMININE ADHERENTS OF THE REBEL CAUSE DISPLY THEIR ENTHUSIAM AT THE FALL OF SAN SEBASTIAN: WOMEN WITH INSURGENT FLAGS HEADING THE FIRST COLUMN OF TROOPS TO ENTER THE TOWN.

The fall of San Sebastian, recently entered by the rebels without opposition, was fortunately not accompanied by an orgy of destruction, on the part of the retreating defenders, such as that which occurred at the neighbouring town of Irun, the capture of which opened the way to the rebel troops. In a message of September 13 from St. Jean de Luz (to "The Daily Telegraph"), Mr Christopher Martin wrote: "San Sebastin is today in the hands of the insurgents. The Government militia, with 60,000 men, women and children, have abandoned it without any attempt at defence. Throughout yesterday and last night the population was in headlong flight,

by road, rail and sea, towards Bilbao and other towns to the West of the city still in Government hands. The last of the militia, with their wives and children, were brought to the France in fishing vessels . . . Basque Nationalists, who, though they belong to the Popular Front, are really Conservatives, prevented the anarchists from burning and sacking the city as they sacked Irun. They seized petrol which the anarchists had collected from the purpose and poured it into the sewers. Nevertheless, the anarchists started a few isolated fires."

THE CIVIL WAR IN SPAIN: FRATRICIDAL STRIFE – FROM BOTH SIDES.

(LEFT), THE SURRENDER OF BADAJOZ – FOLLOWED BY A PITILESS REVENGE: YOUNG REBEL SOLDIERS DISPLAYING A WHITE FLAG WITH WHICH THE GOVERNMENT FORCES DEFENDING THE TOWN INDICATED THEIR SUBMISSION.

(RIGHT), A GRIM TASK INSIDE FOR GUADALUPE AT FUENTERRABIA AFTER ITS CAPTURE BY THE REBELS; RED CROSS WORKERS COLLECTING BODIES OF HOSTAGES EXECUTED BY THE GOVERNMENT DEFENDERS BEFORE ITS FALL.

CIVIL WAR: PHOTOGRAPHS FROM FOUR ZONES

THE ALCAZAR AT TOLEDO, HELD BY SPANISH REBELS, AND SAID TO BE MINED BY THE GOVERNMENT FORCES: THE CITY DOMINATED BY THE FAMOUS OLD FORTRESS.

AN ORGY OF WANTON DESTRUCTION BY "RED" PARTISANS AT VICH, A TOWN NEAR BARCELONA: A PILE OF ECCLESIATICAL STATUES AND TREASURES TORN FROM THE BISHOP'S PALACE READY TO BE BURNED IN THE MARKET PLACE.

The Government claim, made as early as July 23, to have stamped out rebel resistance in Toledo was not substantiated by later news. On August 6 it was stated that the town was almost wholly occupied by Government forces and that the Cadets with a number of Civil Guards still held out in the Alcazar. The message of August 6 added that the rebels had some three hundred civilians with them in the Alcazar, including women and children.

According to a description sent with this photograph, not only were paintings and sculptures destroyed on this occasion, but archives containing documents of historical and archaeological value of the fourteenth, fifteenth, and sixteenth centuries and a collection of old Mass books were burnt. Certainly the Museo Episcopal in the Bishop's palace contained a number of artistic treasures. Whether these have all perished is not known.

A HELMETED PRIEST CONFESSING ONE OF TWO SPIES ABOUT TO BE SHOT: A POIGNANT SCENE NEAR EIBAR.

THE PRESIDENT OF THE PROVISIONAL REBEL GOVERNMENT, GENERAL CABANELLAS (WITH BEARD) GIVING HIS RING TO A GOLD COLLECTION FOR THE CAUSE, AT BURGOS.

"LA PASIONARIA" TO VISIT ENGLAND?

Senora Dolores Irriburi, the left-wing leader, known in her country as "La Pasionaria" has been visiting Paris and Brussels, conducting propaganda on behalf of the Spanish Government. She plans to come to London shortly.

On Oct. 1 General Franco was invested with the title of Commander-in-Chief of the insurgent army and Chief of the Spanish State at the headquarters of the insurgent junta at Burgos. He made a speech to the crowds assembled, saying that, although one of authority would govern for the Spanish people, his party did not mean to uphold the privileges of capitalism. General Franco, it is interesting to note, visited London as the military representative of the Spanish Government at the funeral of King George. He marched in the procession immediately behind the Soviet representative, Marshal Tukhachevsky. General Franco made his career in Morocco, and at the time of his promotion, was stated to be the youngest Spanish general. Later, he was appointed Governor of the Canary Isles. He is forty-five. The new Chief of the State has conveyed an assurance to the British Government that he will respect the *status quo* in Morocco. He contradicted reports that the insurgents had promised bases in Morocco to foreign powers.

GENERAL FRANCO BECOMES "CHIEF OF THE SPANISH STATE": THE INSURGENT LEADER TAKING THE OATH AT BURGOS – THE ARCHBISHOP OF BURGOS IN THE CENTRE; AND THE BEARDED GENERAL CABANELLAS ON THE RIGHT.

LEAVES FROM THE WORLD'S SCRAP-BOOK.

SENTENCED TO DEATH AND SHOT FOR ANTI-STALINIST CONSPIRA-
CY: MR. KAMENEFF.

The trial opened in Moscow on August 19 of Zinovieff, Kameneff, and
fourteen others, charged with being the leaders of "underground"
Revolutionary groups. They are stated to have acknowledged their guilt.

M. ZINOVIEFF, THE FORMER BOLSHEVIST LEADER, OF THE 1924
"RED LETTER" FAME.

MIKHAIL TOMSKY, A LEADER WHO COMMITTED SUICIDE WHEN
ABOUT TO BE ARRESTED.

According to the indictment, at the end of 1932 the heads of the
Zinovieffist and Trotskyist groups formed a united centre, agreeing on
terrorist acts against Russian leaders, with instructions from Trotsky.
Stalin, Voroshiloff, Kagnovitch, Ordjonikidze, Kiroff, and others were
to be murdered. All were convicted and shot on August 24.

TROTSKY'S POSITION IN NORWAY: THE FORMER BOLSHEVIK LEAD-
ER (RIGHT), ALLEGED TO HAVE BEEN CONCERNED IN PLOTS
AGAINST STALIN.

The Soviet Government demanded the expulsion of Trotsky from
Norway, as a sequel to the "Trotskyist plot" trials in Moscow. The
Norwegian Government, however, decided to allow Trotsky and his wife
to remain in Norway, provided they gave up their private villa at
Hoenefoss, lived in a place selected by the Government, made no use of
the telephone, received no visitors except those permitted by the
Government, had their mail supervised, and did not move without a
police guard.

GENERAL VITOVTA PUTNA.

According to a Reuter message from Moscow, General Vitovia Putna,
the Soviet military attaché in London, was arrested and charged with
complicity in the "Trotskyist plot" against Stalin. During the Zinovieff-
Kamenoff trial, a prisoner alleged that Putna had had relations with
Trotsky.

M. ALEXANDRE OSERSKY

It was stated on August 29 that M. Osersky, head of the Soviet Trading
Delegation to Great Britain, had been recalled to Moscow, and his post
in London filled. His recall was widely taken to be connected with the
investigations into the "Trotskyist plot", although denied by the Russian
Embassy. He was said to be returning to London.

THE SIGNING OF THE GERMAN-JAPANESE PACT: HERR VON RIBBEN-
TROP (CENTRE) AND VISCOUNT MUSHAKOTI; WITH GERMAN AND
JAPANESE DIPLOMATS.

An agreement between Germany and Japan was signed in Berlin, on
November 25, by Herr von Ribbentrop, German Ambassador in
London, and Viscount Mushakoyi, Japanese Ambassador in Berlin. The
agreement was a declaration of common determination to resist Bolshevism. It was denied that there were any secret military or economic
clauses.

THE MARCH OF THE JARROW UNEMPLOYED TO LONDON: THE
MARCHERS PASSING THE MARBLE ARCH, WITH A BANNER.

The Jarrow unemployed marchers completed their tramp to London on
October 31. They proceeded along Edgware Road in heavy rain,
displaying a "Jarrow Crusade" banner. They held a demonstration in
Hyde Park on November 1, at which speeches were made by Mayor of
Jarrow and Miss Ellen Wilkinson, MP.

THE PRESIDENT AS VOTER: MR. FRANKLIN D. ROOSEVELT AND HIS
MOTHER, MRS. SARA DELANO ROOSEVELT, ARRIVING AT THE
POLLING STATION IN NEW YORK.

It was announced on November 4 that Mr. Franklin D. Roosevelt, the
Democratic candidate had been re-elected President of the United
States, for the second time, by one of the most decisive triumphs in the
history of American elections; greater than that of any other Presidential
candidate since James Monroe 116 years ago.

THE EPIC OF THE SPANISH WAR: THE DEFENCE OF THE TOLEDO ALCAZAR

The epic of the Spanish Civil War has been the heroic defence of the Alcazar at Toledo by a rebel garrison during a seventy-days siege by Government forces, until the town was captured by insurgent troops under General Varela on September 28 and the Alcazar was relieved. The defenders had with them about 400 women and children and it was stated that about 150 people were found alive in the fortress. The garrison was commanded by Colonel Moscardo. Its losses during the siege were given as 80 killed and 500 wounded. When it was known that deliverance was at hand the surviving cadets, though weak from privations, sailed out to help their rescuers. One of the defendants of the Alcazar, describing their experiences during the siege, stated afterwards (as reported in "The Times"): "First of all we hid the women and children in the safest part of the fortress. Most of them showed extraordinary fortitude and endurance, but their nerves were strained to breaking-point when they heard the noise of pick and drill coming ever nearer and realised that the building was being mined. Each blow, heard with terrifying clarity in the building above, was as excruciating as a dentist's drill . . . But without the women our position would have been even worse. They repaired our clothes and made our food. They insisted on being treated upon terms of absolute equality with the men."

LIKE A CITY DESTROYED BY AN EARTHQUAKE: A GENERAL VIEW OF THE RUINED ALCAZAR AT TOLEDO, PART OF WHICH WAS MINED AND BLOWN UP BY THE GOVERNMENT FORCES THAT BESIEGED IT.

THE "GRANDMOTHER" OF THE ALCAZAR GARRISON: AN OLD DAME EIGHTY YEARS OF AGE WHO LIVED THROUGH THE LONG SIEGE, WITH A YOUNGER COMPANION.

THE HEROES AND HEROINES OF THE ALCAZAR LIVED DURING THE SEVENTY-DAYS' SIEGE: TYPICAL CONDITIONS IN A VAULT OF THE FORTRESS WHICH WAS USED AS A HOSPITAL: A VIEW SHOWING IMPROVISED BARRICADES AT THE WINDOWS.

DAZZLED BY THE SUN ON SEEING IT FOR THE FIRST TIME AFTER SEVENTY DAYS WITHIN THE WALLS OF THE ALCAZAR: A MEMBER OF THE LONG-BELEAGURED GARRISON, WITH A GIRL AMONG SOLDIERS OF THE RELIEF FORCE.

A GROUP INCLUDING A BABY BOY BORN (ON SEPTEMBER 9) DURING THE SIEGE AND NAMED "ALCAZAR": SERGEANT CONZALEY AND HIS FAMILY IN THE LONG-BELEAGURED FORTRESS.

THE BATTLE FOR MADRID: THE CAPITAL OF SPAIN

MADRID FROM THE SOUTH-WEST: A PANORAMA SHOWING (IN FOREGROUND) LAND WEST OF THE MANZANARES RIVER AND NEAR THE CASA DE CAMPO, WHERE SEVERE FIGHTING RECENTLY OCCURRED: (IN LEFT CENTRE) THE FORMER ROYAL PALACE LATELY BOMBED FROM THE AIR; AND (TO RIGHT OF THE PALACE) HIGH BUILDINGS OF THE GRAN VIA – A GENERAL VIEW OF A CITY THAT PRESENTED A DIFFICULT OBJECTIVE FOR ATTACK, WITH BUILDINGS THAT RISE TIER UPON TIER, CONSTITUTING FORMIDABLE BATTLEMENTS.

It was not until October 20 that the people of Madrid realised to the full the imminent danger they were in; felt the pressure of General Franco's advancing armies; knew the relentlessness of the closing "pincers" movement of the insurgents. On that day the newspapers wrote freely, and the Communist "El Mundo Obrero" declared: "The enemy is at our gates." Then many more men and women volunteered and additional trenches were dug near the city. On the following day women demonstrated against idlers and demanded that Señor Largo Caballero should mobilise the city immediately, shouting in chorus, says the "Daily Telegraph": "All men must work at the front and all women must work at the rear". At long last, in fact, Franco's fighting power was recognised. Two significant things followed. General Franco, sure of his success, decided that white volunteer troops should be the first to enter the capital on its surrender, not Foreign Legionaries or Moors; and on Sunday, October 25, came the assertion, or at least the understanding, that Germany and Italy would recognise the Government of General Franco immediately his troops had captured the capital.

It was announced on November 9 that the Spanish Government had two days previously withdrawn from Madrid to Valencia and that supreme power in Madrid had been vested in a Junta under the presidency of General Miaja. The British Embassy, it was then stated, was still guarded by National Republican Guards, formerly called the Civil Guard. There were about 125 people in the Embassy, including members of the Scottish ambulance, but half the British colony were still at home. On November 4 there was a fierce fight at Getafe, one of Madrid's main aerodromes, which was eventually captured by General Franco's forces. Led by

ON THE VALENCIA ROAD, MADRID'S LAST LINK WITH THE COAST: TWO RED CROSS AMBULANCES AT WORK IN A BURNING VILLAGE SHELLED BY GENERAL FRANCO'S ARTILLERY IN AN ATTEMPT TO CUT THIS LINE OF COMMUNICATION.

tanks, they stormed the trenches, and dynamited a Government armoured train. All the aerodrome buildings were described as being in ruins. A report on the Government side stated that the aerodrome had been evacuated after having been previously rendered useless by dynamite.

In their assault on Madrid General Franco's forces encountered strong opposition, especially along the river Manzanares, the city's western boundary. As recently as November 9 it was reported that they had so far failed to cross the river bridges, despite reckless charges by Moors and prolonged attack by aircraft and artillery. On both banks of the river the Government defenders held an elaborate system of concrete trenches, well provided with machine-guns, while the attacking troops had to cross an open plain dominated by these riverside trenches and buildings beyond. Another account, however, stated that a column had broken through the Government trenches at one point and occupied the Northern Railway Station and the University City. From Madrid, heavy shelling was visible across the Manzanares towards the road to Valencia, the last road then open to connect Madrid with the coast. Vallecas, on this road, was bombed by aircraft.

A Reuter correspondent's message of November 9 stated: "Punctually at 8 a.m. the first shells and the first air-raid sirens sounded simultaneously. The principal targets were Government buildings and the main streets, including the Puerta del Sol (Madrid's Piccadilly Circus), the Gran Via, the Alcala, near the War Office and the Recoletos, the popular boulevard on the eastern side of the city. I watched the bombardment from a roof-top."

MADRID'S FOOD SUPPLIES: SHEEP CROSSING THE TOLEDO BRIDGE (LEADING TO THE CALLE DE TOLEDO AND THE PUERTA DEL SOL) OVER THE RIVER MANZANARES, WHICH WAS DEFENDED BY ELABORATE TRENCHES ON BOTH BANKS.

On the previous day, the "Daily Telegraph" Madrid correspondent had cabled: "This afternoon (November 8), seven insurgent bombers, escorted by four pursuit planes, flew low over Madrid and dropped about ten bombs. I clearly saw the bombs, looking like silver bullets, falling from beneath the planes. All fell in the old part of the town between the Plaza Mayor and the River Manzanares. One is said to have hit the Palace, but not to have exploded. Another exploded near the Palace . . ." The British Chargé d'Affaires in Madrid, Mr. Ogilvie-Forbes, in a report to the Foreign Office in London, stated that the attacking forces had been held up at the Toledo and Segovia bridges across the river, both of which were mined and barricaded.

The parts of Madrid which suffered most from the aerial bombardment by General Franco's Forces and the shelling appeared to be the wealthy quarters round the Retiro Park, the Puerta del Sol (the centre of the city's life), the Gran Via, and, of course, all the western quarters, which were practically in the fighting line. The Gran Via is in ruins. One big department store is reported as having had all its huge plate-glass windows smashed. Cases have occurred where bombs penetrated into the underground railway. Bursts on the streets played havoc with water-mains, as well as with trees and lamp-posts. Added to these was the tearing-up of pavement blocks for use in barricades. The effect of shells and bombs hitting the big blocks of flats, which are as numerous in Madrid as in other modern cities, can only be imagined. A "Times" correspondent quotes the experience of a witness who was in the telephone building during a raid. "The great steel and cement skyscraper shivered like a ship struck by a wave when three large bombs struck the earth almost simultaneously in its vicinity, and a shower of smaller incendiary flares descended on the city like diminutive meteors." Incendiary bombs caused fierce fires in many part of the city.

THE MISERY OF THE MADRID POPULATION UNDER THE CONTINUOUS BOMBARDMENT: HOMELESS FAMILIES LIVING GIPSY LIVES IN THE GRAN VIA UNDERGROUND STATION: WITH A BACKGROUND OF STRIDENT GOVERNMENT AND MARXIST POSTERS.

THE CONVERGING POINT OF THE CIVIL WAR.

A SCENE TYPICAL OF THE DEVASTATION CAUSED IN MANY PARTS OF MADRID BY AIR BOMBS AND GUN-FIRE: RUINS OF A CHURCH COMPLETELY DEMOLISHED IN THE CALLE MENDIZABAL.

Since November 5, inhabitants of Madrid have had to endure practically continuous aerial bombardment and shelling from General Franco's troops – over five weeks of horror and devastation. Many thousands have been evacuated but those that remain, it seems, are now threatened with serious food shortage. It appears that some of the lines are still running services intermittently, a circumstance that can hardly add to the comfort of the wretched refugees. Report states that "by December 1 between one-third and a quarter of the houses of Madrid were estimated to have been destroyed". The tendency to fratermisation between opposing forces in the Civil War that occurred in some parts of Spain on the approach of Christmas did not apparently extend to the capital. At the time of writing, as message from a "Times" correspondent there states: ". . . The hatred is too deep, the issues at stake on either side too divergent for any settlement by negotiations . . ."

THE BURNING OF THE CRYSTAL PALACE: THE MOST SPECTACULAR FIRE SEEN IN BRITAIN FOR MANY YEARS.

THE CELEBRATED HOME OF FIREWORK DISPLAYS ITSELF BECOMES A GIGANTIC PYROTECHNIC "SET PIECE": THE AWE-INSPIRING SPECTACLE OF THE CRYSTAL PALACE ABLAZE FROM END TO END, SENDING UP FLAMES AND GLOWING SMOKE-CLOUDS TO AN ALTITUDE DOUBLE THE HEIGHT OF THE TWO GREAT TERMINAL TOWERS, AND SEEN BY OBSERVERS AS FAR AWAY AS THE DEVIL'S DYKE, NEAR BRIGHTON, AND FROM AN AEROPLANE CROSSING THE CHANNEL NEAR MARGATE, AS WELL AS BY HUNDREDS OF THOUSANDS OF LONDONERS.

THE DESTRUCTION OF ONE OF THE WORLD'S LANDMARKS: THE DRAMA OF THE CRYSTAL PALACE FIRE AT ITS HEIGHT – WATER JETS PLAYING NEAR THE SOUTH TOWER, WHICH THREATENED TO COLLAPSE.

THE TRAGIC END OF THE CRYSTAL PALACE: AN AIR VIEW AFTER THE FIRE, SHOWING THE SOUTH TOWER IN THE FOREGROUND, THE NORTH TOWER IN THE BACKGROUND, AND BETWEEN THEM NOTHING BUT A MASS OF SMOULDERING RUINS.

The Crystal Palace on Sydenham Hill, a landmark famous not only to Londoners but throughout the world, was destroyed by fire on the night of November 30. Only the two great towers, 282 ft. high, one at each end, were eventually left standing above the ruins of the huge structure, which covered 25 acres. The fire broke out about 8 p.m. and spread with astonishing rapidity. Some 500 firemen were engaged, with over ninety fire-fighting appliances – a record for a London fire. At one time it was feared the South Tower might collapse into streets crowded with spectators.

By 3 a.m. on December 1 nothing was left of the Palace but the two lofty towers, one at either end. All the rest of the enormous building, except a portion of roof at the northern end still left in position, had been reduced to a mass of twisted metal, red-hot, and here and there still breaking into flame. During the war, it may be recalled, the Crystal Palace was used as an R.N.V.R. training "ship". It was feared then that it might be bombed, but German airmen have since stated that it was too valuable as a landmark for raiders to be destroyed. After the fire the Air Ministry warned pilots to avoid low flying over the ruins.

FROM KING TO PRINCE AND DUKE OF WINDSOR: A VOYAGE OF TRANSITION.

INSTRUMENT OF ABDICATION

I, Edward the Eighth, of Great Britain, Ireland, and the British Dominions beyond the Seas, King, Emperor of India, do hereby declare My irrevocable determination to renounce the Throne for Myself and for My descendants, and My desire that effect should be given to this Instrument of Abdication immediately.

In token whereof I have hereunto set My hand this tenth day of December, nineteen hundred and thirty six, in the presence of the witnesses whose signatures are subscribed.

SIGNED AT
FORT BELVEDERE
IN THE PRESENCE
OF

ONE OF A NUMBER OF GATHERINGS OUTSIDE BUCKINGHAM PALACE, WHERE SOME LOYAL DEMONSTRATORS FROM THE CITY SANG "GOD SAVE THE KING" AND "HE'S A JOLLY GOOD FELLOW".

(RIGHT), THE INSTRUMENT OF ABDICATION SIGNED BY KING EDWARD VIII, AND WITNESSED BY HIS THREE BROTHERS, THE DUKES OF YORK, GLOUCESTER, AND KENT: A DOCUMENT UNIQUE IN BRITISH IMPERIAL HISTORY.

As recorded in the document itself, this Instrument of Abdication was signed at Fort Belvedere on the morning of December 10, the day on which the announcement was made in Parliament. It will be noted that the Duke of York's signature was "Albert", although as King he has taken the title of George VI. His full Christian names are Albert Frederick Arthur George. Those of the Duke of Gloucester, who signs as "Henry", are Henry William Frederick Albert. The Duke of Kent signed the document as "George", his full names being George Edward Alexander Edmund. After giving the terms of the Instrument in his Message to Parliament, King Edward VIII went on to say: "I deeply appreciate the spirit which has actuated the appeals which have been made to me to take a different decision and I have, before reaching my final determination, most fully pondered over them. But my mind is made up. Moreover, further delay cannot but be most injurious to the peoples whom I have tried to serve as Prince of Wales and as King and whose future happiness and prosperity are the constant wish of my heart."

KING EDWARD AND MRS SIMPSON DURING THEIR CRUISE IN THE YACHT "NAILIN" THIS YEAR: A SNAPSHOT TAKEN AT TROGIR (TRAU), ON THE DALMATION COAST.

MRS. SIMPSON WHEN SHE WAS LIVING IN THE UNITED STATES, THE COUNTRY IN WHICH SHE WAS BORN FORTY YEARS AGO.

AT ASCOT LAST YEAR: KING EDWARD (THEN PRINCE OF WALES) PHOTOGRAPHED WITH MRS. SIMPSON AT THE MOST FASHIONABLE OF ALL RACE MEETINGS.

The life of Mrs. Ernest A. Simpson may be summarised as follows. Born in Baltimore in 1896, daughter of Mr. and Mrs. T. Wallis Warfield, and named Bessie Wallis. Married Lieut. (now Commander) Earl Winfield Spencer, U.S.N., in 1916. Obtained a divorce from him in 1925. Meantime, presented at Court in this country, in 1926. Married Mr. Ernest A. Simpson in London in 1928. First met King Edward (then Prince of Wales) in 1934. This year filed a divorce petition against Mr. Simpson in Ipswich, and was granted a decree nisi on October 27. On December 7 issued at Cannes, through Lord Brownlow, the statement: "Mrs. Simpson, throughout the last few weeks, invariably wished to avoid any action or proposal which would hurt or damage his Majesty or the Throne. Today her attitude is unchanged, and she is willing, if such action would solve the problem, to withdraw forthwith from a situation that has been rendered both unhappy and untenable." On December 11, the day after his abdication, King Edward VIII left his home at Fort Belvedere late at night and motored to Portsmouth, arriving soon after midnight. About 2 a.m. on December 12 he left Portsmouth in the destroyer "Fury" which had been waiting under sealed orders. The "Fury" reached Boulogne at 3.55 p.m. on that day, part of the crossing having been through thick fog. Meantime, at his Accession Council on December 12, King George VI had announced that his first act as Sovereign would be to confer a dukedom on his brother, who would henceforth be known as the Duke of Windsor. The transition from King to Duke may thus be said to have occurred at sea. The Duke of Windsor remained on board the "Fury" at Boulogne till about 8 p.m. when he landed and entered a special Pullman car in the Basle express. His train reached Vienna at 10.15 p.m. on the 13th. Thence he motored to Enzesfeld.

A BRITISH DESTROYER BRINGING THE SELF-EXILED MONARCH (NOW H.R.H. THE DUKE OF WINDSOR) TO FRANCE AFTER HIS ABDICATION: H.M.S. "FURY" ENTERING THE HARBOUR AT BOULOGNE ON DECEMBER 12.

THE ILLUSTRATED LONDON NEWS

"CIVILISED MAN"

This satirical study representing a typical outcome of modern civilisation – Red Cross men in helmets and gas-masks equipped to deal with the effects of man's latest death-dealing invention, the bomb- and gas-dropping aeroplane – is included, under the heading of Pictorial Photography, in the 82nd Annual Exhibition of the Royal Photographic Society of Great Britain in its galleries at 35 Russell Square.

1937

New British defence plans published — Franco fails to capture Madrid and is visited by British M.P.s — captures Malaga and Oviedo — Coronation of King George VI — "Hindenburg" airship disaster — Guernica bombed, reportedly by German aircraft — the "Deutschland" incident — further executions in Russia — Amelia Earhart lost on round world flight — Royal Commission plans partition of Palestine — Japan crosses the Great Wall — Peking abandoned — Tientsin taken — Bilbao and Gijon fall to Franco — piratical attacks on neutral shipping in the Mediterranean attributed to Italian submarines — Treaty of Nyon establishes multinational patrols — Italy a reluctant signatory and attacks cease — Masaryk, the founder of modern Czechoslovakia, dies — Lord Halifax visits Hunting Exhibition in Berlin and talks to German leaders — tragedy in Shanghai as Chinese aircraft drop bombs by mistake in International Settlement killing over 1000 people, mainly Chinese — Japan captures Shanghai and bombs Carton and Nanking — an American gunboat sunk by Japanese troops advancing on Nanking — Italy leaves the League of Nations.

NEWS FROM HOME AND ABROAD:
THE CAMERA AS RECORDER OF RECENT EVENTS.

LAID WITHOUT CEREMONY AT WALKER-ON-TYNE: THE FIRST KEEL-PLATE OF THE BATTLESHIP "KING GEORGE V" LOWERED INTO POSITION.

LAID WITH CEREMONY AT BIRKENHEAD: THE DIRECTOR OF NAVAL CONSTRUCTION DRIVING IN THE FIRST RIVET OF THE "PRINCE OF WALES".

The Washington and London Naval Treaties, prohibiting the building of capital ships, expired on January 1. Immediately the keel-plates of the two new battle-ships "King George V" and the "Prince of Wales" were laid at naval yards in Walker-on-Tyne and Birkenhead, respectively. The ships will be of 35,000 tons, carrying a main armament of 14-in. guns. Their estimated speed will be 30 knots and will take 3 years to build.

ORDERED LAST YEAR BY THE ADMIRALTY: SUPERMARINE "WALRUS": A BOAT-HULLED TYPE OF AMPHIBIAN WITH FOLDING WINGS.

The Supermarine "Walrus", its metal constructed, with Pegasus air-cooled engine and folding wings for economy in stowage space. An extensive series of Service trials, which continued for over a year, were carried out.

A TANK DEMONSTRATION LAST MAY BEFORE FOREIGN ATTACHÉS AT LULWORTH: A DETACHMENT COMING INTO ACTION AGAINST MOBILE TARGETS WITH THREE-POUNDERS AND MACHINE-GUNS.

MANOEUVRES WHICH PROVED SINGAPORE "INVULNERABLE".

THE COMBINED LAND, SEA, AND AIR MANŒUVRES AT SINGAPORE, WHICH, IT IS CLAIMED, PROVED THAT THIS GREAT NEW BRITISH BASE IN THE EAST IS IMPREGNABLE BY DIRECT SEA ATTACK; AN ANTI-AIRCRAFT DETACHMENT WATCHING FOR "ENEMY" AEROPLANES IN OPEN COUNTRY AT DAWN, NEAR PADIR.

The recent large-scale land, air, and sea manœuvres at Singapore, appear to have demonstrated that this base is practically invulnerable to direct sea attacks. The plan of the operations, which lasted three days, and were taken part in by 30,000 men of the Navy, in twenty-five warships, 90 warplanes, and 7000 troops on land, was a sudden attack on the base by a hitherto friendly State. This imaginary State, situated 1200 miles south-east of Singapore, had a small but efficient fleet. There was no declaration of war, but Singapore warned the fleet that it if approached within 200 miles it would be regarded as a hostile act. On the second day air patrols located enemy ships within the 200-miles' limit, and small parties were landed from destroyers. These were adjudged to have been repelled with heavy loss. The operations were confined to an air combat on the third day. That

night landing parties got ashore at several points on the coast-line, but before daylight the defenses had got the upper hand. The invading transports were bombed and torpedoed from the air, and in the end the attacking fleet retired under cover of smoke screens after engagements with the guns of the fortress. The fleet defending Singapore ("Red Land") consisted only of the 15-in. monitor "Terror", four destroyers, and four submarines. They were heavily outnumbered by the "Blue Land" fleet consisting of the heavy cruisers "Cumberland" and "Dorsetshire", the aircraft-carrier "Hermes", five destroyers and six submarines. The attack was led by Vice-Admiral Sir Charles Little, C.-in-C. China Station.

THE PRICE OF PEACE – £1,500,000,000: BRITISH DEFENCE PLANS VISUALISED.

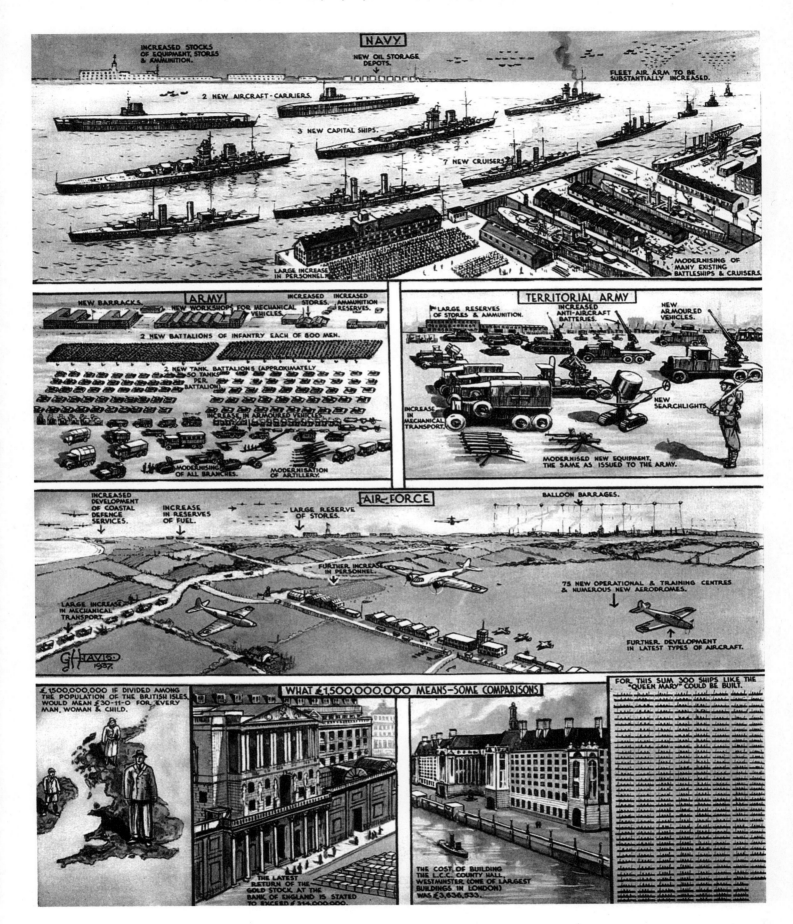

DETAILS OF THE GOVERNMENT'S FIVE-YEAR DEFENCE SCHEME, AS AFFECTING THE NAVY, ARMY AND AIR FORCE, IN PICTORIAL FORM: THE CHIEF EXPENSES; WITH COMPARISONS TO INDICATE THE PURCHASING POWER OF £1,500,000,000.

Our artist shows here, in pictorial form, the main items of the Government's defence plans affecting the three fighting Services, with some interesting comparisons indicating what could be done in other ways with £1,500,000,000 the sum mentioned in the White Paper (issued on February 16) as the contemplated "total expenditure on defence during the next five years". On the 11th, it may be recalled, the Chancellor of the Exchequer (Mr. Neville Chamberlain) had announced in Parliament that the Government proposed to raise £400,000,000 of the amount required by borrowing. On the 17th Mr. Chamberlain moved a resolution to give effect to the Government's programme, which he frankly admitted was unprecedented in time of peace. In the course of his speech he said: "The White Paper shows where and how the cost is going to be incurred . . . Even this figure of £1,500,000,000 cannot be regarded as final for certain. If circumstances should change and allow us to slow down or reduce our programme, all the better; we shall be thankful enough to do it. On the other hand, as conditions have changed to our disadvantage since we first contemplated this programme, they may change again, and it may be that in the end we shall find that even £1,500,000,000 has not represented the total amount that this country has been compelled to spend." Later, Mr. Chamberlain declared: "This is a measure for the preservation of peace . . . Everybody knows that the British Empire stands for peace, and that it never will use its forces for aggressive purposes. On the contrary, it will exert all its influence to preserve peace not only for itself but for others as well."

CHRISTMAS IN SPAIN: FRANCO'S AND GOVERNMENT TROOPS.

GENERAL FRANCO'S ARTILLERY AT WORK AFTER A HEAVY SNOW-STORM: STEEL-HELMETED GUNNERS
GETTING A BATTERY OF FIELD-GUNS INTO POSITION AT NOVACERRADA, FOR A FRESH ATTACK ON
MADRID.

WINTER CONDITIONS ON THE GOVERNMENT SIDE OF THE LINE: MEN AT THEIR MEAGRE DINNER
ROUND A PIONEER'S "TABLE" PHOTOGRAPHED IN THE VALDEMURO-PINTO SECTOR.

Central Spain is notorious for its violent extremes of temperature. Heat and dust in summer, icy winds in winter have wrecked many military enterprises in the history of the Peninsula. The Madrid country is no exception. The sufferings of the men of both sides in the recent fighting can be imagined by all who had experience of trench warfare on the Western front; due account being taken of the fact that, in Spain, the men are probably very much worse equipped – with the exception of General Franco's German "volunteers". There seems no doubt that these troops are being embodied in the insurgent forces in very large numbers. A total of five divisions has been mentioned. Italian "volunteers", it would appear, are much less numerous, but both the German, Italian, Portuguese and Russian Governments are being urged by Britain and France to stop the departure of their nationals as "volunteers" for Spain.

MADRID'S ORDEAL –
33 AIR RAIDS IN 10 WEEKS!

SEARCHING FOR PERSONAL BELONGINGS: PARTY OF HOMELESS *MADRILEÑOS.*

AFTER AN AIR RAID: BODIES LYING IN THE STREET AND RESCUE CARS AT WORK.

Recent accounts of conditions in Madrid state that, since the Government's removal to Valencia, and with the gradual evacuation of civilians, the capital has become, politically, a backwater, though life goes on despite air raids and bombardment. The ruins caused by bomb and shell are cleared away almost as quickly as the human victims are picked up and removed to hospital. In an earlier report a "Times" correspondent there wrote: "Madrid has suffered 33 aerial bombardments in 10 weeks, a unique and unenviable record for a great city. This represents a total of some 50 tons of high explosive, besides the daily shelling from the enemy at the gates

. . . Madrid has not yet been and let us hope never will be gassed . . . Modern bombs cut through seven-storey houses like cheese . . . A vast quantity of incendiary bombs has been showered on Madrid. Except in certain cases . . . they have not proved effective. In one of the night raids the Prado Gallery was hit by nine incendiary bombs, without much damage beyond broken glass. Three heavy bombs that made huge holes in the roadway near the building would have wrecked it had they fallen on top. Thanks to the foresight of the Government the art treasures had been removed."

A RUSSIAN TANK, CAPABLE OF 12 M.P.H., CAPTURED BY FRANCO'S MEN NEAR MADRID: A WEAPON WHICH, IT IS STATED, IS
BEING COMBATED WITH LIGHTED PETROL; WITH OTHER TANKS UNDER TARPAULINS.

WITH THE BRITISH M.P.'S
WHO VISITED
FRANCO'S FORCES

The photograph reproduced here was taken by Mr. Harold Mitchell (Conservative M.P. for Brentford and Chiswick) while visiting the country controlled by General Franco in Spain. Salient facts which struck a visiting Englishman, while behind General Franco's lines, were enumerated in an extremely interesting article by Mr. Anthony Crossley (Conservative M.P. for Stretford) recently printed in the "Manchester Guardian". In this he noted that there were now few Moors left in General Franco's army; but that the Spanish Foreign Legion is as impressive a force as ever. Of war materials General Franco has German guns and tanks, Italian light tanks, German bombing aeroplanes (slow, and probably out of date) and good Italian fighting machines. The Government has Russian bombers and fighters, both very fast; Russian tanks which, it seems, can easily be destroyed at close quarters, but carry a good gun; Czechoslovak rifles and French ammunition. Mr. Mitchell writes that the captured tank (stated to be Russian) seen in his photograph has a speed of 12 m.p.h., which makes it difficult for artillery to knock it out. "The method of dealing with tanks", he writes, "is for a man to creep up near and hurl a bottle of petrol at the rubber on the caterpillar wheels, followed by a bomb. The fire which follows usually destroys the rubber and immobilises the tank. Also the heat inside is such that the men are usually forced to come out."

THE FALL OF MALAGA: A DRAMATIC CHANGE IN SPANISH CIVIL WAR AFTER LONG WINTER QUIESCENCE.

WITH THE SPANISH FLAG FLYING AS A SIGN OF VICTORY: TROOPS OF GENERAL FRANCO'S ARMY ENCAMPED NEAR MALAGA, WHOSE CAPTURE CAUSED GREAT ENTHUSIASM.

MEN TO WHOM THE ARRIVAL OF THE INSURGENT FORCES BROUGHT LIBERTY: REJOICING IN THE STREETS OF MALAGA.

Malaga was occupied by General Franco's forces, under General Queipo de Llano, supported by the fleet, on February 8. A message from Gibraltar reported that the Government militia defending various approaches to Malaga had retreated "in panic" on the previous night, and in the morning white flags were flying over the city in sign of surrender, whereupon the Nationalist troops marched in "almost without incident". According to the Government reports, on the other hand, their troops "fought heroically against great odds" and "retired in good order to new positions". In a personal account written on the 8th near the scene of action, Mr.

Christopher Martin stated (in the "Daily Telegraph"): "Hardly a shot was fired in the capture of Malaga, for the Government defenders realised that their position was hopeless. I understand that the Defence Committee of Malaga tried to escape to sea, but were intercepted by General Franco's warships, which now control the harbour . . . Nationalists make no secret that they intend to deal with the utmost severity the Government leaders, who are said to have put to death 6000 people in Malaga during their seven months' occupation of the city."

WITH THE HARD-FIGHTING ASTURIAN MINERS AT OVIEDO: THE FAMOUS 'DINAMITEROS'

WITH THE FAMOUS DYNAMITE SQUADS FORMED FROM ASTURIAN MINERS AT OVIEDO: LIGHTING THE FUSE OF A CRUDE BOMB WITH A CIGARETTE.

THE RENEWED STRUGGLE FOR OVIEDO: ASTURIAN MINERS, WHO CONSTITUTE A LARGE PART OF THE GOVERNMENT FORCES, FIGHTING IN THE SAN LAZARO QUARTER.

Desperate fighting again broke out round Oviedo, the mining centre in the Asturias, on February 21. The Asturian miners, who had clung to the districts round the city since it was relieved by General Franco's forces early in the winter, tried to create a diversion to draw troops away from Madrid. The Valencia authorities persistently stated that the miners were gaining ground in their attacks. The Government forces were described as fighting with armoured cars through the suburbs. Bomb-throwing figured largely in the house-to-house advance. On February 26 the position (according to reports from Valencia via Bilbao and Gijon) was that some of the surrounding heights were in Government hands and that a battle had raged all day for the San Lazaro quarter, lying to the south of the inner city, part of which was reported to have been taken. Here tanks were used for mopping up machine-gun nests. It was claimed that the insurgents in Oviedo were practically cut off

from their own forces to the South. Basque troops were fighting by the side of the Asturian miners with their famous squads of "dynamiters"; while, on the other side, the insurgents organised their own bombing units. All the reports of Government advances were contradicted by the insurgents. General Aranda, the insurgent commander in Oviedo, issued a denial of February 27 that the attackers had made any material progress, and even stated that at certain points his own men had advanced their positions. At Salamanca, General Franco's headquarters, it was estimated that the Government forces had suffered more than 15,000 casualties in the earlier stages of the fighting, while General Aranda's casualties amounted to some 3500 dead and several thousand wounded.

THE FLOODS IN AMERICA: PROTECTIVE DYNAMITE; DESTRUCTIVE FIRE.

DYNAMITING A MISSISSIPPI LEVEE TO DRAIN OFF FLOOD-WATER INTO A PRE-ARRANGED AREA OF LOW-LYING LAND TO RELIEVE PRESSURE ON THE THREATENED TOWN OF CAIRO AT THE MISSISSIPPI-OHIO CONFLUENCE.

DURING THE GREAT FLOODS ON THE OHIO, IN WHICH OVER 400 PEOPLE PERISHED AND A MILLION WERE RENDERED HOMELESS: A CITY THAT SUFFERED ALSO FROM FIRES CAUSED BY IGNITED OIL FLOATING ON THE WATER.

DEBRIS OF THE FLOOD SWIRLING ROUND A GENERAL STORE. IN PORTSMOUTH, OHIO, A TOWN WHICH WAS PARTIALLY FLOODED BY THE AUTHORITIES TO RELIEVE PRESSURE ON THE RIVER WALLS.

As a result of the floods in the United States, a million people are homeless and, in the majority of cases, destitute. The extent of the damage and the amount of land inundated can be easily visualised, but the suffering and hopeless condition of these people is not so readily understood. As the Ohio River rose they passed sleepless nights, fearing that at any moment a levee would break and drive them to the higher floors of their houses to wait, perhaps for hours, for rescue. Added to this was the dread of some deadly epidemic breaking out.

A NURSE INOCULATING CHILDREN IN KENTUCKY AGAINST TYPHOID FEVER, WHICH IT WAS FEARED MIGHT RESULT FROM THE LACK OF CLEAN DRINKING WATER AND THE FLOODING OF THE SEWERS.

A TEXAS SCHOOL DESTROYED BY EXPLOSION WITH OVER 450 LIVES:

AFTER THE HEART-RENDERING CATASTROPHE AT THE LONDON CONSOLIDATED SCHOOL, NEW LONDON, TEXAS, THE WORLD'S LARGEST RURAL SCHOOL, WHERE THE MAIN BUILDING COLLAPSED ON SOME SEVEN HUNDRED CHILDREN: THE SCENE DURING THE REMOVAL OF WRECKAGE AND THE SEARCH FOR THE BODIES OF VICTIMS.

No more terrible disaster is recorded in the annals of education than that which occurred, on March 18, at the London Consolidated School at New London, Texas, when a terrific explosion, attributed by some to a gas heating system, destroyed the main building which collapsed upon its 700 occupants. The death-roll was given on March 21 as 455, mostly children, but including also some 17 teachers. The number of injured was estimated at nearly 100. The institution is described as the largest rural school in the world for, although New London itself is a comparatively small place, it served a number of other towns and villages in the East Texas oilfields, among them Overton, Shilch, Longview, Tyler and Kilgore. The disaster happened only ten minutes before the pupils were due to be dismissed. The force of the explosion pushed the walls outward and the roof of the two-storey structure fell in. The district was placed under martial law and more than a thousand men worked all night clearing the wreckage and searching for bodies. Scores of doctors and nurses and over 100 ambulances arrived from neighbouring towns and were joined by Red Cross workers.

THE WORLD'S LARGEST AIRSHIP A BLAZING WRECK

THE FIRST PHASE OF THE CATASTROPHE, A TERRIFIC EXPLOSION AT THE AFTER END OF THE HUGE ZEPPELIN AS SHE APPROACHED THE MOORING-MAST AT LAKEHURST.

BELOW: THE FORE PART OF THE BLAZING WRECK, SINKING TO THE EARTH, WITH FUGITIVES DIMLY VISIBLE (IN THE LEFT BACKGROUND).

After the destruction of the great German airship "Hindenburg", which exploded while mooring on arrival at Lakehurst, New Jersey, some fifty miles from New York, on May 6, it was announced that the United States Government would hold investigations into the cause of the disaster. Meanwhile Germany sent to New York a special commission of experts, under Dr. Hugo Eckener, the airship's designer and former commander and chairman of the Zeppelin Company. An official statement gave the total number of people aboard the "Hindenburg" as 97 (61 crew and 36 passengers) and the number of dead and missing as 20 crew, 11 passengers and one groundsman. Further deaths occurred among the injured, and the total of dead was given later as 35. It will be realised that the "Hindenburg" had been cruising round for about an hour, owing to a thunderstorm, before approaching the mooring-mast, and that when she did so, as the weather improved, a terrific explosion occurred at the after end of the airship which crashed in flames. The news aroused strong sympathy in this country, and the King sent a message of condolence to Herr Hitler. It was officially announced in Berlin on May 9 that all services of the "Graf Zeppelin" would be suspended pending an enquiry by General Göring, the Air Minister, into the fate of the "Hindenburg". It was reported also that he had ordered the speeding-up of the construction of her successor, to be finished this autumn, and that three more airships would then be built. The "Hindenburg" was the largest airship in the world, and had safely accommplished 10 Transatlantic flights. The "Graf Zeppelin", half her size, has crossed the Atlantic 90 times between Germany and Brazil. Dr. Eckener was reported to have said that henceforth airships must use the non-inflammable gas, helium, instead of hydrogen. Helium has less lifting power and is more expensive.

THE CORONATION OF HIS MAJESTY KING GEORGE THE SIXTH

THE ROYAL FAMILY IN CORONATION DRESS: A HISTORIC PORTRAIT GROUP. FROM LEFT TO RIGHT ARE SEEN THE PRINCESS ROYAL, THE DUCHESS OF GLOUCESTER, THE DUKE OF GLOUCESTER, QUEEN MARY, THE KING, PRINCESS MARGARET, PRINCESS ELIZABETH, THE QUEEN, THE DUKE OF KENT, THE DUCHESS OF KENT, AND QUEEN MAUD OF NORWAY, SISTER OF KING GEORGE V.

THE CEREMONY IN THE ABBEY

THE RETURN TO THE PALACE

His Majesty King George the Sixth was crowned in Westminster Abbey on May, by the Archbishop of Canterbury. After the Crowning and Inthronization of the King, homage was done to him by the Lords Spiritual and Temporal. Later the Overseas contingents marched at the head of the return procession from the Palace. First came the Colonial Contingent, then the Burma Contingent, then the contingents of Southern Rhodesia and Newfoundland, then the South African contingent, followed by those of New Zealand, Australia, Canada and India. There were also detachments of the King's Own Malta Regiment, the Bermuda Militia and Channel Islands units in the procession. Mounted escorts from Southern Rhodesia, India, South Africa, New Zealand, Australia and Canada accompanied the representatives of these countries.

(RIGHT), FORCES OF THE EMPIRE IN THE PROCESSIONS: (ABOVE) THE ROYAL CANADIAN MOUNTED POLICE; REPRESENTATIVES OF INDIAN REGIMENTS PASSING THROUGH ADMIRALTY ARCH; (BELOW) AUSTRALIAN TROOPS.

THE FLEET ILLUMINATED
IN HONOUR OF THE CORONATION REVIEW BY THE KING.

THE SPLENDID SPECTACLE OF RED, WHITE AND BLUE ROCKETS BURSTING HIGH IN THE AIR IN FIERY SHOWERS ABOVE LINES OF WARSHIPS PICKED OUT WITH LIGHT. A GENERAL VIEW OF THE FLEET'S
DISPLAY ON THE EVENING OF THE ROYAL REVIEW AT SPITHEAD.

AN UNPRECEDENTED SCOTTISH OVATION
FOR THE KING AND QUEEN.

EDINBURGH'S GREAT WELCOME TO KING GEORGE VI. AND QUEEN ELIZABETH, THE FIRST SCOTTISH
QUEEN GREETED THERE SINCE MARY STUART IN 1561: THE ROYAL CARRIAGE PASSING THE SCOTT
MONUMENT IN PRINCES STREET.

The King and Queen were received with the utmost enthusiasm in Edinburgh, where they arrived at Princes Street Station at 10 a.m. on July 5 for their Coronation visit to Scotland. After the King had received the keys of the city from the Lord Provost, and had handed them back according to custom, their Majesties, accompanied by Princess Elizabeth and Princess Margaret, drove to Holyroodhouse in an open landau drawn by four Windsor greys, with an escort of the Royal Scots Greys and the Scottish horse. Not since Mary Queen of Scots landed at Leith in 1561 had Edinburgh greeted a Scottish Queen.

DRAGONS PARADE TO HONOUR THE KING:
REJOICINGS IN HONG KONG.

THE CHINESE CORONATION PROCESSION IN HONG KONG: CUNNINGLY CONSTRUCTED DRAGONS MAKING THEIR TORTUOUS WAY THROUGH THE NARROW, CROWDED STREETS, TO PERFORM EVOLUTIONS ON THE LAWN OF GOVERNMENT HOUSE.

The Coronation of King George VI. was celebrated in Hong Kong not only by a combined review of the Army, Navy and Air Force at Happy Valley, where the salute was taken by the Acting Governor, but also by the Chinese population. Their rejoicings took the form of a procession of dragons winding their way through the narrow streets, to perform complicated evolutions on the lawn of Government House. There were some 500,000 spectators. At night the ships lying off the mainland, including H.M.S. "Eagle" which had arrived two days before, were outlined with electric lights, forming an impressive spectacle.

MADRID IN THE FIGHTING LINE: IN THE INTERNATIONAL BRIGADE'S SECTOR.

The "International Brigade" has played a prominent part in the defence of Madrid. It consists of anti-Fascists from all over Europe. It was formerly commanded by General Kleber, the "Saviour of Madrid", who was of French-Canadian extraction and had experience of organising Communist forces in Germany and China. Less, however, has been heard of General Kleber recently. The Brigade is stated to be composed of French, Germans, Poles, Italians and British. It includes not a few veterans of the Great War. The Germans and the Italians are, of course, anti-Fascist exiles. Many of the latter, it is alleged, have been induced to volunteer for service in Spain by the promises of French Left Wing authorities to obtain French nationalisation papers for them as a reward. The British contingent of the Brigade is apparently represented by the "Saklatvala" battalion (named after the Indian who was at one time Communist M.P. for Battersea), according to the reports of some prisoners taken not long ago by General Franco's forces. A statement issued by the Lancashire Committee of the Communist Party pointed out that over a hundred men had gone from Lancashire to serve in the International Brigade. The Brigade seems to have repeatedly given a very good account of itself, and, notably, played a large part in stopping the last of General Franco's offensives against Madrid. One account said that only 80 men survived out of the 650 in the British battalion after this battle.

(LEFT), THE INTERNATIONAL BRIGADE IN THE DESOLATED OUTSKIRTS OF MADRID: TWO MEN OF THIS FAMOUS VOLUNTEER FORCE, WHICH INCLUDED THE ENGLISH "SAKLATVALA" BATTALION SQUATTING BESIDE A BARRICADE.

GUERNICA DESTROYED

THE DESTRUCTION OF GUERNICA, AN INCIDENT IN THE SPANISH WAR WHICH HAS AROUSED THE WORLD'S SYMPATHY AND STARTED A FIERCE CONTROVERSY: STREETS IN THE LITTLE TOWN, FORMERLY THE CAPITAL OF THE BASQUES; SHOWING THE UTTER HAVOC WROUGHT.

Guernica, the little town near Bilbao, which is the focus of Basque patriotism, was laid in ruins during the operations on the Basque front. The Basques asserted that it was destroyed by systematic bombardment from the air, in the course of which non-combatants attempting to escape were machine-gunned. Eye-witnesses came forward claiming to have seen machines of German type bombing the town. General Franco's headquarters, however, strongly denied that aeroplanes of his forces had been responsible, asserting that the havoc was the work of "Red" elements fighting with the Basques. The matter has aroused much controversy in this country, in Germany, Italy and even, to a certain extent, in the United States.

400 CHILD REFUGEES UNDER CANVAS IN ENGLAND

BASQUE GIRLS ENJOYING THEIR FIRST MEAL IN CAMP AT NORTH STONEHAM.

The evacuation of children, old men and women from Bilbao, in order to save these helpless non-combatants from air-raids and shelling, has met with almost universal approval, although it has been called by General Franco "a Russian ruse to get rid of the population so as to wreak destruction in the city". France has already proved an asylum for many thousands, and the National Joint Committee for Spanish Relief arranged to evacuate 4000 children to England. The Spanish Compañía Transatlantica liner "Habana" was commissioned to take them to Southampton, where she arrived on May 23. Meanwhile, volunteers had prepared a camp at North Stoneham, seven miles from the city, where the children will be housed until other arrangements are made.

THE "DEUTSCHLAND" BOMBED AND ALMERIA BOMBARDED BY THE GERMANS.

The German Note to the Non-Intervention Committee stated: "On Saturday, May 29, the armoured vessel "Deutschland" was peacefully at anchor in the roadstead of Iviza . . . Bombs were suddenly dropped by two aeroplanes of the Red Valencia authorities . . . Twenty-two dead and 83 wounded were the result of this assault. The attack came entirely as a surprise. The ship had not fired at the aeroplanes. In retaliation for the criminal assault . . . German vessels this morning shelled the fortified port of Almeria." Announcing these events in Parliament Mr Eden said that about twenty badly wounded German seamen from the "Deutschland" were being cared for in the military hospital at Gibraltar. In a Note to the League Council the Valencia Government gave a different version of the affair, stating that their aeroplanes were first fired on by a German warship at Iviza and "retaliated by bombing the aggressor vessel". The Note said later: "A cruiser and four destroyers fired 200 shots at Almeria. Thirty-five buildings have been entirely destroyed. Up to the present, 19 dead have been found among the ruins."

(RIGHT), MEMBERS OF THE CREW OF THE GERMAN "POCKET BATTLESHIP" "DEUTSCHLAND" (BOMBED AT IVIZA) SUN-BATHING ON DECK: A SCENE WHILE THE SHIP WAS ON PATROL DUTY OFF THE COAST OF SPAIN.

THE GREAT MASSED TANK PARADE IN PARIS

The Fête Nationale was celebrated with the traditional military review in Paris on July 14. The Algerian and Moroccan cavalry provided a splendidly picturesque spectacle, but the greatest interest was centred in the aeroplanes and tanks. Squadrons of bombers and fighters flew by in close formation. No fewer than 500 aeroplanes, in groups of seven, passed at great speed over the roofs. The roar of their engines was succeeded by the tremendous din of the mechanised forces as they went by. These included motor machine-gun detachments, tractors with infantry, anti-aircraft guns, wireless lorries; and then mechanised artillery of different calibres. The procession was completed by about 200 tanks.

THE GERMAN AIR FORCE AND ITS METHODS OF TRAINING: INGENIOUS DEVICES FOR INSTRUCTION IN BOMB DROPPING AND MACHINE-GUN FIRE.

THE BOMB-AIMING PRACTICE METHOD: A CARPET, REPRESENTING A LAND SURFACE, MOVING ON ROLLERS AT THE SPEED AT WHICH THE AEROPLANE WOULD FLY.

THE MECHANICAL ARM IN THE MILITARY PARADE IN PARIS ON THE FOURTEENTH OF JULY: TANKS PAINTED IN CAMOUFLAGE COLOURS, ON THE MOVE IN REVIEW ORDER.

A GERMAN FIGHTER AT FIRING PRACTICE: THE MACHINE DIVING ON TO GROUND TARGETS – AN OPERATION IN WHICH THE MARKSMAN HAS A FEW FRACTIONS OF A SECOND IN WHICH TO HIT THE MARK, AND RISE CLEAR OF THE EARTH.

THE MASSED MECHANIZED FORCES IN THE FOURTEENTH OF JULY REVIEW IN PARIS: ARMOURED CARS, LIGHT TANKS AND MOTOR CYCLISTS DRAWN UP, WAITING TO PROCEED.

These photographs, recently to hand from Germany, show the methods of instruction now in use in the German Air Force. An explanatory note supplied with the illustrations states: "Germany is training her Air Force at full pressure, and bringing her 'planes up to date in every detail. Her bombers are large, heavy, and usually fitted with several motors; they all carry a crew of several men, and are equipped with instruments which enable them to fly in all weathers, day and night, open or blind. Each man of the crew has his special duties, but each must be thoroughly trained at the machine-gun, bombing and sighting, so as to be able to carry out attack or defence with equal efficiency. These bombers have two tasks: fighting other 'planes in the air with machine-guns and bombing the enemy territory beneath them. There is no doubt that Germany today has an extremely efficient Air Force. She believes that any future was must be, primarily, a war in the air and she acts accordingly."

A LITTLE-KNOWN ELEMENT IN THE SPANISH CIVIL WAR: VOLUNTEERS FROM AMERICA, CUBA AND THE PHILIPPINES.

A MACHINE-GUN POST OF THE AMERICAN "LINCOLN" BATTALION WITH THE GOVERNMENT FORCES: STEEL-HELMETED MACHINE-GUNNERS ON THE LOOK-OUT IN THEIR TRENCHES.

The above photographs, which have been supplied to us by an Amsterdam agency known as Associated Correspondents of the Press, are accompanied by descriptive notes in which it is stated: "Among the innumerable volunteers in the International Brigade on the side of the Spanish Government, in the Civil war in Spain, is the Battalion of American Volunteers, to which belong North Americans, South Americans, Cubans, Mexcians and men from the Philippine Islands. Every three days the volunteers in the first line are withdrawn and other battalions take their place for the next three days. Behind the lines, the American Battalion has a ground for games and sports. From time to time a political instructor visits each formation of the Government's army to tell the troops about the meaning of the war, and the feeling among the Spanish people and in the world generally. One of the most important factors on the Government side is the employment of propagandists, who go into the front lines with megaphones and call across No Man's Land to the rebels, appealing to them to come over. All the photographs were taken with the American Battalion on the Motata front on July 12."

THE FALL OF BILBAO: THE MUCH-TRIED CITY AFTER THE ENTRY OF GENERAL FRANCO'S FORCES

PROPAGANDA BETWEEN THE OPPOSING LINES: A CUBAN WITH THE AMERICAN BATTALION APPEALING TO NATIONALIST TROOPS TO COME OVER TO THE GOVERNMENT.

MADRID IN THE FIRING LINE: SHELLS – AND NONCHALANCE.

THE FALL OF BILBAO: A PEACEFUL STREET SCENE AFTER THE BLOODLESS OCCUPATION OF THE CITY BY GENERAL FRANCO'S TROOPS AND TANKS, ONE OF WHICH IS SEEN ON THE LEFT.

IN THE PUERTA DEL SOL – STILL THRONGED ON SUNDAYS – AFTER A SHELL HAD FALLEN: A GROUP OF PASSERS-BY DISCUSSING THE EVENT.

General Franco's forces entered Bilbao on June 19 and received the submission of some 1200 Basque militiamen, who had taken control of the city and hoisted the white flag, after driving out Asturian and Anarchist extremists bent on house-to-house resistance. No shots were fired, and the entry was made in such a way as to reassure the population and show that they had nothing to fear. Thousands of men, women, and children were gathered in the streets to cheer the victors, and there was general relief that the miseries of the siege had ended. When Nationalist officers entered in small groups they found themselves welcomed as friends by the crowds, who organised impromptu processions in their honour. Later, some tanks and armoured cars drove into the Old Town, a detachment of the "Black Arrow" brigade came in from Las Arenas, and a battalion of Requests and Falangists. People could be seen munching bread given them by soldiers.

DIVIDED PALESTINE: NEW STATES PLANNED BY THE ROYAL COMMISSION

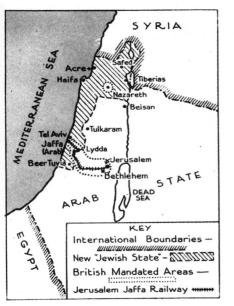

THE PROPOSED NEW DIVISION OF PALESTINE: A SKETCH MAP SHOWING THE PROBABLE RECOMMENDATIONS OF THE ROYAL COMMISSION.

The recently issued Report of the Palestine Royal Commission recommends the division of the country into three parts – (1) an Arab State, including Transjordan: (2) a Jewish State: and (3) territory under permanent mandate to Britain, including the Holy Cities of Jerusalem, Bethlehem and Nazareth. This mandatory enclave, held as "a sacred trust of civilisation", would afford free access from Jaffa to those cities, and to the Sea of Galilee. The Report shows many advantages both to Jews and Arabs under the scheme, but each side has raised certain objections. Some Arabs complain that the Report offers the Arab State nothing but rock and desert, and leaves between 300,000 and 400,000 of their people outside it, while the valuable Arab orange groves south of Jaffa would be handed over to the Jews. They also contend that the Arab State will be cut off from direct access to the sea, minimising their possession of Jaffa and the use offered them of Haifa. The Arabs also dispute the need of a permanent British Mandate over the Holy Places.

JERUSALEM FROM THE AIR, WITH THE TEMPLE AREA AND THE DOME OF THE ROCK (IN FOREGROUND); THE HEART OF THE HOLY LAND, IN THE PROPOSED MANDATE AREA.

The Jews likewise found fault with the Report and one Hebrew paper, commenting on the exclusion of Jerusalem from the Jewish State termed it "Zionism without Zion". Other Jewish complaints were that the area alloted to the Jews, only one-fifth of Palestine affords insufficient scope for immigration: that the Jordan Power Station and the Dead Sea Potash Works, two most important Jewish enterprises, are included in the Arab area.

FURTHER EXECUTIONS OF RED ARMY LEADERS REPORTED.

| GENERAL PUTNA | GENERAL YAKIR | MARSHAL TUKHACHEVSKY | GENERAL UBOREVICH | GENERAL KORK |

SENTENCED TO DEATH ON CHARGES OF ESPIONAGE AND HIGH TREASON: PROMINENT RED ARMY LEADERS WHO HAVE BEEN EXECUTED.

On June 11 Marshal Tukhachevsky and Generals Yakir, Uborevich, Kork, Eidemann, Putna Feldman and Primakoff, of the Soviet Army, were condemned to death by the supreme military court in Moscow on charges of espionage and high treason. The sentences have since been carried out in secret. Marshal Tukhachevsky was a former Assistant Commissar for Defence. He was to have attended the Coronation, but was prevented by a chill. General Yakir recently took over the Leningrad command. General Kork was Commandant of the Military Academy, General Uborevich was G.O.C. of Minsk, Western Command. General Putna, formerly Military Attaché in London, had been imprisoned for ten months, having been implicated in the Zinoviev trial. General Primakoff was reported to have been arrested last November. It is stated that the accused confessed to betraying the military secrets of Russia to a neighbouring State.

MISS AMELIA EARHART MISSING: SHIPS OF THREE NATIONS SEARCH.

THE FIRST WOMAN TO FLY THE ATLANTIC SOLO REPORTED MISSING IN THE PACIFIC: AMELIA EARHART (MRS. PUTNAM).

MISS EARHART WITH HER NAVIGATOR, CAPTIAN NOONAN (LEFT): A PHOTOGRAPH TAKEN AT KARACHI, WHILE THEY WERE ON THEIR WORLD FLIGHT.

Hope for the safety of Miss Amelia Earhart (Mrs. G.P. Putnam) and her navigator, Captain Fred Noonan, was revived by the news that a radio signal from them had been received at Honolulu on July 5, after a message had been transmitted asking them to reply by a given signal, whereby it was hoped to locate them. Later the U.S. coastguard cutter "Itasca", searching for the missing 'plane, reported having received signals giving its call letters. This message was also said to have been received on Howland Island, towards which the 'plane had been flying when it ran short of fuel. Meanwhile, the biggest air rescue expedition on record was on its way to the vicinity – the battleship "Colorado", carrying three 'planes, the aircraft-carrier "Lexington", with fifty-four 'planes, and four destroyers. Japanese warships and fishing vessels also joined in the search. On July 6 it was stated that the "Itasca", the British steamer "Moorby" and an American minesweeper had reached the position indicated by signals but found no trace of the missing 'plane. Miss Earhart and Captain Noonan left Lae, New Guinea, for Howland Island on the last stage of her round-the-world flight and were last heard of on July 2, when a radio message was received stating they were a hundred miles from the Island and could not sight land.

LITTLE MORE THAN A SANDBANK IN THE VAST PACIFIC: HOWLAND ISLAND, TO WHICH MISS EARHART WAS FLYING WHEN SHE DISAPPEARED.

Howland Island is little more than a sandbank in the vast expanse of the Pacific. It appears that no aeroplane has ever alighted there, although it was hoped to use it as a base on the Hawaii-Australia service.

NEWS PICTURES OF SPECIAL INTEREST.

THE NEW "HOUSE OF GERMAN ART" INAUGURATED BY HERR HITLER AT MUNICH: THE IMPOSING BUILDING ON THE SITE OF THE OLD "GLASS PALACE".

THE "NORMANDIE" REGAINS THE BLUE RIBAND OF THE ATLANTIC: THE GREAT FRENCH LINER FLYING THE PENNANT OF TRIUMPH OFF SOUTHAMPTON.

The chief event of the three-days' festival of German Art, which began at Munich on July 16, was the official opening by Herr Hitler of the newly completed House of German Art. In his speech he claimed that the Nazis had effected a Renaissance in German Art by destroying individualism and Liberal, Bolshevist, Jewish and Marxist influences. Some modern pictures, he suggested, could only have been painted by people with abnormal eyesight and if they really painted in this manner because they felt they saw things that way, then these unhappy persons should be handed over to the department of the Ministry of the Interior, where sterilisation of the insane was dealt with.

On her first return trip from the U.S.A. after her extensive overhaul, the French liner "Normandie" regained the Blue Riband of the Atlantic by beating the "Queen Mary's" record of last year, and her own record of last June. Her average speed was 30.99 knots, as against the "Queen Mary's" 30.63. The "Normandie" has had new propellers fitted. These are four-bladed, in place of the three-bladed ones which formerly drove her, and are considerably lighter in weight.

WHERE CONTAINERS ARE BEING MADE FOR 30,000,000 GAS-MASKS: ONE OF THE WOMEN EMPLOYED AT THE BLACKBURN FACTORY WEARING A COMPLETED GAS-MASK.

THE BRITISH FASCIST LEADER STONED: SIR OSWALD MOSLEY (WITH ARM RAISED TO WARD OFF MISSILES) FACING A LIVERPOOL CROWD FROM A LOUD-SPEAKER VAN ROOF.

THE PARIS EXHIBITION OFFICIALLY OPENED BY PRESIDENT LEBRUN.

On January 12 Mr. Geoffrey Lloyd, Parliamentary Under-Secretary to the Home Office, opened the Government factory for mass production of gas-mask containers. Mr. Lloyd said that, if needed, the gas-masks would be issued free to everyone in danger, and would stop every poison gas known to the Government usable in war.

Sir Oswald Mosley was badly injured at an open-air meeting in Walton, Liverpool, on October 10. When about to speak from the roof of a loud-speaker van he was received with a shower of stones, and one struck him on the temple. He lay down, and another stone cut the back of his head. He was taken to Walton Hospital, where a minor operation was successfully performed. Meanwhile the police made fifteen arrests. Next day one man was charged with feloniously wounding Sir Oswald.

The great Paris Exhibition was officially inaugurated on May 24 by M. Lebrun, President of the French Republic. The President crossed the Pont d'Iéna and embarked in a motor-launch which, preceded by an escort of five naval launches, led a river procession to the Ile des Cygnes, on which stand the Colonial Pavilions and returned up-stream to a landing-stage beside the Grand Palais, in which the inaugural ceremony took place. In his speech the President expressed the hope that the Exhibition, in which forty nations are participating, would promote the cause of international peace.

THE MAN WHO INAUGURATED A NEW ERA IN HUMAN INTERCOURSE: THE LATER MARCHESE MARCONI ON BOARD HIS FAMOUS YACHT "ELETTRA", IN WHICH, DURING RECENT YEARS, HE HAD CARRIED OUT MANY SECRET EXPERIMENTS LEADING TO NOTABLE ADVANCES IN THE PRACTICAL DEVELOPMENT OF WIRELESS COMMUNICATION, ESPECIALLY IN REGARD TO THE USE OF ULTRA-SHORT WAVES.

THE ATTEMPT TO ASSASSINATE DR. SALAZAR, PRIME MINISTER OF PORTUGAL.

The news of the Marchese Marconi's sudden death in Rome, on July 20, was received with deep regret throughout the world. All nations owe him gratitude, not least for his contribution to life-saving at sea.

An attempt to assassinate Dr. de Oliveira Salazar, Prime Minister of Portugal, was made on July 4 as he was going to attend Mass in Lisbon. A bomb which had been placed in a drain exploded as he left his car and, although the pavement was damaged in each direction for some one hundred yards, Dr. Salazar was uninjured. Our photograph shows the crater caused by the force of the explosion.

RENEWAL OF THE CONFLICT BETWEEN JAPAN AND CHINA –
PEKING ABANDONED BY THE NANKING GOVERNMENT

TURNED INTO A PUBLIC PARK IN 1925: AN AERIAL VIEW OF THE PEIHAI (NORTH SEA LAKE) SHOWING (IN THE FOREGROUND) HORTENSIA ISLAND, WITH THE WHITE PAGODA DESCRIBED BY MARCO POLO AND (IN THE BACKGROUND) THE FORBIDDEN CITY.

THE COMIC UMBRELLA OF THE CHINESE SOLDIER BECOMES AN IMPORTANT PIECE OF MILITARY EQUIPMENT: (LEFT; ABOVE) MEN OF THE 29TH ARMY, NEAR PEKING, WITH GREEN UMBRELLAS WHICH ARE FOUND USEFUL FOR CAMOUFLAGE AGAINST AERIAL OBSERVATION, PARTICULARLY IN OPEN COUNTRY.

On July 8, Japanese troops, engaged on manoeuvres near Liukouchiao, ten miles south-west of Peking, were fired on by Chinese troops and, in the subsequent fighting, three Japanese officers and seven soldiers were killed and twenty-two were wounded; while the Chinese lost about a hundred men. Japan presented an ultimatum to General Sung Cheh-yuan calling upon him to withdraw the North China troops. This was rejected on July 27. The Japanese forces then launched an attack on Peking, after having assured the British Embassy that no bombs or artillery would be used against the City itself. On July 29 the Nanking Government troops abandoned the City and retired to Paoting-fou. British women and children had been advised, however, to take shelter in the Embassy. During the negotiations, minor skirmishes and "incidents" were common.

SOLDIERS OF THE 29TH ARMY RETREATING FROM PEKING; ONE WITH MACHINE-GUN BELTS OF CARTRIDGES SLUNG ABOUT HIM AND SWORD ON HIS BACK.

THE MARCO POLO BRIDGE, SCENE OF THE EARLY SINO-JAPANESE FIGHTING, WITH ONE OF THE GATES OF WANPINGSHIEN SEEN IN THE DISTANCE: A GRACEFUL MARBLE STRUCTURE WHOSE ELEVEN ARCHES SPAN THE YUNGTING RIVER.

The Marco Polo Bridge, which was the scene of the early Sino-Japanese fighting, has at one end a gate leading into the town of Wanpingshien, the object of a Japanese bombardment, from which the Chinese eventually withdrew their troops. Opposing the Japanese was the famous 29th "Route" Army, which put up a gallant resistance against Japanese troops at Shanghai some time ago. Liukouchiao is only ten miles south-west of Peking, and, when news of the clash was received, the city was placed under martial law and the gates were closed and guarded. Meanwhile, sandbag emplacements for machine-guns were hastily built at strategic points along the broad thoroughfares and narrow alleys. However, in the early morning of July 29, the Chinese troops abandoned the city and the defence works were pulled down. The photographs on this page show men of the 29th Chinese Army, a force which bore the brunt of much of the fighting round Peking. Its ill success there was apparently due principally to lack of organisation and co-ordination.

THE FIERCE SINO-JAPANESE FIGHTING IN TIENTSIN

PRECAUTIONS AT THE BRITISH CONCESSION IN TIENTSIN: A ROAD CLOSED BY A BARBED-WIRE BARRIER DESIGNED TO CHECK RUSHES OF REFUGEES, WHO ARE SEEN WAITING THEIR TURN TO ENTER.

A JAPANESE POST, NEAR THE EAST STATION, TIENTSIN – WHERE VERY HEAVY FIGHTING OCCURRED: RIFLEMEN MANNING A HIGH BREASTWORK OF SANDBAGS; AND A LIGHT MACHINE-GUN BEING OPERATED THROUGH A LOOPHOLE.

Japanese control of Northern China was made complete on August 19, when the Hopei-Chahar Political Council was suspended. This severed the last administrative link of the Peking-Tientsin area with Nanking. An important step in the establishment of Japanese domination was their occupation of Tientsin at the end of July. This was not accomplished without some savage fighting. The fighting in Tientsin began with intense rifle and machine-gun fire, and ended with the Japanese shelling and bombing six points that were being used by

Chinese troops as bases. The Chinese were driven out or overcome, the remnants of their forces retreating south-west. Chinese Central Government Division which have been sent north appear to be concentrating far inland, to the west of Peking. Fighting has been going on near the Nankow Pass, and the Chinese claim to have resisted Japanese attacks.

FIGURES SATIRISING NON-INTERVENTION, FRANCO AND FASCISM EXHIBITED AT VALENCIA.

THE CHIEF BASQUE ARMS-PRODUCING TOWN FALLS: REINOSA OCCUPIED.

MEMBERS OF THE NON-INTERVENTION COMMITTEE GROUP: THE GERMAN (LEFT), A PICKELHAUBE SPIKE SPROUTING FROM HIS HEAD AND A TANK UPON HIS KNEE (LABELLED "VERY FRAGILE IN GUADALAJARA"); AND AN ITALIAN WHO HAS A CAPRONI BOMBER AS A PRESENT FOR GENERAL FRANCO.

THE CAPTURE OF REINOSA, THE BASQUES' MOST IMPORTANT ARMS-MANUFACTURING TOWN IN SANTANDER PROVINCE, WHICH FELL, AFTER SLIGHT RESISTANCE, DURING THE NATIONALISTS' ADVANCE ON SANTANDER: GENERAL FRANCO'S SOLDIERS STOPPING A CAR WHILE PATROLLING THE, APPARENTLY, LITTLE DAMAGED STREETS OF THE TOWN.

FRANCO'S FINAL VICTORY IN THE NORTH: GIJON.

EFFECTS OF THE FIGHTING AT GIJON, WHICH WAS SEVERELY DAMAGED IN MANY QUARTERS: BUILD-INGS RAZED PRACTICALLY TO THE GROUND.

WITH GENERAL FRANCO'S VICTORIOUS TROOPS IN THE ADVANCE ON GIJON: TWO TYPES OF NATIONALIST TANKS.

MEDITERRANEAN "PIRACY": A MAP SHOWING SCENES OF OUTRAGES.

"PIRACY": A MAP SHOWING THE ATTACKS THAT HAVE BEEN MADE UPON SHIPPING IN THE MEDITERRA-NEAN – THE BULK OF THEM BEFORE THE NYON CONFERENCE, WHICH WAS CONVOKED TO ORGANISE ANTI-PIRACY MEASURES, NAVAL BASES AND TRADE ROUTES.

Piratical attacks on shipping in the Mediterranean, principally the work of submarines, led Britain and France to invite Mediterranean and other interested powers to a conference at Nyon. Nine powers signed the agreement at Nyon on September 14. Britain and France agreed to undertake the patrolling of the main trade routes in the Mediterranean. The other signatory powers, Greece, Turkey, Rumania, Egypt, Russia, Bulgaria, and Yugoslavia agreed to patrol their territorial waters. Patrol vessels are authorised to attack and destroy submarines, surface-craft and aeroplanes illegally attacking non-Spanish merchant ships. Italy was also invited to join the patrol. At first she returned a doubtful answer, but later agreed to enter into discussions. The Nyon conference coincided with a remarkable decline in the number of piratical attacks in the Mediterranean, only one occurring after it met, until the attack on the British destroyer "Basilisk" on October 4.

A FATE WHICH THE MEDITERRANEAN PATROL IS DESIGNED TO PREVENT BEFALLING NON-SPANISH SHIPS: THE DESTRUCTION OF A SPANISH OIL-TANKER, BLOWN UP AND SUNK OFF THE TUNISIAN COAST.

CZECHOSLOVAKIA MOURNS DR. MASARYK.

The death of Dr. Masaryk, the liberator of his country and the first President of the Republic of Czechoslovakia, plunged the nation into deep mourning. The body was brought from Castle Lany to Prague and lay in state for three days in the Pillar Hall of the Hradschin, the presidential residence of Dr. Benesh. Pilgrims flocked into the city and queues some two or three miles long were formed in the streets. Altogether, several hundreds of thousands of people must have passed by the bier with the simple coffin covered with a flag bearing the words "The truth wins". On September 21 President Benesh delivered the funeral oration in the forecourt of the Castle, where the coffin had been placed in a great catafalque: and later the coffin was borne slowly through the crowded streets of the city and placed on a train for Lany, where Dr. Masaryk was interred, in the little village cemetery, near his wife, who died in 1923. Mr. Newton, the British Minister in Prague, represented the King: and the British Government was represented by Lord Winterton, Chancellor of the Duchy of Lancaster.

THE MEETING OF THE DUCE AND THE FÜHRER: MUNICH'S FERVID WELCOME.

Signor Mussolini was welcomed in Munich with immense fervour when he arrived there, on September 25. As he descended from his train at the station, Herr Hitler greeted him and they walked together to inspect the guard of honour drawn up outside. Then they entered a car and drove to the Prince Karl Palace, where Signor Mussolini rested awhile before going to visit Herr Hitler at his private residence. There the Duce presented his host with a commission as Honorary Corporal in the Fascist Militia, the highest honour Fascismo can bestow. The Duce created this rank for himself, and was then wearing the uniform. The commission praised Herr Hitler's work for Germany and his friendship towards Italy. Later the Führer reciprocated by bestowing on him the highest Nazi honours, decorating him with the Golden Medal of Sovereignty of the Nazi Party – an eagle mounted on the swastika – formerly worn only by the Führer himself and conferring on him also the first Grand Cross of the Order of the German Eagle, with special insignia in gold and brilliants not to be repeated for any future holder.

THE DEATH OF DR. MASARYK: SOME OF THE HUNDREDS OF THOUSANDS OF PEOPLE WHO WAITED IN PRAGUE TO FILE PAST THE COFFIN IN THE PILLAR HALL OF THE CASTLE.

SIGNOR MUSSOLINI AND HERR HITLER WALKING TOGETHER AMID A STORM OF ACCLAMATION AND NAZI SALUTES: THE DUCE'S ARRIVAL FOR HIS VISIT TO GERMANY.

THE NAZI "RALLY OF WORK"

LORD HALIFAX'S ORIGINAL BERLIN OBJECTIVE: THE HUNTING EXHIBITION

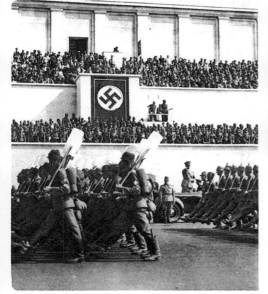

INVITED TO A SERIES OF EXPLORATORY TALKS WITH HERR HITLER IN BERLIN: LORD HALIFAX.

It was arranged that Lord Halifax should go to Berlin on November 16, in order to have a series of exploratory talks with Herr Hitler. Originally he was invited to attend the Hunting Exhibition and the proposal that he should also meet the Führer arose from this fact. Plans for the visit, which was, as Sir John Simon stated in the House of Commons, "entirely private and unofficial" were discussed between the Prime Minister, Lord Halifax, Lord President of the Council and Mr. Eden.

INCLUDING SPECIMENS WHICH WON FIRST PRIZES: SAFARI TROPHIES SENT TO THE EXHIBITION BY THEIR MAJESTIES THE KING AND QUEEN.

Owing to its success, the International Hunting Exhibition in Berlin has been extended to November 28. It was arranged that Lord Halifax, whose original invitation to attend the Exhibition was extended to include exploratory talks with Herr Hitler, should be shown round by the British Ambassador on November 17 before his meeting with the Führer. The British section, which was organised by "The Field", was, with Poland, awarded a prize for the best national exhibit and the specimens shown received 141 international first prizes and eleven special prizes, with further results still to be announced.

ONE OF THE MOST SPECTACULAR EVENTS OF THE NAZI PARTY RALLY: "SOLDIERS OF THE SPADE" (REICH LABOUR SERVICE) MARCHING PAST THE FÜHRER.

The National-Socialist Congress at Nuremberg, held this year under the title of "Rally of Work", was opened on September 7 by Herr Hess, in the presence of Herr Hitler. On the following day, Herr Hitler reviewed some 40,000 members of the compulsory Reich Labour Service, his "soldiers of the spade".

SHANGHAI'S ORDEAL: THE INTERNATIONAL SETTLEMENT AFTER BOMBING

THE HORROR OF WAR: THE TERRIBLE EFFECT OF BOMBS DROPPED IN THE INTERNATIONAL SETTLE-MENT, SHANGHAI – THE BODIES OF DEAD CHINESE REFUGEES COVERING THE GROUND AFTER THE GREAT WORLD AMUSEMENT PARK HAD BEEN HIT.

The opening of the Sino-Japanese conflict at Shanghai was marked by a terrible calamity: the falling of bombs on the International Settlement on August 14 which was crowded with Chinese refugees at the time. Some 1040 people, including eleven foreigners, were killed. In the morning the Japanese flagship the "Izumo" and another warship were attacked by Chinese aircraft, the bulk of whose bombs dropped in the river. In the afternoon the aircraft returned and were received with fierce anti-aircraft fire. From one Chinese aeroplane two bombs were seen to fall on the boundary between the Settlement and the French Concession. These bombs killed 450

SHANGHAI A CENTRE OF FIERCE WARFARE: JAPAN "BLASTS HER WAY FORWARD"

people and wounded 850. Later, two more bombs were dropped between the Cathay Hotel and the Palace Hotel, causing hundreds of casualties.

Shanghai has suffered terribly, both in casualties and damage to property, as one of the chief centres of recent hostilities between the Chinese and Japanese. On September 12 it was stated that very severe fighting had occurred on the previous day on all the eastern and northern sectors of the Shanghai front.

On September 13, the Chinese at Shanghai executed a retirement to their main line of defence, the Japanese having at last landed sufficient men and guns to force them away from the shore. The fighting went on as bitterly as before. A "Daily Telegraph" correspondent gave a description of truckloads of Japanese dead and wounded being brought into the North-East International Settlement, and added: "Japanese nurses at the field hospitals state that the number of deaths from wounds is appalling". Chinese losses, doubtless, were even heavier. News from Shanghai on October 3 stated that throughout that day severe fighting had occurred north-west of the city, and that the Chinese had withdrawn. Tanks and artillery were used on each side, and the Japanese were assisted by fire from their warships in the Whangpoo River. Nearly all day the flagship "Izumo" bombarded Chinese positions with her 6-inch guns, and the whole city was shaken by the firing. Later reports on October 4 said that the Japanese were making great efforts to break the Chinese resistance, concentrating on two points – Kiangwan (5 miles from the International Settlement) and the native quarter of Chapei. Despite 40 hours of continuous bombing and bombardment, however, the Chinese had so far held their positions; they had received reinforcements of heavy artillery and opened an intense fire on the enemy lines, scoring a direct hit on the Japanese landing headquarters.

The Japanese advance which broke through the Chinese positions north of Shanghai, and produced the retreat to the Soochow Creek, was preceded by a long bombardment of Chinese back areas and communications by artillery and from the air. Eye-witnesses described the Japanese methods as "blasting their way forward" through a stubborn defence. Naturally the Markham Road junction, received the close attention of the attackers. Three big fires were started there on October 26, and when the Chinese evacuated it they appear to have fired large areas systematically and also mined certain points. Chapei and the Markham Road Station are now in Japanese occupation.

Following through, the Chinese began to get clear of the Kiangwam Salient, where threatened with being surrounded and during the night they evacuated Chapei. The retreat appears to have been made in good order. A few groups of volunteers elected to remain behind to hold up the Japanese pursuit. One of these was the "dare-and-die" battalion which won world-wide fame by their defence of a warehouse in the south-eastern corner of Chapei on the border of the International Settlement. The situation was the most extraordinary one, the attempts of the Japanese to shell and bomb out the defenders taking place under the eyes of a large "audience" which installed itself in the International Settlement. Finally, after holding out stubbornly for nearly four days, the defenders were given the order to retire by Marshal Chiang Kai-shek himself.

CHINA'S LIMITED MODERN ARMAMENT REDUCED BY CASUALTIES: A CAPTURED TANK STATED TO BE OF BRITISH MAKE: THE ARROWS INDICATING THE PLACES WHERE THE ARMOUR HAS BEEN PIERCED.

THE JAPANESE ATTACK ON CHAPEI, A CHINESE QUARTER OF SHANGHAI THAT HAS AGAIN SUFFERED HEAVILY, AS DURING HOSTILITIES SOME YEARS AGO: JAPANESE GUNNERS IN ACTION IN THE STREETS, BEHIND A SANDBAG BARRICADE; SHOWING (IN THE CENTRE) A FIELD-GUN SHIELD.

ON THE DEFENDING SIDE OF THE STREET FIGHTING IN CERTAIN DISTRICTS OF SHANGHAI: A CHINESE SOLDIER BEHIND A TIMBER BARRICADE AT A POINT WITHIN EARSHOT OF THE JAPANESE LINES.

PHOTOGRAPH TAKEN AT THE STORMING OF A CHINESE TOWN, WHERE HAND-TO-HAND FIGHTING OCCURRED: JAPANESE TROOPS ADVANCING UNDER COVER OF A SMOKE-SCREEN AFTER THEIR EN-GINEERS HAD BRIDGED A CREEK FOR MACHINE-GUN SQUADS TO CROSS.

NANKING AND CANTON: WHOSE BOMBING EVOKED THE BRITISH GOVERNMENT'S "PROFOUND HORROR"

AFTER THE GREAT JAPANESE AIR RAID ON CANTON, WHICH CAUSED IMMENSE DESTRUCTION AND LOSS OF LIFE: HAVOC IN A POOR DISTRICT, WITH A PAGODA INTACT AMID THE WRECKAGE.

The systematic bombing of Nanking by Japanese aeroplanes began on September 22 and that of Canton on September 23. Heavy as was the damage inflicted on the Chinese capital, it was surpassed by the appalling effects of the raids on Canton – a huge city with a bigger population than any in the British Isles, bar London. As we write, the raids appear to be continuing, but, so far, no military objectives worth mentioning are reported to have been hit. These raids have called forth widespread vehement protests, which culminated in that registered by the Far Eastern Advisory Committee of the League at Geneva. In its resolution the Committee solemnly condemned such acts, and declared that they had aroused horror and indignation throughout the world. Lord Cranborne, the British Under-Secretary of State for Foreign Affairs, was even more downright. "Words cannot express (he said) the feelings of profound horror with which the news of these raids had been received by the whole civilised world. They are often directed against places far from the actual area of hostilities. The military objective, where it exists, seems to take a completely second place. The main object seems to be to inspire terror by the indiscriminate slaughter of civilians . . . The extension of air-bombing in China represents a menace not only to the unhappy people who are suffering so grievously from it today, but to the whole world. If this tendency is to continue, and is to be intensified, can civilisation survive? His Majesty's Government in the United Kingdom desire, here in Geneva, to place on record their profound horror at the bombing of open towns which is now taking place in China, and to express their hope that this Committee may condemn such practices in no uncertain terms. The effect on world opinion is, I suggest, a factor which those responsible would do well to take into account."

THE JAPANESE ADVANCE ON NANKING: 200 MILES IN A MONTH

THE OCCASION OF PRESIDENT ROOSEVELT'S MESSAGE OF PROTEST, WHICH HE REQUESTED SHOULD BE CONVEYED TO THE EMPEROR OF JAPAN HIMSELF: THE U.S.S. "PANAY", A 450-TON RIVER GUNBOAT, BOMBED AND SUNK BY JAPANESE AIRCRAFT ON THE YANGTZE, WITH LOSS OF LIFE.

H.M.S. "SCARAB": ONE OF THE 625-TON RIVER GUNBOATS THAT FIRED ON JAPANESE AIRCRAFT AFTER THEY HAD BOMBED BRITISH MERCHANT SHIPS IN COMPANY WITH THE GUNBOATS ON THE YANGTZE BETWEEN NANKING AND WUHU.

THE JAPANESE ADVANCE FROM SHANGHAI TO NANKING – AND "INCIDENTS": A PICTORIAL MAP, LOOKING WESTWARDS, SHOWING THE ROUTES TAKEN BY THEIR COLUMNS; AND THE NANKING-WUHU STRETCH OF THE YANGTZE, IN WHICH BRITISH AND UNITED STATES VESSELS WERE ATTACKED.

The Japanese advance from Shanghai to Nanking was made by two main columns; while Japanese naval forces proceeded as far up the Yangtze as possible. The Chinese defensive lines north and south of the T'a Wu Lake and Soochow do not seem to have held up the enemy for long. The strategic position of these lines was not strong, as they were divided in the centre by the T'a Wu Lake, with flanks liable to be turned by movements from the sea or the Yangtze. Indeed, the southern Japanese column, probably composed of troops which had landed at Hangchow Bay, made rapid progress. The chief obstacle offered by the country to military movement – the innumerable small canals – was turned to their own advantage by the Japanese, who utilised these waterways for their communications, by means of numerous motor sampans and captured junks. The Japanese

captured Nanking on December 13 but, apparently, they got to Wuhu some days earlier. Immediately they were on this stretch of the Yangtze they committed a series of outrages upon neutral shipping which could not fail to have most serious consequences. The sinking of the U.S. gunboat "Panay" took place not far below Taiping (Taipingfu). At a spot between Nanking and Wuhu a concentration of British ships, with the gunboats "Cricket" and "Scarab", were attacked by aircraft, and there were a number of incidents at Wuhu.

BASED ON THE NINE-POWER TREATY:
THE INTERNATIONAL FAR-EASTERN CONFERENCE.

The International Far-Eastern Conference opened on November 3. There were present representatives of all the Great Powers, with the exception of Japan and Germany, who had refused the invitation to attend. Mr. Anthony Eden represented Great Britain; and Mr. Davis the United States. The Italian delegate suggested that it was impossible to establish facts and that the Conference should invite the two warring nations to get into "direct contact". It was ultimately decided to send a Note to Japan inviting her to discuss the conflict with a small working committee, and assuring her that the discussions taking place were based on the provisions of the Nine-Power Treaty.

ENDEAVOURING TO FIND PEACEFUL MEANS OF ENDING THE SINO-JAPANESE CONFLICT: THE INTERNATIONAL FAR-EASTERN CONFERENCE IN SESSION, WITH M. SPAAK IN THE CHAIR, IN THE PALAIS DES ACADEMIES, BRUSSELS.

GERMANY'S GRIEVANCE OVER COLONIES: LOST LANDS SHE WANTS BACK

As we write, the German "enlightenment campaign" on the colonies question – in effect, an agitation for the return of her pre-war colonies – is in full swing. Persistent rumours are abroad that Herr Hitler will shortly summon the Reichstag to hear a statement from his own lips. Dr. Goebbels, Minister of Propaganda, opened the German campaign with a speech before 20,000 people in the German Sports Palace at Berlin on November 5. "Germany", he said, "came off badly in the division of land. Not because we were too weak, or cowardly, but because we had no political thinkers and no political leaders to mould the nation in unity. Some other countries in Europe have only thirty-two inhabitants per square mile, while we have to get people into the same area . . . That is why there is sometimes a shortage of butter one month and beef or margarine the next . . . Other nations have anxieties on score. Rich England and rich France, they can afford things. They have whole continents at their disposal. They swim in wealth. They have space to sow and reap, supplies of gold and Heaven knows what."

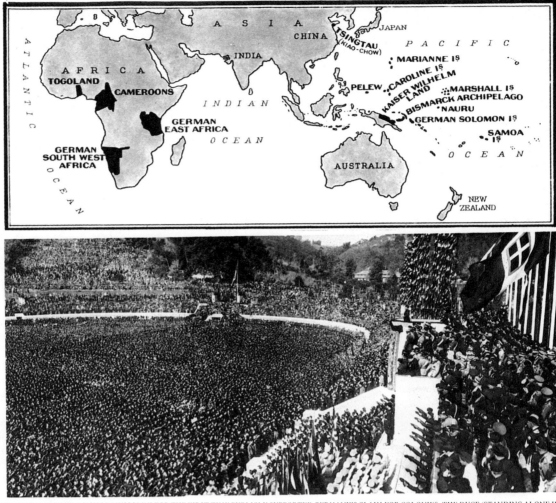

The fifteenth Fascist anniversary was celebrated on October 28 in the Foro Mussolini and the vast assemblage included 100,000 Hierarchs (officials) from every part of Italy. Great honour was paid to the German delegation present, and in his speech Signor Mussolini, discussing peace, said: "A great people such as the German people must regain the place which is due to it, and which it used to have beneath the sun of Africa."

THE OCCASION WHEN SIGNOR MUSSOLINI FOR THE FIRST TIME PUBLICLY SUPPORTED GERMANY'S CLAIM FOR COLONIES: THE DUCE (STANDING ALONE IN THE LOFTY ROSTRUM ON THE RIGHT) ADDRESSING 100,000 FASCIST "HIERARCHS" IN THE FORO MUSSOLINI ON THE ANNIVERSARY OF THE MARCH ON ROME.

ITALY LEAVES THE LEAGUE OF NATIONS.

ANNOUNCING THE GRAND COUNCIL'S DECISION FROM A BALCONY OF THE PALAZZO VENEZIA: SIGNOR MUSSOLINI DELIVERING HIS ATTACK ON THE LEAGUE AFTER AN ACCIDENT WHICH DISCONNECTED THE MICROPHONE FROM THE LOUD-SPEAKERS.

AFTER HIS SPEECH DECLARING "WE WILL ACCEPT DICTATION FROM NONE": MR. EDEN (RIGHT) LEAVING FOR THE BRUSSELS CONFERENCE ON THE FAR EAST.

The Foreign Secretary is here seen with Mr. Malcolm MacDonald, Dominions Secretary, and the Belgian Ambassador. In his speech Mr. Eden had said: "There is an inclination to threaten, to issue orders from the house-tops, to proclaim what is virtually an ultimatum, and call it peace . . . We are not prepared to stand and deliver at anyone's command . . . We offer co-operation to all, but we will accept dictation from none."

Italy's long-anticipated decision to leave the League of Nations was made public on December 11 after a meeting of the Fascist Grand Council and a telegram announcing the fact was immediately sent to the Secretary-General. It is expected that Italy will fulfil her contractual obligations which stipulate for two years' notice. Signor Mussolini's speech, which was broadcast throughout the country and also delivered to a vast crowd in the Piazza Venezia, was somewhat marred in the beginning by an unfortunate accident to the microphone. A preliminary announcement was made by Signor Starace, Secretary of the Fascist Party, who, on leaving the balcony, stumbled over a wire, and thus disconnected not only the loud-speakers in the square, but also the broadcasting circuit! This was not noticed at the time and the crowd heard nothing of the opening sentences of Signor Mussolini's speech and had to be content to watch his familiar gestures. When the fault was remedied, there followed a speech, lasting some twelve minutes, in which the Duce attacked the League as a "tottering temple". From time to time, the crowd interrupted with cheers for the speaker and hisses for the League.

THE ILLUSTRATED LONDON NEWS

FANATICISM.

HITLER YOUTHS WHO HAVE ATTAINED THE AGE OF EIGHTEEN SWORN IN AS MEMBERS OF THE NAZI PARTY IN THE SPORTS STADIUM AT NUREMBERG.

1938

In Spain Government temporarily recaptures Teruel and a Nationalist cruiser is sunk — Nationalist aircraft, including the Italian Legion, bomb Castellon and Barcelona — Franco's armies reach the sea at Castellon, cutting off Barcelona from Valencia — in Germany Hitler takes personal control of the Armed Forces — Chancellor Schuschnigg of Austria is invited to Berchtesgaden and demands are made of him — calls plebiscite on his return to confirm Austria's independence from Germany — Germany sends ultimatum — Schuschnigg and President Miklas resign — Nazis take control in Vienna — German troops arrive by air and road — Hitler visits Austria and proclaims union with Germany — Eden resigns as Foreign Secretary — the first President of Eire installed in Dublin — Germany announces support for Sudeten German separatist movement in Czechoslovakia — King George VI and Queen Elizabeth visit Paris and World War I battlefields — Germany accelerates construction of Siegfried Line and calls up reservists — a "very grave step" according to still-exiled Winston Churchill — Konrad Heinlein, leader of Sudeten Germans, summoned to Berchtesgaden — attempts coup which is suppressed by Czech Government — flees to Germany — Chamberlain flies to Berchtesgaden to meet Hitler — intense pressure on Czechoslovakia to permit peaceful secession of Sudeten Germans rather than risk war into which France and Great Britain would be drawn by Treaty obligations — further meeting between Chamberlain and Hitler at Bad Godesberg — trenches dug in Hyde Park — children evacuated from London — Mussolini agrees to "mediate" — Germany, France, Italy and Great Britain sign Munich Agreement — Czech frontier areas (and her defences) handed over to Germany — Polish troops seize Teschen — British troops clear terrorists out of Jerusalem — Japanese take Canton and Hankow — strikes in France — mass retaliation against Jews in Germany for shooting of German diplomat in Paris.

THE TIDE OF CONQUEST IN CHINA: CHINA'S "VICTORY" ARMY

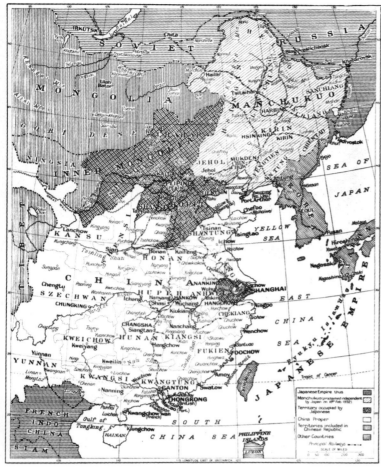

THE PRESENT EXTENT OF THE JAPANESE OCCUPATION OF CHINA

THE MODERN, GERMAN-TRAINED CORE OF THE CHINESE NATIONAL GOVERNMENT'S "VICTORY" ARMY: A WELL-EQUIPPED MOTORISED UNIT BEING ADDRESSED BY ITS COMMANDER BEFORE A MARCH.

In an interview with Reuter's correspondent last month, General Chiang Kai-Shek outlined his plans for the defence of China. "I am training a new army", he then stated. "It will take me two months to rebuild the divisions shattered at Shanghai. Henceforth our resistance will not be concentrated on certain key points. We shall utilise the size of our country and harass the Japanese Army continuously. We shall have to withdraw further into the West of China, but we shall go on fighting. All the Chinese Government leaders are united on this. The main purpose of my operations will be to keep a large Japanese army on Chinese soil. As the months go by, Japan will find this an increasing strain." Previously, in December, he had emphasised the same side of his strategy, saying "Prolonged resistance is not to be found in Nanking nor in the big cities, but in the villages throughout China and in the fixed determination of the people. The time must come when Japan's military strength will be completely exhausted, thus giving us ultimate victory."

This map gives a clear exposition of the areas of China occupied by the Japanese. A Provisional Government has been set up in Peking and the Japanese are reported to have crossed the Yellow River at Tsinan, the capital of Shantung province, probably a preliminary step towards the occupation of this province. The Japanese hold on the westerly Peking-Chengchow railway, however, is more precarious, while in Shansi they are reliably reported to be on the defensive; with continuous Chinese guerrila activity in areas nominally occupied by them. Further inland, a new State – the "Inner Mongolian Autonomous Republic" – has been set up under Japanese auspices, headed by Prince Teh and Prince Yun. This threatens to interrupt Chinese communication with Russia. The Japanese are credited with the intention of linking up their forces which have crossed to the north of the Yangtze, near Nanking, with those which have penetrated into Shantung, and thus depriving Chiang Kai-Shek and China of all the Northern coastal provinces.

HARASSING THE JAPANESE BEHIND THE LINES COMMUNIST GUERRILLA FIGHTERS IN SHANSI

CROQUET – THE FAVOURITE RELAXATION OF THE IMPLACABLE COMMUNIST GUERILLAS. ONE OF THE BOY VOLUNTEERS, KNOWN AS "SMALL DEVILS", MAKING A SHOT WITH HIS MAUSER HOLSTER PROMINENTLY DISPLAYED.

"THE JAPANESE GOVERNMENT . . . LOOK FORWARD TO THE ESTABLISHMENT AND GROWTH OF A NEW CHINESE RÉGIME . . . WITH WHICH . . . THEY WILL WARMLY CO-OPERATE": THE EMPEROR OF JAPAN IN COUNCIL WITH THE CHIEFS OF HIS NAVY (ON THE LEFT) AND ARMY (ON THE RIGHT).

The Japanese Imperial Conference – the first held for 34 years, and only the third in the last 70 years – met on January 11. On the left in the photograph are Admiral Prince Fushimi, Chief of the Naval General Staff (next to the Emperor), the Minister of the Navy and two Adjutants: on the right are General Prince Kanin, Chief of the Army General Staff, the Minister of War and two Adjutants. No decisions were announced, but on the 16th an official statement declared: "The Japanese Government . . . look forward to the establishment and growth of a new Chinese régime, harmonious co-ordination with which can really be counted upon. With such a régime they will warmly co-operate for the adjustment of Sino-Japanese relations and the building-up of a rejuvenated China. This involves no change in the policy of respecting the territorial integrity and sovereignty of China, as well as the rights and interests of other Powers."

The Chinese Eighth Route Army, composed of Chinese Communist troops, has become famous for its guerilla operations against the Japanese in the remote North-West, whence little reliable news ever reaches European newspapers. These Communists, who have allied themselves with the Chinese Central Government in face of the common foe, came originally from areas south of the Yangtze. By an amazing march – or, rather, mass-migration – of over 6000 miles through Szechwan and Kansu and the wilds of the interior, the Communists arrived 20,000 strong in Shensi, in the distant North-Western hinterland. How many tens of thousands perished in the course of this "trek" will never be known. The "Sian incident", when Chiang Kai-Shek was held captive by Chang Hsueh-liang, led to an agreement between the Reds and the Central Government. When the Japanese invaded Northern China the Communist forces turned their aptitude for guerilla warfare against them. Exactly how successful they have been is difficult to tell. Although Japanese forces claim to have penetrated deep into Shansi, it seems that in much of the occupied area they hold little more than the railway-lines.

THE WAR IN SPAIN BLAZES UP AFRESH
TERUEL CAPTURED BY THE GOVERNMENT: TERUEL RETAKEN BY FRANCO

Weather conditions played a great part in the fall of Teruel to the Government troops. Not only did bad weather enable them to penetrate the outposts on December 15, but heavy falls of snow and the intense cold held up the mechanised vehicles of the Nationalist relief force which attempted to break through the Government lines. After Teruel had been entered, the Nationalists took refuge in the Seminary, the Santa Clara Convent, and the Civil Government building. On January 6 it was reported that a large part of the convent had been captured by soldiers armed with hand-grenades, and on the following day the Nationalist commander, Colonel Rey, after a gallant defence of nineteen days, asked for permission to evacuate the women, children and wounded. This was followed the same evening by his offer to surrender, which was accepted by the Government commander, General Hernandez Sarabia, who gave his promise that "the Republican Army would respect the prisoners, care for the wounded and ill, assist the civilian refugees and guarantee the lives of all under the laws of the Republic." Colonel Rey's own conduct has been severely censured by Nationalist headquarters, but this is undoubtedly due to the feeling of optimism which inspired General Franco's New Year message, in which he stated: "The chain of victories of the year now ended has been clasped with the Teruel brooch." Instead it has proved to be the greatest achievement of the Government's new Army, and their most decisive victory for many months.

The Spanish Nationalists re-occupied Teruel on February 22. The town was found to have suffered severely. The buildings in which Colonel Rey and his men held out for three weeks against the Republicans were in ruins. The Cathedral, the Seminary and the Convent of Santa Clara were all badly damaged. The famous Mudejar Tower of S. Martin, though pitted with shell-holes, was found to be standing. The "Lovers of Teruel" – the two mummified figures formerly preserved at the Church of S. Pedro – had disappeared. A "Daily Telegraph" correspondent gave a graphic description of the scene, which was appalling: "Dead dogs and mules lay in the streets, which were littered thickly with debris, cartridges, paper, straw and such abandoned personal belongings as hats, books, clothes, sunshades, bedsteads and family photographs." The Government authorities, it appeared, had evacuated the civilian population from the town when they occupied it and no attempt had been made to restore normal conditions.

ALL THAT WAS LEFT OF A NATIONALIST STRONGHOLD IN TERUEL AFTER THE ASTURIAN MINERS HAD FINISHED WITH IT: THE "GOBIERNO CIVIL" BUILDING REDUCED TO A MOUNTAIN OF RUBBLE WHEN THE GARRISON WOULD NOT SURRENDER.

THE SINKING OF FRANCO'S CRUISER "BALEARES"

The course of the Naval action off Cape Palos, in which the Spanish Nationalist cruiser "Baleares" was sunk, appears to have been as follows. The cruisers "Baleares", "Canarias" and "Almirante Cervera" left Palma on March 5. They were sighted by Spanish Government aircraft, which reported their position to Cartageua and to Government destroyers, which went out to attack them, and backed by the cruisers "Libertad" and "Mendez" The Nationalist vessels, counting on their superior gun-power (and efficiency), opened the action by firing star shells. The Republicans did not wait, but opened fire at once; and the destroyers delivered their torpedo attack. The destroyers seem to have gone in with great boldness. They fired twelve torpedoes. The "Baleares" was hit amidships; fires were started in her oil bunkers and she was reduced to a sinking condition. She appears to have received no help from the other Nationalist vessels, but the British destroyers "Kempenfelt" and "Boreas" came up and rescued some of her crew, although by this time the sinking ship was being attacked by Republican aeroplanes. The "Boreas", unfortunately, had a seaman killed by a bomb splinter while survivors picked up from the Spanish insurgent cruiser "Baleares" were being transferred to the Spanish insurgent cruiser "Canarias", during which operation the "Canarias" was attacked by aircraft.

THE DOOMED CRUISER "BALEARES", SINKING IN FLAMES AND KEELING OVER, WITH HER STERN RISING OUT OF THE WATER – A PHOTOGRAPH SHOWING THE HEADS OF SOME OF HER CREW STRUGGLING IN THE OILY SEA.

"CONTRARY TO THE PRINCIPLES OF INTERNATIONAL LAW"

BARCELONA AFTER THE AIR RAIDS WHICH DREW A DENUNCIATION FROM THE U.S.A. SECRETARY OF STATE.

The severe bombing of Barcelona by aeroplanes fighting for General Franco began at 10 p.m. on March 26. Numerous other air raids followed. According to "The Times" correspondent, those which created the worst havoc were not aimed at military objectives, but at a section of the Old City in which the poor lived huddled together, and at the boulevards and open spaces to which the citizens throng to enjoy their leisure. The same correspondent wrote later: "A visit to the newly-bombed parts reveals that the aeroplanes were systematically raking the city with their bombs, section by section. The scenes of desolation and ruin which I described yesterday I witnessed again today. One saw buildings smashed to the ground, others burning, the wreckage strewn about everywhere. In every street were throngs fleeing as yesterday, only in much greater numbers. Some of the streets were black with men, women and children struggling bravely to carry their poor belongings and sometimes their cats. Long queues waited to catch omnibuses to suburban points. The Red Cross is working in circumstances of great strain. As every few hours the raiders, between 15,000 ft. and 20,000 ft. pass, dropping their deadly load, a fresh call is made on the devoted service." It was officially stated that 815 people had been killed and 2200 injured after some three days raiding. Mr. Chamberlain, giving information in the House of Commons about these raids said he did not think that anyone could read the newspaper reports of what had happened there without horror and disgust. The British Government sent a "communication" – in fact, a protest – to General Franco. Sir Robert Hodgson, the British Chief Agent at Salamander was instructed to tell the Nationalist authorities of the horror and disgust with which the Government and the British people learned of the attacks and of the killing of civilians. The protest curtly reminded General Franco that such direct and deliberate attacks were contrary both to the principles of international law as recognised by civilised peoples and Governments and to the laws of humanity and the dictates of public opinion. The French Government made a similar protest and the Vatican was requested to join in a united appeal for an end to be put to the bombing of open towns. It was not, however, thought likely the Vatican would agree to do this. These terrible devastations also drew a denunciation from the United States Foreign Secretary. In a statement made on March 21, Mr. Cordell Hull said that the reports from Barcelona left no doubt of the appalling loss of life among civilian men, women and children. The American position was based first on considerations of humanity, and secondly on the consideration that no theory of war could possibly excuse such conduct. "On this occasion", he went on, "when the loss of life among non-combatants is perhaps greater than even before in history, I feel that I am speaking for the whole American people when I voice a sense of horror at what has taken place in Barcelona, and when I express the earnest hope that, in future, civilian centres of population will not be made the objectives of military bombardment from the air."

DEVASTATION IN THE STREETS OF A CITY WHICH WAS FORMERLY NOTED FOR ITS GAIETY AND ANIMATION: A TRAM-CAR COMPLETELY WRECKED BY AN EXPLOSION WHICH HAS ALSO BROUGHT DOWN HOUSE-FRONTS.

PERSONALITIES IN THE GERMAN CRISIS:
RETIREMENTS AND APPOINTMENTS.

DR. HEINRICH
LAMMERS

HERR HIMMLER

THE PRESIDENT OF THE NEW SECRET CABINET COUNCIL: BARON VON
NEURATH CONGRATULATED BY HERR HITLER ON HIS SIXTY-FIFTH BIRTHDAY
RECENTLY.

DR. JOSEF GOEBBELS

HERR RUDOLF HESS

Dr. Lammers is one of the members of the Cabinet Council which was established by Herr Hitler in the recent   . Dr Lammers holds the office of Reich Minister of the Reich

Herr Himmler is Chief of the German Police, the Secret Police and the Black Guards. He has been an active member of the Nazi Party since 1925 and is said to have been "the chief executive in the crushing of the 'mutiny' in 1934".

Baron von Neurath, who has been succeeded as Minister for Foreign Affairs by Herr von Ribbentrop, has been nominated by Herr Hitler as President of the new secret Cabinet Council to advise on foreign political questions. He was Ambassador in London from 1930 to 1932, when he became Foreign Minister. He attended King George V's funeral.

In announcing the names of members of the secret Cabinet Council, Herr Hitler mentioned "the Reich Minister for National Enlightenment and Propaganda, Dr. Josef Goebbels".

Herr Hess, who is one of the members of the secret Cabinet Council established by Herr Hitler, holds the official position of Deputy of the Führer.

ADMIRAL RAEDER

HERR JOACHIM VON
RIBBENTROP

GENERAL
WILHELM KEITEL

GENERAL
VON BRAUSCHITSCH

In his Decree appointing the new secret Cabinet Council, Herr Hitler named among its members "Commander-in-Chief of the Navy, General Admiral Dr. Raeder".

Herr von Ribbentrop, the new Foreign Minister, and German Ambassador in London. He is a close personal friend of Herr Hitler.

General Keitel will be Chief of the High Command of the Armed Forces, and will co-ordinate the Army, Navy and Air Force.

As a member of the secret Cabinet Council, Herr Hitler named "the Commander-in-Chief of the Army, Colonel-General Walter von Brauschitsch".

THE GERMAN "PURGE": HERR HITLER, WHO IS NOW SUPREME HEAD OF THE WHOLE ARMED FORCES, AND THE NEWLY-PROMOTED FIELD-MARSHAL GÖRING, A
MEMBER OF THE NEW SECRET CABINET COUNCIL.

A sensation was caused by the announcement, on February 4, of sweeping changes at the control of the German Forces and the direction of foreign policy. Herr Hitler's first Decree stated: "From now on I exercise personally the command over the whole Armed Forces. The Wehrmacht Office in the War Ministry becomes the High Command of the Armed Forces and comes immediately under my command as my military staff." A second Decree an announced: "To advise me in the conduct of foreign policy I set up a secret Cabinet Council," and in naming its members he included "the Prussian Minister–President, Minister of Aviation and Commander-in-Chief of the Air Force, General Field-Marshal Göring". Field-Marshal Göring is the first German to attain that rank without ever having been a Staff Officer, having risen from the rank of captain

within five years. Another announcement made on February 4 was that Herr Hitler had decreed a reorganisation of the Ministry of Economics "in view of the powers given to the Commissioner of the Four-Year Plan, Field-Marshal Göring." In that capacity the latter is still busy co-ordinating German trade and industry under State control. The chief sensations of the crisis were the resignations of Field-Marshal von Blomberg, the Minister of War and General von Fritsch, Commander-in-Chief of the Army. Besides those, thirteen other Generals of the Army and Air Force are being retired. All the new arrangements were regarded in Berlin as a victory for Nazism over reactionary elements in the Army high command.

MASS TREASON AND MURDER TRIAL OPENS IN MOSCOW

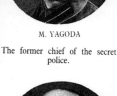

M. YENUKIDZE

M. BUKHARIN

Former Editor of both *Pravda* and *Isvestia*.

M. YAGODA

The former chief of the secret police.

M. KARAKHAN

Sentenced to death by the Soviet Military Collegium without a trial and executed. Accused of being an active member of the "Trotzkyist-Bukharinite spy organisation" and of preparing terrorist acts. Was a former "Speaker" of the Soviet Parliament.

THE MASS TREASON TRIAL IN MOSCOW: M. RAKOVSKY (ABOVE), FORMER AMBASSADOR IN LONDON AND PARIS; AND FOUR OTHERS OF THE TWENTY-ONE SOVIET LEADERS ACCUSED.

The biggest treason and murder trial yet held at Moscow opened in public on March 2. The twenty-one accused include seven former members of the Soviet Government, Yagoda, the former Chief of the Ogpu, who was himself responsible for assembling the victims of the last big treason case and many former friends of Lenin.

Executed without receiving a trial after being sentenced to death by the Soviet Military Collegium on December 16. Accused of selling State secrets of exceptional importance to Fascist intelligence services. Was formerly the Soviet Ambassador to Turkey.

M. RYKOV

Former President, the Council of People's Commissars.

M. GRINKO

Former Commissar for Finance.

THE PROLOGUE TO THE AUSTRO-GERMAN DRAMA:
DR. SCHUSCHNIGG VISITS HERR HITLER

THE MAN OF THE MOMENT: DR. SCHUSCHNIGG, THE AUSTRIAN CHANCELLOR, WHOSE SUDDEN VISIT TO HERR HITLER REVIVED THE VEXED QUESTION OF NAZI INFLUENCE IN AUSTRIA.

Only a week after the German "purge" of February 4, another sensational event occurred on the 12th. An official Berlin communiqué stated: "The Austrian Chancellor, Dr. Schuschnigg, accompanied by the Foreign Secretary, Dr. Guido Schmidt, and Herr von Papen, German Ambassador to Austria, visited Herr Hitler at Obersalzberg today. Herr von Ribbentrop, German Foreign Minister, was present. The visit was paid on Herr Hitler's invitation. This informal meeting was occasioned by a mutual wish to confer on all questions concerning relations between the Reich and Austria." Hitches arose later over Herr Hitler's terms.

As we write it is stated that two pro-Nazis are in the rearranged Austrian Cabinet – Dr. von Seyss-Inquart, who becomes Minister of the Interior, and Herr Glaise-Horstenau (his predecessor in that office), who becomes Vice-Chancellor.

The two Chancellors had never met before. Dr. Schuschnigg assumed office in 1934, at the early age of thirty-six, on the assassination of Dr. Dollfuss. He served with distinction in the Great War.

HERR HITLER WITH HERR VON PAPEN, GERMAN AMBASSADOR AT VIENNA, WHO SUGGESTED THE SCHUSCHNIGG INTERVIEW, AT BERCHTESGADEN.

Although Herr von Papen was mentioned among Ambassadors to be recalled, at the time of the German "purge" of February 4, he continued his duties at Vienna, pending appointment of a successor. It was reported on the 12th that a week previously he had gone to Herr Hitler's villa at Berchtesgaden, and persuaded the Führer to invite Dr. Schuschnigg to the now famous interview. Herr von Papen was concerned in the Austrio-German Pact of 1936.

THE CHANCELLOR: "AUSTRIA WILL REMAIN FREE"

WITH BANNERS EMBLAZONED WITH THE AUSTRIAN CROSS: MEMBERS OF THE WORKERS' FRONT MARCHING THROUGH THE RINGSTRASS, VIENNA, ON THE NIGHT OF THE CHANCELLOR'S SPEECH.

The Austrian Chancellor, Dr. Schuschnigg, was acclaimed with immense enthusiasm on February 24 when he explained and defined the new agreement with Germany resulting from his recent interview with Herr Hitler. "The Government", he said, "stands unalterably by the Constitution of May1 1934. It regards as its first unquestionable duty to maintain with all its strength the freedom and independence of the Austrian Fatherland intact . . . "Austria will remain free, and for this we will fight to the death. Because we are resolved, there is no doubt about our victory. Till death, the red-white-and-red – Austria!"

THE NAZIS TAKE CONTROL IN VIENNA

The event that brought to a head political tension in Austria, and led to the German coup, was the speech delivered at Innsbruck on March 9 by the then Chancellor, Dr. Schuschnigg, who announced the decision to hold a plebiscite of the Austrian people on the following Sunday, March 13, to pronounce upon his policy. They were to answer "Yes" or "No" to the question "Are you for a free and German, independent and social, Christian and united Austria, for peace and work, for the equality of all those who affirm themselves for the people and Fatherland?"

On March 11 Dr. Schuschnigg received a German ultimatum to postpone his proposed plebiscite. On endeavouring to make conditions, he was further required to resign the Chancellorship in favour of Dr. von Seyss-Inquart, the Minister appointed at Herr Hitler's behest. Later, Dr. Schuschnigg broadcast an address announcing his own resignation and stating that President Miklas, who later also resigned, had charged him to say that they yielded to force to avoid spilling German blood. Immediately after this announcement, the Nazi groups took possession of Vienna.

NAZI STORM TROOPERS MARCHING INTO THE CHANCELLERY AT VIENNA PAST TWO SENTRIES: A FORCE WEARING CIVILIAN CLOTHES WITH SWASTIKA ARMLETS, ARMED WITH RIFLES, AND LED BY TWO MEN CARRYING AMMUNITION

"SIEG HEIL!": AUSTRIAN NAZI DEMONSTRATIONS

POLITICAL EXPRESSION WHICH HAS SINCE BEEN BANNED: AUSTRIAN NAZIS, ON THEIR WAY TO A MEETING AT GRAZ, WEARING FLAGS OF THE AUSTRIAN WHITE AND RED WITH A SWASTIKA SUPERIMPOSED.

After Herr Hitler's speech to the Reichstag on February 20, the Austrian Nazis, who are naturally jubilant at Dr. Schuschnigg's acceptance of the Führer's demands, organised demonstrations throughout Austria. In Vienna a crowd marched past the German Legation shouting "Heil Hitler!" and "Sieg Heil!" (Hail Victory!), but the activity of the police prevented any violence. In Graz, where Dr. Rintelen, who was sentenced to twenty years' imprisonment for his alleged part in the Nazi putsch of 1934, has been received as a hero on his release under the general amnesty, some 10,000 people bearing swastika flags took part in a torchlight procession and similar scenes were witnessed at Innsbruck. These political meetings have now been banned by the Austrian Government as from February 22, but, as they were already illegal and Dr. Seyss-Inquart, Minister of the Interior, is Herr Hitler's nominee, it is unlikely that the ban will be effective.

AUSTRIA INVADED BY GERMANY: THE VANGUARD REACHES VIENNA BY AIR

GERMAN BOMBERS OVER VIENNA: UNITS OF THE FORCE OF SCORES OF MACHINES WHICH DROPPED LEAFLETS OR LANDED TROOPS ON MARCH 12.

RAISING THE FRONTIER BARRIER AS GERMAN TROOPS MARCH INTO AUSTRIA: THE SCENE AT KUF-STEIN, ONE OF THE MAIN POINTS OF ENTRY.

Vienna awoke on the morning of March 12 to the roar of the engines of scores of German bombers, which proceeded to drop leaflets – bearing messages such as "The Nationalist Socialist Germany greets the new National Socialist Austria!" – and, happily, nothing more lethal. By breakfast time troop-carrying aeroplanes had begun landing German infantrymen at Aspern airport, outside Vienna. By 3.30 there were 2000 Germans at Aspern. Two hundred machines are said to have been used, and to have arrived at the rate of fifty every hour. These men constituted the vanguard of the German Army, which was already moving into Austria in several columns. Troops continued to pour into the country in vast numbers: the great display of force showing that the Germans were determined not to permit demonstrations against the new régime; and also, perhaps, to discourage any of Austria's neighbours from interfering.

THE END OF AUSTRIAN INDEPENDENCE: HERR HITLER PROCLAIMING THAT "MY HOMELAND HAS NOW ENTERED THE GERMAN REICH" ON THE VIENNA "HEROES' SQUARE".

Herr Hitler entered Vienna at 5.40 in the evening of March 14. By order of the Cardinal Archbishop, all the churches rang their bells. The Führer drove in procession through throngs of excited people to the Hotel Imperial, where he spent the night. On March 15 the ceremonial announcement of the incorporation of Austria into the Reich was staged. For this Herr Hitler drove from his hotel to the Heldenplatz, the great square in which stands the memorial to the Austrian unknown soldier. There he was welcomed by Dr. von Seyss-Inquart, formerly Chancellor, and now Reichstatthalter (Governor) of Austria. Herr Hitler spoke from the balcony of the former Royal Palace. His words included the following: "German men and women! In the last few days a change has been accomplished in the German community, the importance of which will only be gauged by future generations. I now proclaim a new mission for this land. This 'East March' will from now on be the youngest bulwark of the German nation. For centuries it has been the bulwark against invaders from the east. For centuries to come it shall be our guarantor for the safety and freedom of the German Reich! This land is German and has understood its mission. In this hour I can make before the German people the greatest report of my life on a task carried out. As Leader and Chancellor of the German Reich, I report before German history that my homeland has now entered the German Reich."

THE AUSTRIAN ARMY SWEARS ALLEGIANCE TO HERR HITLER: OFFICERS OF THE TYROL JAEGER REGIMENT TAKING THE OATH AT INNSBRUCK DURING A SPECTACULAR MILITARY PARADE IN THE ADOLF HITLER PLATZ.

THE GERMAN PLEBISCITE:
VOTERS FROM BRITAIN POLL ON BOARD SHIP.

The "Greater Reich" Plebiscite on the annexation of Austria, held throughout Germany and Austria on Sunday, April 10, resulted in a sweeping victory for Herr Hitler. Out of an electorate of 49,546,950 the total votes cast were 49,326,791, of which 98.08 per cent were in his favour. The final figures were – For, 48,799,269. Against 452,180; Spoiled papers 75,342. The above photographs illustrate only that section of the Plebiscite specially arranged for voters resident in Britain, and held on board the 24,000-ton German liner "Wilhelm Gustloff", of Hamburg. She carried nearly 2000 Germans and Austrians, mainly from London, but some from the provinces and as far north as Edinburgh and Glasgow. Women outnumbered men by about three to one, most of the Austrian voters being domestic servants. The company on board had an enjoyable trip, with dancing and processions on deck, down the Thames from Tilbury to a point outside the 3-mile limit of British territorial waters, where the poll took place. The voting occupied 3 hours and gave a percentage of 99.4 in favour of Herr Hitler. The result was greeted with loud cheers. At the end of the cruise the ship's band played "God Save the King" and the German National Anthem.

(LEFT), DANCING ON DECK TO THE STRAINS OF AN ACCORDION: REJOICING AMONG THE CROWD OF VOTERS ON BOARD THE "STRENGTH THROUGH JOY" SHIP, "WILHELM GUSTLOFF", ON HER WAY DOWN THE THAMES.

THE GERMAN MARCH ON AUSTRIA:

PERSONALITIES OF THE CRISIS

DR. GOEBBELS BROADCASTING HERR HITLER'S PROCLAMATION.

On March 12 a proclamation by Herr Hitler was broadcast by Dr. Goebbels, the Minister for Propaganda. It read: "Since this morning, the soldiers of the German Armed Forces are marching over all the German-Austria frontier".

DR. SEYSS-INQUART

Has become Governor of the Austrian State within the German Reich. Was appointed Minister of the Interior after the Berchtesgaden Agreement.

HERR HITLER ENTERING BRAUNAU, IN UPPER AUSTRIA, WHERE HE WAS BORN: RECEIVING A BOUQUET.

One of the towns through which the Führer passed on his way to Vienna was Braunau, in Upper Austria. It was the first time that he had visited it since 1912 and he received an enthusiastic reception from the inhabitants.

TAKING OVER THE AUSTRIAN YOUTH ORGANISATION: HERR BALDUR VON SCHIRACH.

Herr Baldur von Schirach, the Reich Youth Leader, arrived in Vienna on March 13 and took possession of the Austrian Youth organisation.

FRAU DOLLFUSS WITH HER TWO YOUNG CHILDREN – REFUGEES FROM THE NAZI RÉGIME IN AUSTRIA.

Frau Dollfuss, the widow of the late Austrian Chancellor who was murdered by Nazis in 1934, fled from Austria when the National-Socialists assumed power and arrived in Budapest on March 13.

NOW FOREIGN MINISTER FOR BOTH GERMANY AND AUSTRIA: HERR VON RIBBENTROP; WITH HIS WIFE.

On March 15 Herr Wolff, Austrian Foreign Minister, handed over his office to Herr von Ribbentrop. During his stay in London, Herr von Ribbentrop was in close touch with Lord Halifax.

THE ALL-NAZI GOVERNMENT OF AUSTRIA, WHICH TOOK OFFICE ON MARCH 12: DR. SEYSS-INQUART (CENTRE; WITH CLASPED HANDS); AND MINISTERS.

THE LAST HEAD OF AN INDEPENDENT AUSTRIAN STATE: DR WILHELM MIKLAS, THE FEDERAL PRESIDENT, WITH HIS WIFE AND ONE OF HIS SONS.

An all-Nazi government took office in Austria on March 12. They are (l. to r.): Dr. Michael Skubl, Police Minister; Dr. Wilhelm Wolff, Foreign Minister; Dr. Rudolf Neumayr, Finance Minister; Dr. Franz Huber, Minister of Justice; Dr. Artur von Seyss-Inquart, Chancellor, Minister for Defence and Public Security; Professor Oswald Menghin, Minister of Education; Dr. Anton Reinthaler, Minister of Agriculture; Dr. Edmund von Glaise-Horstenau, Vice Chancellor; Dr. Hugo Jury, Minister for Social Welfare; and Dr. Fischbok, Trade and Communications. Dr. Wilhelm Miklas, Federal President of Austria, resigned on March 13.

ATLANTIC TO MEDITERRANEAN: FRANCO'S ADVANCES IN SPAIN

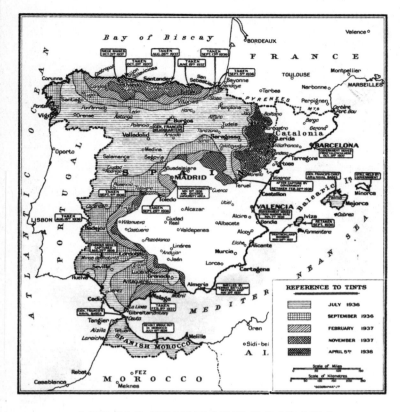

The revolt in Spain began with the murder by "Shock Police" of a Fascist leader, Sr. Calvo Sotelo, on July 13, 1936. On July 17 the Foreign Legion in Morocco revolted under General Franco, who flew there from the Canaries. It was followed by various garrisons in Spain, notably at Burgos in the north-west, in Saragossa, and in the Balearics. The Army officers attempted to rise in Barcelona and Madrid, but were overcome by popular resistance. From the first, Morocco formed a base for the insurgents. Their forces in the south of Spain then started by capturing isolated towns. Badajoz fell in August, and the southern forces joined up with General Mola's in the north-west. In September Iran and San Sebastian were taken in the north-east; and in the centre an attack launched up the Tagus Valley. Toledo was reached on September 28. By November the Nationalists were at the gates of Madrid. On November 15 they crossed the Manzanares River and entered the University City, but got no further. In 1937 an advance was made in the south, and Malaga fell in February. After an attempt to cut off Madrid had failed at Guadalajara, General Granco turned his attention to the weak and isolated Republican forces on the north coast. Bilbao fell on June 19, Santander on August 26, and Gijon, the last Government city in the north, on October 21. This year opened with a Government counter-attack. The Nationalists lost Teruel, but soon regained the ascendant. Teruel was recaptured and a new offensive was started which carried them into Catalonia. Lerida fell on April 3. Gaudesa, a place about twenty-five miles from the coast, was taken on April 4; and, as we write, the Nationalists are reported to be threatening Tortosa and the last remaining road linking Catalonia with the rest of Republican Spain. A relief offensive has been started by the Madrid army on the Guadalajara front, but it seems unlikely that this will prevent General Franco from reaching the Mediterranean.

AERIAL WARFARE IN SPAIN:
WITH THE ITALIAN "LEGIONARY AIR FORCE".

A TYPICAL BOMBER OF THE ITALIAN "LEGIONARY AIR FORCE" IN SPAIN: A MACHINE MARKED WITH THE NATIONALIST BLACK SALTIRE; AND AN "M" ON THE TAIL, PERHAPS INDICATING THAT IT IS PILOTED BY MUSSOLINI'S SON.

IN CASTELLON, REPORTED TAKEN BY FRANCO:
"AIR-RAID PRECAUTIONS".

AT CASTELLON, WHICH, IT WAS REPORTED, GENERAL FRANCO'S TROOPS RECENTLY ENTERED: AN AIR-RAID WARNING SOUNDS AND CIVILIANS RUN FOR COVER FROM NATIONALIST BOMBS.

BARCELONA'S ELECTRICITY IN FRANCO'S HANDS

THE TREMP BARRAGE IN THE VALLEY OF THE RIVER NOGUERA.

The capture of the village of Tremp, in north-eastern Spain between Lerida and the Pyrenees, by Navarrese troops of General Franco, was officially announced on April 7. With reference to this action, a "Times" correspondent wrote: "The big electric power plant and the large reservoir, a few miles outside the village, which supplies the greater part of the electric power to Barcelona and the rest of Catalonia, has also been surrounded."

The Spanish Nationalist resumed their offensive on the front between Teruel and the sea on June 7 and succeeded in advancing by gradual stages south-westward, their immediate objective being Castellon, a coastal town on the road to Valencia. They made gradual advances with the Galician Army Corps and the First and Fourth Navarrese divisions, in spite of prepared Government defences, which they appear to have outflanked by moving through the mountains. By June 9 they claimed to be within 12 miles of Castellon. On June 10, although their progress was retarded inland, they still went forward in the coastal sector. General Miaja, famous as the defender of Madrid, hurried to the Castellon sector to co-ordinate the Government efforts. The position there, however, was so precarious that a start was made with blowing-up bridges and destroying surplus transport. As we go to press, Nationalist reports claim that their troops are in possession of the town. The latest Government reports mention fighting four miles outside the town, the defenders finding themselves harassed by great numbers of Nationalist aeroplanes.

MR. EDEN RESIGNS.

MR. ANTHONY EDEN AFTER RESIGNING THE OFFICE OF FOREIGN SECRETARY: LEAVING HIS HOME ON HIS WAY TO THE HOUSE OF COMMONS TO EXPLAIN HIS DIFFERENCES WITH THE PRIME MINISTER.

Mr. Anthony Eden, the Foreign Secretary, handed his resignation to the Prime Minister on the evening of Sunday, February 20. He explained his action in the House of Commons on the following day. "There are occasions", he said, "when political convictions must override all other considerations . . . the ultimate aim of us all . . . is, and must always be, the maintenance of peace." He gave examples of the difficulties he had had in negotiating with Italy, notably over the Spanish question: and he argued: "In the light of the present international situation this is a moment for this country to stand firm . . . The conviction has steadily grown upon me that there has been too keen a desire on our part to make terms to others rather than others to make terms to us." Mr. Eden is the youngest Foreign Secretary of modern times, taking office at the age of thirty-eight. After distinguishing himself in the war, he entered politics and won Warwick and Leamington by a big majority in 1923. He became Parliamentary Private Secretary to Sir Austen Chamberlain in 1926.

ANGLO-ITALIAN PACT SIGNED.

A GREAT MOVE TOWARDS EUROPEAN PEACE: THE ANGLO-ITALIAN AGREEMENT – COUNT CIANO, THE ITALIAN MINISTER, SIGNING THE DOCUMENTS, WITH LORD PERTH, THE BRITISH AMBASSADOR (EXTREME RIGHT).

The Anglo-Italian Agreement, signed in Rome on April 16, and known there as the "Easter Pact" has been welcomed not only as putting an end to tension and misunderstanding between the two countries, and reviving their traditional friendship, but as a contribution of high importance to the cause of general peace in Europe. Germany regards it in that light, while France has taken steps towards negotiating a Franco-Italian Pact on similar lines. The ceremony of signature took place in the Sala della Vittoria in the Palazzo Chigi, the Italian Foreign Office, at a table on which stood a bronze figure of Winged Victory. Count Ciano signed first on the Italian text of the documents, and the Earl of Perth on the English text. Those relating to Egyptian interests were in triplicate and were signed first by the Egyptian Minister. On leaving the Palace, the British Ambassador was loudly cheered by the crowd outside.

EIRE'S FIRST PRESIDENT INSTALLED.

THE FIRST PRESIDENT OF EIRE INSTALLED IN DUBLIN CASTLE: A VIEW OF THE CEREMONY IN ST. PATRICK'S HALL, WITH DR. DOUGLAS HYDE TAKING THE OATH OF LOYALTY TO THE STATE BEFORE RECEIVING THE SEAL OF OFFICE FROM CHIEF JUSTICE SULLIVAN.

The new Constitution of the Irish Free State – now to be known as Eire – came into force on December 29. No public celebrations took place at the time, but Mr. de Valera drove from Government Buildings in Dublin, with an escort of mounted infantry, to the Pro-Cathedral, where he and his Ministers attended a votive Mass, while a salute of 21 guns was fired at the Royal Hospital at Kilmainham. The Presidental Commission (to function pending the election of a President) held its first meeting in Dublin Castle. The British Government issued a statement announcing that they were prepared, in common with the Dominions, to treat the new Constitution as not fundamentally altering the position of the State as a member of the British Commonwealth, but they could not recognise that the adoption of the name "Eire", or "Ireland", affects the position of Northern Ireland as an integral part of the United Kingdom.

By the signing of the Anglo-Irish Agreement on April 25, many outstanding questions between this country and Eire have been satisfactorily settled – among them the problem of the Land Annuities, which has been responsible for an economic "war" lasting six years. Much of the credit must necessarily go to Mr. Malcolm Macdonald, the Dominions Secretary, whose personal relations with Mr. de Valera have undoubtedly contributed to a satisfactory settlement.

DEMONSTRATING ITALY'S AIR FORCE TO HITLER

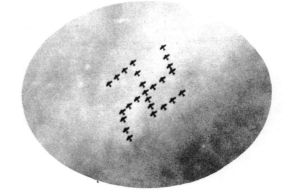

AERIAL MIGHT TO HERR HITLER: A SWASTIKA FORMED BY AEROPLANES – AN ELABORATE COMPLIMENT PAID TO THE GERMAN VISITORS.

Herr Hitler witnessed the great parade of Italian military might in Rome on May 6. For two hours standing on a platform facing the ruined palace of the Caesars, he returned the turned the salute of 50,000 troops, including infantry, colonial cavalry, mechanised heavy artillery, and labour battalions. He was on the right of his host, King Victor Emmanuel and on the left of the Duce. The parade opened with the marchpast of 10,000 boys and youths of the pre-military organisations breaking into the Roman "goose-step" as they neared the saluting-base.

Herr Hitler's magnificent welcome in Rome culminated in a State banquet at the Palazzo Venezia on May 7, when he and Signor Mussolini reaffirmed German-Italian friendship. They afterwards appeared together on the balcony to acknowledge acclamations. The Duce said in his speech: "Your visit to Rome fulfils and seals the understanding between our two countries". In his reply the Führer declared: "Germany and Italy are closely bound to one another by their common ideology".

GREATER GERMANY: PROPAGANDA MAPS;
CZECHOSLOVAKIA'S GERMAN MINORITIES.

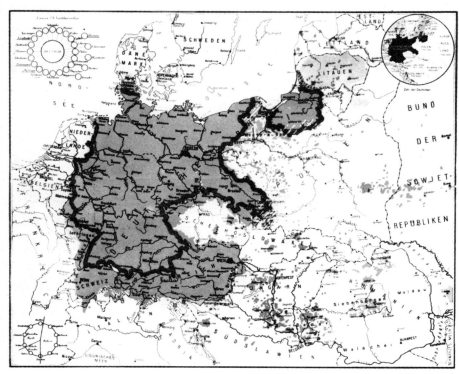

The working of the Pan-German conception of Central Europe can be described and illustrated by a series of maps. Since the invasion of Austria, speeches by German leaders have left no doubt as to the continued influence of Pan-German ideas. For instance, Herr Hitler, speaking in Berlin on March 28, reiterated his claim that all Germans in Europe should be united with the Reich, saying that by the Peace Treaties 10,000,000 of them had been made "stateless". On the left we deal with recent German propaganda; notably, a scientific-looking language map arranged to "emphasise" the German's place in Europe. It is beautifully printed in numerous colours. It is misleading in several ways. Thus, although ostensibly only a language map, it makes no differentiation between the High German and Low German dialects (a division usual in maps of this type), yet separates the Walloon-speaking area, though Walloon is only a French dialect, and divides Great Russia from White Russia – again only a matter of dialects. It also separates absolutely Czechs from Slovaks – a favourite contention of German propaganda, totally unjustified by the facts. It is more or less subtly misleading with regard to German minorities in Czechoslovakia, Poland, and Alsace-Lorraine, showing solid German speaking blocks, where this is not the case. With regard to the Germans in Switzerland, the author of the map admits (in a column of descriptive matter) that "at times a strong sentiment of nationality largely obliterates the sentiment of common ancestry and cultural heritage". Germany is shown bordered by "Germanic peoples" – such as Swedes, Danes, Dutchmen, and Flemings – another somewhat misleading category.

LINGUISTIC MAP OF EUROPE CALLING ATTENTION TO THE GERMAN-SPEAKING GROUPS – INCLUDING THOSE IN FRANCE, SWITZERLAND, HUNGARY, RUMANIA, CZECHOSLOVAKIA, POLAND AND RUSSIA.

The Nazi move towards dominating Austria has set everyone asking "What is the position of Czechoslovakia in the altered circumstances?" On March 4, the Czechoslovak Prime Minister, Dr. Hodza, vigorously expressed his country's determination to maintain her independence. His words were: "I emphasise in full consciousness of the consequences of this declaration that our frontiers are absolutely inviolate . . . We would be doing a poor service to Central Europe and to our own relations with Germany if we did not make it perfectly clear that Czechoslovakia will never . . . tolerate interference with its domestic affairs. Czechoslovakia wishes to leave no room for doubt as to its firm determination to defend with all its power the attributes of its Statehood . . . If we are faced with the necessity of defending ourselves, we will defend, defend, defend." Opportunity of emphasising this determination was taken by President Benesh in a special interview printed in the "Sunday Times" on March 6. He there made the following points: Czechoslovakia can never discuss the minority problem with Germany officially; she recognises, nevertheless, the moral right of Europe to take an interest in a question so important for peace; regards good relations with Germany as a vital interest; is prepared, therefore, to make her contribution in any general European settlement; but excludes as impossible federal autonomy for the 3,000,000 Germans within her borders. These statements had been preceded by a significant pronouncement by General Ludwig Krejci, chief of the Czech General Staff. He said: "We are aware of the possibility of a war against the Republic without formal declaration of war. The Army is well prepared and will not be taken by surprise by such a war, which may take the form of a sudden and brutal onslaught of motorised and mechanised units against the most vulnerable regions of the country. The standards of the Army, of the country's defence works, and of its armaments industry are so highly perfected that any enemy would do well to think twice whether a surprise attack will have any prospects of quick success. In view of her great geographical distance from her allies, Czechoslovakia cannot count on their assistance during the first phase of such a war and will, at least during the first days, have to make her stand alone. The General Staff has, therefore, erected a huge barrier of permanent fortifications and defence works along the whole frontier, whereby time will be secured for a general mobilisation and to move troops into position. A detailed scheme for the mobilisation of all the country's war industries for war purposes is ready. The famous Czech Skoda armament works are already being moved from danger zones into districts which afford greater military advantages. Eight aircraft factories have been constructed and are working at full speed. A detailed scheme for the food supply of the entire population in the event of war has been worked out and can be operated whenever necessary."

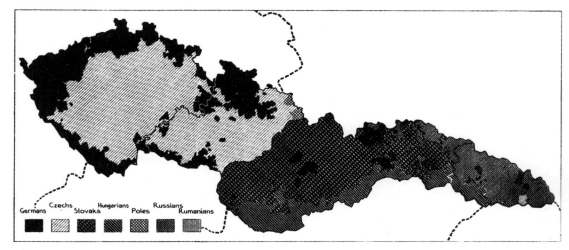

Germans   Czechs   Hungarians   Russians
         Slovaks   Poles   Rumanians

THE BURNING QUESTION OF MINORITIES IN CZECHOSLOVAKIA: A GERMAN PROPAGANDIST MAP WHICH GIVES THE IMPRESSION THAT THE GERMAN COMMUNITIES ARE MORE NUMEROUS THAN, IN FACT, THEY ARE AND THAT CZECHS AND SLOVAKS FORM SEPARATE NATIONS; AND ALSO EMPHASISES HUNGARIAN AND RUTHENIAN MINORITIES.

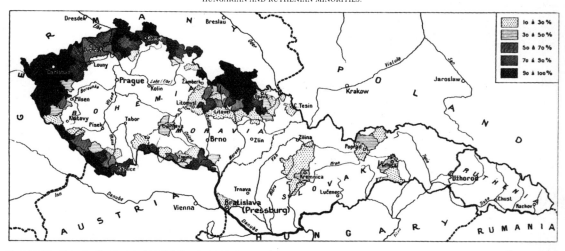

10 à 30 %
30 à 50 %
50 à 70 %
70 à 90 %
90 à 100 %

PART OF THE TEN MILLION GERMANS LIVING OUT OF THEIR OWN COUNTRY WHOM HERR HITLER HAS SAID THE REICH WOULD PROTECT: A MAP OF CZECHOSLOVAKIA (PREPARED IN FRANCE) SHOWING THE VERY VARIABLE DENSITY OF THE GERMAN POPULATION, WHICH IS ONLY LARGE IN CERTAIN FRONTIER DISTRICTS.

Looking at the map of Czechoslovakia it will be seen that its weakest feature, strategically speaking, is its narrow "waist" – scarcely 100 miles across from Southern Silesia, in the north, to Austria in the south. Should an enemy succeed in getting possession of this "waist", the country could be cut in two, and the halves, Bohemia and Slovakia, dealt with separately. It happens, too, that this "waist" coincides both on the north and the south with gaps in the moutain barriers on the frontier, the "Oder gap" in the north and the "Moravian gateway" in the south. But the Oder gap is half in Polish territory, and all that is left is a narrow bottle-neck twenty-five miles wide. This the Czechs have transformed into one of the strongest fortified areas in Europe, so tht it cannot easily be rushed. The Czechoslovak frontier with Austria, on the other hand, has, up till now, been only lightly fortified, Austria having been hitherto regarded as a friend and possible ally. Special measures are now being taken to ensure the protection of the Moravian gateway.

CZECHOSLOVAKIAN DEFENCES:
FRONTIERS SECURED BY FORTIFICATIONS.

THE ARTILLERY OF THE CZECH ARMY – REPUTED TO BE EXTREMELY EFFICIENT AND WELL-EQUIPPED: A HEAVY HOWITZER WITH THE GUN CREW IN THE NEW TYPE OF CZECHOSLOVAK STEEL HELMET RESEMBLING THE GERMAN.

A HEAVY MORTAR – A TYPE OF GUN IN WHICH THE SKODA ARMS WORKS OF CZECHOSLOVAKIA HAVE ALWAYS SPECIALISED. A HUGE WEAPON (PROBABLY OF 21 CM–I.E. 8.2 IN CALIBRE) ABOUT TO BE FIRED.

The peace-strength of the Czech Army is fourteen divisions; and this could be doubled in answer to an act of war, provided that mobilisation was not interfered with by enemy sabotage and air action. The population of the country is 15,000,000; including the German minority of 3,000,000. The army is formidable, on account of its thoroughly up-to-date equipment. Czechoslovakia is one of the great arms-manufacturing countries of the world. The huge 30.5 cm and 21 cm mortars are a special feature of the Czech artillery; and it will be recalled that mortars from the Skoda works won some notable successes for the Central Powers in the Great War. The remainder of the Czech artillery is armed with 15 cm guns and howitzers, both with motor traction; 10 cm and 10.5 cm "light" and "heavy" field guns; and mountain guns. There are also several "special" artillery regiments, some being armed with anti-aircraft guns. Czechoslovakia has also made considerable progress in developing her tank strength, while the effectiveness of her light machine-guns is vouched for by the fact that our own army when investigating different types to replace the Lewis gun, chose a model from the Brno factories which was developed into the Bren gun now in use. The Czechoslovak Air Force has been steadily expanding for many years. It now comprises six regiments, with about 550 first-line machines, and a thousand all told. It is backed by an extremely efficient aviation industry, quite independent of foreign imports, and with an annual productive capacity of over a thousand machines, which could be considerably increased in emergency.

THE NAZI MOVEMENT IN CZECHOSLOVAKIA

Herr Conrad Henlein joined the Austrian Army in 1914 and saw service on the Italian front. He was made prisoner and sent to a camp in Sardinia, where he spent two years. After the war he became a bank clerk in Bohemia; but all his spare time was devoted to the new gymnastic youth movement among the Germans in Czechoslovakia, known as the Turnbewegung. By May 1935 Herr Henlein found himself at the head of the Sudeten German organisation, at the time of their great success in the Czechoslovak Parliamentary elections.

(RIGHT), A DEMONSTRATION BY MEMBERS OF THE SUDETEN GERMAN PARTY, WEARING WHITE SHIRTS, WITH BLACK TROUSERS AND CAPS, AS SUBSTITUTE FOR A FORBIDDEN UNIFORM.

THE "FÜHRER" OF THE SUDETEN PARTY AMONG THE GERMAN MINORITY IN CZECHOSLOVAKIA, WHOSE ACTIVITIES ARE OF MOMENTOUS IMPORTANCE IN EUROPE: HERR CONRAD HENLEIN SPEAKING AT A SUDETEN DEUTSCH GATHERING.

TENSE DAYS IN CZECHOSLOVAKIA:
THE SUDETEN "MARTYRS'" FUNERAL

Considerable relief was felt throughout Europe when the funerals of the two Sudeten farmers who were shot by Czech frontier guards after defying their orders to halt, passed off without awkward incident. The town of Eger, on the north-western border of Bohemia, was packed with mourners of the Sudeten party and all houses were hung with black flags. The Czechoslovak authorities withdrew not only the police and the gendarmerie, but even the sentries outside the barracks. In the centre of the main square, where is situated the inn from which the dead men set out on their last journey, was a great catafalque of black and red. Herr Hitler's wreaths displayed the Swastika and the Chancellor's standard. Herr Henlein, the Sudeten German leader, two deputy leaders, Colonel Toussaint, the German Military Attaché, and Major Moericke, the German Air Attaché, marched side by side in the procession.

THE FUNERAL OF TWO SUDETEN FARMERS SHOT BY CZECH FRONTIER GUARDS, ANXIOUSLY WATCHED BY ALL EUROPE, AN "INCIDENT" BEING FEARED: DENSE CROWDS OF SUDETEN SYMPATHISERS IN THE MAIN SQUARE OF EGER.

THE STATE VISIT OF THE KING AND QUEEN TO FRANCE.

THE "ENCHANTRESS", WITH THEIR MAJESTIES ON BOARD, ESCORTED ACROSS THE CHANNEL: A PHOTOGRAPH SHOWING BRITISH AEROPLANES AND BRITISH DESTROYERS WHICH HANDED OVER THE DUTY TO FRENCH VESSELS AT A POINT HALF-WAY.

THE DEPARTURE FROM BOULOGNE FOR PARIS: THEIR MAJESTIES HONOURED IN THE ROYAL TRAIN AS IT MOVED OUT – THE ROYAL ARMS VISIBLE ON A PLAQUE ON THE LEFT.

JULY 19; AFTERNOON: THE ROYAL CARS, ESCORTED BY A DETACHMENT OF THE MOUNTED GARDE REPUBLICAINE AND FLANKED BY MOTOR-CYCLISTS, CROSSING THE PONT DE LA CONCORDE EN ROUTE TO THE QUAI D'ORSAY.

PRELUDE TO THE ROYAL VISIT:
A JULY 14 "REHEARSAL" FOR VERSAILLES.

"BASTILLE DAY" IN PARIS: "DAZZLE-PAINTED TANKS PASSING THROUGH THE ARC DE TRIOMPHE DURING THE REVIEW OF THE FRENCH DEFENCE FORCES.

On July 22 the King unveiled the Australian National War Memorial at Villers Bretonneux, on ground known in the war as "Hill 104", the scene of a brilliant counter-attack by Australian troops. President Lebrun described the site as "this plot of French soil, now become Australian". His Majesty said, in the course of his moving speech: "This ridge, on which we stand, surveyed those hard-fought actions and the monument which crowns it will commemorate them for all time . . . It looks down a hallowed field, beneath whose soil, consecrated to God and to their glorious memory, lie the men who came from every corner of the earth to fight for ideals common to the whole Empire. They rest in peace, while over them all Australia's tower keeps watch and ward . . . It is also a symbol, marking the first entry into history of a young and vigorous nation – the gateway through which Australia passed from youth to manhood."

The customary celebration of the fall of the Bastille was linked in Paris this year with the royal visit. The capital was thronged by sightseers examining the special and beautiful decorations; and this national holiday became, as one paper described it, a "Franco-British July 14", for there were as many Union Jacks displayed as tricolour flags. The annual parade of troops from all parts of France and her colonies and units of the Navy and Air Force assumed a new significance: it not only emphasised France's share in the "Entente Cordiale", but served as something of a rehearsal for the great military review at Versailles, on July 21, at which the King, accompanied by the President, arranged to be present.

THE KING'S TRIBUTE TO AUSTRALIA'S DEAD: HIS MAJESTY PLACING A WREATH AT THE AUSTRALIAN WAR MEMORIAL AT VILLERS BRETONNEUX JUST AFTER HE HAD UNVEILED IT.

THE MAGINOT LINE: THE VAST DEFENCE SYSTEM ON THE EASTERN FRONTIER OF FRANCE.

THE SIEGFRIED LINE: GERMANY'S REPLY TO THE FRENCH MAGINOT LINE.

POINTING EASTWARD TOWARDS GERMANY: SHOWING PORT-HOLES FOR OBSERVATION.

A NEW TYPE OF ROAD BARRIER: A CONCRETE OBSTACLE WITH "COG-WHEEL" TEETH; AND (BEYOND) A BELT OF ANTI-TANK PYRAMIDS, FIVE DEEP, ZIGZAGGING ACROSS COUNTRY.

In view of the European situation, it is hardly necessary to stress the immense importance of the Maginot Line, that vast system of subterranean fortifications – named after the late M. André Maginot, French Minister of War at the time of its inception – which is considered to make the eastern frontier of France impregnable against invasion. Mr. Robert Leurquin writes: "France is on guard in the Maginot Line: surprise is impossible. A visitor . . . can, with the aid of binoculars, look across the Rhine to the other side, where are the observation posts of the Reichswehr. There columns of German workmen are making a system of defence identical with the French. These defences are a reassuring guarantee of peace to the West. Before 1914 both sides of the eastern frontier strove to prepare the most powerful jumping-off places for attack. Today on both sides they are digging for defence."

According to an account published in the "Angriff", the Berlin newspaper founded by Dr. Goebbels, Reich Minister of Propaganda, there is in front "a line of steel and concrete pyramids, running like a road over hills and down valleys from the north to the south extremities of the western frontier", while further back is "a secondary line of ferro-concrete forts, largely sunk in the ground and practically invisible to the naked eye". The pyramids, which are arranged in connected sets, are designed to obstruct tanks, and are believed to be quite impassable. Behind them lie chain after chain of machine-gun nests. The German Command, it is said, does not favour an entirely underground system like the French. Great importance is attached to camouflage, and bushes have been planted to screen forts and gun positions. The "Angriff" writer says that such precautions are necessary, as observers in the Maginot Line command an extensive view into German territory.

DISCUSSED BY ALL EUROPE: GERMANY'S GREATEST POST-WAR MANOEUVRES.

PREPARING THE GUNS FOR ACTION DURING THE GERMAN ARMY MANOEUVRES: A BATTERY OF MEDIUM ARTILLERY CAMOUFLAGED AND IN POSITION.

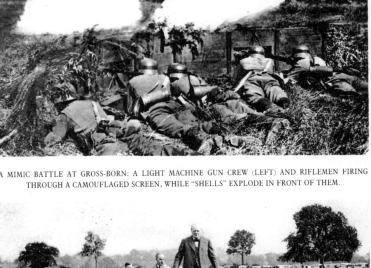

A MIMIC BATTLE AT GROSS-BORN: A LIGHT MACHINE GUN CREW (LEFT) AND RIFLEMEN FIRING THROUGH A CAMOUFLAGED SCREEN, WHILE "SHELLS" EXPLODE IN FRONT OF THEM.

"TO PLACE OVER 1,500,000 SOLDIERS UPON A WAR-FOOTING IS A VERY GRAVE STEP": MR. WINSTON CHURCHILL SPEAKING AT THEYDON BOIS.

The autumn manoeuvres of the German Army, which began on August 14, are expected to last ten weeks and are intended mainly to serve the purpose of training reservists. Most marked interest in these exercises was shown in other countries when it became known that 750,000 reservists were to be called to the Colours; that a certain number of conscripts whose service would normally end in September were to be retained indefinitely; that all men of military age (under 65) were forbidden to leave Germany; and that food, horses and motor-vehicles were being requisitioned on a large scale. These measures and the registration of women and other non-combatants may be regarded as a partial trial mobilisation. As the reserve divisions are training as units, it was necessary to draw upon civilian resources for their needs, for they are not equipped with military transport of their own. Officially described as "small manoeuvres", each of the 52 divisions of the German Army will carry out divisional training in its own area until September and then each of the 18 Army Corps which form Germany's peace establishment will train independently as a unit until September 25. The peace establishment of the German Army, together with that of the former Austrian Army, is some 600,000 men and by the middle of September probably over 1,000,000 men will be under arms. Herr Hitler is taking a keen personal interest in the technical side of the exercises and on August 15 he visited Juterborg, some forty miles from Berlin, where units of the Third Army Command (Berlin) began divisional training, as did other troops in all parts of the Reich. On August 17 the Führer watched a battalion exercise at the Infantry School at Doberitz, near Berlin, and on August 19 he began a two-day visit to units of the 11. Army Corps at Gross-Born, in Eastern Pomerania. He was accompanied by the Commander-in-Chief, Colonel-General von Brauchitsch.

In a speech at Theydon Bois on August 27, Mr. Winston Churchill declared that the whole state of Europe was moving steadily towards a climax could not be long delayed. "War is certainly not inevitable", he said, but he argued that danger to peace would not be removed until the vast German armies which had been called up had been dispersed. "Our anxieties and our hopes centre upon the extraordinary man at the summit of Germany."

CZECHOSLOVAKIA: THE TENTH SOKOL FESTIVAL AT PRAGUE.

The tenth Sokol Festival coincided with the twentieth anniversary of the founding of the Czechoslovak Republic, and extensive preparations were made in Prague to make the four days' Congress a success. The Masaryk Stadium was enlarged to enable 30,000 performers to give displays at a time and to accommodate 150,000 spectators. Representatives of the Sokol (Falcon) Association abroad came from the United States, France, Belgium, Bulgaria, Poland, Lithuania and Yugoslavia and from Vienna and Berlin. The displays at the Stadium began on July 3 in the presence of President Benesh, members of the Cabinet and the whole of the Diplomatic Corps. The Sokol movement dates from 1862.

A DISPLAY OF COUNTRY DANCING IN THE IMMENSE MASARYK STADIUM AT PRAGUE DURING THE TENTH SOKOL FESTIVAL: WOMEN, DRESSED IN WHITE BLOUSES AND RED SKIRTS, PERFORMING A MAYPOLE DANCE.

A GYMNASTIC DISPLAY BY YOUNG GIRLS FROM SIX TO FOURTEEN YEARS OF AGE: MASSED EXERCISES BY PERFORMERS WHO, IN SPITE OF THEIR YOUTH, TOOK UP THEIR POSITIONS WITH ASTONISHING PRECISION.

THE SUDETEN GERMAN PROBLEM IN CZECHOSLOVAKIA: A MENACE TO THE PEACE OF CENTRAL EUROPE.

AN ATTACK ON DEMOCRACIES AT THE ANNUAL CONGRESS OF THE ORGANISATION OF GERMANS LIVING ABROAD: HERR HESS SPEAKING AT STUTTGART.

The annual congress of the Nazi organisation for Germans living abroad began at Stuttgart on August 28. In a speech at the opening ceremony, Herr Hess, Herr Hitler's deputy, made a violent attack on democracies. His references to the "martyrdom" and "suffering" of Sudeten Germans in Czechoslovakia were also warmly applauded by the audience. Herr Bohle, the leader of the organisation, made a threat to deprive "Aryan" Germans living abroad of their nationality if they did not demonstrate their adherence to National Socialism more loyally. He also threatened drastic reprisals against Germans who "from the safety of a foreign residence", write for anti-Nazi newspapers criticising the National Socialist regime. Foreign observers, however, noted that, generally speaking, the same enthusiasm was not observable among the delegates to the congress as in previous years.

SIR JOHN SIMON'S SPEECH AT LANARK: THE BRITISH CHANCELLOR OF THE EXCHEQUER MAKING HIS EAGERLY AWAITED DECLARATION ON THE GOVERNMENT'S ATTITUDE WITH REGARD TO THE PROBLEM OF CZECHOSLOVAKIA.

In his important speech at Lanark on August 27, Sir John Simon spoke of the Government's determination to make every effort to maintain peace. Mr. Chamberlain's declaration of March 24 with regard to Czechoslovakia, he said, held good today. In this declaration, it will be remembered, the Prime Minister refused to admit that British would automatically be drawn into any conflict over Czechoslovakia; but, he added, "where peace and war are concerned, legal obligations are not alone involved, and if war broke out . . . it would be quite impossible to say where it would end and what Governments might become involved." Sir John Simon's speech was received with anger and disappointment in Berlin; welcomed in Prague and approved in Paris.

AT A MOMENT OF VERY GREAT GRAVITY: SPEECH AND DISCUSSION.

negotiations with the Prague Government . . . After his long conversation with Herr Hitler, Herr Henlein travelled back to Prague, and later had a private talk with Mr. Ashton-Gwatkin, of the British Mission. It was reported that nothing had been said at Berchtesgaden to rule out a peaceful solution of the Czech problem. In the above photograph Dr. Goebbels, German Minister of Propaganda, is seen standing (with arms folded) between Herr Hitler and Herr Henlein, and in the middle of the group on the right (with hand on arm) is Herr von Ribbentrop, the Foreign Minister.

In his broadcast appeal to the nation, made at Prague on September 10, Dr. Benesh said: "I am talking to all of you. Czechs, Slovaks, Germans . . . Never has the responsibility of every one of us been greater. Show the world that not one of us wishes to be held responsible for increasing the present European tension . . . I believe that the German people as well as the Czechs, Slovaks, and all others truly desire to work together in quiet. That is why I believe that on the basis of the new proposals the Government will come to terms with all nationalities and will guarantee the Republic a future of prosperity."

A MEETING CONCERNING THE EUROPEAN CRISIS: HERR HITLER (LEFT) AND HIS MINISTERS DISCUSSING THE CZECH QUESTION WITH THE SUDETEN GERMAN LEADER, HERR HENLEIN (IN CENTRE, FACING THE CAMERA), ON THE TERRACE OF THE FÜHRER'S VILLA AT BERCHTESGADEN.

An official German *communiqué* issued in Berlin on September 2 stated: "The Führer received today at the Berghof the Leader of the Sudeten Germans, Konrad Henlein, who at Lord Runciman's desire gave him a sketch of the present state of the

DR. BENESH, PRESIDENT OF CZECHOSLOVAKIA, APPEALING TO ALL CONCERNED TO KEEP CALM AND AVOID DISPUTES.

IN GERMANY DURING THE CRISIS:
NUREMBERG SPEECHES AND PARADES.

The Nuremberg Congress reached its climax on September 12 with the anxiously awaited speech of Herr Hitler. Sir Nevile Henderson, the British Ambassador to Germany, attended the Congress. Full reports of his previous conversations in Germany had been received by the Cabinet in London and showed that the British Government's views on the Czech crisis had been conveyed to the proper quarter. Field-Marshal Goering's speech to 30,000 members of the Labour Front, on September 10, was provocative in certain references to Czechoslovakia, Russia and the democracies. He also said: "Never before in history has Germany been so strong and united as she is now . . . We shall be ready to obey unflinchingly the orders of our Führer wherever he leads us . . . We do not want to hurt anybody, but we will not suffer any harm to our brethren from anyone." One the same evening Dr. Goebbels, Minister of Propaganda, addressed a Nazi Party rally and referred to what he called "the Bolshevik menace in Czechoslovakia". After the Hitler Youth gathering in the Sports Stadium, Herr Rudolf Hess enrolled several thousand boys and girls of eighteen as members of the Nazi Party.

In the course of his momentous speech in the Congress Hall on September 12, Herr Hitler, dealing with the subject chiefly in the minds of the statesmen and peoples of the world, said "Among the majority of the nationalities which are being supressed in this state (Czechoslovakia) there are 3,500,000 Germans . . . In no circumstances shall I be willing any more to regard with endless tranquility a continuation of oppression of German compatriots in Czechoslovakia . . . I have not raised the claim that Germany may oppress three and a half million French, or that three and a half million English shall be surrendered to Germany for oppression. But I demand that the oppression of three and a half million Germans in Czechoslovakia shall cease and be replaced by the free right of self-determination . . . It is up to the Czechoslovak Government to discuss matters with the representatives of the Sudeten Germans.

HERR HITLER MAKING HIS FATEFUL PRONOUNCEMENT, IN WHICH HE DEMANDED THE RIGHT OF SELF-DETERMINATION FOR THE SUDETEN GERMANS OF CZECHOSLOVAKIA.

ON THE HITLER SPEECH NIGHT: DOWNING ST. CROWDS RECALLING 1914.

MR. JOSEPH KENNEDY

MR. CHURCHILL

MR. ANTHONY EDEN

A SCENE PARALLELLED ONLY BY THOSE OF THE EVE OF THE GREAT WAR: A SECTION OF THE BIG CROWD WHICH BEGAN TO ASSEMBLE IN DOWNING STREET IN THE EARLY AFTERNOON OF SEPTEMBER 12 AND REACHED SUCH PROPORTIONS BY THE EVENING THAT THE POLICE HAD TO CLEAR THE STREET.

Anxiety over the German-Czechoslovak crisis caused great activity among British Ministers and their advisers, especially during the weekend preceding the date (September 12) fixed for Herr Hitler's fateful speech at Nuremberg. There was much coming and going at the Prime Minister's residence in Downing Street, and large crowds collected outside to watch the arrival and departure of visitors. Among those who called at the Foreign Office to see Lord Halifax was Mr. Joseph Kennedy, the American Ambassador, who later had a talk with Mr. Chamberlain. It was stated in official circles that the sympathy of the United States was valued more than ever at this difficult moment and that Anglo-American relations had never been more cordial. Mr. Churchill and Mr. Eden were said to be the only two British statesmen not in office who joined in the discussions. The meetings of the Cabinet attracted a number of interested spectators; but the scenes in Downing Street and Whitehall on September 12 have only been paralleled by those on the eve of the Great War. The crowds began to assemble in the afternoon and by the evening filled the street. Shortly before 9.30, when Sir John Simon, Lord Halifax and Sir Samuel Hoare arrived to confer with the Prime Minister on Herr Hitler's speech, mounted police cleared the crowd from Downing Street and formed a cordon across the entrance. In Whitehall reports of the speech were eagerly read, passed from hand to hand, and discussed by the public, many of whom had been waiting there for some hours.

THE PRIME MINISTER'S VISIT
TO THE FÜHRER AT BERCHTESGADEN.

"A FLYING MESSENGER OF PEACE": MR. NEVILLE CHAMBERLAIN ON THE WAY TO GERMANY TO SEE HERR HITLER.

Believing, as he does, in personal contact for settling disputes, Mr. Chamberlain, on September 14, sent a message to Herr Hitler in which he said: "In view of the increasingly critical situation, I propose to come over at once to see you with a view to trying to find a peaceful solution". The Führer suggested September 15, so the Prime Minister, who is sixty-nine, made his first air journey (600 miles) from Heston to Munich, accompanied by Sir Horace Wilson and Mr. William Strang, of the Foreign Office. At Munich airport the party were met by Herr von Ribbentrop, German Foreign Minister, and Dr. von Dirksen, German Ambassador in London. Mr. Chamberlain then went by special train to Berchtesgaden, and proceeded at once to the Grand Hotel. Presently he drove to the Führer's chalet. Herr Hitler, who was waiting on the steps, welcomed him warmly and led the way into the house, where tea was taken in the great hall. The party included Sir Nevile Henderson, British Ambassador in Berlin. Afterwards the two statemen retired to Herr Hitler's study, and a conference took place lasting till 8 p.m. Next day Mr. Chamberlain returned to consult the Cabinet. He drove to Munich and thence came by air. On landing at Heston he said: "I had a long talk with Herr Hitler. It was a frank talk; it was a friendly one and I feel satisfied now that each of us fully understands what is in the mind of the other . . . Later on, I am going to have another talk with Herr Hitler only this time it is his intention to come half-way to meet me."

THE PRIME MINISTER AS A GUEST AT THE FÜHRER'S TABLE: (LEFT TO RIGHT) MR. CHAMBERLAIN, HERR HITLER, AND (EXTREME RIGHT) SIR NEVILE HENDERSON, BRITISH AMBASSADOR TO GERMANY, AT TEA.

As he left the aeroplane, the Premier was handed a personal letter from the King, and later he had an audience of his Majesty at Buckingham Palace. Mr. Chamberlain's next meeting with the Führer was expected to take place at Bad Godesberg.

AGITATION IN SUDETEN GERMAN AREAS OF CZECHOSLOVAKIA.

"INCIDENTS" OF THE CZECH CRISIS: 1. THE SUDETEN DEMONSTRATION AT MARISCH OSTRAU ON SEPTEMBER 7TH. 2. SUDETEN FLAGS AT MARISCH OSTRAU. 3. BOMB DAMAGE ON SEPTEMBER 9TH IN A CZECH TECHNICAL SCHOOL AT HULTSCHIN. 4. WHERE HENLEINISTS KILLED THE COMMANDANT AND THREE OF HIS MEN: THE GENDARMERIE POST AT HABERSBERG. 5. 6 AND 7. BILINGUAL NOTICES AT EGER DEFACED, WITH CZECH WORDS OBLITERATED. (6) A SCHOOL DENTAL CLINIC NOTICE; AND (7) A PLACARD. 8. CZECH POLICE MAKING ARRESTS AT MOST, A MINING VILLAGE IN NORTH BOHEMIA.

We illustrate here various "incidents" and clashes that occurred in the Sudeten German areas of Czechoslovakia, both before and after Herr Hitler's speech at Nuremberg on September 12. On September 13 the Czech Government imposed martial law in certain Sudeten German districts after the outbreak of disorders. Later in the same day Herr Henlein, the Sudeten German leader, sent an ultimatum to President Benesh demanding the immediate revocation of martial law, withdrawal of the State and Special Police, and the confinement of troops to barracks. This ultimatum expired at midnight, and the Government decided not to revoke the measures taken. On the 14th it was stated that Herr Henlein had informed the Czech Premier, Dr. Hodza, that further negotiations were not possible. Later Herr Heinlein was reported to have fled to Germany.

FRANCO-BRITISH CONSULTATIONS
AND SUPPORT FROM ITALY

THE FRENCH PREMIER'S ARRIVAL IN LONDON FOR CONSULTATIONS WHICH RESULTED IN COMPLETE AGREEMENT BETWEEN FRANCE AND BRITAIN OVER THE CZECH CRISIS: M. DALADIER WELCOMED AT CROYDON BY MR. CHAMBERLAIN.

"ITALY KNOWS ON WHICH SIDE SHE WILL BE": SIGNOR MUSSOLINI AT TRIESTE, WHERE HE SPOKE ON THE INTERNATIONAL SITUATION.

M. Daladier, the French Prime Minister, with M. Bonnet (seen in the photograph next to right), arrived at Croydon by air from Paris on the morning of Sunday, September 18, in response to the British Cabinet's invitation. The French Ministers were met by Mr. Chamberlain in person accompanied by Lord Halifax (seen above in the left foreground) and M. Corbin, the French Ambassador. They spent the whole day in consultation with Mr. Chamberlain and other British Ministers, or among themselves, and heard Mr. Chamberlain's account of his talk with Herr Hitler. Shortly after midnight the following *communiqué* was issued from 10, Downing Street: "After full discussion of the present international situation the representatives of the British and French Governments are in complete agreement as to the policy to be adopted with a view to promoting a peaceful solution of the Czechoslovak question. The two Governments hope that thereafter it will be possible to consider a more general settlement in the interests of European peace." MM. Daladier and Bonnet flew back to France on Monday, September 19.

Speaking at Trieste on September 18, Signor Mussolini reviewed the international situation and stated: "The solution of the problem which is tormenting Europe at the moment has only one name, plebiscites, plebiscites for all the nationalities which want them . . . We still hope for a peaceful issue. We hope that if that is not possible the conflict may be localised, but if that cannot be done and a front is formed either for or against Prague, Italy knows on which side she will be." He also referred to Mr. Chamberlain's visit to Herr Hitler and stated: "The need for quick action was realised by the Prime Minister, who went from London to Munich, a flying messenger of peace."

THE CHAMBERLAIN-HITLER CONVERSATIONS:
THE PREMIER AT GODESBERG.

At their conferences on the Czechoslovak crisis, held at the Hotel Dreesen in Godesberg during the Prime Minister's second visit to Germany, he and Herr Hitler made much use of maps in discussing the situation. In the above photograph Mr. Chamberlain is seen leaning on the table to examine the map of Europe while a point in the Führer's remarks is explained by Dr. Schmidt, of the German Foreign Office (acting as interpreter) who is standing between the two statemen.

MR. CHAMBERLAIN AND HERR HITLER CONSULT THE MAP OF EUROPE DURING THEIR DISCUSSION OF THE CZECHOSLOVAK PROBLEM: AN INCIDENT OF THE GODESBERG CONVERSATIONS.

The conference between Mr. Chamberlain and Herr Hitler, begun recently at Berchtesgaden, were resumed on September 22 at Godesberg. That night the British delegation issued a *communiqué* stating: "The Prime Minister had a conversation with the German Führer, which, beginning at 4 o clock, was continued until shortly after 7 p.m. It is intended to resume the conversations to-morrow morning. In the meantime the first essential, in the opinion of the Prime Minister, is that there should be a determination on the part of all parties and of all concerned to ensure that the local conditions in Czechoslovakia are such as not in any way to interfere with the progress of the conversations. The Prime Minister appeals most earnestly, therefore, to everybody to assist in maintaining a state of orderliness and to refrain from action of any kind that would be likely to lead to incidents."

The intention referred to in the *communiqué* of September 22 to resume the talks between Mr. Chamberlain and Herr Hitler next morning was not fulfilled, and their next meeting did not take place til 10.40 p.m. Commenting on the delay. "The Times" stated: "Yesterday (the 23rd) was a day of the most acute suspense. Mr. Chamberlain remained in his hotel on the mountains. Herr Hitler in his hotel by the river bank. Messengers between the two hotels were ferried across the river and driven up and down the steep slopes of the Petersberg . . . No official information was obtainable as to the reasons for the hitch . . . Later the explanation came. Mr. Chamberlain, it was announced, had sent a letter to Herr Hitler, to which the Führer would reply. The resumption of the negotiations was accordingly postponed until later in the day." After the meeting, a joint official *communiqué* stated: "Friendly conversations between Herr Hitler and Mr. Chamberlain ended today with the handing over of a German memorandum containing Germany's final attitude regarding the situation in the Sudeten-German territory. Mr. Chamberlain undertook to transmit the memorandum to the Czech Government. The Führer took the opportunity to express to Mr. Chamberlain his personal gratitude and that of the German nation for his efforts in favour of a peaceful settlement of the Sudeten question."

THE END OF THE FATEFUL GODESBERG MEETING BETWEEN THE PREMIER AND THE FÜHRER: MR. CHAMBERLAIN, WITH HERR HITLER, LEAVING THE HOTEL DREESEN AFTER THE MIDNIGHT CONVERSATION.

BRITAIN PREPARES FOR EMERGENCIES:
GAS-MASKS; AND OTHER PRECAUTIONS.

A CHEERFUL RESPONSE TO THE NATION'S CALL: PROSPECTIVE ARMY RECRUITS SURGING TOWARDS THE DOOR AT NEW SCOTLAND YARD.

MAKING READY, IN CASE OF EMERGENCY, TO JOIN IN THE DEFENCE OF LONDON AGAINST POSSIBLE AIR RAIDS: TERRITORIALS GETTING THEIR ANTI-AIRCRAFT GUN INTO POSITION.

HYDE PARK PROVIDES A VAST REFUGE AREA FOR LONDONERS AGAINST THE THREAT OF AIR ATTACK: MEN DIGGING THE TRENCHES – WORK THAT WENT ON BY NIGHT AND DAY.

EAGER TO JOIN UP: A CROWD OF YOUNG MEN BESIEGING A.R.P. AND TERRITORIAL RECRUITING OFFICERS AT THE MANSION HOUSE.

THE DISTRIBUTION OF GAS-MASKS IN LONDON: A TYPICAL SCENE OUTSIDE CHELSEA TOWN-HALL – WOMEN GOING IN TO BE FITTED.

AIR-BELLOWS WHICH ARE OPERATED BY THE MOVEMENT OF THE PET WITHIN: A GAS-PROOF CHAMBER FOR ANIMALS.

THE MOST SPECTACULAR OF LONDON'S A.R.P. MEASURES: THE DIGGING OF LINES AND TRENCHES IN THE ALMOST SACROSANCT PRECINTS OF ST. JAMES'S PARK; THE GERMAN EMBASSY SEEN AT THE BACK (LEFT CENTRE).

We illustrate here various precautions taken by the authorities in view of the European crisis, all showing Britain's readiness to face emergencies. On September 26 the War Office called out officers and men of Anti-Aircraft and Coast Defence Units of the Territorial Army. It was emphasised that this was a precautionary measure and quite distinct from general mobilisation. On the same day two information bureaux were opened – at the Mansion House and the Duke of York's headquarters, Chelsea – for men wishing to join the Territorials,

and there was a rush of prospective recruits. The Home Office also on the 26th issued instructions to many London and provincial centres for the immediate distribution of gas-masks. It was stated that a total of thirty-five million gas-masks had been stored at Home Office depots in London and a number of other centres in different parts of the country.

LONDON SAFEGUARDS HER CHILDREN: AND HER ART TREASURES

Details of a plan for evacuating some two million people, including half a million school-children, from London in an emergency were made known by the Home Office on September 29. The L.C.C. had already set a similar plan in operation on the previous day and on September 29 one thousand children between the ages of two and five were taken from London nursery schools into the country to the homes of people who had offered to billet them. A parent or teacher accompanied every ten children.

SOME OF THE ONE THOUSAND SMALL CHILDREN EVACUATED BY THE L.C.C.: LABELLED TODDLERS FROM THE SHERBORNE NURSERY SCHOOL, KENTISH TOWN, AT EUSTON STATION.

SAFEGUARDING NATIONAL ART TREASURES AT THE VICTORIA AND ALBERT MUSEUM: OFFICIALS TAKING A RARE TAPESTRY TO A PLACE OF SAFETY.

PRAGUE HAILS THE NEW NATIONAL DEFENCE GOVERNMENT UNDER SYROVY.

ACCLAIMING SPEAKERS FROM ALL PARTIES AND OF VARIOUS NATIONALITIES WHO APPEARED ON THE BALCONY OF THE PARLIAMENT BUILDINGS AFTER THE ANNOUNCEMENT THAT A NEW GOVERNMENT OF NATIONAL DEFENCE HAD BEEN FORMED: AN EXCITED CROWD IN THE WENCESLAS SQUARE, PRAGUE.

After the resignation of the Hodza Government early on September 22, an enormous crowd assembled in the Wenceslas Square, Prague, to await a broadcast by President Benes. Troops who arrived in the Square to take up positions in front of the loud-speakers were welcomed with shouts of "Long live the Army!" and some were carried shoulder-high. In his speech, President Benes said that the Hodza Government would be succeeded by a Government of National Defence, on a broad basis, and concluded with these words: "Have no fear about the future of our Fatherland. Let everyone return to his post. Do not listen to rumours and provocations. The nation has deep roots, and I will close with the words of our national poet: 'Czechoslovakia will not perish.' "

THE SUDETEN *FREIKORPS*:
FIREBRANDS IN EUROPE'S POWDER-MAGAZINE.

THE SUDETEN *FREIKORPS* INCURSIONS ON THE CZECH FRONTIER: THE SCENE AT HASLAU, NEAR EGER, IN THE NORTH-WEST, AS ARMED SUDETENS MARCHED BACK INTO THEIR HOME DISTRICTS.

UPROOTED BY THE RUMOURS OF WAR: REFUGEES FROM THE SUDETEN AREA OF CZECHOSLOVAKIA IN A HASTILY PREPARED CAMP IN PRAGUE.

Refugees from the Sudeten areas have been arriving in Prague, uprooted from their homes by the fear of war; while members of the Sudeten German Party, whose revolt was crushed by the Czech police, have been crossing the frontier into Germany. Herr Henlein has formed a Volunteer Corps of Sudeten troops from these fugitives – the *Freikorps* – and units of this are reported to have attacked some customs posts on the frontier. The *Freikorps* numbered 40,000 men organised in four divisions armed and equipped with German weapons.

Competent observers regarded this figure with scepticism. General Syrovy's first act after taking over the Prime Ministership of Czechoslovakia was to move troops up to the frontier, since the gendarmerie could no longer hold the frontier posts against the sporadic inroads. There was heavy fighting in places, and in one town, Graslitz, over 200 men are stated to have been kidnapped.

WORDS ON WHICH ALL EUROPE HUNG: HERR HITLER'S BERLIN SPEECH.

THE FÜHRER SALUTES HIS BERLIN AUDIENCE: A CLOSE-UP VIEW OF THE NAZI LEADERS ON THE ROSTRUM – (FROM LEFT TO RIGHT) DR. GOEBBELS, HERR HITLER (WITH UPRAISED ARM), HERR HESS, FIELD-MARSHAL GÖRING, HERR VON RIBBENTROP, DR. FRICK, HERR HIMMLER, AND HERR RUST.

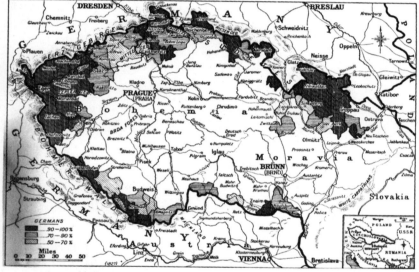

THE SUDETEN DISTRICTS OF CZECHOSLOVAKIA, THE CESSION OF WHICH, IT IS UNDERSTOOD, FORMED THE BASIS OF THE ANGLO-FRENCH PLAN OF SEPTEMBER 18: THE AREAS WITH MORE THAN 50 PER CENT OF SUDETEN INHABITANTS: FOR COMPARISON WITH BOUNDARIES DEMANDED IN HERR HITLER'S MEMORANDUM OF SEPTEM-BER 23, GIVEN IN THE MAP ON RIGHT.

A MAP OF WESTERN CZECHOSLOVAKIA, SHOWING THE EVACUATION AND PLEBISCITE AREAS IN ACCORDANCE WITH HERR HITLER'S MEMORANDUM OF SEPTEMBER 23: DEMANDS REPRESENTING A SUBSTANTIAL INCREASE IN CZECH TERRITORIAL CONCESSIONS, OVER THOSE PROPOSED IN THE ANGLO-FRENCH PLAN.

On September 24 the French Ministry of Defence promulgated an order recalling certain classes of reserves to the Colours. In an official statement the Ministry said: "In consequence of the development of the foreign situation, the Government has been led to reinforce the precautionary measures already taken to assure the safety of our north-eastern frontier. In particular, it has decided to call up urgently certain categories of reservists of all classes. This is by no means a general mobilisation. Simultaneously with the measure and with the object of assuring to the troops the necessary means, requisitions have begun on part of the national territory." Immense crowds watched reservists leave from the Gare de l'Est, Paris, on September 25. In his speech in Berlin on September 26, Herr Hitler asserted that there was no difference, apart from procedure, between the memorandum on Czechoslovakia he handed to Mr. Chamberlain on September 23 and the Anglo-French plan of September 18. That this is inaccurate, and that his memorandum represents an increase in the concessions demanded of Czechoslovakia, may be gathered from a glance at the maps on this page. The Anglo-French plan contained, it is understood, the following proposals: (a) Transfer without a plebiscite of areas with more than 50 per cent Sudeten German inhabitants, adjustments to the frontier being made by some international body: (b) an exchange of populations: (c) a guarantee of Czechoslovakia's security if she agreed to these conditions. The German memorandum on Czechoslovakia which Herr Hitler handed to Mr. Chamberlain on the night of September 23 included the following demands (1) Withdrawal of the whole Czech armed forces, police, gendarmerie, etc. from the area to be evacuated, as designated on the map (reproduced above). This area to be handed over to Germany by October 1. (2) The evacuated territory to be handed over in its present condition: (3) The Czech Government to discharge at once all Sudeten Germans serving in the military forces or the police, anywhere in Czech territory: (4) The German Government to permit a plebiscite to take place in areas to be more

definitely defined before, at latest, November 25, the plebiscite to be carried out under the control of an international commission. Thus, it will be seen that the German memorandum, like the Anglo-French plan, contemplated the cession of certain areas without a plebiscite. Under the Anglo-French plan the areas to be thus ceded outright are those in which 50 per cent of the population, or more, are German-speaking. The German memorandum specifies larger areas, which are shown in the right hand side map. In fact, the new frontier demanded gives to Germany nearly all of Czechoslovakia's main defences and a number of strategic points, which would have remained on the Czech side of the frontier contemplated by the Anglo-French plan. The German demands also include plebiscites in further areas, most of which adjoin those in which total annexation is claimed. A vital proviso of the Anglo-French proposals – namely, an international guarantee of the new frontiers, is absent from the German scheme. Moreover, while the Anglo-French plan stipulated no date for the transfer, the German demand made to-day, Saturday (October 1), the time limit.

During his speech, Herr Hitler also said: "We have no interest in breaking the peace." He recalled the naval agreement with Britain "to secure a lasting peace between the two peoples," and declared: "We do not want war with France . . . Alsace-Lorraine does not exist any more for us. The best relations will prevail between France and Germany so long as they work together." On the Czech crisis, he said: "I have now placed at the British Government's disposal a Memorandum with the final German proposal . . . The contents . . . are the practical execution of what Herr Benesh has promised . . . He will have to hand over this area to us on October 1 . . . I am grateful to Mr. Chamberlain for all his efforts, and I have assured him that the German people want nothing but peace . . . and that, when this problem is solved, Germany has no more territorial problems in Europe."

THE MOST DRAMATIC SCENE IN THE HOUSE OF COMMONS SINCE 1914.

"I HAVE NOW BEEN INFORMED BY HERR HITLER THAT HE INVITES ME TO MEET HIM AT MUNICH TOMORROW MORNING, HE HAS ALSO INVITED SIGNOR MUSSOLINI AND M. DALADIER": MR. NEVILLE CHAMBERLAIN MAKING HIS MOMENTOUS AND UNEXPECTED ANNOUNCEMENT WHICH REVIVED HOPES OF PEACE AND EVOKED INTENSE ENTHUSIASM.

Since the "eve of war" debate in Parliament in 1914, nothing has occurred there so intensely dramatic as the scene when Mr. Chamberlain, during his speech on the European crisis on September 28, unexpectedly received Herr Hitler's invitation to Munich, and announced it to the House. "I have now been informed by Herr Hitler that he invites me to meet him at Munich to-morrow morning. He has also invited Signor Mussolini and M. Daladier. Signor Mussolini has accepted, and I have no doubt M. Daladier will also accept. I need not say what my answer will be." At these words the House rose and broke into a storm of cheers. Expressing the emotion of the moment, Mr. Chamberlain said: "There can be no hon. member who did not feel his heart leap that the crisis has been once more postponed, to give us once more an opportunity to try what reason and good will and discussion will do.

Mr. Speaker, I cannot say any more. I am sure that the House will be ready to release me now to go and see what I can make of this last effort." Then came another great outburst of cheering. On behalf of the Opposition, Mr. Attlee welcomed the Premier's statement, and agreed to an adjournment, which followed

shortly. As "The Times" pointed out afterwards, in reference to the arrival of Herr Hitler's invitation: "This was the crucial moment. That peace would follow the Munich negotiations was almost a foregone conclusion once a dictator had made the difficult renunciation of consenting to treat after he had announced his last word. The message so dramatically brought to Mr. Chamberlain in the House of Commons marked the true climax and ended the threat of war." Queen Mary (not visible in the drawing) was in the Speaker's Gallery, with the Duchess of Kent. The Duke of Kent (shown just to right of the clock) was in the Peers' Gallery next to Lord Baldwin, beyond whom were Lord Halifax and the Archbishop of Canterbury. Behind Mr. Chamberlain, to right, are members of the Cabinet, among whom will be recognised Mr. Ernest Brown, Sir Kingsley Wood, Sir John Simon, Sir Samuel Hoare, and Mr. Hore-Belisha. Behind the last-named is Mr. Churchill, and, next to right, Lord Dunglass. The Speaker is in the extreme left foreground. Facing Mr. Chamberlain across the table are members of the Opposition, seated, with Mr. Attlee third from left.

THE SURPRISE SEND-OFF TO MUNICH: THE CABINET CHEER THE PREMIER.

SMILING MINISTERIAL FACES AT THE START OF MR. CHAMBERLAIN'S MUNICH FLIGHT: THE PREMIER WITH SIR KINGSLEY WOOD BESIDE HIM; AND BEHIND (L. TO R.) LORD HAILSHAM, LORD MAUGHAM, SIR JOHN SIMON, MR. HORE-BELISHA, LORD HALIFAX, AND MR VINCENT MASSEY (REPRESENTING CANADA); AND (AT BACK) SIR PHILIP SASSOON, MR. W.S. MORRISON, MR. DUFF COOPER, MR. LESLIE BURGIN, MR. WALTER ELLIOT, AND MR. OLIVER STANLEY.

A REMARKABLE DEMONSTRATION BY BRITISH CABINET MINISTERS: LORD HALIFAX LEADING HIS COLLEAGUES IN CHEERING MR. CHAMBERLAIN; WITH THE SOUTH AFRICAN HIGH COMMISSIONER (RIGHT; BEHIND) AND SIR KINGSLEY WOOD.

The Prime Minister's departure for the Munich conference was marked by a public demonstration of his Cabinet's good wishes which was without precedent. Unknown to him, some sixteen Ministers had agreed amongst themselves to give him a united send-off from Heston, as a gesture of their appreciation of his efforts for peace. The Prime Minister's pleasure at this was evident. Ministers and their wives crowded round him,

patting him on the shoulder: there were warm handshakes; and a great cheer was given as Mr. Chamberlain walked towards his aeroplane. Besides members of the Cabinet were the High Commissioners for Canada, Australia, and Eire, and many members of the Diplomatic Corps, including the French Ambassador and the German Charge d'Affaires. Immediately after the Prime Minister had exchanged greetings with his colleagues, Count Grandi, the Italian Ambassador, came up to offer his sincere wishes for success.

A TURNING-POINT IN EUROPEAN HISTORY.

THE CONFERENCE THAT BROUGHT PEACE TO WAR-MENACED EUROPE:
IN SESSION IN THE FÜHRER'S HOUSE AT MUNICH: MR. CHAMBERLAIN, HERR HITLER, SIGNOR MUSSOLINI, COUNT CIANO (SEEN FROM BEHIND), HERR VON RIBBENTROP AND M. DALADIER (LEFT TO RIGHT).

The first sitting of the Four-Power Conference at Munich began shortly before 1 p.m. on September 29, with Herr von Ribbentrop, the German Foreign Minister, and Count Ciano taking part with the heads of the British, German, Italian and French Governments. The reconciliation of Germany's demands with the British and French ideas of what the Czechoslovak Government could reasonably be asked to accept was undertaken. The Agreement was signed at 12.30 a.m.

CO-OPERATING FOR EUROPEAN PEACE: THE DUCE AND PREMIER.	WESTMINSTER ABBEY: PRAYERS AT THE UNKNOWN WARRIOR'S GRAVE.	AUTHOR OF TWO APPEALS TO HERR HITLER: PRESIDENT ROOSEVELT.

SIGNOR MUSSOLINI MEETING MR. NEVILLE CHAMBERLAIN IN MUNICH.

PRAYERS FOR PEACE AT THE TOMB OF THE UNKNOWN WARRIOR ON THE DAY OF THE MUNICH CONFERENCE: A SCENE IN THE ABBEY.

A CHAMPION OF PEACE BY NEGOTIATION: PRESIDENT ROOSEVELT, WHO PLEADED WITH HERR HITLER THAT THE CZECHOSLOVAK PROBLEM SHOULD BE SOLVED BY A RESORT TO REASON, RATHER THAN BY FORCE.

At the Four-Power Conference at the Führer's House in Munich on September 29–30, Mr. Chamberlain met Signor Mussolini for the first time. In his now historic speech in the House of Commons on September 28, the Prime Minister said "In reply to my message to Signor Mussolini, I was informed that instructions had been sent by the Duce to the Italian Ambassador in Berlin to see Herr von Ribbentrop at once and to say that while Italy would fulfil completely her pledges to stand by Germany, yet, in view of the great importance of the request made by his Majesty's Government to Signor Mussolini, the hoped Herr Hitler would see his way to postpone action for at least 24 hours so as to allow Signor Mussolini time to re-examine the situation and endeavour to find a peaceful settlement. In response, Herr Hitler has agreed to postpone mobilisation for 24 hours. Whatever views Hon. Members may have had about Signor Mussolini in the past, I believe that everyone will welcome his gesture of being willing to work with us for peace in Europe."

During the international crisis, a period of unbroken prayer for peace began in Westminster Abbey on September 15. The above photograph was taken on the 29th, the day on which the Prime Minister attended the Four-Power Conference at Munich. In a broadcast message on the previous night, the Archbishop of Canterbury said: "Let me ask you all to accompany him with your prayers. To-night before you go to rest, pray for him with full hearts; . . . Continue these prayers to-morrow, when this conference, on which the hopes of the world depend, will be meeting in Germany. Surely this so sudden and unexpected lifting of the burden which weighed so heavily upon us this very morning is itself an answer to the great volume of prayer which has been rising to God . . . None can tell or measure the power of prayer."

The part played by the United States of America in bringing about the Four-Power Conference at Munich will never, perhaps, be fully revealed, but the two appeals addressed by President Roosevelt to Herr Hitler undoubtedly contributed to that event. The first was sent on September 26 and in it Mr. Roosevelt said: "I am persuaded that there is no problem so difficult or so pressing for a solution that it cannot justly be solved by a resort to reason rather than by a resort to force." To this the Führer replied: and Mr. Roosevelt felt himself constrained to send a second message on September 27 stating: "The Government of the United States has no political involvements in Europe . . . Yet in our own right we recognise our responsibilities as part of a world of neighbours."

THE SIGNING OF THE FOUR-POWER AGREEMENT AT MUNICH.

HERR HITLER SIGNING THE MUNICH AGREEMENT BETWEEN GERMANY, GREAT BRITAIN, FRANCE AND ITALY.

FOR GREAT BRITAIN: MR. NEVILLE CHAMBERLAIN PRIME MINISTER SIGNING THE AGREEMENT CONCLUDED WITH GERMANY, FRANCE AND ITALY REGARDING THE SUDETEN TERRITORY IN CZECHOSLOVAKIA.

"Agreement between Germany, Great Britain, France and Italy, concluded in Munich on September 29, 1938. The conversations which the chiefs of the Governments of Germany, Italy, France and Great Britain began on Thursday noon have found their conclusion in the late evening. The agreements which were reached, and which are laid down in the following documents, have been immediately transmitted to the Czech Government. Germany, the United Kingdom, France and Italy, taking into consideration the settlement already agreed upon in principle concerning the cession of the Sudeten German districts, have agreed on the following conditions and procedure and the measures to be taken, and declare themselves individually held responsible by this agreement for guaranteeing the steps necessary for its fulfilment: (1) The evacuation begins on October 1. (2) The United Kingdom of Great Britain, France and Italy agree that the evacuation of the region shall be completed by October 10, without destruction of any of the existing installations, and that the Czechoslovak Government bear the responsibility for seeing that the evacuation is carried out without damaging the aforesaid installations. (3) The conditions governing the evacuation will be laid down in detail by an International Commission composed of representatives of Germany, the United Kingdom, France Italy and Czechoslovakia. (4) The occupation by stages of the predominantly German territories by German troops will begin on October 1. Four territories marked on an attached map will be occupied by German troops (in stages to be completed by October 7) . . . The remaining territories of predominantly German character will be ascertained by the afore said International Commission forthwith and be occupied by German troops by October 10. (5) The International Commission referred to in paragraph 3 will determine the territories in which a plebiscite is to be held. These territories will be occupied by international bodies until the plebiscite has been completed. The same Commission will fix the conditions in which the plebiscite is to be held, taken as a basis the conditions of the Saar plebiscite. The Commission will also fix the date at the end of November on which the plebiscite will be held. (6) The final determination of the frontiers will be carried out by the International Commission. This Commission will also recommend to the four Powers – Germany, the United Kingdom, France and Italy – in certain exceptional circumstances, minor modifications in the strictly ethnographical determination of the zones which are to be transferred without plebiscite. (7) There will be a right of option into and out of the transferred territories, the option to be exercised within six months of the date of this agreement. A German-Czechoslovak Commission shall determine details of the options, and consider ways of facilitating the transfer of populations and certain questions of principle arising out of the said transfers. (8) The Czechoslovak Government will, within the period of four weeks from the date of this agreement, release from the military and police forces any Sudeten Germans who may wish to be released; and the Czech Government will, within the same period, release Sudeten German prisoners who are serving terms of imprisonment for political offences." An annexe to the agreement states: "His Majesty's Government in the United Kingdom and the French Government have entered into the above agreement on the basis that they stand by the offer contained in Paragraph 6 of the Anglo-French proposals of September 19 in relation to an international guarantee of the new boundaries of the Czechoslovak State against unprovoked aggression. When the question of the Polish and Hungarian minorities in Czechoslovakia has been settled Germany and Italy, for their part, will give a guarantee to Czechoslovakia. The heads of the Governments of the four Powers declare that the problems of the Polish and Hungarian minorities in Czechoslovakia, if not settled within three months by agreement between the respective Governments, shall form the subject of a further meeting of the heads of Governments of the four Powers here present." A supplementary declaration says: "All questions which may arise out of the transfer of the territories shall be considered as coming within the terms of reference of the International Commission."

FOR ITALY: SIGNOR MUSSOLINI SIGNING THE AGREEMENT CONCLUDED WITH GERMANY, GREAT BRITAIN AND FRANCE FOR THE SETTLEMENT OF THE CZECHOSLOVAK QUESTION – SHOWING HERR VON RIBBENTROP ON THE RIGHT.

FOR FRANCE: M. EDOUARD DALADIER, PRIME MINISTER SIGNING THE AGREEMENT CONCLUDED WITH GERMANY, GREAT BRITAIN AND ITALY; WITH HERR VON RIBBENTROP (RIGHT) LOOKING ON.

The historic document which put an end to the Czechoslovak crisis, and averted the imminent danger of a European war, was concluded in the Führer House at Munich on September 29, but was not actually signed until 12.30 a.m. on the following morning. Here we show the representatives of Germany, Great Britain, France and Italy in the act of affixing their signatures. The essential part of the text of the Agreement is also given here.
Herr Hitler has undoubtedly increased his prestige by acceding to the general desire for a peaceful settlement of the Czech question and convening the Four-Power Conference.

M. DALADIER'S RETURN TO PARIS: THE PREMIER'S TRIUMPHAL DRIVE.

M. DALADIER'S TRIUMPHAL DRIVE THROUGH THE STREETS OF PARIS TO THE WAR MINISTRY ON HIS RETURN FROM MUNICH: THE FRENCH PREMIER ACKNOWLEDGING THE CHEERS OF AN ENTHUSIASTIC CROWD WHICH LINED THE ROUTE AND, AT TIMES, FORCED THE CAR PRACTICALLY TO A STANDSTILL.

"I BELIEVE IT IS PEACE FOR OUR TIME": MR. CHAMBERLAIN'S RETURN.

"I HAD ANOTHER TALK WITH HERR HITLER, AND HERE IS A PAPER WHICH BEARS HIS NAME AS WELL AS MINE": THE DOCUMENT MR. CHAMBERLAIN READ AT HESTON.

SIGNOR MUSSOLINI'S RETURN TO ROME: AN UNPRECEDENTED OVATION.

THE GREATEST AND MOST SPONTANEOUS WELCOME EVER GIVEN TO THE DUCE BY THE ITALIAN PEOPLE: THE VAST CROWD IN THE PIAZZA BEFORE THE PALAZZO VENEZIA (RIGHT), SHOWING THE BALCONY, WITH FASCIST SYMBOLS, ON WHICH HE SAID: "AT MUNICH WE WORKED FOR PEACE BASED ON JUSTICE."

THE HISTORIC MOMENT WHEN MR. CHAMBERLAIN – JUST BACK FROM MUNICH STOOD ON THE BALCONY OF BUCKINGHAM PALACE, WITH THEIR MAJESTIES AND HIS WIFE, RECEIVING LONDON'S GRATITUDE FOR PEACE.

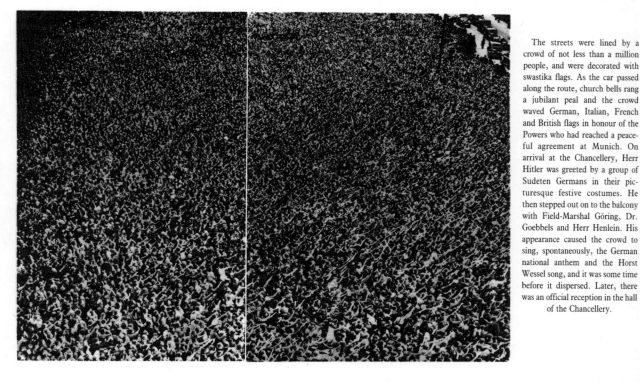

The greatest and most whole-hearted ovation that Herr Hitler has ever received from the German people was given to him when he returned to Berlin on October 1 from Munich after having signed the Agreement and the Anglo-German Declaration. Coupled with the joy that the Führer had obtained the Sudeten areas of Czechoslovakia for the Reich was the feeling of tremendous relief that the tension of the previous days had eased and that peace was assured. The Leader arrived at the Anhalter Station, where the German Cabinet had assembled to welcome him, and was greeted first by Field-Marshal Göring and then by Herr Henlein. After receiving bouquets from two little Sudeten girls, he entered his car and drove slowly to the Reich Chancellery.

The streets were lined by a crowd of not less than a million people, and were decorated with swastika flags. As the car passed along the route, church bells rang a jubilant peal and the crowd waved German, Italian, French and British flags in honour of the Powers who had reached a peaceful agreement at Munich. On arrival at the Chancellery, Herr Hitler was greeted by a group of Sudeten Germans in their picturesque festive costumes. He then stepped out on to the balcony with Field-Marshal Göring, Dr. Goebbels and Herr Henlein. His appearance caused the crowd to sing, spontaneously, the German national anthem and the Horst Wessel song, and it was some time before it dispersed. Later, there was an official reception in the hall of the Chancellery.

THE GERMAN PEOPLE ACCLAIM THE PEACEFUL SOLUTION OF THE SUDETEN PROBLEM EXPRESSING THEIR RELIEF BY SALUTES AND CHEERS: A SECTION OF THE IMMENSE CROWD THAT WELCOMED HERR HITLER ON HIS RETURN TO BERLIN.

CZECH "MAGINOT LINES" NOW GERMAN.

GERMAN TROOPS ENTER THE SECOND ZONE OF OCCUPATION – IN NORTHERN BOHEMIA: THE CROWD WELCOMING BEFLOWERED, GOOSE-STEPPING INFANTRY AT RUMBURG.

HERR HITLER INTERESTED IN THE TECHNICAL DETAILS OF THE "PILL-BOXES" IN THE DEFENSIVE LINES ON THE OLD FRONTIERS OF CZECHOSLOVAKIA – DURING A VISIT TO SOUTH BOHEMIA: THE FÜHRER DISCUSSING PLANS OF STRONG POINTS DRAWN ON BLACKBOARDS.

At 2 p.m. on October 1 German troops began to march into the first of the four special zones on the Czechoslovak frontier which were to be first occupied from the Munich agreement. This lies on the southern frontier of Bohemia. German troops entered the second zone (in the north of Bohemia) on October 2. The occupation took place peacefully and without incident. As was the case with the first zone, the troops did not penetrate deeply into the area. The Czechoslovak troops retired in good order, preceded by swarms of refugees – Czechs, Social-Democrats and Jews – who took with them what belongings they could. At Tetschen (North Bohemia) the town was apparently left in the hands of the Sudeten Corps police and Freikorps authorities. But, according to the accounts of British observers, many of the inhabitants were bewildered, having supported the Sudeten movement with a view to obtain local autonomy and not annexation by Germany. German troops

began to enter the third area of occupation (North-Western Bohemia) on October 3. Later, Herr Hitler entered the new German territory near Asch. The streets were carefully guarded. He arrived at Eger at about 1 p.m. and stood up to acknowledge the cheers of the crowd. It was known that the former frontier of Czechoslovakia was defended by "Maginot lines" of concrete forts and pill-boxes. Large sectors of these lines, being in Sudeten territory, have now been taken over by the German Army, and photographs, such as the one reproduced here, taken of them. The Czech systems of fortification won praise from the Germans and one officer, a major, was reported to have said to a Reuter correspondent, while showing him one of the forts on the Schoberline: "Even the German Army would have found this fort almost impregnable."

THE PLIGHT OF REFUGEES IN CZECHOSLOVAKIA:

In his letter announcing a Mansion House Fund for refugees in Czechoslovakia, the Lord Mayor said: "Tens of thousands of factory workers and farmers, with their families, are suddenly rendered homeless. Without provisions, savings, or more bedding than can be carried on the back, worn out by their journey, men and women and children are streaming into Prague for shelter. To all who realise how much they owe to the self-sacrifice of these refugees and to the calmness of the Czech Government, I appeal for a gift to the Fund." The photograph was taken at Steti, near Melnic, on the new Czecho-German frontier, where over 1,500 refugees were temporarily housed. They had to be content with straw and pillows on the floor as bedding. It was reported on October 9 that Berlin demanded that all Sudeten Germans, including Socialists and Communists, who had left the occupied districts, should be compelled to return, as Germany was "not prepared to renounce its claims to any Germans." Prague officials, however, later denied that such a demand had been made directly or formally from Germany. Refugees claimed that, under the Munich agreement, they had the right of option for Czech or German nationality, and could remain outside the German areas. It was suggested that the Czech authorities feared the creation of a new German minority in this way might cause further intervention.

PEOPLE WHOSE STRONG CLAIMS TO BRITISH SYMPATHY HAVE BEEN RECOGNISED BY THE OPENING OF A MANSION HOUSE-FUND: A TYPICAL GROUP OF REFUGEE FAMILIES FROM THE SUDETEN AREAS OF CZECHOSLOVAKIA.

THE CZECHS ACCEPT POLAND'S CLAIMS:
POLISH TROOPS ENTER TESCHEN.

A MECHANISED SECTION OF THE POLISH FORCES THAT OCCUPIED THE TERRITORY CEDED TO POLAND BY CZECHOSLOVAKIA: A LINE OF POLISH TANKS DURING THE ENTRY INTO TESCHEN.

THE PRESIDENT OF CZECHOSLOVAKIA, WHO HAS DWELT ON HER IMMENSE SACRIFICES FOR THE CAUSE OF PEACE IN EUROPE: DR. BENES (LEFT) WITH GENERAL SYROVY, THE PRIME MINISTER.

It was announced on October 2 that all the Polish Government's demands, in a Note sent to Prague by aeroplane on September 30, regarding the cession of territory, had been accepted by the Czechoslovak Government. In a broadcast address on October 1, Colonel Beck, the Polish Foreign Minister, said: "With the restoration of the old Polish territory beyond the Olza we shall have no further grievances against

Czechoslovakia." On October 2 Polish military and civil authorities took possession of the first zone, covering part of the Powiat of Teschen within about ten miles of the town. It was officially stated that the occupation of further territory, comprising the rest of this Powiat, part of that of Frystat, and the Bohumin railway junction, would be carried out gradually and completed by October 10.

THE "SERIOUS DETERIORATION" IN THE SITUATION IN PALESTINE:
WHICH HAS NECESSITATED THE DESPATCH OF ADDITIONAL BRITISH TROOPS.

THE FIRST OPEN SESSION OF THE PALESTINE PARTITION COMMISSION, IN JERUSALEM: A PHOTOGRAPH SHOWING THE MEMBERS SEATED ROUND THE TABLE, WITH (L. TO R.) MR. REED, SIR ALLISON RUSSELL, SIR JOHN WOODHEAD (THE CHAIRMAN), MR. WATERFIELD AND MR. LUKE (SECRETARY).

The Palestine Partition Commission arrived in Palestine in May to study the technical details of what is the accepted Government policy. Their task is simply to enquire how partition may best be effected in view of the racial, religious, economic and military difficulties. The Jews are, officially, prepared to discuss the partition proposal: but the Arabs reject partition as being impracticable. It is stated that even moderate Arabs (as represented by the National Defence Party) have refused to appear before the Commission.

SECURING THE NORTHERN FRONTIER OF PALESTINE AGAINST THE INFILTRATION OF REBELS FROM SYRIA: THE DENSE BARBED-WIRE BARRIER KNOWN AS "TEGART'S WALL" – OVER SIXTY MILES IN LENGTH.

THE POLICY OF RETAINING CERTAIN HORSED REGIMENTS OF CAVALRY IN THE BRITISH ARMY PROVES ITS WORTH IN PALESTINE: TROOPERS OF THE ROYAL SCOTS GREYS PATROLLING THE RAILWAY NEAR SARAFAND.

THE ARMY "CLEANING-UP" IN THE OLD CITY OF JERUSALEM.

MEETING THE MENACE OF SNIPERS: MEN OF THE COLDSTREAM GUARDS AND BLACK WATCH LINING THE LOOPHOLES OF ONE OF A SECTION OF JERUSALEM'S SIXTEENTH CENTURY BATTLEMENTS WHILE A PUPPY UNCONCERNEDLY PLAYS AMONG THEM.

The restoration of orderly government in Jerusalem stands as a masterly achievement of the British Army. On October 18 the utmost anxiety was felt, since parts of the Old City were hotbeds of terrorism and the Arabs were boasting that the rebels dominated the whole of it. The troops went in on the 19th and that evening practically the whole of the Old City was secured. Indeed, the worst of the dangers were past in two hours. Only the sacred Haram-esh-Sherif area presented a problem. On the following day it was clear that Arab resistance had evaporated. Some twenty-two Arabs were killed in these operations and twenty-five wounded. The total British casualties could be counted on the fingers of two hands. The operations left the inhabitants of the Old City, which presents an extraordinary difficult police problem, practically unharmed. The secret of this quick and effective work lay in very careful preparation, and the use of adequate forces.

ARAB SUSPECTS: MEN WHO WERE UNABLE TO PROVE RESIDENCE IN JERUSALEM BROUGHT OUT OF THE DAMASCUS GATE FOR EXAMINATION, LIGHTLY TIED TOGETHER.

"TO YOUNG CHINA AN EL DORADO":
YENAN'S PATRIOTIC CAVE-DWELLERS – A WONDERFUL TROGLODYTE "UNIVERSITY" FOR YOUNG CHINESE PATRIOTS:

THE "MAINSPRING" OF YENAN'S FERVID ACTIVITY: MAO TSE-TUNG, THE COMMUNIST LEADER, WHO, AFTER LONG WARFARE AGAINST CHIANG KAI-SHEK'S GOVERNMENT, JOINED HIM IN FORMING A NATIONAL FRONT.

DISTINGUISHED BY DECORATIVE WOODWORK, INCLUDING THE SOVIET STAR OVER THE DOOR: THE ENTRANCE TO THE OFFICE OF THE PRESIDENT OF THE "RESIST JAPAN" UNIVERSITY AT YENAN, SITUATED, LIKE THE STUDENTS' QUARTERS, IN A CAVE.

The little walled city of Yenan, in the northern part of the province of Shensi, is the centre of a system of political and military training of high importance for the future of China. It is the headquarters of the Chinese Communist Party. For ten years the so-called "Red" forces, which were driven to this region in December 1936, were at war with the Central Government troops, but eventually the Government was induced to call off the campaign and to form a National Front against the Japanese invaders. The significance of that agreement with the leaders of the "Red" Army (now known as the Eighth Route Army) is becoming more and more evident. The outstanding feature at Yenan is that the various institutions established there, and the students that attend them, are housed in caves excavated in the loess hills. These institutions comprise the North Shensi Academy (the main training school for political organisers), the "Resist Japan" University (a military training school), an Art Academy, a School of Dramatic Art, and a Hospital. A considerable proportion of the students at Yenan are girls, who dress like the men and live under the same conditions.

THE FALL OF CANTON –
ABANDONED TO JAPAN A BLAZING RUIN.

Japanese troops in South China entered Canton on October 21. The Chinese forces abandoned the city, after blowing-up the great Pearl River bridge, built by British engineers at a cost of £425,000, and setting fire to many buildings. The electricity plant, cement works, and military barracks were also damaged. The fires in Canton spread rapidly and whole districts were destroyed. On the 23rd the flames reached two huge ammunition dumps, and the city was rocked by terrific explosions. Debris fell in the Shameen settlement, half a mile away. Twenty buildings in the Foreign Settlement, including the oldest English church in China, Christ Church, were severely damaged and the western area of the British Concession was evacuated.

THE SYSTEMATIC DESTRUCTION OF CANTON BY THE CHINESE WHEN COMPELLED TO EVACUATE THE CITY: RUINS NEAR THE WONGSHA STATION YARDS, WHERE BIG MUNITION DUMPS EXPLODED.

GREAT BRIDGE ACROSS THE PEARL RIVER THAT WAS DESTROYED BY THE RETREATING CHINESE: AN AIR VIEW OF CANTON, GREATEST CITY, RECENTLY CAPTURED.

HANGKOW EVACUATES CHILDREN:
LITTLE CHINESE MOVED *EN MASSE.*

The Japanese advance on Hangkow began in June and lasted the best part of five months. The Japanese were led to undertake the enormous task of capturing Hangkow by advancing up the Yangtze when their attempt to get at the city from the north was foiled on the Yellow River. It will be recalled that floods in this sector brought their progress to a standstill. At the beginning of July the Japanese announced the capture of Hukow, which provided them with a base for attacking Kiuklang. Kiuklang, the big port about 200 miles below Hangkow, fell to them at the end of July. The Japanese efforts were resumed later in August. At the same time, the Japanese northern wing was carrying out a drive for the Hangkow-Peking Railway, which they aimed at cutting at Sinyang, about 100 miles north of Hangkow. Kichow, some 130 miles below Hankow apparently fell about October 10, but Chinese batteries ten miles further up stopped operations there. At this time the Japanese landed in South China and began to advance on Canton, a move which seriously weakened the Chinese resistance round Hangkow. On October 18 the Japanese captured Yangsin, about eighty miles to the S.E. of Hangkow, and began an overland drive to cut the Hangkow-Canton railway. The naval forces, still far ahead of land operations, attacked the Hwangshihkang defences (90 miles below Hangkow) on October 19. General Chiang Kai-shek, who had previously had his headquarters at Hangkow, and Mme. Chiang Kai-shek left by aeroplane, it was believed for Chungking. Hangkow was partly occupied by Japanese forces on the afternoon of October 25. The Chinese military authorities had decided not to defend the city, which had previously been their headquarters. Charges were laid under all public utility concerns, Japanese-owned buildings and strategic centres, including the great arsenal and the steel works at Hanyang. The Chinese Government began to evacuate the civil population from the Wuhan district (Hangkow, Wuchang, and Hanyang) as early as last July. Since then, it is estimated, some 50,000 Chinese have gone up the Yangtze to Chungking alone. Thousands of others have scattered westward through the countryside. On September 15 a census revealed that only 158,897 families remained in residence.

LITTLE BOYS LINED UP BEFORE THE MOVE: THE YOUNGEST WEARING STOCK OVERALLS OF THE SIMPLEST TYPE, AND EACH HAVING HIS IDENTITY LABEL SECURELY ATTACHED.

THE "QUEEN MARY" REGAINS THE ATLANTIC BLUE RIBAND FOR BRITAIN, AFTER BREAKING THE RECORD FOR THE FASTEST CROSSING OF THE ATLANTIC IN BOTH DIRECTIONS: THE CUNARD WHITE STAR LINER "QUEEN MARY" DOCKING AT SOUTHAMPTON IN THE EARLY HOURS OF AUGUST 15, ON HER RETURN FROM NEW YORK.

The "Queen Mary" docked at Southampton at 2.52 a.m. on August 15, at the end of her record-breaking run from New York. She had traversed nearly 3000 miles of ocean to the Bishop Rock, Scilly Isles (the terminal point for record purposes), nearly half a knot faster than the "Normandie," which made the previous record a year ago with an average speed of 31.20 knots. The "Queen Mary's" average speed to the Bishop Rock was 31.69 knots. On the outward voyage she had averaged 30.99 knots, against the "Normandie's" 30.58, and made the fastest westbound crossing, the fastest day's run, and, in actual steaming time, the fastest crossing in either direction.

HUTTON'S SOUVENIR OF THE ASTONISHING TEST MATCH, IN WHICH HE BROKE MANY BATTING RECORDS: THE TWENTY-TWO-YEAR-OLD YORKSHIRE BATSMAN WHO PLAYED THE MOST BRILLIANT INNINGS IN ENGLISH TEST CRICKET WHEN HE MADE 364 IN THE FINAL TEST MATCH. RUNNING BACK TO THE PAVILION WITH ONE OF THE STUMPS, SECURED AFTER A FRIENDLY STRUGGLE.

GERMANY'S NEW £50 CAR, FOR THE MASS PRODUCTION OF WHICH HERR HITLER HAS FOUNDED A GOVERNMENT FACTORY: THREE TYPES PARADED FOR INSPECTION.

At Fallersleben, Brunswick, on May 26, Herr Hitler laid the foundation-stone of a Government factory for cars costing 990 marks, or about £50, purchasable by weekly payments. "The new motor-car," he said, "is one of the means of providing German people with an article of definitive value, which they may buy with their wages. It will give joy to millions and supply a means of transport. I therefore name it the 'Strength through Joy Car,' after the organisation which has done so much to fill the great mass of the people with happiness". British manufacturers have protested against its possible importation.

FROM THE WORLD'S SCRAP-BOOK: NEWS ITEMS OF TOPICAL INTEREST.

A SHIP LIFTED ABOVE WATER BY A BOMB EXPLOSION BESIDE HER: AN AMAZING PHOTOGRAPH TAKEN AT THE ACTUAL MOMENT OF IMPACT.

During their campaign in China the Japanese air forces have made a practice of systematically bombing Chinese vessels plying up and down the River Yangtze. The above photograph was taken just at the moment when a heavy bomb fell close alongside a small steamer, and shows how the tremendous force of the explosion lifted the vessel clean out of the water!

HER VON RIBBENTROP AND M. GEORGES BONNET SIGNING WITH GOLDEN PENS ON SPECIAL VERSIONS PRINTED ON VELLUM: IN THE SALON DE L'HORLOGE AT THE QUAI D'ORSAY.

Herr von Ribbentrop arrived in Paris on December 6 to sign the Franco-German Declaration which began by pledging both countries to further relations with the other, and to recognise as definite the frontier between them as it now runs. It also stated that both Governments were resolved. "without prejudice to their special relations to other Powers, to remain in touch with one another as regards all questions concerning their two countries, and mutually to consult if the future development of these questions should lead to international difficulties."

THE FIRST NON-STOP FLIGHT FROM BRITAIN TO SOUTH AFRICA: THE "MERCURY" TAKING OFF FROM THE TAY ON THE BACK OF THE "MAIA."

"Mercury", the upper component of the Mayo Composite Aircraft, took off from the Tay on the back of the lower component, "Maia," on October 6, in an attempt to fly non-stop to the Cape. Shortage of petrol forced her down on the Orange River on October 8, 325 miles from her destination. She thus failed to beat the world's long-distance record, but set up a new record for seaplanes. It was the first non-stop flight from Britain to South Africa.

THE LABOUR UNREST IN FRANCE: STRIKES IN PARIS AND THE NORTH.

Strikes broke out in France as a result of the French Government's decree-laws, particularly as they were regarded as an attack on the forty-hour working week. The General Confederation of Trades Unions threatened the Government with a twenty-four-hour general strike, to take place on November 30, and in the north miners and metal-workers stopped work and occupied the factories. At Denain railway trucks were used as a barricade and the strikers repulsed an attack by Mobile Guards. The Sub-Prefect asked the Communist Mayor of Denain to negotiate with the workmen, who decided to evacuate their position on the withdrawal of the Mobile Guards. On November 24 30,000 men employed at the Renault works at Billancourt, near Paris, ceased work and occupied the buildings. Early on November 25, 5000 Mobile Guards attempted to eject them and a pitched battle ensued. The workmen were driven out and 290 were charged with "organised rebellion against the public authority." Later, when the men returned to the factory to start work they were locked out, a notice stating: "In view of the fact that the staff has broken the agreement signed with the firm on May 2, 1938, the works are closed until further notice." The general strike collapsed in face of the measure taken by the Government, business, trade and public services throughout the country. In a subsequent broadcast, M. Daladier declared that France had triumphed over her uncertainties at home, and emerged stronger than ever she was before. The strikers were most widespread in the mines, metal and textile industries and in the docks. The dockers' strike was most serious at Bordeaux, where there was a stoppage, in which the seamen participated. At Toulon there was a "folded arms" strike in some departments of the arsenal. At Le Havre the docks were paralysed by the strike of 2500 men. Perhaps the most dramatic incident in the strikes and their aftermath was the stopping of the sailing of the giant liner "Normandie". The "Normandie" was due to leave Havre on December 3 for New York, but she was taken out of commission as a result of the seamen defying M. Daladier's requisition order; 200 of the "Normandie's" passengers were sent by special train to Cherbourg, where they embarked on the Cunard White Star liner "Aquitania." Warrants were issued for the arrest of four of the leaders of the "Normandie" strike, which spread to several other liners.

THE FRENCH GOVERNMENT'S FINANCIAL DECREES OPPOSED: STAY-IN STRIKERS RESTING AMONG THE MACHINERY AT THE CRESPIN STEEL WORKS IN THE VALENCIENNES DISTRICT.

THE GERMAN "LABOUR SERVICE" – A NAZI INSTITUTION THE SOLID ACHIEVEMENTS OF THE LABOUR CAMPS AND THEIR LESS ADMIRABLE "MILITARISM."

The compulsory period of service in the Nazi Labour Corps is six months and this is usually taken between the ages of eighteen to twenty. No exemption whatever is obtainable except on the ground of a medical certificate expressly certifying unfitness. On October 15 the majority of the men start their military training, lasting for two years. On arrival in the camps the men are given a complete outfit, that they will require during the period which have to be handed back in proper condition before leaving. They receive an allowance of 25 pfennigs (about 3d.) per working day, and the cost of maintenance for each man is calculated at 94 pfennigs per day. The life in the camps is arduous. In the summer the men get up at five (in the winter at six) and go immediately for a run. Half an hour is allowed for dressing, bed-making, room-duty and preparation for breakfast. After breakfast is the morning parade, with a ceremonial hoisting of the flag and orders for the day. At 6.30 the men set out, on bicycles for their work. They work, with a short break at 10.30, until it is time to return for dinner at two. After dinner there is half an hour's rest interval. This is followed on alternate days by drill or games, lasting for about an hour. The drill is entirely military, consisting of exercises in-parade formations and weapon drill (in this case with spades) similar to those practised in the O.T.C., and approximately the same standard is attained. Then follows a period of political instruction, dealing with the outlines of Nazi statecraft and achievements. At six is the evening parade, with a ceremonial sinking of the flag and the veneration (complete with obituary notice) of an historic German figure noted for prowess. After that – supper, followed by a sing-song or special duty, and bed at ten. With the exception of the rest-interval, the men are under constant supervision and under orders throughout the day. Orders, reprimands, or pieces of information are retailed to the men, collectively or individually, with the stentorian tones of a sergeant-major putting a parade in its place. The only permissible reply to a command or a piece of abuse is *Jawohl*.

(LEFT), THE NAZI LABOUR SERVICE, WHICH ALL YOUNG GERMANS HAVE NOW TO PASS THROUGH BEFORE DOING THEIR MILITARY SERVICE: A PARTY AT WORK UPON A MOUNTAIN ROAD IN THE BLACK FOREST.

ANTI-JEWISH OUTBREAKS IN GERMANY: "RETRIBUTION" FOR AN ASSASSINATION.

The anti-jewish outbreaks began in Germany on November 10. Veritable pogroms occured in revenge for the shooting, in Paris, of the German diplomat, Herr vom Rath, a young Polish Jew. The savagery of the mobs, it appears, was not restrained by the police. Many important synagogues throughout the country were burnt to the ground; scarcely a Jewish shop escaped being wrecked; looting occured on a great scale and parts of the fashionable shopping centre of Berlin were reduced to ruins. In Vienna search for concealed arms was used as a pretext upon which thousands of Jewish homes were entered, and the inmates were in many cases taken to police stations followed by shouting mobs. On November 11 mass demonstrations were held in Munich against Jews, and also against Roman Catholics. Decrees were subsequently issued imposing further disabilities on Jews. These laid a collective fine of £84,000,000 upon the Jewish community; barred them from wholesale and retail trade; confiscated their insurance claims and ordered them to pay for damage done in the riots.

(LEFT), THE DESTRUCTION OF SYNAGOGUES, WHICH OCCURRED THROUGHOUT GERMANY: THE GREAT BUILDING ON THE PRINZREGENTENSTRASS, BERLIN, GUTTED.

(RIGHT), ANOTHER BIG BERLIN SYNAGOGUE BURNT OUT: THE DOME OF THE FASANENSTRASS BUILDING, AND A COLLAPSED ROOF.

THE ILLUSTRATED LONDON NEWS

THE POLISH INFANTRYMAN IN FULL WAR-KIT: A TYPE OF SOLDIER WHO CAN ENDURE PRIVATION, MAKE LONG MARCHES WITHOUT DIFFICULTY, AND PREFERS HAND-TO-HAND FIGHTING.

Poland's ability to remain firm over the Danzig question rests on her vast resources of man-power which enable her to rank as the fifth military power in the world. Today 66 per cent of the population are under thirty years of age, and with a total of only 34,000,000, Poland can mobilise an army larger than that of France. The strength of the standing army in 1938 was 18,738 officers and 255,150 other ranks, and on a war footing, it could easily be increased to 2,000,000 men. There are thirty infantry divisions, recruited for the most part from Poland's peasantry – men inured to fatigue and able to live on the country. These troops can march thirty to forty miles daily without difficulty, and are animated with a spirit which makes them prefer hand-to-hand fighting with the enemy. Two divisions consist of mountain troops trained as independent units.

1939

President Roosevelt warns Congress of dangers of not actively resisting aggression — Chilean earthquake kills 30,000 — British rearmament continues — Barcelona surrenders — many refugees and remnants of Republican army in Catalonia cross to France — Great Britain recognises Nationalists as Government of Spain — Madrid falls and Republican Government resigns — Dr. Tiso, the Slovak premier, arrested by Czech troops and charged with attempted secession — released and flees to Germany — Hitler invites Czech President Dr. Hacha to Berlin — requires him to sign over all rights of government in Bohemia and Moravia to Germany on pain of air bombardment of Prague — Hacha signs and German troops enter Prague unopposed — Hungary annexes Ruthenia — Italy annexes Albania — Germany annexes Memel — King George VI and Queen Elizabeth visit Canada and the U.S.A. — spend weekend with President Roosevelt at Hyde Park — Germany lays claim to Danzig — Britain calls up militia — and Naval Reserve — the Danzig Heimwehr reinforced by German "tourists" and a German ship arrives on "courtesy visit" — Germany unexpectedly signs "Non-Aggression Pact" with Soviet Russia, and invades Poland — Britain and France send ultimatum and, when it expires, declare war.

SPEECHES OF STATESMEN WHICH HAVE CAUSED WORLD-WIDE COMMENT.

"WAR TO-DAY . . . OUGHT NEVER TO BE ALLOWED TO BEGIN": MR. NEVILLE CHAMBERLAIN SPEAKING AT THE BIRMINGHAM JEWELLERS' ASSOCIATION DINNER, WHEN HE MADE AN APPEAL FOR PEACE.

WHEN PRESIDENT ROOSEVELT VOICED HIS COUNTRY'S DETERMINATION TO UPHOLD DEMOCRACY IN AMERICA, AND HINTED AT MODIFICATIONS IN THE U.S.A.'S NEUTRALITY LEGISLATION: THE GREAT SPEECH TO CONGRESS.

The Prime Minister, Mr. Neville Chamberlain, speaking at the Birmingham Jewellers' Association dinner at Birmingham on January 28, made an appeal for peace to the Powers, and stated: "We cannot forget that though it takes at least two to make a peace, one can make a war, and until we have come to clear understandings . . . we must put ourselves in a position to defend ourselves." Mr. Chamberlain then reviewed the progress of our rearmament programme and observed that in the last few months we had actually doubled the rate of aircraft production. "Our motto," he said, "is not defiance . . . it is not, either, deference. It is defence."

President Roosevelt, in the first part of his message to Congress delivered on January 4, warned Americans of the dangers threatening the foundations of their civilisation from aggressor states, and suggested that the possibility of America's remaining isolated from the troubles of the rest of the world had become much reduced. He made the following points: the three institutions "indispensable to Americans, now as always" – religion, democracy and international good faith – were directly challenged by undeclared wars, military and economic . . . The god-fearing democracies of the world which observed the sanctity of treaties and good faith could not safely be indifferent to international lawlessness anywhere. But the mere fact that we decline to intervene with arms, to prevent acts of aggression does not mean that we must act as if there were no aggression at all. We have learned that, when we deliberately try to legislate neutrality, our neutrality laws may operate unevenly and unfairly – may actually give aid to an aggressor. The instinct of self-preservation should warn us that we ought not to let that happen. From this suggestion of a needed change in the neutrality laws, Mr. Roosevelt passed to the necessity of the U.S.A. being united and strong.

THE CHILEAN EARTHQUAKE, 30,000 KILLED: HELP BY THE BRITISH NAVY.

After the Great War a number of United States warships became redundant and were laid up at various ports as being of no further use. It has now been found that in an emergency some of these vessels could be put into service and the authorities have ordered them to be reconditioned. Our lower photograph shows forty-eight 1200-ton destroyers, which were laid up at San Diego, being overhauled and re-equipped to form a war reserve.

REDUNDANT SINCE THE GREAT WAR BUT NOW BEING PREPARED TO SERVE AS A RESERVE IN AN EMERGENCY: FORTY-EIGHT DESTROYERS, BUILT FOR THE UNITED STATES NAVY IN THE WAR, UNDERGOING RECONDITIONING AT SAN DIEGO, CALIFORNIA.

THE SCENE OF ONE OF THE WORST DISASTERS IN THE EARTHQUAKE: THE REMAINS OF THE CONVENT OF SAN FRANCISCO AT CONCEPCION, WHERE 280 CHILDREN WERE KILLED WHEN THE STRUCTURE WAS SHATTERED.

Great devastation and heavy loss of life were suffered during the catastrophic earthquakes in Chile on January 24. Several towns and countless villages are in ruins; the earthquake having shaken practically the whole of the populous and fertile valley south of Talco – an area the size of Ireland. Concepcion, the third largest city in Chile, lost fully a quarter of its population of 80,000; but Chillan had the heaviest death-toll. The first shock was felt in Santiago near midnight. In Concepcion people rushed into the streets from their houses and were buried in the falling debris. The latest figures give the death-toll of the earthquake as 30,000, though this may well have been increased by the sufferings endured by the refugees, who numbered at least 100,000 homeless people. The crews of two British cruisers, the "Exeter" and "Ajax," co-operated actively in transporting survivors from Concepcion to Valparaiso. The United States and Argentine Governments despatched large quantities of anti-gangrene and anti-tetanus serums; in addition to the quantities of food and clothing sent by train over the Andes. All the Central and South American countries also sent help in one way or another; and Japan, mindful of the assistance she received from Chile on the occasion of a similar disaster just over fifteen years ago, made a special relaxation of currency restrictions to enable Japanese people to remit money to earthquake victims. The Chilean Congress was faced with a request for £21,000,000 for relief work.

On March 3 Mr. Gandhi began to fast as a protest against the refusal of the Thakore Saheb, ruler of Rajkot, to accede to his demands for a more democratic form of government in the State. On March 7 the Viceroy, Lord Linlithgow, succeeded in effecting a settlement of the dispute, and the Mahatma broke his fast after being four days without food. It was later stated that the Victory would receive Mr. Gandhi on March 15.

PARTAKING OF A LAST MEAL BEFORE BEGINNING HIS FAST: MR. GANDHI PREPARES FOR HIS PROTEST IN THE RAJKOT DISPUTE.

THE GROWTH OF A.R.P.: THE BALLOON-BARRAGE AND PASSIVE DEFENCE.

  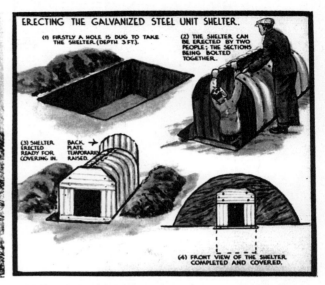

A PUBLIC DEMONSTRATION OF BALLOON-BARRAGE FLYING AT HORNCHURCH R.A.F. STATION: A FULLY INFLATED BALLOON.

A REMARKABLE PHOTOGRAPH SHOWING A BARRAGE-BALLOON JUST AFTER IT WAS STRUCK BY LIGHTNING: AN INCIDENT DURING A DEMONSTRATION AT STANMORE.

THE STEEL SHELTERS FOR SMALL HOUSES ABOUT TO BE ISSUED BY THE GOVERNMENT.

A demonstration of barrage-balloon flying was given by various Balloon Squadrons of the Auxiliary Air Force on February 26. Large crowds collected to watch the winch-crews at work lowering and raising the balloons and the operations were carried out with complete success. Two balloons were, however, struck by lightning and, falling to the ground in flames, were destroyed. One of these balloons was stationed at Chigwell, Essex, and the other at Stanmore, Middlesex. The balloon at Stanmore was being hauled down when a flash of lightning apparently struck the winch and ran up the steel cable. The fabric caught fire and then the hydrogen in the balloon ignited. The balloon fell on the roof of a hanger containing balloon-barrage lorries and trailers fitted with gas-cylinders but the blazing fabric was pulled clear of the roof by the cable attached to it and the emergency fire-engine put out the fire. The balloon at Chigwell fell in a clear space and no damage was done.

The A.R.P. department of the Home Office announced its plans for the rapid distribution of steel air raid shelters to small houses throughout twenty-three big cities, on February 9. These shelters are capable of holding from four to six persons. They are constructed of strong galvanised corrugated steel sheets, and have been subjected to rigorous tests to ensure that their strength when erected will be sufficient to take the weight of any debris that might fall upon them from the type of house which they are designed.

The first delivery of the Government's steel air-raid shelters in London took place on February 25 when they were distributed to residents in Tiber Street and Carlsbad Street, Islington. The sections were brought on drays, and were carried with much difficulty through the houses into the small backyard behind. The instructions for erecting the shelters state that they should be buried three feet in the ground, but as these backyards are for the most part paved with concrete it is anticipated that it will require considerable labour to carry the instructions into effect. The shelter stands on steel foundation channels and the sections are joined together with nuts and bolts.

THE FIRST DELIVERY OF STEEL AIR-RAID SHELTERS IN LONDON: A LONG LINE OF DRAYS IN TIBER STREET, ISLINGTON.

ERECTING ONE OF THE GOVERNMENT'S STEEL AIR-RAID SHELTERS IN A SMALL GARDEN: WORKMEN PLACING THE SECTIONS IN POSITION.

THE PALESTINE CONFERENCES OPENED: ARAB AND JEWISH DELEGATIONS.

THE OPENING OF THE PALESTINE CONFERENCES AT ST. JAMES'S PALACE: THE BRITISH DELEGATION WITH ARAB REPRESENTATIVES FROM PALESTINE AND NEIGHBOURING STATES.

THE SECOND OPENING OF THE PALESTINE CONFERENCES: THE JEWISH REPRESENTATIVES AT ST. JAMES'S PALACE.

The Prime Minister, Mr. Neville Chamberlain, opened the Palestine Conference at St. James's Palace on February 7. There were two ceremonies, as the Arab delegates had refused to meet the Jewish representatives. It is expected that the negotiations will continue for some weeks. In his speech to the Arabs the Prime Minister said: "My policy is one of peace. It is the task of statesmanship . . . to achieve a compromise on the basis of justice." Our photograph (left) shows (reading from l. to r. of the top table and then clockwise) the British

delegation; Sir Lancelot Oliphant, Mr. R.A. Butler, Under-Secretary of State for Foreign Affairs; Lord Halifax, the Foreign Minister; Mr. Neville Chamberlain (chairman); Mr. Malcolm MacDonald, Colonial Secretary; Lord Dufferin and Ava, Under-Secretary of State for the Colonies; Sir Cosmo Parkinson. With them are delegations from Saudi Arabai, Iraq, Trans-Jordan, Egypt, the Yemen and a delegation of Palestinian Arabs. The Prime Minister addressed the Jewish representatives after the Arab delegates had left.

"MASS PRODUCTION" METHODS TO MEET THE DEMANDS MADE BY THE EXPANSION OF THE R.A.F.: AIRCRAFT UNDER CONSTRUCTION.

VICKERS-SUPERMARINE "SPITFIRES" FOR FIGHTER SQUADRONS OF THE AIR FORCE – THE METHOD OF CONSTRUCTION FACILITATING THE INTERCHANGEABILITY OF COMPONENTS.

"MASS PRODUCTION" AT THE DE HAVILLAND WORKS AT HATFIELD: A LONG LINE OF D.H. "TIGER MOTH" TRAINING AIRCRAFT NEARING COMPLETION FOR DELIVERY TO ROYAL AIR FORCE FLYING TRAINING SCHOOLS.

FORMIDABLE TWIN-ENGINED BOMBERS IN LARGE-SCALE PRODUCTION AT THE ARMSTRONG-WHITWORTH WORKS AT COVENTRY (HAWKER SIDDELEY GROUP): ARMSTRONG-WHITWORTH "WHIT-LEYS" NEARING COMPLETION – A TYPE OF MACHINE WHICH HAS A RANGE OF 1315 MILES AND IS ARMED WITH FIVE MACHINE-GUNS.

PROVIDING STRIKING EVIDENCE OF THE SIZE AND SCOPE OF AIRCRAFT OUTPUT FOR THE R.A.F.: STANDARD BRISTOL "BLENHEIMS" IN THE ROOTES FACTORY AT SPEKE WHERE THESE FAST TWIN-ENGINED BOMBERS ARE BEING RAPIDLY CONSTRUCTED UNDER A SYSTEM OF "FLOW" PRODUCTION.

The photographs shown above are of exceptional interest, for they provide convincing evidence that the British aircraft industry is not lagging behind the programme of expansion with which the Royal Air Force is now faced. Quite apart from the need to build more front line aircraft (fighters and bombers), which has been the subject of many of our articles in recent years, an important feature of this activity is the provision of training machines for the instruction of the many new pilots at the R.A.F. Flying Training Schools who have to undergo a course lasting approximately ten months before they are qualified to handle the fast fighters with speeds of over 300 m.p.h.

NAVAL OCCASIONS: NEW WARSHIPS LAUNCHED.

THE "KING GEORGE V." LAUNCHED BY THE KING: THE NEW 35,000-TON BATTLESHIP MOVING DOWN THE SLIPWAY IN THE WALKER YARD OF VICKERS-ARMSTRONGS ON THE TYNE.

THE LAUNCH OF THE LARGEST BRITISH AIRCRAFT-CARRIER TO BE DESIGNED AS SUCH: H.M.S. "ILLUSTRIOUS", A 23,000-TON VESSEL, TAKING THE WATER AT BARROW.

A new British aircraft-carrier, the "Illustrious", was launched at Messrs. Vickers Armstrongs works at Barrow on April 5. She is the biggest vessel yet built as an aircraft-carrier for the Navy, and also the largest vessel ever launched at Barrow. She has a displacement of 23,000 tons. She is similar in many respects to the "Ark Royal", commissioned last year – but slightly larger, being the first of a new group of big aircraft-carriers now being built.

BARCELONA FALLS TO FRANCO: NATIONALIST TROOPS WELCOMED.

General Franco launched his great offensive on the Catalan front on December 23 and since that date the Nationalist forces have made steady progress towards their objective, Barcelona. On January 15 the important port of Tarragona was captured and arrangements were immediately made for feeding the population of the town, who eagerly surrounded the lorries from which bread was distributed. On January 22 the town of Igualada was taken, regarded as the key position to the outermost line of defences and by the evening the troops advancing from Tarragona were within twenty-five miles of Barcelona, while the Government troops had withdrawn to the fortified line running from Solsona to Manresa. On January 23 Nationalist troops were only ten miles from Barcelona, and attacks were being made in the direction of Manresa and Solsona, with the purpose of cutting Catalonia's communications with the French frontier.

Following the retreat of the Government forces from Barcelona, the city was occupied by the Nationalist troops on January 26. There was little resistance and, after light tanks and armoured cars had entered the city, the infantry columns marched in unopposed. In fact, although at first the inhabitants of Barcelona seemed apathetic, the arrival of food supplies soon caused vast crowds to gather and the incoming soldiers were greeted with the Fascist salute while Nationalist flags and portraits of General Franco were displayed. The decision to keep the Italian and Moorish units outside the city undoubtedly determined the attitude taken by the inhabitants to the victorious troops.

The British Government's decision to recognise General Franco's Government was announced in the House of Commons by Mr. Chamberlain on February 27.

LEFT BEHIND IN THE RETREAT AND PROVIDING AN UNUSUAL INCIDENT IN THE CIVIL WAR: THE BAND OF A GOVERNMENT REGIMENT HEADS A NATIONALIST COLUMN ON ITS MARCH INTO THE CITY, PLAYING NATIONALIST TUNES!

WHEN THE SPANISH WAR REACHED A CLIMAX OF MISERY:

TYPICAL OF THE HUGE NUMBERS OF REFUGEES, SOME 35,000 OF WHOM ENTERED FRANCE ON THE FIRST TWO DAYS THE FRONTIER WAS OPENED: A CROWD OF ALL TYPES, INCLUDING SOME SOLDIERS, HERDED TOGETHER, NEAR A FRONTIER POST.

THE SURVIVORS OF THE INTERNATIONAL BRIGADE REACH FRANCE: THE LONG COLUMN OF DISARMED MEN, MOST OF THEM CZECHS, GERMANS, AND EASTERN EUROPEANS, MARCHING IN GOOD ORDER ALONG THE ROAD NEAR PERTHUS.

The exodus of refugees from Catalonia into France was followed by the crossing of the Catalan army. For the most part the retreat was orderly, the pursuers being held up by well-planned demolitions. Among the first Republican military units to seek refuge in France were air squadrons deprived of their bases in Catalonia. The aeroplanes were stripped of their machine-guns and the pilots given shelter at local barracks. Some seventy up-to-date machines, many of them of Russian make, were gathered at the military aerodrome at Toulouse. Then came artillery. A convoy of nineteen heavy guns drawn by six-wheel lorries passed into France on February 7; followed by another of thirteen guns. During the following night a train-load of fifty guns came over. There was a striking scene at Perthus when 1000 men of the International Brigade marched smartly in, headed by their standard-bearers and led by 300 veterans of the Italian Garibaldi Battalion. In the early hours of February 10, Colonel Modesto, Commander of the Republican Ebro Army, crossed the frontier near La Serra, followed by his troops comprising 10,000 Spaniards and 350 members of the International Brigade.

MADRID FALLS TO GENERAL FRANCO AFTER 33 MONTHS OF WAR

On March 29, the Nationalist wireless station at Burgos broadcast the announcement: "The war has ended". On the previous day General Franco's forces had entered Madrid without a shot being fired, and so brought to a close the battle for the city which had lasted for thirty-three months. The troops defending Madrid had surrendered at dawn and soon white flags appeared on the principal buildings, while secret supporters of General Franco in the city dressed themselves in Falagist uniforms and took over police duties. The city was occupied by some 10,000 troops, led by the Italian General Gambara, who were welcomed by cheering crowds waving Nationalist flags. Perhaps the most welcome sight for the inhabitants of the city were the long columns of lorries organised by the "Auxilio Social" service, from which loaves, tins of meat and sardines were distributed to the hungry crowds, many of whom had received no food since their ration two days previously. In the streets, Republican soldiers could be seen returning to their homes and passing Nationalist soldiers with scarcely a glance in their direction. An unusual feature of the occupation was the entry of certain Nationalist officials by parachute. They were dropped from aeroplanes and, on landing, took over control of the power stations. Other officers arrived in the capital by taking the tube train with Republican troops. Madrid quickly settled down under the new authorities and on the day after the surrender civilians were wandering about the front lines, shortly before the scene of fierce fighting, while children searched for souvenirs among the débris. It is estimated that a sum of £50,000,000 will be needed for the reconstruction of Madrid, and that of the 200,000 buildings in the city, over 70,000 have been completely destroyed. On March 30, General Franco placed Madrid under martial law.

General Franco's victory parade was held in Madrid on May 19. More than 150,000 troops took part. The parade was led by General Saliquet, commander of the Nationalist Army of the Centre. General Gambara, leader of the 21,000 Italian "legionaries", followed with his four divisions, the Littorio, the Black Arrows, the Blue Arrows and the Green Arrows. Several hundred field guns, lorries and ambulances separated the different sections. They took 75 minutes to pass. After them came military cadets and marines and representative groups from the Southern and Levant army corps; 30,000 Carlists led by General Solchaga; General Valino's Moors; the First Army Corps; Spanish lancers; Moorish cavalry and near the end the German "Condor" legion under Colonel von Richthofen.

GENERAL FRANCO TAKING THE SALUTE OF AN ITALIAN PACK BATTERY FROM AN ELABORATE TRIBUNE HUNG WITH TAPESTRY, IN FRONT OF WHICH STAND SUB-ALTERNS WITH ANCIENT SPANISH BANNERS AND MOORISH GUARDS.

THE END OF THE CZECHS' INDEPENDENCE.

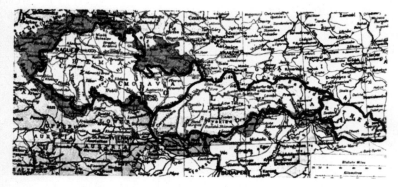

CZECHOSLOVAKIA IN THE MELTING-POT: A MAP SHOWING THE FRONTIERS AFTER MUNICH; AND THE BOUNDARIES OF SLOVAKIA AND SUB-CARPATHIAN UKRAINE.

An acute crisis arose in Czechoslovakia on March 10, when Dr. Tiso, the Slovak Premier, was arrested on the orders of the Czechoslovak President, on a charge of attempting to establish an independent Slovakia. Czech troops occupied key positions in Bratislava, after clashes with hlinka Guards, the Slovak Storm Troops. Dr. Tiso smuggled an appeal for aid to Herr Hitler from his place of custody and another dismissed Minister, Dr. Durcansky, escaped to Vienna from Czechoslovakia. He broadcast an appeal to the Slovaks to resist the Czechs. A new Slovak Cabinet came into office, headed by Dr. Sidor. Dr. Tiso was released and flew to Berlin on March 13, where he had a conference with Herr Hitler. He was accompanied into Germany by Herr Karmarsin, the leader of the Germans in Slovakia. Dr. Tiso returned from Berlin on March 14 and was proclaimed President of an independent Slovakia. At the same time, the Czech Cabinet resigned. The situation was further complicated by a series of clashes between Germans and Czechs and Hungarians and Czechs in many districts.

Of all the actors who played a part in the miserable tragedy of the invasion of Czechoslovakia Dr. Hacha, President of the Czechoslovak Republic, merits the most sympathy. He and Dr. Chvalkovsky, the Foreign Minister, were informed by the German Minister in Prague on March 14 that it was thought that it would be useful if they could come to Berlin for conversations. On arrival they were met with military honours. According to a "Daily Telegraph" correspondent, they were then confronted by a document which when signed would abdicate all rights of government in favour of Germany.

Herr Hitler explained that the decisions reached by the German Government were irrevocable and that Prague would be occupied by German troops next morning at nine o'clock, and Bohemia and Moravia become a German protectorate. Herr Hitler then affixed his signature to the document and left the room. In spite of vehement protests the German Ministers were quite pitiless and hustled the Czechs round the table continually thrusting pens into their hands, threatening that if they continued to withhold their signatures half of Prague would be laid waste by air bombardment within two hours. In the end Dr. Hacha's physical resistance was broken and he signed to save his country from ruthless aerial bomardment. The occupation of Prague began on March 15, when an advanced guard of tanks entered the city, to be followed shortly afterwards by armoured cars, motorised troops and motor-cyclists. The Czechs greeted the German soldiers with jeers and derisive shouts of "Shame! Why don't you go home", as they passed through the streets,but here and there little groups of Germans welcomed them with the Nazi salute. Czech troops remained in their barracks awaiting orders and there were no incidents apart from natural expressions of resentment by the populace. The first motorised column entered the city at 9 o'clock in the morning, having occupied the civil airport at Ruzyne. It was snowing heavily at the time, but the tank detachments arrived looking as if they were on parade and the discipline of the troops was excellent. The German Secret Police occupied the Hotel Alcron and at once began searching for "wanted" men. On March 15 Herr Hitler left Berlin in a special train to join the German troops marching into the Czech provinces. The Führer arrived in Prague in the evening, closely following his Army of Occupation, and drove through the streets to the Hradschin Castle, the former residence of the Presidents of the Czechoslovak Republic. On March 16 Herr Hitler made a proclamation on the new Constitution of the "Protectorate of Bohemia and Moravia" and stated that the German people, by their greatness and qualities, were alone fitted to "re-establish the bases of a reasonable Central European order".

DR. HACHA LEAVING BERLIN AFTER HIS TERRIBLE EXPERIENCE WHEN HE WAS FORCED TO SIGN AWAY HIS COUNTRY'S INDEPENDENCE: AND PAID THE EMPTY COMPLIMENT OF A GUARD OF HONOUR.

HERR HITLER WELL GUARDED DURING HIS TRIMPHAL DRIVE THROUGH BRNO: THE FÜHRER STANDING IN HIS CAR IN ORDER TO BE SEEN BY THE GERMAN INHABITANTS, WHILE BEHIND HIM ARE CARS CONTAINING HIS BODYGUARDS, SOME OF WHOM ARE STANDING ON THE RUNNING-BOARDS.

Brno, the capital of the Czech province of Moravia and a German minority centre, was occupied by German troops from Austria at 6 a.m. on March 15. Behind the advanced guard of motorised troops came long columns of infantry who were greeted with enthusiasm by the German inhabitants. The Czechs watched the German invaders in silence, being too overwhelmed by the rapid march of events to protest. On March 16 Herr Hitler left Prague for Brno. He arrived there on the morning of March 17 and drove in triumph through the streets to the Town Hall amid the acclamations of the German minority. As in Vienna after the Anschluss, some of the Czech street names were changed: thus, "Freedom Square" was renamed "Adolf Hitler Platz" – an unconsciously ironic commentary on the annexation.

Although Czechoslovakia was always regarded as a small State, it has an armaments industry comparable to that of a Great Power. Apart from the economic advantages which Germany has gained by establishing a protectorate, the German Army has now added to its equipment the material obtained from the disarmed Czechoslovak forces. The "Daily Telegraph's" military correspondent stated recently: "At the time of the September crisis the Czechoslovaks mobilised 34 divisions. Exact calculations are difficult, but this would probably represent a minimum of 200,000 rifles, with machine-guns – light and heavy – in proportion and probably not less than 3500 guns of various calibres." There are twenty-five factories in Czechoslovakia making artillery and nine employed in constructing tanks and armoured cars. These are to become German, including the famous Skoda works. The Czechoslovak Air Force consisted of a first-line strength of approximately 650 machines and about 1500 aeroplanes in all should be available to increase Germany's air power. At a meeting of the Foreign Affairs Committee of Government supporters in the House of Commons on March 16 Mr. Amery said that he computed the gain to Germany in aircraft and air force material amounted to three months' output in Britain. Germany does not increase her manpower, however, as the Czechs will be exempt from military service in the Germany Army.

CZECHOSLOVAKIA DISINTEGRATES: RUTHENIA ANNEXED BY HUNGARY.

On March 14 the Hungarian Government sent an ultimatum to Prague demanding the withdrawal of Czech troops from Ruthenia and later, without waiting for a reply, Hungarian forces invaded Ruthenia and advanced towards the Polish frontier. The Hungarian troops were opposed by Ruthenian irregulars and snow also added to their difficulties, but on March 16 the long-desired common frontier with Poland was formally established at Tucholska, a town on the south Polish border. Hungarian officers, commanding an armoured train and three companies of infantry, were welcomed by the Polish General Biurata-Spiechowicz and the Polish frontier guard turned out and saluted as the column marched by. During the occupation of the country the Hungarians had 200 killed and a large number wounded, owing to the resistance offered by Ukranian Storm Troopers. Father Volosin, the Ruthenian Premier, was stated to have appealed to the Rumanian Government and also to Herr Hitler for aid, but without success. The former Czechoslovak province had declared its independence on the day it was invaded.

(RIGHT), A COMMON FRONTIER FORMALLY ESTABLISHED BETWEEN HUNGARY AND POLAND: THE OFFICER COMMANDING AN ADVANCED COLUMN OF HUNGARIAN TROOPS BEING GREETED BY THE POLISH GENERAL BIURATA-SPIECHOWICZ WHEN THE REACHED THE FRONTIER TOWN OF TUCHOLSKA, ON THE SOUTH POLISH BORDER.

THE ANGLO-ITALIAN AGREEMENT VIOLATED: THE CONQUEST OF ALBANIA.

At dawn on April 7 Italian troops from Bari and Brindisi invaded Albania. The troopships were escorted by a large force of Italian warships which covered the landing parties as they went ashore at the four seaports of Durazzo, Valona, Santi Quaranta and San Giovanni di Medua. Meanwhile some 400 aeroplanes flew overhead dropping leaflets advising the Albanians not to resist. However, the troops had to fight their way into the centre of the towns and their advance was made only with the assistance of light tanks which were quickly unloaded from the transports. A *communiqué* explaining the reason for the invasion stated: "During the past few days, and while conversations were proceeding between the Italian Government and King Zog for the conclusion of a closer agreement, threatening demonstrations by armed bands took place at Tirana and elsewhere and were a serious danger to the personal safety of Italians living in Albania."

After the invading army had swept inland, vast quantities of munitions and stores arrived at Durazzo, where they were rapidly unloaded and reinforcements were brought from Italy by air. Heavy artillery has now been installed at Valona which, with batteries on the Italian side, will enable the entrance to the Adriatic to be closed without the assistance of warships. Albania's oil-wells were protected by troops sent by air from the coast. The Italian invasion of Albania may be interpreted as being a violation of the Anglo-Italian Agreement of April 1938, whereby both countries undertook to exchange information regarding any distribution of their armed forces in overseas territory in or with a seaboard on the Mediterranean and to preserve the status quo in the Mediterranean as defined in the Anglo-Italian declaration of January 1937. On April 7 the Earl of Perth, British Ambassador in Rome, handed a Note to Count Ciano in which the British Government is believed to have expressed this view. The invasion of Albania closely followed the method which Herr Hitler has made so familiar. It was reported that the Italian Government desired to take possession of that part of the Albanian

THE LIBERATORS OF OPPRESSED ALBANIANS WELCOMED IN TIRANA: ITALIAN TROOPS MARCHING BETWEEN THE THIN RANKS OF SILENT AND BEWILDERED SPECTATORS.

coast opposite the Gulf of Otranto as a means of holding Yugoslavia in check and as a safeguard in the event of war. These demands led to anti-Italian demonstrations which were made a pretext for the invasion. To ensure the "personal safety of Italians living in Albania", 20,000 troops were sent from Bari and Brindisi, escorted by a large number of warships and preceded by hundreds of aeroplanes.

In an article in the "Giornale d'Italia", Signor Gayda recently stated: "King Zog and his circle of politicians showed a growing tendency to govern away from the people . . . Implacable enemy of all Albanians who were not under his immediate influence, he appropriated . . . financial assistance which Italy had furnished for his people's needs". This effort to justify the Italian invasion of Albania does not seem to be supported by the evidence of some of the photographs on this page, which show only a small number of people lined up to welcome their "liberators" as the Italian troops marched into Tirana. In fact, the spectators were silent and seemed bewildered by the sudden invasion of their country by a nation which they had always regarded as an ally.

Following the invasion of Albania by Italy on April 7, Italian troops were sent to strategic points near the Greek frontier. Speaking in the House of Commons on April 13, the Prime Minister stated that these troops movements had caused the Greek Government to become uneasy as to the intentions of the Italian Government. As a consequence, Lord Halifax pointed out to the Italian Chargé d'Affaires that the British Government would take a serious view of any threat to the independence of Greek and subsequently Signor Mussolini instructed the Italian Chargé d'Affaires in Athens to assure the Greek Government that Italy intended to respect the territorial and insular integrity of Greece. Before the Italian forces reached Tirana the Royal Family fled and an Albanian mob broke into the palace and sacked it. On April 12 the Albanian Constituent Assembly offered the crown to King Victor Emmanuel in order to form a personal union between the two countries. On the following day the Fascist Grand Council approved the King of Italy's acceptance.

OPPOSED BY GROUPS OF HURRIEDLY ARMED ALBANIANS WHOSE RESISTANCE WAS BROKEN BY MECHANISED FORCES AND BY SHELLING FROM THE ITALIAN WARSHIPS WHICH ESCORTED THE TRANSPORTS: ITALIAN INFANTRY SHELTERING BEHIND TREE-TRUNKS NEAR THE HARBOUR DURING THE FIGHT FOR DURAZZO.

ANOTHER NAZI INVASION:
THE ANNEXATION OF MEMEL BY THE THIRD REICH.

THE ITALO-GERMAN TREATY SIGNED IN BERLIN

THE RATIFICATION OF THE ITALO-GERMAN TREATY: THE SCENE IN THE HALL OF AMBASSADORS AT THE NEW REICH CHANCELLERY IN BERLIN SHOWING (L. TO R.) COUNT CIANO, HERR HITLER AND HERR VON RIBBENTROP.

The Italo-German Treaty, which takes the form of a political and military alliance, was signed on May 22 in the Hall of Ambassadors, at the new Reich Chancellery in Berlin. Count Ciano, the Italian Foreign Minister, and Herr von Ribbentrop sat on either side of Herr Hitler at a long table with Field-Marshal Göring, General-Admiral Raeder and other high officials standing behind them. When Count Ciano and he himself had affixed their signatures to the documents, Herr von Ribbentrop turned to Herr Hitler and said: "My Führer, I report to you the completed signature of the German-Italian Pact of Alliance". The Führer then grasped Count Ciano's hand and shook it warmly and presented him with the Grand Cross of the Order of the German Eagle in gold. This is the highest order that Herr Hitler can bestow. Later the two Foreign Ministers broadcast short statements on the Treaty.

NAZI SAILORS JOIN FOR THE FIRST TIME IN OCCUPYING TERRITORY CEDED TO THE REICH: A LANDING PARTY MARCH THROUGH MEMEL; PART OF THE BALTIC FLEET WHICH ESCORTED HERR HITLER.

Herr Hitler's long-awaited march into Memel took place on March 23. On March 21, an ultimatum had been presented to the Lithuanian Foreign Minister in Berlin, M. Urbsys, giving the Lithuanian Government a space of approximately four days to make up their minds to cede Memel. Sir Samuel Hoare, speaking in the House on March 22 for the Prime Minister, stated he understood that "in the event of resistance or application for support elsewhere, the matter would be dealt with not diplomatically but in a military sense". (This presumably meant the immediate bombing of Kaunas.) Lithuania is officially to retain certain rights in Memel; any form of alliance with Poland, however, will be frowned upon; and the familiar Nazi fiat that if internal disorder occurred it would be followed by German intervention went forth. On March 23, escorted by the whole of the Baltic fleet, Herr Hitler paid a three-hour visit to Memel. Within four days of this the Lithuanian Government resigned. Thirteen per cent of Memel's population (c. 150,000) were Jews and Lithuanians. By the Convention of 1924, England, France, Italy and Japan guaranteed Lithuanian sovereignty of Memel (1099 sq. m.), with a measure of local autonomy.

HITLER ANSWERS PRESIDENT ROOSEVELT: THE FÜHRER SPEAKING.

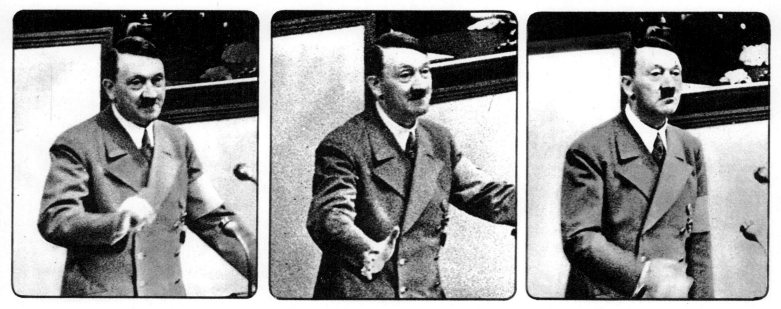

HERR HITLER ADDRESSES THE REICHSTAG IN THE KROLL OPERA HOUSE: THE FÜHRER'S GESTURES AND EXPRESSIONS.

The speech delivered by Herr Hitler before the Reichstag in the Kroll Opera House, Berlin, on April 28, was punctuated by applause and laughter at the Führer amused himself by making a number of debating points at the expense of President Roosevelt's proposals for obtaining a period of peace in Europe. On this page we show some of Herr Hitler's facial expressions and gestures during the course of an address in which he denounced two pacts, one a ten-year pact of non-aggression with Poland, and the other the Anglo-German Naval Pact, by which Germany accepted a limitation of the total tonnage of her Fleet to 35 per cent of the aggregate tonnage of the naval forces of the British Empire.

HERR HITLER'S BROKEN PLEDGES: AN AMAZING RECORD.

Speaking at the Sportpalast, Berlin, some days after his meeting with Mr. Chamberlain at Godesberg, last September, Herr Hitler told his hearers, with reference to the German occupation of Sudetenland: "THIS IS THE LAST TERRITORIAL CLAIM WHICH I HAVE TO MAKE IN EUROPE", and again: "I HAVE ASSURED MR. CHAMBERLAIN, AND I EMPHASISE IT NOW, THAT WHEN THIS PROBLEM IS SOLVED GERMANY HAS NO MORE TERRITORIAL PROBLEMS IN EUROPE". He added: "I have further assured him that at the moment when Czechoslovakia has solved its other problems – that is, when the Czechs shall have come to an understanding with their other minorities – I SHALL NOT BE INTERESTED IN THE CZECH STATE ANY MORE, AND THAT AS FAR AS I AM CONCERNED, I CAN GUARANTEE IT. WE DO NOT WANT ANY CZECHS ANY MORE". In the same speech he also said: "We have assured all our immediate neighbours of the integrity of their territory as far as Germany is concerned. That is no hollow phrase; it is our sacred will". All these assurances only confirmed what Herr Hitler had already told Mr. Chamberlain at Godesberg. Speaking with great earnestness, Herr Hitler repeated what he had previously said at Berchtesgaden – namely, that this was the last of his territorial ambitions in Europe, and that he had no wish to include in the Reich people of other races than Germany.

1934

SPEAKING BEFORE THE REICHSTAG ON JANUARY 30, 1934, HERR HITLER SAID: "AFTER IT (THE SAAR) HAS BEEN SETTLED THE GERMAN GOVERNMENT IS READY TO ACCEPT NOT ONLY THE LETTER BUT ALSO THE SPIRIT OF THE LOCARNO PACT". IN A NOTE TO FRANCE ON MARCH 13 OF THE SAME YEAR HE WROTE: "THE GERMAN GOVERNMENT HAS NEVER QUESTIONED THE VALIDITY OF THE TREATY OF LOCARNO". GERMANY'S WILLINGNESS TO FULFIL HER LOCARNO OBLIGATIONS WAS FURTHER CONFIRMED BY HERR HITLER IN HIS SPEECH OF MAY 21, 1935, WHEN HE ALSO MADE A SPECIFIC REFERENCE TO HER ACCEPTANCE OF THE DEMILITARISED ZONES.

1935

IN HIS SPEECH IN THE REICHSTAG ON MAY 21, 1935, HERR HITLER SAID: "GERMANY NEITHER INTENDS NOR WISHES TO INTERFERE IN THE INTERNAL AFFAIRS OF AUSTRIA, TO ANNEXE AUSTRIA OR TO CONCLUDE AN ANSCHLUSS". IN THE SAME SPEECH HE ALSO SAID THAT THE TERRITORIAL DECLARATIONS, OF VERSAILLES COULD NOT BE RENOUNCED UNILATERALLY AND THAT GERMANY WOULD UNCONDITIONALLY RESPECT THEM. THE INDEPENDENCE OF AUSTRIA WAS LAID DOWN AT VERSAILLES.

1936

IN HIS REICHSTAG SPEECH OF MARCH 7, 1936 THOUGH DENOUNCING THE TREATY OF LOCARNO, HERR HITLER PROMISED THIS SHOULD BE THE END OF GERMANY'S DEMANDS, WITH THE WORDS: "AFTER THREE YEARS I BELIEVE I CAN REGARD THE STRUGGLE FOR GERMAN EQUALITY AS CONCLUDED TODAY . . . WE HAVE NO TERRITORIAL DEMANDS TO MAKE IN EUROPE. WE KNOW THAT ALL THE TENSIONS WHICH ARISE FROM WRONG TERRITORIAL PROVISIONS . . . CANNOT BE SOLVED IN EUROPE BY WAR. WE HOPE THAT HUMAN WISDOM WILL HELP TO . . . ALLAY THE TENSIONS BY THE METHOD OF GRADUAL EVOLUTION IN FRIENDLY CO-OPERATION".

1936

IN SPITE OF THE ASSURANCES QUOTED ABOVE, HERR HITLER DENOUNCED THE LOCARNO PACT IN MARCH 1936 AND ORDERED THE MILITARY REOCCUPATION OF THE RHINELAND DEMILITARISED ZONE. HERE THE GERMAN TROOPS ARE SEEN MARCHING INTO COLOGNE.

MARCH 1938

IN SPITE OF THE PLEDGES QUOTED ABOVE, AUSTRIA WAS INVADED BY GERMAN TROOPS IN MARCH 1938. THIS PHOTOGRAPH WAS TAKEN AS A UNIT CROSSED THE BORDER AT KUFSTEIN ON THE ROAD TO INNSBRUCK.

SEPTEMBER 1938

IN SPITE OF THESE ASSURANCES, BY SEPTEMBER 1938 HERR HITLER WAS DEMANDING THE EVACUATION OF THEIR SUDETEN AREAS BY THE CZECHS, AND AT THE BEGINNING OF OCTOBER THE GERMAN ARMY MARCHED IN. THEIR TROOPS ARE HERE SEEN ENTERING FRIEDLAND.

Herr Hitler's cynical disregard of past promises, and his practice of accompanying every *coup* with soothing assurances for the future, are reminiscent of Napoleon, a conqueror whose triumphs of cunning and "realism" only brought him to destruction. As with Napoleon, considerations of justice, good faith and the rights of nations are only operative so long as they can be called in to justify the aggressor's actions and hoodwink future victims. On this page we show three occasions on which Herr Hitler has broken his own word, freely given. On the opposite page he is seen speaking at the Sportpalast in Berlin last September, when he gave the pacific assurances then believed sincere in this country, and now shown to have been nothing but "blinds" to gain time for the organisation of the complete overrunning of Czechoslovakia. The facts are undeniable. His speeches stand recorded. Mr. Chamberlain made a stern reference to these broken pledges in his speech at Birmingham and asked: "If it is so easy to discover good reasons for ignoring assurances so solemnly . . . given, what reliance can we place upon any such assurances that come from the same quarter?"

THE ROYAL VISIT TO CANADA

"NO CEREMONY COULD MORE COMPLETELY SYMBOLISE THE FREE AND EQUAL ASSOCIATION OF THE NATIONS OF OUR COMMONWEALTH": THE HISTORIC OCCASION WHEN THE FIRST REIGNING SOVEREIGN VISITED A DOMINION PARLIAMENT, SHOWING THE KING AND QUEEN SEATED IN STATE IN THE SENATE CHAMBER OF PARLIAMENT HOUSE IN OTTAWA, CAPITAL OF THE DOMINION.

The King and Queen arrived in Ottawa, the capital of the Dominion, from Montreal, on May 19 and in the afternoon drove to Parliament House where his Majesty was to give the Royal Assent to certain Bills in the Senate. For this ceremony the King was in Field-Marshal's uniform, while the Queen wore a magnificent crinoline dress with the Riband of the Order of the Garter. Their Majesties were conducted to their thrones in the Senate, where Members of the Upper House and their wives were assembled and sat facing the Judges of the Supreme Court, who occupied the circular Woolsack. The Commons was then summoned to the Bar of the House, and the Clerk of the Crown in Chancery read out a list of the Bills passed by the Senate and Commons and requested their Majesties resumed their drive, stopping for tea at the Chalet, on Mount Royal, from which a fine view of the city can be obtained. At the Stadium 85,000 French-speaking children greeted the King and Queen with mass singing of "God Save the King", and a similar demonstration of loyalty was given by

Jubilee, the unity of the British Empire is no longer expressed by the supremacy of the time-honoured Parliament that sits at Westminster. It finds expression today in the free association of nations enjoying common principles of government . . . and bound together by a common allegiance to the Crown . . . It is my earnest hope that my present visit may give my Canadian people a deeper conception of their unity as a nation."

The most historic single act of their Majesties' visit to Canada was their attendance at the Dominion Parliament in Ottawa on May 19. Here the King gave the Royal Assent to certain Bills in the Senate. This was the first time that a King had personally given his Assent to legislation in any of the Dominions and the act constituted an impressive symbol of the unity of the Empire under the Crown. This photograph has another unique interest for it was flown across the Atlantic in the "Yankee Clipper" on the first regular Transatlantic Mail Service.

THE ROYAL TOUR: THEIR MAJESTIES IN MONTREAL AND TORONTO.

THE KING AND QUEEN IN MONTREAL: THEIR MAJESTIES DRIVING IN AN OPEN CAR ROUND MOLSON PARK, WHER 35,000 ENGLISH-SPEAKING CHILDREN HAD GATHERED TO DEMONSTRATE THEIR LOYALTY AND GREETED THE ROYAL PROCESSION WITH MASS SINGING OF "GOD SAVE THE KING".

THEIR MAJESTIES' ARRIVAL AT THE WOODBINE RACECOURSE, TORONTO, TO SEE THE KING'S PLATE, CANADA'S BIGGEST RACE: THE KING AND QUEEN DRIVING ROUND THE COURSE IN A STATE LANDAU WITH AN ESCORT OF ROYAL CANADIAN DRAGOONS.

The King and Queen arrived in Montreal from Quebec on May 18 and drove in an open car through the greater part of the city before calling at the City Hall to sign the Golden Book and attend a civic reception. After these ceremonies their Majesties resumed their drive, stopping for tea at the Chalet, on Mount Royal, from which a fine view of the city can be obtained. At the Stadium 85,000 French-speaking children greeted the King and Queen with mass singing of "God Save the King", and a similar demonstration of loyalty was given by

English-speaking children gathered in Molson Park. Their Majesties arrived in Toronto, Canada's second largest city, on May 22, where they watched the King's Plate run at the Woodbine Racecourse. They drove in a State landau, with an escort of Royal Canadian Dragoons, round the course to the Royal Box. The King's Plate is the oldest fixture in North America to be run continuously.

ROYAL VISIT TO CANADA – THE TOUR ITINERARY

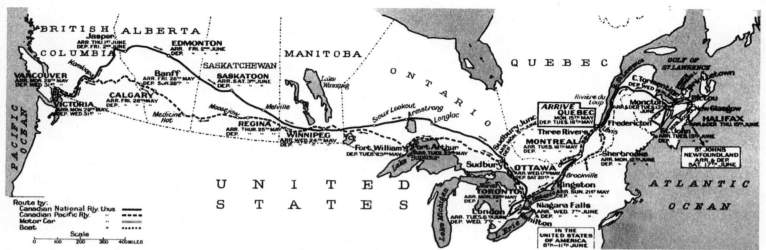

THE KING AND QUEEN'S VISIT TO CANADA: A MAP OF THEIR MAJESTIES' ITINERARY, WITH A KEY SHOWING THE MODE OF TRAVEL ON DIFFERENT SECTIONS OF THE ROUTE, AND THE DATES OF THEIR ARRIVAL AND DEPARTURE AT VARIOUS CENTRES.

EXPRESSING UNAFFECTED ENJOYMENT: THEIR MAJESTIES IN THE U.S.A.

THE KING AND QUEEN TALKING TO MEMBERS OF CONGRESS WHO WELCOMED THEM AT THE RECEPTION IN THE ROTUNDA: THEIR MAJESTIES WITH SENATORS AND OFFICIALS DURING THE CEREMONY.

WITH MAYOR AND MRS. LA GUARDIA AT THE WORLD'S FAIR: THE KING AND QUEEN, OBVIOUSLY ENJOYING THEMSELVES, ABOUT TO LEAVE FOR A TOUR OF THE FAIR GROUNDS IN A TRACTOR-TRAIN.

THE KING AND QUEEN AT HYDE PARK.

A HISTORIC PHOTOGRAPH OF THEIR MAJESTIES' VISIT TO THE ROOSEVELT ESTATE, OVERLOOKING THE HUDSON RIVER: THE KING AND QUEEN WITH MRS. SARAH ROOSEVELT (THE PRESIDENT'S 85-YEAR-OLD MOTHER), MRS. ROOSEVELT (LEFT) AND PRESIDENT ROOSEVELT (RIGHT), ON THE PORCH AT HYDE PARK.

If Americans cherished any doubts about the democratic simplicity of the British Royal Family these were finally dispelled by the visit this month, brief as it was, to Washington and New York of the King and Queen, whose frank and unaffected enjoyment of the tumultuous reception accorded them won the public affection wherever they moved. As the delightful study of the Queen and President Roosevelt together shows, the weather reflected the happy smiles of the royal visitors and their hosts, much of the visit taking place at the height of a June heat-wave. The King by his dignity, naturalness and obvious pleasure, and the Queen by her radiant smile, disarmed all criticism: and a spirit of spontaneous gaiety pervaded every event.

SUNSHINE AND SMILES: A PICTURE OF HAPPINESS, SHOWING THE QUEEN, WITH PRESIDENT ROOSEVELT, SEATED ON THE PORCH OF THE PRESIDENT'S COUNTRY HOME AT HYDE PARK.

AFTER MORE THAN TWO YEARS OF UNDECLARED WAR: A PERSPECTIVE MAP ILLUSTRATING JAPAN'S GAINS IN CHINA.

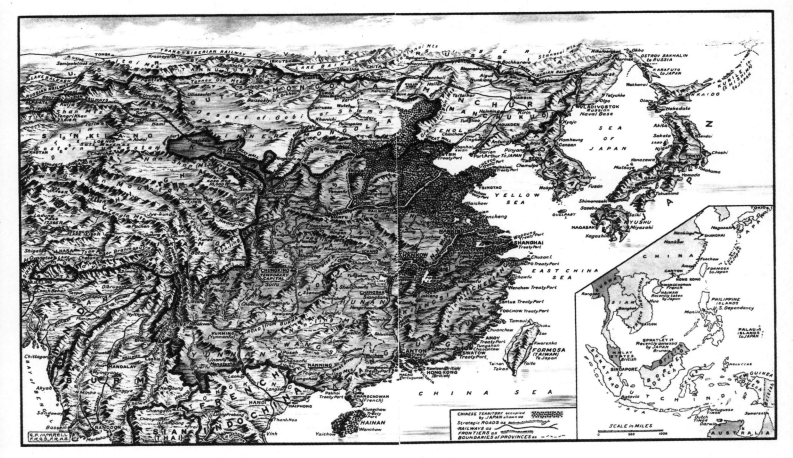

A PICTORIAL RELIEF MAP OF CHINA, SHOWING MAIN STRATEGICAL ROUTES, AND A SCALE KEY MAP ILLUSTRATING THE STRATEGICAL IMPORTANCE TO JAPAN OF THE SPRATLEY ISLANDS.

The Sino-Japanese War entered on its third year last month – though as yet without an official declaration of war by Japan. Yet after two years of costly fighting, Japan occupies but relatively little of China, as can be seen from a glance at the above pictorial map. Inland towns on this map which are open to foreign trade are underlined. The roads from Burma and the newly constructed roads from Indo-China to Central China are indicated together with the roads, northern and western, from Chungking (the present seat of government). The main air routes from China to the west generally follow the line of these roads. The Spratley Islands (in the Scale Key Map) are a group of coral atolls which were seized by Japan at the end of March 1939. They could easily be fortified and thus made of considerable strategic importance to her. Japan claims during the two years to have occupied approximately 270,000 square miles; to have killed nearly 900,000 Chinese and to have wounded or taken prisoner over a million: at a loss of under 60,000 Japanese. China claims that the Japanese dead number 870,000 and that 20,000 prisoners have been made. They also claim to have regained 70,000 square miles in the April offensive, leaving only 120,000 square miles in Japanese possession. Of this they further claim that only 70,000 square miles are completely occupied and that guerilla warfare reigns elsewhere. The Chinese claim would appear to be the more nearly accurate, at least as regards captured territory, and tallies more with our map.

AN ISSUE BETWEEN BERLIN AND WARSAW: DANZIG AND THE "CORRIDOR".

The substance of the proposals made by Herr Hitler to Poland in his Reichstag speech were: the return of Danzig; a road and railway line through the "Corridor possessing the same extra-territorial status for Germany as the Corridor itself has for Poland". He said he has proposed: to recognise all Polish economic rights in Danzig; to ensure for Poland a Free Harbour in Danzig of any size; to accept as permanent the present boundaries between Germany and Poland; conclude a twenty-five year non-aggression pact with Poland and to have the "independence of the Slovak State guaranteed by Germany, Poland and Hungary jointly – which means in practice the renunciation of any unilateral German hegemony in this territory". The Polish Government denied knowledge of the last two proposals. It did not "reject" the others: it submitted alternatives as a basis for discussion: (1) to negotiate concerning the question of a substitute for the Commissioner of the League of Nations (at Danzig) and (2) to consider facilities for the transit traffic through the Corridor. As the Führer himself suggested, the Czecho-Slovak situation of a year ago might be recalled. And, it may justly be pondered, of what use is a fresh pact, even of twenty-five years, when the existing agreement is denounced on so flimsy a pretext as the Anglo-Polish mutual guarantees? Polish counter-demands are foreshadowed which include a Polish Protectorate over Danzig.

Recently agitation has again come to the fore, a German coup, indeed, over last weekend being thought possible by many political observers. Polish Navy Week culminated on June 29 in national demonstrations throughout the country under the slogan "We will not be forced from the sea". On the same day Lord Halifax, speaking at the Royal Institute of International Affairs, emphasised Britain's Continental commitments. "We have assumed obligations", he said, "and are prepared to assume more, with full understanding of their consequences." In Danzig itself, Nazi military preparations were taking place, in the shape of armed "tourists" from the Reich with "Heimwehr" marked on their sleeves; the formation of a Nazi "Free Corps" in which it was reported that all young Danzigers between the ages of fifteen and twenty-five were ordered to enlist, with July 6 as the day by which enrolment had to be completed; and the pouring in from East Prussia of arms, including tanks and heavy guns. Poland, however, refused to be provoked into rash action. Thus the Government informed the Danzig Senate that they saw no objection to the German cruiser "Konigsberg" visiting Danzig on August 25; and a similar line was reported to be taken over Herr Hitler's projected visit to the Free City on or about July 20. Danzig for long has been one of the "danger spots of Europe" and on more than one occasion it has seemed that the danger could no longer be tided over. But such speeches as that on July 2 of the Free City's Nazi Gauleiter, Herr Forster, when he declared that "Danzigers and all Germans in Great Germany have drawn the conclusion that there is nothing for it but to accept the standpoint of force adopted by Britain and her allies", do not materially help in the finding of a peaceful solution.

A MAP OF POLAND SHOWING THE FAMOUS "CORRIDOR" BETWEEN POMERANIA AND EAST PRUSSIA, GDYNIA, THE ONLY PORT OVER WHICH POLAND POSSESSES SOVEREIGNTY, AND DANZIG, BY THE VERSAILLES TREATY A UNIT OF THE POLISH CUSTOMS ADMINISTRATION.

ABOVE CLOUDS: GERMAN DIVE-BOMBERS ON A PRACTICE "STALK".

We illustrate here a group of German dive-bombers, a type of machine which the Luftwaffe (the German Air Force) has recently developed considerably. The machines are Junkers Ju.87s. fitted with Jumbo 600-h.p. twelve-cylinder inverted-V petrol motors. Their performance figures and bomb loads have not yet been revealed but their maximum speed is believed to be somewhere about 220 m.p.h. An interesting feature is the flap-gear seen in the bottom left corner, and the spoiler-gear just outboard of the undercarriage. These are designed to prevent the speed becoming too high in a nearly vertical bombing dive. The Junkers machines seen here mount three machine-guns. The bombs carried are not large – certainly not above 500 lbs. To the layman, dive-bombing is usually associated with naval warfare. In land warfare it is plain that dive-bombers are well adapted to making attacks on small or mobile targets, such as railway stations, road junctions, or troop concentrations. In Spain, dive-bombing is stated to have been used against convoys and troops on the road. The pilots seek to attack with the sun behind them, to increase the difficulties of the anti-aircraft gunners. They will also use low clouds as cover from which to "stalk" their quarry on the ground. Anyone who has watched these bombers at work knows that even the noise made by their breathless dives has a powerful psychological effect and is most unnerving to the gunners on the ground.

DIVE-BOMBERS IN FLIGHT: A TYPE OF MACHINE UTILISED IN THIS COUNTRY AND THE U.S.A. FOR NAVAL WARFARE; BUT DESIGNED IN GERMANY FOR ATTACKING LAND TARGETS SUCH AS RAILWAY STATIONS AND ROAD CONVOYS.

THE GERMAN ARMY: MECHANISED UNITS FOR "LIGHTNING WAR"

On March 16, 1935, Germany repudiated the armament clauses of the Treaty of Versailles, and from that date rearmament in the Reich has been proceeding at an ever-accelerating rate. Immediately on Hitler's accession to power, military service in Germany was made compulsory, beginning from the completion of the eighteenth year of an able-bodied man and lasting to the completion of the twenty-first year. Service in the Regular Army is preceded by service in the labour corps, which usually lasts six months, the conscript entering the Reichswehr in his twentieth year and serving for two years, passing after that to the Reserve for fourteen years and to the Landwehr for nine years. Those men who, for various reasons, have not done military service, form the Ersatz Reserve. In 1938 the army of the old Reich was increased by one army corps and two more army corps were added in consequence of the absorption of Austria. The army is now organised in five groups, with headquarters in Berlin, Frankfort-on-Main, Dresden, Leipzig and Vienna and comprises eighteen army corps and three mobile divisions. The number of trained reserves, which is about one million at present, increases at the rate of 350,000 a year. As we go to press Germany is reported to have over two million men under arms with mobilisation still proceeding.

TANKS AND INFANTRY UNITS IN A SPECTACULAR DISPLAY BY UNITS OF THE REICHWEHR, THE FOUNDATIONS FOR THE ENORMOUS EXPANSION OF WHICH WERE LAID BY THE LATE GENERAL VON SEECKT, THE POST-WAR COMMANDER OF THE GERMAN ARMY AND THE VIRTUAL FATHER OF THE REICHSWEHR.

A LARGE GERMAN MOTORISED UNIT IN PARADE ORDER: IN THE FOREGROUND MACHINE-GUNS AND THEIR CREWS BORNE ON MOTOR-CYCLES, WITH INFANTRY IN SPECIAL LORRIES SEEN BEYOND.

WITH THE GERMAN MECHANISED UNITS ADAPTED FOR A "LIGHTNING WAR": MOTORISED TROOPS CARRIED IN SPECIAL TRUCKS TAKING PART IN A REVIEW IN BERLIN AND RESEMBLING SIMILAR ITALIAN FORMATIONS.

FRANCE DEMONSTRATES HER ARMY'S PREPAREDNESS:
THE "BASTILLE DAY" PARADE IN PARIS.

THE MOST LEGENDARY TROOPS IN THE WORLD MAKE THEIR FIRST APPEARANCE AT A JULY 14 PARADE: A DETACHMENT FROM THE FRENCH FOREIGN LEGION IN PARIS.

"VOICI LES ANGLAIS!" – MARCHING WITH MATCHLESS PRECISION TO A CRESCENDO OF POPULAR APPLAUSE: GUARDS CROSSING THE PLACE DE LA CONCORDE IN THE FÊTE NATIONALE PARADE IN PARIS ON JULY 14.

NATIVE TROOPS OF THE FRENCH EMPIRE: DETACHMENTS FROM THE 12TH AND 14TH BATTALIONS OF SENEGALESE TIRAILLEURS, OF MAGNIFICENT PHYSIQUE, MARCHING ALONG THE CHAMPS ÉLYSÉES.

FRANCO-BRITISH AIR POWER:
THE FÊTE NATIONALE COMBINED FLY-PAST.

ONCE AGAIN IN ALLIANCE WITH BRITISH TROOPS: FRENCH INFANTRY, HEIRS OF THE STALWART POILUS OF 1914–18, MARCHING IN MASS FORMATION.

The most impressive demonstration of French military might that has ever been staged since the Fête Nationale became a tradition filed past the Presidential Tribune in the Champs Élysées on the occasion of the 150th anniversary of the French Revolution. Thirty thousand troops of all arms took part in the parade, which also included a Brigade of Guards' detachment, heading the procession under the command of Lieut.-Col. W.P.A. Bradshaw, D.S.O. – "a splendid, soldier-like figure" – and naval units led by a Royal Marine band. R.A.F. bombers flew above them. The appearance of "les Guards" evoked enormous enthusiasm among the craning multitude along the route which, says "The Times" account, "rose to fever pitch as the crowd took in the full precision of their marching".

THE FLY-PAST OF 315 BRITISH AND FRENCH AIRCRAFT PRECEDING THE FÊTE NATIONALE PARADE IN THE CHAMPS ÉLYSÉES: VICKERS "WELLINGTON" BOMBERS, WHICH LED THE SQUADRONS OVER PARIS.

ROYAL REVIEW OF NATIONAL DEFENCE SERVICES IN HYDE PARK

H.M. THE KING REVIEWS REPRESENTATIVE DETACHMENTS OF THE NATIONAL DEFENCE SERVICES IN HYDE PARK: NURSING AND FIRST-AID SERVICES, FOLLOWED BY THE WOMEN'S LAND ARMY AND (IN BACKGROUND) THE AUXILIARY FIRE SERVICE, PASSING THE SALUTE-POINT DURING THE IMPRESSIVE PARADE.

UNITS OF THE LONDON DIVISION IN THE REVIEW IN HYDE PARK: LIGHT TANKS AND ARMOURED CARS PASSING THE SALUTING-POINT.

REPRESENTING MANY THOUSANDS WHO HAVE RESPONDED TO THE CALL FOR VOLUNTEERS FOR THE CIVIL DEFENCE FORCES: THE A.R.P. CONTINGENT IN THE PARADE – THE NOVEL SPECTACLE OF MEN AND WOMEN MARCHING IN THE SAME RANKS AND WEARING STEEL HELMETS AND BADGES AS UNIFORM.

AN IMPRESSIVE DISPLAY OF TERRITORIAL ARMY EQUIPMENT: FIELD ARTILLERY DRAWN BY TROOP-CARRYING LORRIES APPROACHING THE SALUTING-POINT IN HYDE PARK.

The review of representatives of the National Defence Services by the King in Hyde Park on July 2 presented a striking demonstration of complete national unity in a time of stress. Some 20,000 men and women, representing the many thousands who have responded to the call of National Service, marched past the saluting-point, where the King remained at the salute for long periods as the contingents passed by.

The important part which women play in National Defence was very apparent. Besides the nursing services, women's activities were represented by the Auxiliary Territorial Service, the Women's Land Army. Women were also to be seen in the Auxiliary Fire Service contingent, the Civil Air Guard detachment and the A.R.P. services. After the detachments on foot had passed the saluting-point there was a short interval and then units of the Mobile London Division drove past the King and Queen.

IRISH OUTRAGES IN ENGLAND IN 1939: I.R.A. BOMB EXPLOSIONS

BOMB OUTRAGES THOUGHT TO HAVE BEEN DUE TO THE I.R.A.: (LEFT) THE TWISTED STEELWORK OF HAMMERSMITH BRIDGE, FOLLOWING AN EXPLOSION WHICH SHATTERED WINDOWS IN HOUSES HUNDREDS OF YARDS DISTANT; AND (RIGHT) THE SMASHED SHOP WINDOW OF A SHOE SHOP IN THE EDGWARE ROAD.

We illustrate here further bomb outrages which have recently disturbed London. That on Hammersmith Bridge occurred in the early morning of March 29; that at an Edgware Road shoe shop on April 1, at 5.30 a.m. The latter, which occurred within a few hours of the conviction of seven terrorists at the Old Bailey, was one of five attacks between midnight at 6 a.m.: (12.37 a.m.) "News-Chronicle" offices in Fleet Street: (1.35 a.m.) in Park Lane: (3.2 a.m.) a large furniture shop in Tottenham Court Road: (5.30 a.m.) the shoe shop illustrated in Edgware Road: (6.5 a.m.) Messrs. Coutts Bank in the Strand. The courageous action of a London hairdresser, Mr. Childs, in hurling into the Thames a smoking suitcase left on the bridge, probably saved Hammersmith Bridge from more serious damage. Traffic was suspended and the bridge put under repair. Crude, home-made

bombs appear to have been used; fortunately no lives have been lost.

More recently the outrages at Victoria Station and King's Cross on July 26 took place only two days before the Prevention of Violence Act became law, and are among the most serious of the explosions caused by the I.R.A. The death of Dr. Campbell is the second caused by I.R.A. explosions, the previous one being at Manchester. Sir Samuel Hoare, speaking in the House on July 24, announced that since January there had been 127 outrages; the Government, he said, had reliable information that the campaign was being stimulated by foreign organisations. Sir Samuel also stated that there was a plot to blow up the Houses of Parliament.

"A HISTORIC DAY": THE FIRST GROUP OF MILITIAMEN WELCOMED AT CAMPS AND DEPOTS THROUGHOUT BRITAIN.
BRITAIN MANS THE FORMIDABLE RESERVE FLEET.

BRITAIN'S PREPAREDNESS FOR A WAR OF MOVEMENT: TANKS MANOEUVRING IN MASS FORMATION DURING A REVIEW, PROVIDING A PICTURE OF GRIM EFFICIENCY TYPICAL OF THE NEW ROYAL ARMOURED CORPS, WHICH INCLUDES THE MECHANISED CAVALRY REGIMENTS AND FORMS THE SPEARHEAD OF AN ATTACK.

"BOOTS, BOOTS, BOOTS": PREPARING EQUIPMENT IN READINESS FOR THE ARRIVAL OF MILITIAMEN AT THE CAMP AT ARROWE PARK, BIRKENHEAD.

WITH THE NAVY IN THE MEDITERRANEAN: THE AIRCRAFT-CARRIER "GLORIOUS" ENCOUNTERING HEAVY SEAS, WITH WAVES MOUNTING UPON HER LOFTY FO'C'SLE.

LIKE A SCENE FROM H.G. WELL'S FILM "THE SHAPE OF THINGS TO COME": MEMBERS OF A LONDON ANTI-AIRCRAFT REGIMENT BRINGING A 3-IN A.A. GUN INTO ACTION BY NIGHT, THE MEN FOLLOWING THE TARGET AS DIRECTED BY THE READINGS ON THE PREDICTOR.

On July 15, the first group of over 30,000 militiamen reported for six months' training at camps and depots throughout the country, and it was immediately apparent not only that the men concerned had accepted conscription with a good spirit, but that the Army authorities had done everything possible to assist them to settle down to their new life.

The R.A.F. received its first batch of militiamen on July 17, and in the next two months will receive 2,000 men who will be sent to R.A.F. stations in groups of a hundred. The first contingent consists of skilled tradesmen, who are intended for the ground sections of the R.A.F. Men for the air sections will be called up later in the year. The next group of militiamen will be called up about September 15 and those allotted to anti-aircraft units will report for duty in the first half of October. Speaking at Birmingham on July 15, Major-General J.H. Beith, Director of Public Relations, stated that nearly 1,000,000 men will be under arms in this country by August. 10,500 Naval Reservists have also been called up, and by the time this issue appears, the entire Reserve Fleet of 130 vessels will probably be in commission, ready for the Inspection which the King will hold in Weymouth Bay on August 9. The Reserve Fleet will remain manned and will carry out exercises until towards the end of September.

The experience gained during the mobilisation last September and the realisation that it is undesirable, owing to air attack, for large numbers of men to be kept in the manning depots for longer than it is absolutely necessary, have led to a new refinement or organisation designed to pass the men through depots and out to the Fleet in the minimum of time. The men called up include about 800 of the Royal Naval Volunteer Reserve – not seamen by profession, but civilians who have done special naval training; roughly the same number of the Royal Naval Reserve – merchant seamen and fishermen; 100 men of the Signals Branch, Royal Naval Reserve and 130 Royal Naval Volunteer Wireless Reservists.

(RIGHT), A POWERFUL AID TO GROUND AIR-DEFENCE, WHOSE ALL-SEARCHING RAYS ARE DESIGNED TO FORM A NIGHTLY RAMPART ROUND ENGLAND: SEARCHLIGHT PRACTICE AT AN ANTI-AIRCRAFT BATTALION, R.E., IN LONDON.

POLAND AS A MILITARY POWER: CAVALRY, TANKS AND INFANTRY.

POLAND'S MECHANISED FORCES: TANKS, OF EXCELLENT QUALITY AND HIGH PERFORMANCE, MOVING UP TOWARDS THE FRONTIER, THEIR MOBILITY BEING RESTRICTED, HOWEVER, BY THE LACK OF ROADS AND THE PRESENCE OF WOODS, LAKES AND MARSHES WHICH FORM A NATURAL BARRIER AGAINST AN INVADER.

POLAND'S IMPRESSIVE HORSED CAVALRY – PROBABLY THE BEST IN EUROPE AND EQUIPPED WITH SWORDS, LANCES AND MACHINE-GUNS: AN ARM WHICH HAS BEEN EXTENSIVELY DEVELOPED AND HAS GREATER MOBILITY IN DIFFICULT TERRAIN THAN MECHANISED FORCES BESIDES BEING ABLE TO LIVE ON THE COUNTRY.

OCCUPYING A COMMANDING POSITION IN A VILLAGE STREET: A GUN (ON RIGHT) IN THE BELGIAN FORTIFICATIONS SITED SO THAT IT CAN SWEEP THE ROADWAY IN FRONT.

STRETCHING FOR MILES ALONG THE BELGIAN FRONTIER AND PROVIDING SECURITY AGAINST SUDDEN ATTACK: AN ANTI-TANK BARRIER OF SHORT STEEL POSTS WHICH IS PROTECTED BY BARBED-WIRE ENTANGLEMENTS AND BY MINES.

POLAND PREPARES: INFANTRY ATTACKING AN ENEMY POSITION DURING RECENT MANOEUVRES; SHOWING HOW LIGHT MACHINE-GUNS ARE BROUGHT FORWARD AND USED IN THE OFFENSIVE TO SUPPORT THE ADVANCING TROOPS.

Poland has 3,000,000 trained reserves and could ultimately mobilise a force of 6,000,000 men for service in the army. Every Polish subject who is physically fit is liable to serve between the ages of 21 and 50. Those selected join the active army for two years and then pass to the reserve, in which they remain for eighteen years. At forty years of age they are drafted to the territorial army in which they remain for ten years. Recently Poland has strengthened her mechanised forces and is now producing tanks and armoured cars for her army, whose excellent quality and high performance is widely recognised. The terrain, however, presents difficulties to mechanised and motorised forces and an invader would find his way barred by lakes, woods and marshes, leaving him open to attack by the Polish cavalry which has been extensively developed and is probably the best in Europe. The horsemen are equipped with rifles, bayonets, swords, and lances, and are provided with light machine-guns; while horse artillery and horse-drawn anti-tank and anti-aircraft guns operate with them. There are three regiments of lancers, twenty-seven of Uhlans, and ten regiments of riflemen, and Poland possesses 3,950,000 horses classed as fit for military service.

THE BELGIAN FRONTIER FORTIFICATIONS: A "MAGINOT LINE" WITH MILES OF ANTI-TANK BARRIERS AND MOAT TANK-TRAPS.

A system of fortifications which can be compared with the French Maginot Line and the German Siegfried Line, has been constructed along the frontiers of Belgium. Belgium has a frontier of 831 miles to defend and her intention to make it impregnable was shown when there was an extraordinary budget for 1937 of some £6,600,000 to meet improvements in the fortifications of the eastern frontier. To man the underground fortresses and concrete "pill-boxes" and gun-emplacements in an emergency, Belgium has an Army of 80,000 men, with over 4000 officers, which includes a mechanised cavalry corps and one division of special frontier troops. This photograph shows sentries guarding concrete gun emplacements.

INUNDATION – NEUTRAL HOLLAND'S MAIN DEFENCE.

TESTING ONE OF HOLLAND'S MOST IMPORTANT DEFENCES AGAINST INVASION: THE DUTCH C.-IN-C. (LEFT), INSPECTING INUNDATIONS NEAR UTRECHT.

Although Germany has emphasised that she will respect the integrity of neutral countries, the Dutch Government have tested one of Holland's main defences against invasion – that of inundation – in some of the country near Utrecht. Above is seen the C.-in-C. of all the Netherlands Forces, Baron J.J.G. van Vooert Tot Vooert inspecting the result. Dutch waterways have been allowed to reach a higher level than before.

DANZIG GREETS A GERMAN WARSHIP

THE DANZIG NAZI HEIMWEHR
ELABORATELY EQUIPPED INFANTRY

THE HEIMWEHR, OR "S.S. HOME DEFENCE CORPS", IS A BODY RECENTLY CREATED OSTENSIBLY FOR THE DEFENCE OF DANZIG AND ALLEGEDLY FROM THE LOCAL MALE POPULATION, BUT IS BELIEVED TO BE ALMOST WHOLLY MANNED BY GERMANS INTRODUCED INTO THE FREE CITY AS "TOURISTS".

Supported by a virulent campaign in the German newspapers against Poland, the renewed tension under which Europe has been labouring has also been fostered by the activities of the Bavarian-born Gauleiter of Danzig, Herr Albert Forster, whose speeches, delivered before the marshalled throngs of the Free City on his return from interviewing the Führer at Berchtesgaden, heightened the acuity of the crisis. On August 18, after presenting regimental colours, Herr Forster carried out in Danzig the first official inspection of the local Heimwehr, or Home Defence Corps, which has been largely recruited from the legion of German "tourists" introduced into Danzig since early July. Speaking at the opening of the ceremony, the Reich representative declared that Danzig was now protected against any attack by another State, adding significantly, "We are now able to show our weapons – the world's most modern weapons – for the first time since the last German troops moved out of the city twenty years ago". On the following day, Herr Forster opened a new pontoon bridge across the Vistula, constructed in eight weeks to afford passage for heavy traffic to the East Prussian frontier.

A GERMAN NAVAL TRAINING SHIP ARRIVES AT DANZIG AT A FATEFUL HOUR: THE "SCHLESWIG-HOLSTEIN", WHICH IS ARMED WITH 11-IN. GUNS, ENTERING THE HARBOUR ON AUGUST 25.

SIGNING THE WORLD-STAGGERING PACT: RUSSO-GERMAN SMILES.

A COMPLETE REVERSAL OF GERMAN POLICY: HERR VON RIBBENTROP FLIES TO MOSCOW TO NEGOTIATE A NON-AGGRESSION PACT.

Herr von Ribbentrop, German Foreign Minister, arrived in Moscow by air at 1 p.m. on August 23. He was met at the airport by the Assistant Commissar for Foreign Affairs and a number of other high Soviet officials, German and Italian diplomatists. The absence of Japanese representatives was noted. The Swastika Flag was displayed next to the Red Flag on this occasion. An ironical touch was lent to the proceedings by the fact that Herr von Ribbentrop stayed at the former Austrian Legation, almost next door to the house occupied by the British and French Military Missions. The German-Russian non-Aggression Pact was signed in the presence of M. Stalin that evening. The clauses of this document are now widely known and it is unnecessary for us to detail them here. Particular attention has been drawn to Article 4, by which the two Powers bind themselves not to join "any other group of Powers directly or indirectly if directed against one of the two". Herr von Ribbentrop spend the next morning sight-seeing in Moscow and then left by air for Germany.

HERR HITLER'S FOREIGN MINISTER SHAKES HANDS WITH THE GENERAL SECRETARY OF THE COMMUNIST PARTY IN SOVIET RUSSIA: M. STALIN AND HERR VON RIBBENTROP.

The news of the project for a non-aggression Pact between Germany and Soviet Russia resulted in intense activity in Whitehall. Mr. Chamberlain had already returned to London in view of the deterioration of the international situation. On August 21 he saw Lord Halifax and also Mr. Greenwood, the acting Leader of the Opposition. Mr. Hore-Belisha hurried back from the South of France, stopping in Paris for consultations with the French authorities, and concluding his journey by air. On August 22 Mr. Chamberlain took his usual morning walk before 10 o'clock, and Mrs. Chamberlain accompanied him. Callers at No. 10 that morning included Sir Kingsley Wood, Secretary of State for Air, Sir John Simon, and Dr. Kordt, the German *Chargé* *d'Affaires* in London. Mr. S.M. Bruce, High Commissioner for Australia had an interview with the Premier. A Cabinet meeting began at 3 p.m. A *communiqué* issued afterwards included the statement that a non-aggression Pact between Germany and Russia would in no way affect our obligations to Poland; and that Parliament would be summoned and asked to pass the Emergency Powers (Defence) Bill. In some quarters it is believed that the whole diplomatic balance of Europe will be altered by the pact. Should Germany feel justified by what she considers a diplomatic triumph in making an attempt to seize Danzig, it would undoubtedly lead to the gravest consequences.

POLAND PREPARES FOR AIR RAIDS: TRENCH-DIGGING IN WARSAW

STRENUOUS WORK IN WHICH ALL CLASSES WILLINGLY JOINED: MEN, WOMEN AND CHILDREN DIGGING TRENCHES IN AN OPEN SPACE IN WARSAW TO PROVIDE SHELTER FROM RAIDING GERMAN AIRCRAFT – A PRECAUTION TAKEN IN LONDON DURING THE CRISIS LAST SEPTEMBER.

EVACUATING LONDON'S CHILDREN: TO THE COUNTRY BY ROAD AND RAIL.

THE GREAT "TREK" TO THE COUNTRY: MOTOR-BUSES, TAKEN OFF THEIR ORDINARY ROUTES FOR THE OCCASION, AT A SUBURBAN UNDERGROUND TERMINUS, READY TO CONVEY PARTIES OF CHILDREN ARRIVING FROM LONDON TO A MAIN LINE STATION.

LONDON EVACUATED A FIRST "WAVE" OF 400,000 CHILDREN ON SEPTEMBER 1, IN CHARGE OF 22,000 TEACHERS; OTHERS GOING ON LATER DAYS. HERE A PARTY IS SEEN ENTRAINING AT A MAIN LINE STATION IN THE SUBURBS, EQUIPPED WITH GAS-MASKS AND CARRYING THEIR BELONGINGS IN BAGS AND HAVERSACKS.

WAR'S IMPACT ON LONDON: FAMILIAR STREETS IN UNUSUAL GUISE.

A "MODERN" DESIGN IN A.R.P. FOR SHOP WINDOWS – STRIPS OF ADHESIVE PAPER, WHICH SERVE TO PREVENT SPLINTERING.

USING BOOKS INSTEAD OF SOIL FOR SANDBAG FILLING; APPROPRIATE VOLUMES IN THIS DEFENCE "LIBRARY" BEING HITLER'S "MEIN KAMPF".

LIKE A MESSENGER FROM MARS: MEMBERS OF THE AUXILIARY FIRE SERVICE, ONE WEARING GAS-MASK, ON DUTY IN LONDON.

GERMANY INVADES POLAND – BRITAIN AND FRANCE DECLARE WAR.

HORSE-DRAWN GERMAN ARTILLERY ADVANCING THROUGH A BURNING POLISH VILLAGE, THE POLISH ARMY HAVING WITHDRAWN TO STRONG DEFENSIVE POSITIONS.

NEARING WARSAW: GERMAN INFANTRY, MOTORISED AND MECHANISED, ADVANCING THROUGH THE DESERTED STREETS OF A SMALL TOWN SOUTH-WEST OF WARSAW.

GERMAN ADVANCE-GUARDS ON MOTOR-CYCLES – THE MOTORISED NATURE OF THE GERMAN TROOPS WAS RESPONSIBLE FOR THEIR ADVANCE – BUT THE POLISH ARMY HAS REMAINED INTACT.

Above we reproduce two pictures of the German advance on the Polish front and showing the waste and desolation brought to Poland by the war. Germany has attempted to put in practice her doctrine of *Blitzkrieg*; but Polish spirit remains unbroken and the Polish Army is still intact.

THE SWASTIKA OVER WESTERPLATTE – CAPTURED AFTER AN EPIC DEFENCE.

THE RT. HON. NEVILLE CHAMBERLAIN, PRIME MINISTER, WHO MADE UNREMITTING BUT UNAVAILING EFFORTS TO SAVE PEACE.

Mr. Chamberlain's unsparing but finally unavailing efforts for peace are too well known to need quotation. "You can imagine", he said, when he broadcast to the nation, on September 3, that England was at war with Germany, "what a bitter blow it is to me that all my long struggle to win peace has failed". "We are ready", he declared the same day in the House. "It is a sad day for all of us, sadder for none than for me."

GERMAN ENTRENCHMENTS JUST OUTSIDE WARSAW – TRAMCARS SUGGESTING THE NEARNESS TO THE CAPITAL'S CENTRE.

Warsaw, in its epic defence against the German attack, became almost at once a city in the front line. By September 14, the Germans had claimed to have cut off the capital, and to be approaching Praga, the north-eastern suburb. On the 16th the city was given twelve hours to surrender, after which it would be treated as war territory; a week later the Lord Mayor, M. Skarzynski, was declaring the city's determination to fight on.

POLAND STABBED IN THE BACK: THE RED ARMY IN THE FIELD.

THE NAZI BANNER FLYING ABOVE THE RUINS OF WESTERPLATTE, THE POLISH MUNITIONS DUMP AT THE MOUTH OF DANZIG HARBOUR WHOSE HEROIC DEFENCE EARNED GERMAN PRAISE.

The garrison of Westerplatte had been besieged for six days, remaining firm against overwhelming odds. Finally, it was reported, boat companies from the German warship "Schleswig Holstein" made an assault on the depot under cover of heavy fire, while, simultaneously, a battalion of pioneers attacked from the land.

TROOPS OF THE SOVIET ARMY, WHICH CROSSED THE POLISH FRONTIER ALONG ITS WHOLE LENGTH ON SEPTEMBER 17 ON THE PRETEXT OF THE "DISINTEGRATION" OF THE POLISH STATE: RUSSIAN INFANTRYMEN AND THEIR OFFICERS.

Russian troops crossed the Polish frontier along its whole length on September 17. In a note handed to the Polish Ambassador in Moscow the Russian Government stated that, owing to the "disintegration" of the Polish State, they felt it their "sacred duty" to protect their blood relations living on Polish territory.

THE WAR CABINET OF NINE –
AND OTHER MINISTERIAL APPOINTMENTS.

MINISTER FOR CO-ORDINATION OF DEFENCE IN THE WAR CABINET: ADMIRAL LORD CHATFIELD.

SECRETARY OF STATE FOR AIR IN THE WAR CABINET: SIR KINGSLEY WOOD.

SECRETARY OF STATE FOR WAR IN THE WAR CABINET: MR. L. HOPE-BELISHA.

MINISTER WITHOUT PORTFOLIO IN THE WAR CABINET: LORD HANKEY.

LORD PRIVY SEAL IN THE WAR CABINET: SIR SAMUEL HOARE, WHO WAS FORMERLY HOME SECRETARY.

FIRST LORD OF THE ADMIRALTY IN THE WAR CABINET: MR. WINSTON CHURCHILL ARRIVING AT THE ADMIRALTY; WHERE HE HELD OFFICE IN AUGUST 1914.

PRIME MINISTER AND FIRST LORD OF THE TREASURY: MR. NEVILLE CHAMBERLAIN, WHO RECONSTITUTED THE CABINET ON SEPTEMBER 3.

RETAINING HIS OFFICE OF SECRETARY OF STATE FOR FOREIGN AFFAIRS: LORD HALIFAX, ON HIS WAY TO THE HOUSES OF PARLIAMENT.

SIR JOHN ANDERSON: HOME SECRETARY; MINISTER, HOME SECURITY (NOT IN WAR CABINET).

SIR T. INSKIP (FORMERLY DOMINIONS SECRETARY): LORD CHANCELLOR (NOT IN WAR CABINET).

CHANCELLOR OF THE EXCHEQUER IN THE WAR CABINET: SIR JOHN SIMON.

MR. ANTHONY EDEN: SECRETARY OF STATE FOR DOMINION AFFAIRS (NOT IN THE WAR CABINET).

LORD STANHOPE: LORD PRESIDENT OF THE COUNCIL (NOT IN THE WAR CABINET).

It was officially announced on September 3 that the Prime Minister had decided to reconstitute the Government and set up a War Cabinet on the lines of the War Cabinet established in December 1916. The nine members of this are all illustrated on this page as well as four other new ministerial appointments which were made later. Mr.

Churchill was First Lord of the Admiralty in August 1914. Lord Hankey was Secretary of the Committee of Imperial Defence throughout the last war. Subsequent ministerial appointments included that of Mr. W.S. Morris as Minister of Food; and Lord MacMillan as Minister of Information.

PROMINENT SUPPORTERS OF BRITAIN'S FIGHT AGAINST NAZI-ISM.

MR. M.J. SAVAGE, PRIME MINISTER OF NEW ZEALAND, WHICH HAS DECLARED WAR ON GERMANY.

MR. MACKENZIE KING, PRIME MINISTER OF CANADA, WHICH HAS DECLARED WAR ON GERMANY.

MR. ROBERT MENZIES, PRIME MINISTER OF AUSTRALIA, WHICH HAS DECLARED WAR ON GERMANY.

THE SULTAN OF OMAN (MUSCAT), RULING OVER 83,000 SQUARE MILES AND 550,000 INHABITANTS, WHO HAS OFFERED HIS ASSISTANCE.

THE SHEIKE OF BAHRAIN, AN IMPORTANT OIL-PRODUCING COUNTRY, WHO HAS OFFERED HIS ASSISTANCE.

THE AGA KHAN, WHO HAS APPEALED TO ISMAILIAN MOHAMMEDANS FOR "UNSTINTED SERVICE".

KING FARUK I. OF EGYPT, WHICH HAS BROKEN OFF DIPLOMATIC RELATIONS WITH GERMANY.

THE MAHARAJA OF JAMMU AND KASHMIR, WHO HAS OFFERED HIS SWORD TO THE KING-EMPEROR.

THE VETERAN SOUTH AFRICAN LEADER WHO HAS RALLIED HIS NATION TO THE SIDE OF GREAT BRITAIN AND FRANCE IN THE STAND AGAINST NAZI AGGRESSION, AND FORMED A NATIONAL WAR GOVERNMENT: GENERAL J.C. SMUTS.

THE MAHARAJA OF BIKANER, WHO HAS OFFERED HIS SERVICES TO THE KING-EMPEROR.

Side by side with Great Britain and France in their fight against Hitlerism stands the Dominions – Canada, Australia, New Zealand and South Africa – all of which have declared war. Moreover, in a message read by the Viceroy at Delhi the King-Emperor expressed his satisfaction at India's attachment to our cause – an attachment existing equally among the Princes, peasants and political leaders. Both Egypt and Iraq, as well as offering pledges, broke off relations with Germany. Nepal, famous for the Gurkha troops who fought with Britain in 1914 – 1918, also offered a contingent.

INDEX OF NAMES AND PLACE NAMES